Handbook of hospitality strategic management

Handbook of hospitality strategic management

Edited by
Michael Olsen
Virginia Tech

Jinlin Zhao
Associate Professor,
School of Hospitality and Tourism Management,
Florida International University, USA

AMSTERDAM • BOSTON • HEIDELBERG • LONDON • NEW YORK • OXFORD
PARIS • SAN DIEGO • SAN FRANCISCO • SINGAPORE • SYDNEY • TOKYO
Butterworth-Heinemann is an imprint of Elsevier

Butterworth-Heinemann is an imprint of Elsevier
Linacre House, Jordan Hill, Oxford OX2 8DP, UK
30 Corporate Drive, Suite 400, Burlington, MA 01803, USA

First edition 2008

British Library Cataloguing-in-Publication Data
A catalogue record for this book is available from the British Library

Library of Congress Cataloging-in-Publication Data
A catalog record for this book is available from the Library of Congress

ISBN: 978-0-08-045079-7

For information on all Butterworth-Heinemann publications
visit our website at elsevierdirect.com

Printed and bound in Hungary
08 09 10 11 12 10 9 8 7 6 5 4 3 2 1

Working together to grow
libraries in developing countries

www.elsevier.com | www.bookaid.org | www.sabre.org

ELSEVIER   BOOK AID
International   Sabre Foundation

Contents

List of contributors

Sander M. Allegro, M.Sc., BHA (The Netherlands, 1968) combines his directorship of innovation at Hotelschool The Hague, international University of Hospitality Management with his privately held consultancy firm Allegro INN ovations. Sander is an accomplished consultant and trainer to the hospitality industry and is experienced in strategic management, workshop facilitation, and the field of organizational learning and development. Sander is visiting professor at various hospitality colleges and is a columnist to two hospitality publications.

Dr. Levent Altinay is a Reader in Strategic Management at the Oxford Brookes University Business School. His research interests include internationalization, international franchising, intrapreneurship, and ethnic minority entrepreneurship. He is currently leading a research project investigating the interaction between culture and entrepreneurship. Dr. Altinay is the co-author of the book Planning Research in Hospitality and Tourism.

Dr. Marvin J. Cetron is founder and president of Forecasting International. Over a career that spans more than 40 years, Dr. Cetron has consulted for more than 350 of the Fortune 500 corporations, 200 academic and professional organizations, and 100 agencies of the US and foreign governments. He has been an advisor to the White House in every administration from the time of President John F. Kennedy to that of Bill Clinton. Dr. Cetron's long-standing corporate clients include many multinational hotel companies. His published more than a dozen of books. His Encounters with the Future sold more than 140,000 copies and was translated into nine languages.

Dr. Prakash K. Chathoth is an Assistant Professor in the School of Hotel and Tourism Management at the Hong Kong Polytechnic University. His research area includes strategic management, applied corporate finance and service management. Prakash received his Ph.D. in 2002 from Virginia Tech, Virginia, USA.

Daniel J. Connolly, Ph.D. is an Associate Professor of information technology and electronic commerce at the University of Denver's Daniels College of Business with a dual appointment in the School of Hotel, Restaurant, and Tourism Management and the Department of Information Technology and Electronic Commerce.

Dr. Jorge Costa is President of the Institute for Tourism Planning and Development, is also Professor of Strategic Management, Founding Director of the Centre for Trends Research in Hospitality & Tourism (CETS-HT) and Post Graduate and Research Director at Fernando Pessoa University, Porto, Portugal. He continues to be actively involved in applied research and management consultancy as a Founding Partner of Future Trends Ltd.

Owen Davies is a forecaster and freelance writer. He has written six books with Dr. Cetron and five books on his own. His independent works include The User's Guide to NEXIS (St. Martin's Press), a manual for users of this complex online database system, and The OMNI On-Line Database Directory (Macmillan), which was a main or alternate selection of seven book clubs, including the Book-of-the-Month Club. A former senior editor at OMNI Magazine, he has written articles for periodicals ranging from Medical World News and Managing Automation to Forbes, Self, and Newsweek International.

Rob de Graaf is innovation facilitator, entrepreneur, and assistant professor the University of Groningen, The Netherlands, at the department of Economics and Business. He is also a freelance teacher at the Hotelschool The Hague, The Netherlands. He holds a Ph.D. in Technology Management and an M.Sc. in Industrial Engineering, both from Eindhoven University of Technology, The Netherlands. In his work, Rob focuses on collaborative innovation processes, ranging from developing strategies, managing innovation projects, to successful introduction of new products and services. He also runs the Innovation Leadership management development programme, which he co-developed.

Dr. Frederick J. DeMicco is Professor and ARAMARK Chair of Hotel & Restaurant Management at the University of Delaware and Conti Professor of Hotel and Restaurant Management at Pennsylvania State University. Dr. DeMicco is author or co-author of more than 75 publications in the area of hospitality. He is ranked 12th among the 119 most cited international hospitality faculty members.

Tevfik Demirciftci completed his undergraduate studies at Bilkent University, Turkey and his graduate studies at University of Delaware specializing in hospitality information management. His area of interest is hotel revenue management.

Dr. Nicolas S. Graf is an Assistant Professor of Hospitality Finance and Strategy at the Conrad N. Hilton College of Hotel and Restaurant Management at the University of Houston. Dr. Graf received his Ph.D. from Virginia Tech and his MBA from the Ecole hoteliere de Lausanne. His research interests include hotel and restaurant valuation and financing.

Dr. Robert J. Harrington is the 21st Century Endowed Chair in Hospitality at the University of Arkansas, USA. He holds a Ph.D. in Strategic Management and MBA from Washington State University; BBA from Boise State University; and is a Certified Executive Chef by the American Culinary Federation. He has more than 18 years of industry experience and his primary research interests include strategic management and innovation, culinary tourism, and food and wine.

Mr. Wei He is a lecturer, research assistant, and doctoral student at Florida International University, School of Hospitality & Tourism Management and Chapman School of Business Administration. He received his first master degree in Hospitality Management from Leeds Metropolitan University, UK, and the second master degree in Information Systems from University of Leeds, UK. Prior to entering the Ph.D. programme, Mr. He had ever worked for several international hotels chains. He currently engages in research on numerous topics in relation to strategic management in service organizations, international hospitality business, and global knowledge management and diffusion for service firms.

Professor Peter Jones, Ph.D. is ITCA Chair of Production and Operations Management in the School of Management at the University of Surrey. He has written, co-authored, and edited numerous books and chapters on the subject of hospitality management, as well as present keynotes and research papers at conferences throughout the world. In 1992 he was the founding President of EuroCHRIE and in 2007/2008 served as International CHRIE President.

Russell Kett is Managing Director of the London office of HVS. Russell has some 30 years' specialist hotel consultancy, investment and real estate experience and generally focuses on the provision of valuation, feasibility, shared ownership, property, brokerage, investment, asset management, strategy and related consultancy services. He is a frequent speaker on the international hotel industry and lectures regularly at leading international hotel schools.

Francis A. Kwansa, Ph.D. is an Associate Professor of financial management at the University of Delaware and Director of Graduate Studies in the HRIM Department. He was previously on the faculty at Virginia Tech and Cornell University. Currently Associate Editor of the Journal of Hospitality Financial Management and former Associate Editor of the Journal of Foodservice Business Research, and serves on editorial boards of five academic journals. He is a member of the Financial Management Committee of the American Hotel and Lodging Association.

Melih Madanoglu, Ph.D., CHE is an Assistant Professor in the Division of Resort and Hospitality Management at Florida Gulf Coast University in Fort Myers, Florida and is the Co-Editor of Resort Industry Review. Dr. Madanoglu earned his doctoral degree from Virginia Tech University. Dr. Madanoglu's areas of expertise include: firm risk analysis, capital budgeting, and value-based management in corporations.

Cynthia R. Mayo is an Associate Professor and Director of the Hospitality and Tourism Management Program, College of Business, Delaware State University. She received her Ph.D. degree from Virginia Polytechnic Institute and State University and MBA degrees from Hampton University and Delaware State University. She has served as Director of the Hospitality Program at Virginia State University. She has also served as co-editor of the Hosteur web-based magazine and The Consortium Journal of Hospitality and Tourism Management. She has co-authored several books related to Hospitality and Tourism Management and Leadership development for Youth.

Kevin S. Murphy is an Assistant Professor of Hospitality Management, specializing in the area of strategy, human resources, and food service. He holds an A.S. degree in Accounting from Bentley College, MA, a Bachelors of Science, Masters of Science, and a Ph.D. in Hospitality Tourism Management from Virginia Polytechnic Institute and State University. Professor Murphy began teaching at the Rosen College in the fall of 2003. Prior to coming to UCF he also served on the faculty of James Madison University and Virginia Tech's Hospitality and Tourism Management departments, teaching primarily in the area of foodservice management. Professor Murphy worked in foodservice and hotel industry for over 20 years and has owned or managed a variety of hospitality establishments including hotels, restaurants, and catering operations. He presently holds the following industry certifications: Certified Executive Chef (C.E.C.) from the American Culinary Federation, Certified Food Safety Manager, and a Certified HACCP Manager from NSF International.

Dr. Fevzi Okumus is currently the interim chair of the Hospitality Services Department at the Rosen College of Hospitality Management, UCF. He completed his Masters degree in International Hotel Management in 1995 and his Ph.D. in Strategic Hotel Management in 2000 at Oxford Brookes University, UK. He has over 90 publications and presentations. He has published in leading journals, including Annals of Tourism Research, International Journal of Contemporary Hospitality Management, Service Industries Journal, Tourism Management, Management Decision, International Journal of Hospitality Management, and Journal of Hospitality and Tourism Research. His publications have been cited over 110 times by other academics and industry practitioners in numerous academic and industry publications. He is the editor of the International Journal of Contemporary Hospitality Management, which is rated as one of the tier one academic journals in the hospitality management field. He also serves on the editorial board of six journals including Annals of Tourism Research. He is the founder editor of an academic journal (Seyahat ve Otel Isletmeciligi Dergisi), which is published in Turkish. His research areas include strategy implementation, change management, competitive advantage, learning organizations, knowledge management, crisis management, cross-cultural management, and destination marketing. His teaching areas include leadership development, strategic management, strategic human resources management, strategic marketing, and international hospitality management.

John W. O'Neill, MAI, CHE, Ph.D., is an Associate Professor in lodging strategy and real estate at The Pennsylvania State University in University Park, Pennsylvania. Previously, Dr. O'Neill was Senior Associate in the Hospitality Industry Consulting Group at the international accounting and consulting firm of Coopers & Lybrand in New York, and prior to that, was Director of Market Planning for Holiday Inn at its Eastern Regional Office in Boston. Previously, he held unit-level, regional-level, and corporate-level management positions with Hyatt and Marriott in Chicago, Kansas City, and Washington, DC.

Michael D. Olsen is a Retired Professor of Strategic Management in the Department of Hospitality and Tourism Management, at Virginia Polytechnic Institute and State University, and Chairman of the Olsen Group Inc., a firm providing strategic visioning leadership to the global hospitality industry. He is a Top researcher and a frequent speaker in the global hospitality industry, published hundreds of publications.

Dr. Michael Ottenbacher is an Associate Professor at San Diego State University, USA. He received his Ph.D. in Marketing from the University of Otago, New Zealand and his Master and Bachelor of Science in Hospitality Management from Florida International University, USA. He has worked in senior hospitality positions in the USA, UK, France, and Germany. Professor Ottenbacher has widely published in leading journals including Journal of Hospitality and Tourism Research and Cornell Hospitality Quarterly.

Chris Roberts, Ph.D. is Professor of Strategic Management at the University of Massachusetts Amherst, Isenberg School of Management, Department of Hospitality and Tourism Management. He has 17 years of hospitality, travel, and telecommunications work experience. Dr. Roberts has published widely in hospitality research journals including the Journal of Hospitality and Tourism Research, the Journal of Travel Research, the Journal of Hospitality and Tourism Education, and the Journal of Hospitality and Leisure Marketing.

Dr. Angela Roper is Savoy Educational Trust Senior Lecturer in Hospitality Management in the School of Management at the University of Surrey, UK. She is an internationally recognized researcher in her field with over 16 years of experience in teaching, learning, and research in the area of the strategic management and the internationalization of hospitality and tourism firms. Over 70 academic papers and conference presentations have resulted from her research and she has been a Guest Editor for several journals. Angela holds Editorial Board positions on all the leading hospitality and tourism management journals and has been a Guest Editor for several journals. She currently holds the position of Vice-Chair on the Council for Hospitality Management Educators (CHME). Before joining the University of Surrey, Angela worked for 14 years at Oxford Brookes University, where she was Reader and Head of the Doctoral Programme in the Business School. Previous to embarking upon an academic career she worked as an Analyst for the Property and Leisure division of part of the Bank of Scotland Group.

Amit Sharma is an Assistant Professor in the School of Hospitality at The Pennsylvania State University's University Park campus. Dr. Sharma teaches financial management courses at the School of Hospitality. His research interests are in corporate finance and economic aspects of hospitality and tourism. He joined Penn State University in August 2006. Before joining Penn State he was an Assistant Professor at Iowa State University for 4 years, and completed his doctoral studies at Virginia Tech in 2002. His education includes a Bachelor in Economics from University of Delhi (India), Higher National Diploma (HND) in Hospitality Management from University of Salford (England), and a Masters in Hospitality Management from Institut de Management Hotelier International (France).

Paul Slattery is a Director of Otus & Co. a company that provides strategic advice and corporate finance services to the hospitality, travel, and transport industries. Paul worked for Dresdner Kleinwort for 15 years until 2002 in both equity research where he was head of hospitality research and in investment banking where he built the bank's franchise in the hospitality arena and advised companies such as Compass Group, Scandic Hotels, Thompson Travel Group, and Whitbread. Otus advises hotel chains, private equity funds, and real estate companies on hotel chain transactions. Otus also advises the major international hotel chains, online travel agencies, and equity providers on strategic progress for the medium to long term, drawing on its economic, hotel demand and hotel supply databases. Early in his career, Paul worked for several international hospitality companies and spent time as an academic. Paul writes regularly for academic and industry publications and is past Chairman of The International Hotel Investment Council.

Marcia Taylor is an Assistant Professor in hotel management, in the Department of Hospitality Management, at East Carolina University. She received her Ph.D. from Virginia Polytechnic Institute and State University in Hospitality Management, with a concentration in strategic management. Prior to teaching, Marcia worked in the hotel industry in various management positions.

Sabina Tonarelli-Frey, PHR, MBA, is an Adjunct Lecturer at Florida International University, School of Hospitality & Tourism Management. Through STF Consulting, Inc., Ms. Tonarelli-Frey is also a Human Resources Management Consultant for the South Florida Community. Before beginning her career as an educator and human resources management consultant, Ms. Tonarelli-Frey worked as Director of Human Resources in the hospitality arena with various major hotel companies, including Loews Hotels and Hilton Hotels. Additionally in 2002 and 2003, Ms. Tonarelli-Frey held the position of President of the South Florida Human Resources Hospitality Association. Ms. Tonarelli-Frey is a graduate of Florida International University's School of Hospitality Management programme and earned her MBA, Master's in Business Administration, from Nova Southeastern University. She received her Certified Professional in Human Resources (PHR) in 1998.

Dr. Joseph J. West is currently serving as Dean of the School of Hospitality and Tourism Management at Florida International University in Miami, Florida. He has been a hospitality educator and administrator for the past 20 years. Prior to that he held leadership positions in two high end restaurant companies and was Director of Dietary Services in three major regional medical centres. He is a retired Naval Officer and resides with his wife, Liz, in Hollywood Florida.

Elie Younes is a member of Starwood Hotels and Resorts' Acquisition & Development team. Prior to that, he was Director with HVS London office, heading the Middle East and Africa region together with Bernard Forster. While working for HVS, Elie has advised on and valued various hotel resorts, and extended stay projects, and has also given strategic advice on mid- and large-scale developments and investment ventures in the Middle East and Africa.

Dr. Jinlin Zhao is an Associate Professor and Director of Graduate Program in the School of Hospitality and Tourism Management at Florida International University, Miami,

Florida. Dr. Zhao has been an active researcher. He has been a contributing author to three IH&RA White Papers on the Global Hospitality Industry. His area of research lies in competitive methods, the international environment and impact analysis, and multinational corporate strategy. He has co-authored books and book chapters and published many articles in top ranking research journals. He has guided many Ph.D. and Master Degree students' researches.

Ian Gamse is a Director of Otus & Co. a company that provides strategic advice and corporate finance services to the hospitality, travel, and transport industries. Ian has worked in investment banking and strategic consultancy for twenty years and is a specialist in the analysis and presentation of complex data. Within Otus he has the primary responsibility for the economic, hotel demand and hotel supply databases and the array of analytical tools that inform Otus's view of the hotel industry.

Dr. Anna S. Mattila is a professor of services marketing at the School of Hospitality Management at the Pennsylvania State University. She holds a Ph.D. in services marketing from Cornell University. Her research interests focus on service encounters with a particular interest in service failures and service recovery. Her work has appeared in the *Journal of the Academy of Marketing Science, Journal of Retailing, Journal of Service Research, Journal of Consumer Psychology, Psychology & Marketing, Journal of Services Marketing, International Journal of Service Industry Management, Cornell Hotel & Restaurant Administration Quarterly, Journal of Travel Research, International Journal of Hospitality Management, Tourism Management* and in *the Journal of Hospitality & Tourism Research.* Dr. Mattila has written several book chapters and currently serves on thirteen editorial boards in journals specializing in services management. She is a recipient of John Wiley & Sons Lifetime Research Award and The University of Delaware Michael D. Olsen Lifetime Research Achievement Award.

Acknowledgements

This *handbook* is a product of 31 internationally known scholars and researchers. We are grateful to and want to express our deep appreciation to these contributors:

Dr. Fred J. DeMicco of the University of Delaware
Dr. Marvin J. Cetron of Forecasting International
Dr. António Jorge Costa, Instituto de Planeamento e
   Desenvolvimento do Turismo of Portugal
Mr. Paul Slattery of Otus & Co. Advisory Ltd., London, UK
Mr. Ian Gamse, Otus & Co. Advisory Ltd., London, UK
Dr. Angela Roper of University of Surrey, UK
Dr. Nicolas S. GRAF of the University of Houston
Mr. Eie Younes of Starwood Hotels & Resorts
Mr. Russell Kett of HVS
Dr. Melih Madanoglu of Florida Gulf Coast University
Mr. Wei He of Florida International University
Dr. Francis Kwansa of the University of Delaware
Dr. Cynthia R. Mayo of Delaware State University
Mr. Tevfik Demirciftci of the University of Delaware
Dr. John W. O'Neill of the Pennsylvania State University
Dr. Prakash K. Chathoth of the Hong Kong Polytechnic
   University
Dr. Robert Harrington of the University of Arkansas
Dr. Michael Ottenbacher of San Diego State University
Dr. Kevin S. Murphy of the University of Central Florida
Dr. Daniel J. Connolly of the University of Denver
Dr. Peter Jones of the University of Surrey
Mr. Mark H. Maloney of Compass Group
Dr. Joseph J. West of Florida International University
Mrs. Sabina Tonarelli-Frey of Florida International University
Dr. Chris Roberts of the University of Massachusetts
Dr. Marcia Taylor of East Carolina University

Mr. Sander Allegro of Hotelschool The Hague, The Netherlands

Dr. Rob de Graaf of the University of Groningen, The Netherlands

Dr. Amit Sharma of the Pennsylvania State University

Dr. Levent Altinay of Oxford Brooks University

Dr. Fevzi Okumus of the University of Central Florida

Many thanks to you all.

Preface

Strategic management has become a very important management tool in today's dynamic competitive business environment. *The Handbook of Hospitality Strategic Management* consists of 20 chapters contributed by 31 internationally recognized, leading researchers, university professors, consultants, and industry leaders. The authors provide thorough reviews of current literature and discussions of mainstream strategic-management-research subject areas. They also apply the theories and concepts by means of hospitality industry cases.

This handbook uses the co-alignment principle of strategic management, which suggests that a hospitality firm wins competitive advantage by co-aligning its opportunities with its competitive strategies, its core competencies, and its implementation process. It identifies its opportunities through environmental-scanning activities. This handbook consists of the following sections: environmental scanning, strategy as investment in competitiveness, core competencies, functional competencies, decision making, implementation, and strategy and multi-unit issues.

Environmental scanning Marvin J. Cetron, Frederick J. DeMicco, and Owen Davies analyse the impact on the hospitality business environment of economics, population change, the labour shortage, market change, technological advantage, the energy issue, and world terrorism. Using this analysis, they predict the environmental impact on the travel and tourism business of vacation patterns, the MICE market, the club market, the medical travel market, theme parks, green travel, the cruise line and airline industries, and health foods.

Jorge Costa, from the theoretical perspective, analyses the concept of business environmental scanning, its process, content, and outcome, and how these relate to the development of strategies. He also discusses major models in the field of environmental scanning and their applications. Costa also proposes a model for continuous environmental scanning and presents the impacts it may bring to hospitality organizations.

Strategy as investment in competitiveness Focused on the economic environment and its impact on hotel demand, supply, and development, Paul Slattery, Ian Gamse, and Angela Roper argue that academics have paid only minor attention to the topic in small, underfunded hotel projects. They introduce a more comprehensive approach, which is based on the continuous tracking of the structure of economies, the hotel demand and supply profiles of all hotel chains. Armed with such longitudinal data, they provide more effective interpretations of the development of international hotel chains in Europe and why they evolve as they do.

Nicolas Graf argues that the Critical Successful Factors (CSFs) approach to strategy implies that companies must do well at the core activities of their business before they can successfully attempt to gain a competitive advantage. In their pursuit of infinite growth, firms may be tempted to trade off some of these principles, but as history shows, a lack of focus on CSFs inevitably ends with long-term performance failure.

Elie Younes and Russell Kett analyse the risk factors at various life stages (development, operating, and obsolescence/exit) related to various hotel asset classes, such as limited, extended stay, shared ownership, full service, and luxury hotels. They argue that, in general, limited service hotels seem to run less risk, while luxury and full-service hotels run higher risks.

Melih Madanoglu suggests two interim solutions for this cost-of-equity conundrum in the emerging markets: The investors and academics should either (1) solely focus on future cash flows of the project, or (2) use simulations, such as Monte Carlo, in order to create multiple scenarios that approximate the investment realities of the emerging markets.

Jinlin Zhao and Wei He review literature relevant to several important concepts and explain how they are interrelated, especially in the context of the international hotel industry. They conduct a comprehensive, in-depth content analysis and summarize major competitive methods employed by multinational hotel firms between 2000 and 2007.

Francis A. Kwansa, Cynthia Mayo, and Tevfik Demirciftci believe that companies that recognize, harness, and leverage intangible assets are rewarded by investors on the stock market. They discuss many intangible assets, such as leadership, strategy execution, brand equity, reputation, network, human capital, and more that help companies maintain competitive advantage as well as sustain their revenues and earnings stream for the future. They analyse the percentage of intangible assets in relation to their total market cap of 10 lodging companies. The analysis shows that there is a rising trend in intangible value among the companies.

From a corporate strategy viewpoint, John O'Neill believes that a hotel's brand contributes significantly to the property's market value. Well-managed hotel brands tend to gain increasing market share. He further discusses brand power, brand as a value creator, brand and satisfaction, brand extension, and brand and franchising.

Prakash K. Chathoth argues that strategic alliances are used as vehicles of growth that provide partners with access to each other's resources and capabilities. He believes that in today's global economy, it is essential that hospitality firms use alliances to access markets globally. Acquiring resources or developing them internally may be a more costly option, which could be done away with if alliances are pursued.

Core competencies Robert J. Harrington and Michael Ottenbacher provide an overview of the current thinking in resource-allocation decisions and organizational structure in the general and hospitality literatures. They compare these issues for the emerging trend of "channel blurring" between retail and foodservice in order to demonstrate the impact of level of control considerations, resource availability, and demand uncertainty on structural decisions. This comparative analysis highlights key resource-allocation decision issues for the strategic option. They also provide a glimpse at factors influencing structural decisions, such as vertical integration, ownership forms, and co-branding opportunities between retail and foodservice.

Functional competencies Kevin S. Murphy and Michael D. Olsen outline the development of a high performance people system (HPPS) within the US hospitality industry and demonstrate those practices which should be included in a firm's HRM core competencies. Firms able to implement such systems possessing complementary internal fit have been shown to increase the intangible value of their human capital (employees) and create greater economic value. Such organizations can compete more effectively in their industry sector. They used Outback Steakhouse Inc. as a case to illustrate their view points.

Daniel J. Connolly argues that information technology (IT) is a resource vital to a firm's success. No longer can it be viewed simply for its support and utility roles dominant in tactical applications, which focus on the use of IT to gain efficiencies, reduce costs, decrease labour, and improve productivity. Instead, IT is increasingly playing a strategic role in organizations, where it either creates competitive advantage or enables new business opportunities. Attention is now being given to IT's ability to differentiate products and services, to create new product and service offerings, and to build and sustain core competencies.

Peter Jones and Alan Parker believe that it might seem slightly surprising that strategic operations management in the hospitality industry is relatively little discussed and not much researched. This is partly because of the "blur" between operations, marketing, and human resources; and partly because it is difficult to separate managing operations from managing operations *strategically*. Nonetheless, when this is attempted, it becomes apparent that firms have developed and adopted a strategic approach to managing their operations, which has contributed greatly to their success. The authors use the Whitbread case to illustrate how a company can compete at a number of levels: at the corporate level, for instance through merger, acquisition and disposal of other firms; at the business unit level, by having an integrated strategy based around operations, human resources and marketing; and specifically through operations, by adopting the right location strategy, ubiquity, or other operations strategies.

Decision making Joseph J. West and Sabina Tonarelli-Frey introduce the concept of leadership and their point of view of effective leadership. They believe effective leaders are highly visible, take responsibility for their actions, and have followers who do the right thing. Leaders are goal-oriented. They are judged by the actions of their followers, glorying in the strength of their followers, and intolerant of poor performance. Effective leaders understand that leadership is situational; they must either modify their behaviour or the situation to successfully attain their goals. They realize that in addition to intelligence and technical skills, they must possess emotional intelligence if they are to be effective in today's complex environment. They understand that emotional intelligence is essential if they are to lead the knowledge workers of today and tomorrow. Effective leaders understand that they are responsible for the ethical behaviour of their organizations.

Chris Roberts believes that organizational culture is recognized as one of the most powerful forces in determining an organization's success. Resistance to goals and strategic plans from those within the organization can doom such efforts before they have any opportunity to succeed. Therefore, understanding what constitutes an organizational culture and how to influence it are key aspects of effectively formulating and implementing strategic plans.

Marcia H. Taylor and Michael D. Olsen investigated the co-alignment between elements of the co-alignment model: strategy choice, firm structure, and firm performance. Based on "resource-based view" literature, they conducted in-depth interviews with general managers and other managers of five hotels, direct observations, guests' surveys and secondary data in Jamaica. They revealed the importance of co-alignment in hotels: Performance was best when co-alignment was present. In addition, the findings indicated that the competitive methods cited by managers as providing the greatest value to the hotels were not always in line with what was most important to the guests.

Implementation Sander Allegro and Rob de Graaf look into three innovative concepts that help make the right decisions around innovation: scenario thinking, the innovator's dilemma, and the development of new services. These concepts have been used in industry for many years and have increased product and service sales and profits. These concepts are applicable to the hospitality industry as well. They present a case study of Qbic hotels, a truly innovative concept that was introduced in the European hotel market

Amit Sharma argues that a large number of small businesses play a very important role in the hospitality and tourism industry; however, most hospitality strategy literature is based on strategy models with a lesser emphasis on small businesses. By default the emphasis has been on studying large businesses. He believes that it is necessary to strengthen hospitality strategy literature by studying small businesses. Researchers will need to expand the existing models and theories, develop a parallel stream of literature focused solely on small businesses, and evaluate strategic process of such businesses.

Strategy and multiunit issues Levent Altinay and Fevzi Okumus discuss and evaluate factors influencing entrepreneurial orientation of ethnic minority SMEs in the tourism and hospitality industry. They believe that owners of ethnic minority SMEs play a crucial role in setting a direction and influencing the culture and management of these firms. They argue that the owners who have a higher level of language proficiency of the host country and business education are better equipped to communicate and understand the stakeholders and develop appropriate strategies. In return, such skills then lead to better performance and a higher growth in their businesses. Therefore, researchers need to understand and evaluate the cultural background, religion, language skills, education, and work experience of these entrepreneurs.

We believe that the depth and coverage of each topic is unprecedented. It is a must-read for any hospitality researchers and educators, students, and industry practitioners interested in the hospitality strategic management.

Michael Olsen, Ph.D., of Virginia Tech
Jinlin Zhao, Ph.D., of Florida International University

Part One

Strategy in general

Travel 2015: scanning the environment—the next big thing in travel and tourism

Marvin J. Cetron[1], Frederick J. DeMicco[2] and Owen Davies[3]

[1]*President, Forecasting International, Arlington, VA, USA*
[2]*Professor & ARAMARK Chair of Global Strategy & Development,
Hotel, Restaurant & Institutional Management,
Lerner College of Business & Economics,
The University of Delaware and Conti Distinguished Professor at
the Pennsylvania State University's School of Hotel,
Restaurant and Recreation Management, Newark, DE*
[3]*Research Associate, Forecasting International,
Arlington, VA, USA*

Introduction

Travel and tourism form one of the largest and fastest growing industries, both in the United States and throughout the world. This sector also is changing rapidly. In this chapter (which has been adapted from a forthcoming book of the name: Travel 2015: The Next Big Thing in Travel and Tourism), the senior authors—one a prominent and widely respected forecaster, the other ARAMARK Chair of Hotel and Restaurant Management at the University of Delaware—offer a clear-eyed and compelling look into the future of this diverse field. In addition, they provide tools with which readers can begin to make useful forecasts for their own companies and careers.

This is a chapter to examine the future of tourism, travel, transportation, and related services.

Overview

The travel and tourism industry is accustomed to good times. Yet for some years, travel suffered. And because it was unprepared for adversity, it suffered more than it needed to. Today, prosperity has returned, but there are warning signs that we still could see another period of declining travel and pinched revenues. This chapter will tell readers what lies in the future and provide an introduction to forecasting, a critical management tool for turbulent times.

The terrorist attacks of September 11, 2001, more than decimated the travel industry. International tourism to the U.S. plunged by 70%. Even such evergreen attractions as Disney World, Washington, and Las Vegas were forced to cut back, and profits collapsed throughout the industry. In the United States, airlines alone laid off an estimated 100,000 workers. Travel-related firms in Europe and Asia suffered similar declines. More recently, SARS and hostility over Europe's position on the Iraq war have aggravated this already-grim situation.

These problems could not have been avoided, but it might at least have been possible to prepare for them. In 1994, author Marvin Cetron and his colleagues at Forecasting International carried out a study of terrorism for the Pentagon. Their report, Terror 2000, specifically predicted events that to many people then seemed unthinkable. These included a massive assault on the World Trade Towers, an attack on the Pentagon using a commandeered airplane, and the delivery of simultaneous blows by Muslim extremists against widely separated targets.

If this study had been undertaken for the hospitality industry, the implications would have been obvious; hotel, resort, and airline executives at least could have managed their resources to weather the coming storm.

Those insights—still vitally important in the post-9/11 world—are only a small part of what this chapter has to offer. This chapter will tell readers what to expect in the travel and tourism industry for the rest of this decade. In this book, we will examine both general issues, such as the state of the economy and the supply of suitable workers, and specific trends that are now changing important industry sectors. We will cover hotels and resorts, airlines, cruise lines, and other aspects of this field. In addition, we will reveal the specific trends that Forecasting International uses to make its forecasts and tell readers how they can be used to predict their own futures.

The pressing need to look ahead is a lesson that many people have learned well in recent years. Economic boom and bust, technological change, international competition, terrorism, and other predictable forces have destroyed some industries, created others, and left none untouched. No one at the level of middle management or above, and no student preparing for a career, can do his job without keeping one eye on the future.

We believe that many executives, teachers, and students in the travel and tourism industry will be eager for an advance look at the years ahead. The next few years will be a challenging time, and these potential readers will need all the help we can offer them.

Part I: common concerns for the hospitality industry

Forecasting, a quick introduction

There is nothing arcane, or even particularly difficult, about anticipating what is to come. However, sound forecasting does require a good sense of what is going on in the world, the ability to look at new information objectively, and some practice at relating general trends to the specific conditions of an industry or company. This chapter will explain the strengths and limitations of forecasting and introduce the methods by which Forecasting International arrives at its insights. This will serve to reassure sceptical readers that the predictions made in this book are worth listening to.

Money matters

The single greatest factor shaping the future of the travel and tourism industry is the condition of the U.S. economy. When Americans are prosperous, the world's hotels, airlines, cruise ships, and destinations flourish as well. When Americans feel poor, the impact is felt around the world. Regionally, the economies of Europe and Japan have similar influence on this consumer-sensitive industry. In the years ahead, the economies of China and India will become nearly as influential as that of the United States.

Forecasting International has long believed that the U.S. economy would be generally strong through at least this decade, with only temporary, relatively mild interruptions. The post-9/11 recession has done nothing to change that view, and current data indicates that a healthy recovery has begun. This augurs well for the travel and tourism industry through at least 2010. Beyond that, the health of the economy depends significantly on federal tax and spending policies in ways that we will make clear.

For other economies, the picture is mixed. We will make concrete forecasts for them late in the production schedule.

Grey power

Throughout the developed world, populations are growing older. The elderly live longer, thanks to healthier living and better medical care, and the vast Baby Boom generation, now nearing retirement, is being followed by much smaller generations. By 2025, the number of people age 15–64 in Germany, Italy, Japan, and Spain—among other countries—will see double-digit declines, while the number of elderly grows rapidly. Japan has the highest average longevity in the world and a birth rate so low that by 2050 its population is expected to decline by 30%, while the senior population grows to nearly 37% of the total. Thus, in 2025 more than 18% of the American population will be age 65 or older, up from 12% today. Throughout the world, the ranks of 60-year-olds and older are growing 1.9% per year, 60% faster than the overall world population. People over 65 made up only 15% of the population in the developed world in 2000, but will grow to 27% of the population in the next half-century.

Add to this the growing concentration of wealth among seniors, thanks to their longer time for earning and investment and the contribution of social security benefits in most of the developed world, and we see a trend that will have a profound impact on hospitality and travel. More and more of the hospitality industry's guests will be seniors. Many will be healthier than their parents and grandparents were at the same age, and they will demand more active, adventurous vacations than previous generations of seniors could endure, much less enjoy. Yet others will be frail or sickly and will need care and assistance that destinations are accustomed to providing. And all are likely to require special accommodations for their changing needs. Hotels will require arthritis-friendly handles on doors and faucets—levers, rather than knobs—brighter lighting, and signs that are easier to read, with larger lettering and less clutter. Restaurants will need to provide meals with more intense flavours suited to the declining acuity of older palates. And personnel throughout the industry will require training to attend better to the needs of the elderly. These and other changing demands will be a continual challenge to travel and tourism.

Personnel

The supply of entry-level and low-wage workers is shrinking throughout the developed world, while the travel and tourism industry continues to need ever more inexpensive, personable, and well-trained people to care for its guests. In the years ahead, the industry will meet this problem by recruiting from among retirees and other relatively underutilized groups of potential employees. Inevitably, it also will recruit from younger generations of workers, whose values and expectations vary significantly from those of their parents, older siblings, and company superiors. Finally, new educational techniques and certification opportunities will change the process of training new employees and teaching them the corporate culture. Many companies will find themselves teaching many of their new hires English as a second language. All these factors will modify personnel and management practices in important and sometimes unexpected ways.

Impact of new travel technology

In the next few years, airliners will grow larger, faster, and more efficient. Cruise ships will become larger, more efficient, and better equipped with high-tech amenities such as instant Internet access. The United States may finally begin to replace regional air travel with high-speed rail. "Intelligent" highways will speed ground transportation throughout the developed world. Rail, too, is becoming ever more important for middle-distance travel as high-speed rail systems proliferate.

And Internet-based marketing will continue to chip away at the travel agents' remaining foothold in the industry. These and other developments will change the way the travel and tourism do business in the years ahead, as this chapter will explain.

Slice and dice marketing

Around the world, more and more travellers are using their vacations to visit places and partake of activities that fewer and fewer of them would be interested in. This is not a paradox; it is the latest thing in market segmentation: niche marketing to ever smaller groups of people who share specific, often unique, interests and values. Poker players, amateur astronomers, fans of mystery fiction, and gays and lesbians all form specialized and lucrative markets that cruise lines and travel destinations have tapped with great success. Serving these niche markets is quickly proving to be one of the most productive trends in travel and tourism.

At least five market segments will be growing fast for the next decade or more: adventure travel, ecotourism, attractions based on tragedy and terrorism, African-American history (in the United States), and so-called medical tourism, which we will examine at much greater length in Chapter 11.

Energy: lifeblood of travel

We see it most clearly in the airlines, which have jammed more seats into the economy sections of their planes, trimmed flight schedules, and added fuel-cost surcharges to their ticket prices. Yet cruise lines, hotels, and other parts of the travel and tourism sector are feeling it as well: with crude oil at nearly $120 in April 2008, the high price of energy began to hurt. Energy costs are likely to remain relatively high for the next year or two.

And in the long run? There is little hope that oil prices will return to the comfortable levels of $30 or $35 per barrel that were standard just a few years ago. In 2015, and for years thereafter, fossil fuels will remain the world's most important energy resources, with oil clearly in the lead.

Yet if energy will never be cheap, neither will it remain as expensive as it has been of late. Contrary to many dire forecasts, there is no evidence that our supply is soon to run out. Proved oil reserves stand just above 1 trillion barrels, enough to keep the plant going for another 20 years or so. They have remained at that level for decades and show no sign of shrinking in the years ahead. More importantly, new refining capacity—the real limiting factor in the world's fuel supply—will at last come online by 2009 or 2010. When it does, the cost of oil will drop significantly. The International Monetary Fund is predicting that oil will cost $34 per barrel in 2010. At Forecasting International, we would not be surprised to see it at $40–$45 per barrel. Yet even this is a big improvement in prices over 2008. It is a cost that the world's travel and tourism operators will easily afford.

"Bang, you're dead!" and they mean it

Wherever extremists aim their guns and bombs, they hit the travel and tourism industry. Sometimes they strike directly, as in Indonesia and Bali, where Jamaah Islamiya bombed a Marriott hotel and a night club full of tourists. Sometimes they strike indirectly, as in the September 11 attacks, which all but destroyed international tourism and air travel even though they were not aimed directly at the industry. This is a problem that will be with us for decades, as the recent plot to blow up airliners travelling from Britain to the United States demonstrates yet again.

In a recent Harris poll, 94% of travellers surveyed understandably said that they now consider security a critical factor when deciding where to stay. Coping with this heightened concern for safety will require important changes in security, personnel, and sourcing practices, not only for airlines, but for hotels, resorts, cruise lines, and other travel facilities. Many organizations have responded slowly or not at all to this grim, still-new reality. Doing so effectively will mean tightening the screening of personnel—not only their own, but those of suppliers—installation of intrusion barriers, and even upgrading standard safety measures such as fire alarms and food storage. This chapter will tell what to expect in the years ahead, and how to cope with the demands increasingly being placed on them.

Part II: sector forecasts

If this is Tuesday, it must be Orlando

Major changes have swept the tourism sector in the recent 2 years. Busy working people are taking smaller vacations and more of them—a long weekend or a 4-day get-away every couple of months, rather than one or two traditional vacations each year. Retirees are travelling in the off-season. Cruise vacations have become the fastest growing sector of the tourism market. And, increasingly, consumers are cutting out the middleman and booking their own vacations online. This has been good news for most of the industry—with the obvious exception of the travel agents—because it has evened out a lot of tourism's customary seasonality.

However, there has been bad news as well. The September 2001 terrorist attacks, the controversy over the Iraq war, and the slow job growth of recent years (compared to the boom years of the 1990s) all are changing travel habits in unwelcome ways. Elective air travel remains depressed, and international tourism to and from the United States is off sharply. Hotel occupancy has fallen more than 25% in Paris, while foreign visitors remain unaccustomedly scarce at the Orlando theme parks. In general, Americans are vacationing within driving distance of their homes, making day trips, and visiting the local amusement park, rather than going farther afield.

Some of these changes will prove transient as September 11 and the Iraq war fade further into the background. Others may be with us for years. This chapter will tell what to expect.

Away on business: the MICE market

Business travellers go to meetings and exhibitions for the "three Cs"—contacts, contracts, and certification—and for a "high-touch" antidote to the sterile pressures of an increasingly high-tech world. As a result, gatherings large and small have long been an essential part of many industries, and they used to be one of the easier, more profitable markets for the hotels and resorts that host them. Booking them meant a block of rooms filled, and payment for them was assured.

Today, the MICE market—for meetings, incentives, certification, and exhibitions—has been struggling with difficult challenges. Video conferencing is quickly replacing in-person meetings, and online instruction allows certification whenever and wherever the student finds most convenient. The market for incentive travel is growing quickly, but it generally offers much smaller sales. For the host destinations, this has meant more effort, smaller profits, and a lot less certainty.

This is a taste of things to come. In the years ahead, the global population will continue to grow and change, science and technology will tighten their hold on business and society, and the world will knit itself ever more tightly into a single market. And all this means that competition and cost cutting will grow ever more intense. As a result, both opportunities and trials will abound in the MICE market.

Club medic

The well-to-do have long visited spas for weight loss, exercise, and general pampering; others have gone to specialized clinics for medical procedures not approved at home. And spas in particular are a fast growing segment of the travel and tourism industry. They are creating new products and penetrating new markets.

However, growing numbers of people are going abroad for more critical forms of care. When they require surgery or dental work, they combine it with a trip to the Taj Mahal, a photo safari on the African veldt, or a stay at a luxury hotel—or at a hospital that feels like one—all at bargain-basement prices. This is medical tourism, and it is one of the hottest niche markets in travel and tourism.

Medical tourists have good cause to seek out care far from home. In some regions, state-of-the-art medical facilities are hard to come by, if they exist at all. For that reason, patients throughout the Middle East are travelling to Jordan or Asia for complicated surgery. In other countries, the public health care system is so overburdened that it can take years to get needed care. In Britain or Canada, the waiting list for a hip replacement can be a year or more long. In Bangkok or Bangalore, you can be in a state-of-the-art operating room the morning after you get off the plane. But for most people, the real attraction is price. The cost of surgery in India, Thailand, or South Africa can be one-tenth of rates in the United States or Western Europe, and sometimes even less.

Under the circumstances, it is no surprise that the medical tourism market is growing rapidly. Ten years ago, it was hardly large enough to be noticed. Today, something over 250,000 patients per year visit Singapore alone; nearly half arrive from the Middle East. Perhaps half a million annually travel to India for medical care; in 2002, it was only 150,000. McKinsey, the consulting firm, estimates that medical tourism could bring India as much as $2.2 billion per year by 2012. Throughout Asia, Africa, South America, and Eastern Europe, clinics and tour directors alike are rushing to tap this lucrative market. They will make medical tourism one of the fastest growing niche markets in the travel and tourism industry for many years to come.

The theme is amusement

It was a good year for the world's amusement and theme parks in 2005, the most recent year for which figures are available. Some 253 million people visited amusement parks that year, up 2.2% from 2004. The years ahead should be even better.

Amusement parks are one of the few travel and tourism markets that cater to visitors who are short of funds and actually prosper in lean times. The proliferation of young families in the next decade, particularly outside the United States, will create a ready market of cash-strapped customers looking for inexpensive entertainment close to home. However, the price of success for parks is constant investment in new rides, stage shows, and other attractions. Today's prosperity will enable them to make these costly commitments, ensuring that the good times continue.

Water, water everywhere—but that is not what they drink

Cruising is hot, hot, hot, and not just when the weather turns sultry. More than 80 ocean-going cruise lines with over 250 ships now visit some 2000 destinations, and bookings are expanding by 8% annually, the fastest growth rate in the travel and tourism industry.

Yet it has not all been clear sailing for the cruise sector. In 2001, some 10 million people booked passage on the world's cruise lines. The terrorist attacks of September 11 slashed that demand. Drastic price cuts have brought business back, but decimated profits. Ticket prices remain depressed, and passengers are beginning to complain that service has suffered as a result. And capacity is rising even faster than demand.

All this brings up obvious questions: Can even these livable times last, or do worse problems lie just over the horizon? How long will cruise prices remain depressed? How can cruise operators turn growing demand into solid profits? How can they adapt to the challenges of a fast-changing world?

Travel goes green

One of the fastest niche markets in the travel industry is ecotourism, where the colour green stands for environmental concern, not dollars spent per minute. Hard data on the ecotourism market is difficult to find, in part because it is not easy to pin down exactly which activities really qualify. However, a few figures offer at least a hint of this market's size and potential. In 1993, the World Tourism Organization estimated that "nature tourism" accounted for just 7% of all money spent on international travel. Just 10 years later, it put the figure at 20% in the Asia-Pacific region. In some areas, such as South Africa, the number of visitors to game and nature preserves is doubling every year. Another report from the WTO estimated that ecotourism is the fastest growing segment of the tourism industry, expanding by about 5% per year. It represents 6% of the global GDP and 11.4% of all consumer spending.

This fast growth is powered by some important trends. One is the health of the developed economies, which provide the vast majority of ecotourists. Another is the youth of the most eco-conscious population segment. Too short of cash to indulge in lavish vacations today, these young families soon will mature into their peak earning years and will set about turning their nature-oriented vacation dreams into reality. It helps also that the Baby Boom generation, which largely invented ecotourism, is the largest generation in history and soon will be the wealthiest.

All this points to major growth in ecotourism in general, and in such subcategories as geotourism, nature-based tourism, and pro-poor tourism. This will bring new prosperity, both to a wide variety of new destinations and to tour operators capable of cashing in on this powerful trend.

Troubled airlines begin to soar

The perpetually earthbound airline industry is one sector that needs a little good news. Fortunately, there is more to offer than many observers recognize. It took a few years, but the passenger shortage that followed the September 11 hijackings has finally been fully made up. In 2005 and 2006, the recovering global economy brought unaccustomed profits to many of the world's airlines, including the financially shaky U.S. carriers. This was made possible by a variety of sound business decisions, including cutbacks in unprofitable routes, imposition of fuel surcharges to compensate for high energy prices, and the packing of still more seats into economy sections.

Paradoxically, the best news may have been the plot to blow up airliners in flight between Britain and the United States. Unlike the successful attacks of 9/11, the potential horror revealed in mid-2006 has had little impact on air travel. Flights from Great Britain were nearly grounded, not for lack of passengers, but because stringent security measures enacted after the incident took so long that few would-be travellers could make their planes without longer waits than most could endure. In the U.S., air passengers accepted hours-long lines with scarcely a murmur of protest. This has to be a good omen for the period, soon to come, when security measures return to normal.

Yet the real payoff will come in 2010 and beyond. By then, fuel costs should be declining, travel demand growing, and the new leanness and efficiency of the world's airlines—enhanced by still more fuel-efficient models from Airbus and Boeing—should bring prosperity at last to the world's long-beleaguered airlines.

Food for thought

Restaurants and food service used to be an afterthought for hotels, resorts, and travel destinations. Given a choice, travellers were likely to stop at a nearby restaurant instead of eating in. Today, that is changing, and restaurants are becoming a significant profit centre for many travel and tourism businesses. This exposes them to the same trends that are affecting free-standing restaurants.

Diners are becoming more health conscious, more quality conscious, and much more interested in convenience and economy. These trends are changing the food from restaurants to the local supermarket. They are most advanced here in the United States, but are beginning to appear in Europe as well.

At home, Americans are looking for meals that are easy to serve, but many are "cuisine literate yet culinary illiterate" due to increased global travel.

Scanning the business environment

Jorge Costa

IPDT – Institute for Tourism Planning and Development, Santa Maria da Feira, Portugal

Introduction

This chapter analyses the concept of business environmental scanning, its process, content, and outcome and how these relate to the development of strategies. The major models in the field of environmental scanning and their applications are also presented and analysed. Finally, a model for continuous environmental scanning is proposed and the impacts it may bring to hospitality organizations who adopt it, are explained.

As research into the environmental scanning activities of organizations started in areas other than those of hospitality and tourism, the majority of the literature on this subject relates to industrial and other service organizations. From the small number of studies on the environmental scanning activities of hospitality organizations, a review of the most relevant is presented.

Strategic planning and environmental scanning

There is no generally accepted definition of strategic planning; different authors use different terms to define the same concept (Mintzberg *et al.*, 2005; Stoner and Freeman, 1986). However, the definition proposed by Wheelen and Hunger (1989, p. 14) provides a good illustration of the process and content of strategic planning while at the same time addressing basically the same aspects as other authors:

... the development of long range plans for the effective management of environmental opportunities and threats in the light of corporate strengths and weaknesses. Such planning includes establishing the corporate mission, specifying objectives, developing strategies, and setting policy guidelines.

According to research (Mintzberg *et al.*, 2005; Mintzberg, 1992; Costa, 1997), the development of strategies is not always carried out in such a formal way. As found by Mintzberg, there are organizations where strategies are not deliberate but emergent. This realized approach to strategy development is likely to result in different attitudes towards the management of environmental opportunities as proposed by Wheelen and Hunger. In addition to considering strategic planning activities, the emergent approach to strategy also requires clarification namely in respect of how an organization's objectives are formally defined and strategies developed. This is also one of the limitations identified by Costa and Teare (2000) and West (1988) in their research on the relationship between strategy, environmental scanning, and performance.

The identification and management of environmental opportunities, however, is seen as fundamental to the competitive positioning of companies (Garland, 2007; Mazarr, 1999; Fahey and King, 1977; Segev, 1977; Kefalas and Schoderbeck, 1973). The identification of business environmental trends can be achieved using environmental scanning, which is seen by Aguilar (1967) as a way to examine information about events and relationships in a company's outside environment. This information can then be used to assist top management in its task of charting the company's future course of action.

The importance of environmental scanning for organizations can be seen by looking at some of its potential outcomes: identification of events and trends in the external environment, and the possible relationships between them. An understanding of the data may help organizations extract the main implications for decision making and strategy development (Van Deusen et al., 2007; Okumus, 2004; Daft et al., 1988; Lenz and Engledow, 1986; Stubbart, 1982). Even though it is an established activity with well-defined elements, environmental scanning is not regularly used by business organizations (Garland, 2007; West and Olsen, 1989; Jain, 1984).

Research on environmental scanning has followed different directions (Okumus, 2004; Olsen and Roper, 1998). Some studies focus their attention on the information-gathering activities of senior-level executives (Miller and Friesen, 1983; Hoffman and Hegarty, 1983; Hambrick, 1982; Segev, 1977; Keegan, 1974; Kefalas and Schoderbeck, 1973; Aguilar, 1967), while others on various analytical techniques and formal strategic planning systems (Stoffels, 1994; Lorange, 1982; Steiner, 1979; Post, 1973). Yet another approach (Narchal et al., 1987) covered the social and psychological processes associated with organizational learning and executive decision making (Dutton and Duncan, 1983; McCaskey, 1982; Weick, 1979; Dill, 1962).

Empirical research also demonstrates that for environmental scanning to succeed it has to be linked to the formal planning process (Evans et al., 2003; Engledow and Lenz, 1989; Jain, 1984; Fahey and King, 1977). Even though organizations regard environmental information as highly relevant for strategic planning the majority still perceive themselves as basically involved in relating environmental phenomena to short-term choices (Okumus, 2004; Costa, 1997; Fahey and King, 1977). Knowing the nature of the link between environmental scanning and strategic planning among hospitality organizations is fundamental in understanding how the information on existing and future trends in the business environment supports strategy development and decision making.

The concept of business environment

The environment of an organization consists of the outside forces that directly or indirectly influence its goals, structure, size, plans, procedures, operations, input, output, and human relations (Van Deusen *et al.*, 2007; Preble, 1978; Segev, 1977). The importance of understanding the environment is demonstrated in research by Bourgeois (1985) where he shows that a firm which examines its environment accurately, tends to achieve a higher than average level of economic performance.

The theory of open systems introduced the concept of the environment and its effect on the organization (West and Anthony, 1990). The concept of an open system is based on the assumption that an organization's growth and survival is dependent on the nature of the environment that it faces (Fahey *et al.*, 1983). It has been recognized that different environments impose different demands and/or opportunities for organizations (Okumus, 2004; Kefalas and Schoderbeck, 1973).

Thomas (1974) suggests that the application of systems theory to the corporate environment can be done by employing the concepts of "resolution levels" or "superordinate systems." These can be grouped into two broad categories: "operating environment" and "general environment." The operating environment[1] can be defined as the set of suppliers and other interest groups which the firm deals with, while general environment is defined as the national and global context of social, political, regulatory, economic, and technological conditions (Johnson *et al.*, 2006; Daft *et al.*, 1988; Fahey and King, 1977; Thomas, 1974). According to Daft *et al.* (1988), sectors[2] in the task and general environment are expected to influence scanning and other organizational activities because these sectors differ in uncertainty.

Thomas (1974) argues that the analysis of the general environment is at least as important as the analysis of the operating environment for purposes of corporate planning. While sharing the same perspective, Fahey and King (1977) go further and consider the general environment as being more relevant to strategic planning and as requiring a greater degree of innovation in the collection of information.

---

[1] The operating environment is sometimes referred to as "specific environment," "immediate environment," and/or "task environment."
[2] Sectors are the main elements comprising both task and general environment, i.e., competitors, suppliers, social, political, and so on.

The concept of environmental scanning

The seminal work in this field was carried out by Aguilar (1967) whose purpose was to look at the ways in which top management gains relevant information about events occurring outside the company in order to guide the company's future course of action. In his study Aguilar (1967, p. vii) refers to environmental scanning as:

scanning for information about events and relationships in a company's outside environment, the knowledge of which would assist top management in its task of charting the company's future course of action.

A similar perspective is proposed by Hambrick (1981) who defines environmental scanning as the managerial activity of learning about events and trends in the organization's environment, conceiving it as the first step in the ongoing chain of perceptions and actions leading to an organization's adaptation to its environment.

The majority of authors agree that the main functions of environmental scanning are: to learn about events and trends in the external environment; to establish relationships between them; to make sense of the data; and to extract the main implications for decision making and strategy development (Costa and Teare, 2000; Olsen and Roper, 1998; Daft *et al.*, 1988; Lenz and Engledow, 1986; Stubbart, 1982; Fahey and King, 1977; Segev, 1977; Keegan, 1974; Thomas, 1974; Kefalas and Schoderbeck, 1973).

Despite being an established activity with well-defined elements, environmental scanning is not in widespread use among business organizations (Okumus, 2004; Costa, 1997; West and Olsen, 1989; Jain, 1984) and the scanning behaviour differs from one company to another (Costa and Teare, 2000; Olsen *et al.*, 1994; Daft *et al.*, 1988; Preble *et al.*, 1988; Lenz and Engledow, 1986; Farh *et al.*, 1984; Hambrick, 1982).

Research shows that the degree of importance of environmental scanning in a company can be inferred by the way scanning activities are integrated into the overall planning process (Costa and Teare, 2000; Okumus, 2004; Fahey and King, 1977). According to Jain (1984) as companies grow in size and complexity their need for formal strategic planning increases accordingly and with it the need for a systematic approach to environmental scanning. Thus, Jain adds that the effectiveness of strategic planning is directly related to the capacity for environmental scanning.

In this context, back in 1977, Terry argued that the most obvious use of environmental scanning was the gathering of data for long-range planning. Terry suggested that being such an important activity it could be also used for organizational development and design, development of agenda for executive boards or boards of management, and management education. The importance of this view is well illustrated more than 30 years later by Garland (2007, p. 4) when he states that "trends combine and interact ... to present your business with wild and unprecedented threats and opportunities." that need constant attention.

As organizations derive their existence from the environment, they should scan and monitor their business environment and incorporate the impact of environmental trends on the organization by reviewing corporate strategy on a continuous basis (Garland, 2007; Jain, 1993). From Jain's standpoint scanning improves an organization's abilities to deal with a rapidly changing environment in various ways:

- It helps an organization capitalize early on opportunities;
- It provides an early signal of impending problems;
- It sensitizes an organization to the changing needs and wishes of its customers;
- It provides a base of objective qualitative information about the environment;
- It provides intellectual stimulation to strategists in their decision making;
- It improves the image of the organization with its publics by showing that it is sensitive to its environment and responsive to it.

The information gathered by the environmental scanning process differs from industry or competitive analysis in two main aspects: it is broad in scope and it is future-directed (Johnson *et al.*, 2006; Costa and Teare, 2000; Stubbart, 1982). As such, environmental scanning should be conceptualized as a process of data collection about the business environment, which may help managers identify opportunities, detect and interpret problem areas, and implement strategic or structural adaptations (Okumus, 2004; Daft *et al.*, 1988).

Scanning characteristics and processes • • •

According to Murphy (1989) there are some characteristics of environmental scanning that can be seen as essential:

- It should be integrative (part of the planning and decision-making system of the corporation);

- It should be relevant to strategic planning (focus on strategic issues and assistance in strategic decision making);
- It should take a holistic approach (so as not to miss any signals).

Terry (1977) and more recently, Costa and Teare (2000) argue that environmental scanning will normally start in existing organizations and, therefore, much relevant data will be readily available, for example, the company's mission and functional plans. These, they assert, should be taken into account in setting up the process of environmental scanning, even though they may be radically altered after the scan has taken place. Consequently, Terry suggests that the following should inform the designing of an environmental scanning process:

- The scan needs to consider all possible influences in the company;
- The purpose of environmental scanning is not to foretell accurately the future but to plot the issues that are likely to have impact on the company so that it can be prepared to cope with them when they arise;
- The results of environmental scanning should be a proactive rather than a reactive stance by the company towards its environment;
- It is not sufficient for managers to understand the plan that results from the environmental scan, it is crucial that they understand the thinking that has led to the development of strategic and tactical key issues;
- It should focus managers' attention on what lies outside the organization and allow them to create an organization which can adapt to and learn from that environment.

Approaches to environmental scanning ● ● ●

There are two distinct approaches within environmental scanning: the "outside-in" or macro-approach, and the "inside-out" or micro-approach (Fahey and Narayanan, 1986). The outside-in approach adopts a broad view of the environment. It looks at all the existing elements in the outside environment facing the organization. Its main concerns are the longer-term trends, the development of alternative views or scenarios of the future environment, and the identification of the implications for the industry in which the firm operates and the implications for the firm itself. The inside-out approach takes a narrow view of the environment. It looks just for some elements in the outside

Table 2.1 The Outside-in and Inside-out Perspectives

	Outside-in	**Inside-out**
Focus and scope	Unconstrained view of environment	View of environment constrained by conception of organization
Goal	Broad environmental analysis before considering the organization	Environmental analysis relevant to current organization
Time horizon	Typically 1–5 years, sometimes 5–10 years	Typically 1–3 years
Frequency	Periodic/ad hoc	Continuous/periodic
Strengths	Avoids organizational blinders Identifies broader array of trends Identifies trends earlier	Efficient, well-focused analysis Implications for organizational action

Source: Adapted from Fahey and Narayanan (1986).

environment as its view is constrained by the internal influences of the organization. For the main differences between these perspectives see Table 2.1.

These same approaches to environmental scanning taken by hospitality organizations were recently confirmed by Okumus (2004) in an extensive review of environmental scanning research and its development in the international hospitality industry.

The content of environmental scanning • • •

The elements most commonly referred to as composing environmental scanning are: political, economic, social, and technological elements, well known as "PEST analysis" (Johnson *et al.*, 2006; Fahey and Narayanan, 1986; Aaker, 1984). The activity through which organizations collect data from these areas can be characterized as Irregular, Periodic, or Continuous in increasing order of sophistication and complexity (Fahey *et al.*, 1983). According to these authors, irregular systems are characterized by the reactive nature of planning as well as environmental scanning. On the other hand, they suggest that periodic systems are more sophisticated and complex, and, while the focus is still on problem-solving, they exhibit greater proactive characteristics. Finally, they believe continuous systems are the ideal systems because attention is directed not only towards mere problem-solving but primarily towards opportunity-finding and the realization that planning systems contribute to the growth and survival of the organization in a proactive way. This view is supported by Garland (2007) in his work on how business can anticipate and profit from the trends in the general environment.

The outcome of environmental scanning • • •

The outcomes of environmental scanning, according to Costa and Teare (2000) and Fahey and Narayanan (1986), are: an understanding of current and potential changes taking place in the environment; the provision of important data for strategic decision makers; and the facilitation and development of strategic thinking in organizations. Jain (1993) emphasizes that scanning serves as an early warning system for the environmental forces that may impact a company's products and markets in the future. As argued by researchers in the field of hospitality (Costa, 1997; Slattery and Olsen, 1984) environmental scanning helps managers to foresee favourable and unfavourable influences and initiate strategies that will enable their organizations to adapt to the environment. These outcomes can be divided into short-term and long-term outcomes. In the short term the outcome is to modify the company's actions in order to better explore opportunities and avoid threats. In the long term the outcome is to inform the development of strategies.

However, while the outcomes of environmental scanning are very important the process of engaging in it is no less important (Okumus, 2004; Fahey and Narayanan, 1986). Undertaking the process, according to these authors, leads to enhanced capacity and commitment in understanding, anticipating, and responding to external changes on the part of the firm's key strategic managers. Environmental scanning can be a powerful tool for strategic planning if it has specific aims and objectives, and the commitment of the key players within the organization (Engledow and Lenz, 1989).

Environmental scanning and strategic planning relationship

As empirical research shows, to succeed environmental scanning activity has to be linked to the formal planning process (Costa and Teare, 2000; Engledow and Lenz, 1989; Jain, 1984; Fahey and King, 1977). However, even though organizations realize and accept the need to relate environmental information to long-range plans, so far most of them still perceive themselves as being primarily involved in relating environmental phenomena to short-term choices (Costa, 1997; Fahey and King, 1977).

Jain (1993) proposes a seven-step approach to explain the link between environmental scanning and corporate strategy in organizations:

1. Keep a tab on broad trends appearing in the environment;
2. Determine the relevance of an environmental trend;
3. Study the impact of an environmental trend on a product/market;
4. Forecast the direction of an environmental trend into the future;
5. Analyse the momentum of the product/market business in the face of the environmental trend;
6. Study the new opportunities that an environmental trend appears to provide;
7. Relate the outcome of an environmental trend to corporate strategy.

As Jain (1993) and Johnson *et al.* (2006) suggest, based on information about environmental trends and their impacts, a company needs to review its strategy on two counts: changes that may be introduced in current products/markets, and feasible opportunities that the company may embrace for action. In fact, the identification of weak signals in the business environment may provide the best opportunities for organizations in the long term (Stoffels, 1994; Ansoff and McDonnell, 1990).

Scanning and the development of strategies

Strategy as a plan and strategy as a pattern have different implications for environmental scanning activities. According to research (Costa, 1997; Daft *et al.*, 1988; Jain, 1984; Fahey and King, 1977; Kefalas and Schoderbeck, 1973), environmental scanning needs to be linked to strategic planning in order to be a successful activity. From this perspective, environmental scanning fits perfectly into the planning process of the organization. However, in organizations where strategies result from consistency in behaviour the design of environmental scanning activities for strategic decision making will have to follow a different process (Okumus, 2004).

As demonstrated by research (Costa and Teare, 2000; Daft *et al.*, 1988; Jain, 1984; Fahey and King, 1977; Kefalas and Schoderbeck, 1973), there is a strong link between environmental scanning and strategic planning. While environmental scanning provides information for strategic decision making, the development of strategies justifies the need for environmental scanning by organizations. This justification is particularly important in periods of economic recession when organizations try to cut down their costs mainly in those departments where the importance of actions can only be assessed in the long term as is the case with environmental scanning (Fahey *et al.*, 1983).

On the other hand, as Mintzberg (1994) argues, there are organizations where strategies are not made explicit or simply do not exist formally. As strategies cannot be purely deliberate and a few can be purely emergent (Mintzberg, 1994), the most logical behaviour for an organization would be to develop some sort of formal planning process. However, considering that organizations will not formalize their strategies just to justify the creation of a scanning activity, the justification will have to originate from managers who must realize the importance of scanning the business environment for better decision making and planning, no matter what kind.

Environmental scanning activities by hospitality organizations

In relation to the hospitality industry Olsen *et al.* (1992) argue that environmental scanning helps managers to foresee favourable and unfavourable influences and initiate strategies that will enable their organizations to adapt to the environment. They state that:

If one accepts the proposition that the environment has the ability to threaten the continued survival of the firm and that managers possess the ability to adapt to these environmental forces through their use of competitive tools, then one must see how important it is for hospitality managers to monitor and accurately perceive their environment.

Despite the prior empirical work and recommendations that companies should undertake environmental scanning activities, research shows a different reality (Okumus, 2004; Costa, 1997; Olsen *et al.*, 1994). In fact, according to Olsen *et al.* hospitality organizations are aware of the need to relate environmental information to long-range plans, but so far the majority is just relating this information to short-term decisions.

Research into the environmental scanning process has also discovered that much of the scanning activity of managers is informal in nature (Costa, 1997; Fahey *et al.*, 1983). Managers are too concerned with the short term, and for this reason, their main goal is to get information about the economy, financing and customer needs and wants, ignoring other sectors of the general environment (Olsen *et al.*, 1994). There are many structural and psychological reasons why this happens. One major reason is that any attempt to monitor both the general and task environments comprehensively is beyond the resources and abilities of all firms (Okumus, 2004).

A study by West and Olsen (1989) into the hospitality industry reported the majority of the companies as having an informal scanning process. This was based on inputs about the environment from other members of staff, market research information or interaction with managers of other companies at professional and trade association meetings. Respondents to the study cited that a major weakness associated with the scanning endeavour was the lack of good, reliable information, and the authors further highlighted that scanning is expensive when engaged in at the highest levels of the firm. These results were later confirmed in a research by Costa and Teare (2000) whose study produced similar findings.

Results from Olsen *et al.*'s study also showed that for hospitality managers environmental scanning was seen as "... time taken away from more tangible pursuits," with "Active problem solving [seen] as much more rewarding to managers than time spent in such 'soft' activities as scanning" (Olsen *et al.*, 1992, p. 58). These statements reflect other deeply ingrained reasons for the lack of commitment towards the scanning process. According to the same authors, another problem affecting formalized environmental scanning is that much of the information processed by the manager during scanning is difficult to evaluate quantitatively "making assessment of its impact upon the firm more of a guessing game than a formal strategic exercise."

As many organizational studies have reported, the inability of executives to assign probabilities to events in the environment with respect to their impact upon the firm dilutes the value of environmental scanning efforts to the decision making process.

(Olsen *et al.*, 1992, p. 58)

The evidence provided (see Okumus, 2004; Costa, 1997; Olsen *et al.*, 1992, 1994; West and Olsen, 1989) reveals that, besides the scarcity of reliable information and the constraints on resources, something more complex is affecting the development of scanning activities in organizations. The lack of a long-term perspective coupled with a commitment to immediate tangible pursuits, and a strong reliance on quantitative data are strong reflexes of the existing organizational culture among hospitality organizations. Perhaps the existing organizational culture rather than the link to the strategic planning process is what makes the difference in the successful implementation of environmental scanning activities. It is clear that the malfunctions of the process are due to a lack of commitment by the organizations to continuously assess their environment in search for other events and trends than just mere statistical information.

It is possible that one way to lead organizations to undertake environmental scanning activities is to design the process in such a way as to fit the organizational structures and needs, and, as argued by Jain (1993), short-term scanning might be useful for programming various operational activities, as opposed to strategic planning activities.

Environmental scanning models and their applications

According to Gilbert (1993) a model can be defined as a theory or set of hypotheses that attempts to explain the connections and interrelationships between social phenomena. From his perspective, models are made up of concepts and relationships between concepts. As Gilbert proposes, a model can be used to make predictions about how the "real world" will respond to changes, and the relationships specified in the model will also serve as an explanation of how the "real world" works.

It can be said that corporate planning models are quite recent when compared with other tools available in the business management field (Johnson *et al.*, 2006; Shim and McGlade, 1989). According to the later authors the definition of a planning model varies with the scope of its application. In this context, the importance of an environmental scanning model resides in its potential to analyse more accurately the external environment and forecast business trends.

The need for a considerable amount of data about the external business environment is obvious when managers have to make certain business decisions. Information derived from within the company has little strategic value when it comes to the analysis of the task or general environment. In situations such as these the collection of external data is a priority (Wu *et al.*, 1998; Young, 1981). In order to better understand the application and use of environmental scanning models, it is important to analyse the existing models as a basis for identifying their benefits and adequacy to hospitality organizations.

Not all of the authors writing on environmental scanning present models for scanning the environment (Okumus, 2004). Some develop models based either on published information on the environmental scanning behaviour of organizations (Camillus and Datta, 1991; Ginter and Duncan, 1990; Narchal *et al.*, 1987; Terry, 1977) or the findings of their empirical research

(West and Olsen, 1989; Fahey and King, 1977; Segev, 1977; Aguilar, 1967), while others present frameworks or processes to follow when undertaking business environmental scanning (Jain, 1993; Murphy, 1989; Nanus and Lundberg, 1988; Aaker, 1983; Keegan, 1974; Thomas, 1974; Kefalas and Schoderbeck, 1973).

Some of these models provide good illustrations of the process of environmental scanning and the limitations to be overcome when undertaking the activity. Five studies in particular (Jain, 1993; Aaker, 1983; Fahey and King, 1977; Segev, 1977; Aguilar, 1967) provide the context and highlight the steps necessary in order to develop an effective environmental scanning process.

In reviewing the environmental scanning models, the following aspects emerge as relevant in developing an environmental scanning process irrespective of the formal or informal approach to strategic planning the hotel chain adopts:

- it should be deliberate and prospective;
- it should look for specific and broad-ranging information;
- it should follow a pre-established plan, procedure or methodology;
- it should be proactive and planning process oriented;
- it should be an ongoing study of the business environment and not crisis initiated;
- there should be a high level of interaction between scanners and decision makers;
- there should be a clear definition of information needs and sources;
- participants should be selected and their role/scanning tasks clearly specified;
- the means of storing, processing, and disseminating information should be clearly defined.

On the other hand, in order for companies to engage in environmental scanning the process has to match its needs and resources. One way to achieve this purpose may be to take an inside-out perspective by selecting the areas where information is needed and identifying the adequate sources to use. It is also important to choose the participants from those members of the organization exposed to relevant information, and to develop a continuous process of environmental scanning that explores the issues arising in the sources under analysis. According to the organizational structure, the information should be analysed, its importance for the organization inferred, and storage/dissemination carried out so that those members of staff playing vital roles in the strategy making process have access to it (Costa and Teare, 2000).

By following these steps it is likely that the process of environmental scanning will perform the important role of providing information for strategic decision making and, at the same time, take into account the major limitations that normally affect the process: too broad scope, lack of resources to undertake such complex task and the difficulty of justifying its existence if not linked to a formal written strategic plan.

An environmental scanning model for hospitality organizations • • •

Based on previous models on environmental scanning and the findings from Costa's (1997) research on the hospitality industry, it is possible to propose a new theoretical model that attempts to conceptualize a formal process of continuous environmental scanning. This model may be used to make predictions about how the "real world" (hotel units/chains) will accept the need for an ongoing process of scanning. The relationships specified in the model will also serve as an explanation on how the model may work in practice.

The model presented in Figure 2.1 is divided into five different phases, from the information function as a process (phase 1), to the planning of the scanning process (phase 2), analysis and processing of information (phase 3), storage, dissemination and sharing of information (phase 4), and finally, the information linkage to strategy development and decision making (phase 5). A more detailed analysis of this continuous environmental scanning process for hotel chains provides a further understanding of the sequences and relationships between the different phases.

Phase 1: Information Function as a Process. One of the main barriers to a formal environmental scanning process is the fact that the information function is regarded as a second-level priority and that other functions have to be performed first. Another barrier is the existing managerial mindset of collecting information by department (function), which is then essentially used by each department, hence limiting the dissemination and sharing of information. By transforming the environmental scanning into a process that collects information for the whole organization, synergies can be achieved and the information will be seen as an organizational asset to be used by everybody who needs it. For this to be possible, a change in decision makers' attitudes towards the importance of information must occur. This change is expected to produce the needed financial resources, trained staff, and a different attitude towards the use of information. The main outcome, however, will be the valorization of the

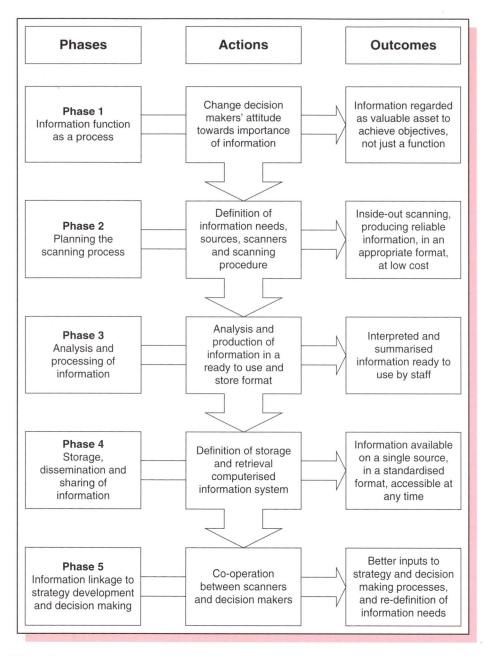

Figure 2.1
A continuous environmental scanning process for hospitality organizations.

information by managers and staff alike, and its use as a valuable asset in achieving hotel chain's objectives.

Phase 2: Planning the Scanning Process. As a consequence of the lack of organization in the collection of information, too much information, sometimes replicated, is available. However, what hotel chain managers need is not "reports produced in duplicate," or "dispersed information," but instead, "summarized information" that "cuts down on the amount of data required." Planning the scanning process allows the definition of information needs (inside-out approach proposed by Fahey and Narayanan, 1986), hence focusing what the organization is looking for. The ideal situation would be an outside-in approach, but as reported in previous research, this is expensive and time-consuming (Olsen *et al.*, 1992; West and Olsen, 1989; Aaker, 1983), making it very difficult to be adopted and implemented. Once the information needs have been defined, the relevant sources are identified and selected. The next step is the identification of those members of staff who will be involved in the scanning process. As suggested by Aaker (1983), these can be selected from those involved in the planning process as well as others who are exposed to useful information sources.

Before initiating the scanning, it is important that a pre-established plan, procedure or methodology is defined so that the best results can be achieved (Stoffels, 1994; Aguilar, 1967). The outcome of this phase is a focused view of the business environment through an inside-out scanning approach, based on reliable sources producing quality information, in a pre-defined format, at a low cost. This is possible because the scanning efforts are directed and the scanning procedures are undertaken by staff that are already scanning but in an undirected and non-integrated way.

Phase 3: Analysis and Processing of Information. The analysis of information should allow the identification and relevance of environmental trends, as not everything occurring in the environment is likely to have the same importance for the organization (Jain, 1993). The analysis and processing of information is also seen by respondents as important to "help with the identification of market trends" and as allowing "greater efficiency." The analysis of information and its availability in a ready-to-use format is regarded as relevant for hotel chains because it can be "provided to the units, board of directors and administration" to "make quicker decisions on the market." This phase of the continuous environmental scanning process will also allow the production of "simple and objective information," which is at the same time "well balanced but also not exaggerated." The outcome will be "better and structured information," which is already interpreted and summarized so that it can provide staff with "better knowledge of market trends."

Phase 4: Storage, Dissemination, and Sharing of Information. Storage and dissemination of information is crucial for the success of the process (Aaker, 1983). The storage process, as proposed by Aaker, can be a simple set of files or a sophisticated computer-based information retrieval system. According to hotel chain managers (Costa, 1997), the ideal process is a "computerized" process where the information is "concentrated on a single source," which allows "quick access to information." The vital characteristic about the storage element is that staff will know where to send the information they have collected (Aaker, 1983). From the respondents' viewpoint, the ideal situation would be the "information inputted by each department director and available to everybody." These are in accordance with Aaker's perspective who proposes that participants should be those executives and staff directly involved in the planning process. The outcome of this phase will be information available on a single source, in a standardized format, which is accessible at any time and "is easy to share." This will also allow what is seen by respondents as a desired outcome of a formal scanning process: "better circulation of information between directors and sharing with employees."

Phase 5: Information Linkage to Strategy Development and Decision Making. The information on environmental trends and their likely impacts will then be used to review strategy, which, according to Jain (1993), can be done on two counts: changes that may be introduced in products/markets, and the exploration of feasible opportunities that the company may embrace for action. This link of environmental scanning to strategy development and decision making is only possible through the co-operation between scanners and planners/ decision makers. The "malfunctions" of a formal scanning process are normally due to a lack of interaction and clear communication between environmental scanners and strategy makers (Segev, 1977). Segev recommends that a closer relationship between the two groups should be developed, so that the translation of environmental scanning into specific strategy changes can be performed co-operatively by analysts and strategy makers. The outcome of this phase will be the production of better inputs to strategy and decision-making processes as well as a re-definition of the hotel chain information needs which will occur through new requests for environmental data. In following this model, it will be possible for environmental scanning to play a direct rather than indirect role in strategy making.

Conclusion

Once hospitality decision makers change their attitude towards the importance of information and move from an information function to an information process paradigm, the development and implementation of a formal environmental scanning process will stand a much higher chance of success. This can be further achieved by focusing on target information needs using an inside-out approach, involving those members of staff in charge or linked to the planning process (either formal or informal) or exposed to relevant information. The selection of the most reliable and relevant sources of information and the definition of the scanning procedures should be carefully undertaken to maximize the success of the process. The following stages should consider the careful analysis and identification of business environmental trends and the storage of the resulting information in a computerized information system making it readily available in a standardized format. This will also allow a higher level of dissemination and sharing of information by having it concentrated on a single source to which staff can have access at any time. Finally, through the development of a close relationship between scanners and planners/decision makers, a better link of the scanning process to strategy development and a re-definition of the information needs can be achieved.

References

Aaker, D. A. (1983). Organizing a strategic information scanning system. *California Management Review*, 25(2), 76–83.

Aaker, D. A. (1984). *Developing business strategy*. New York: Wiley.

Aguilar, F. (1967). *Scanning the business environment*. New York: Macmillan.

Ansoff, I., and McDonnell, E. (1990). *Implanting strategic management* (2nd Ed.). London: Prentice Hall International.

Bourgeois, L. J. (1985). Strategic goals, perceived uncertainty, and economic performance in volatile environments. *Academy of Management Journal*, 28, 548–573.

Camillus, J. C., and Datta, D. K. (1991). Managing strategic issues in a turbulent environment. *Long Range Planning*, 24(2), 67–74.

Costa, J. (1997). *A study of strategic planning and environmental scanning in the multi-unit Portuguese hotel sector*. Unpublished Ph.D. Thesis, Guildford, University of Surrey.

Costa, J., and Teare, R. (2000). Developing an environmental scanning process in the hotel sector. *International Journal of Contemporary Hospitality Management*, 12(3), 156–169.

Daft, R. L., Sormunen, J., and Parks, D. (1988). Chief executive scanning, environmental characteristics, and company performance: An empirical study. *Strategic Management Journal*, 9, 123–139.

Dill, W. (1962). The impact of environment on organisational development. In S. Mailick and E. Van Ness (Eds.), *Concepts and issues in administrative behavior*. Englewood Cliffs, NJ: Prentice-Hall.

Dutton, J., and Duncan, R. (1983). The creation of momentum for change through the process of organizational sense-making. *Working Paper*. J. L. Kellogg Graduate School of Management, Evanston, Northwestern University.

Engledow, J. L., and Lenz, R. T. (1989). Whatever happened to environmental analysis? In D. Asch and C. Bowman (Eds.), *Readings in Strategic Management* (pp. 113–132). London: MacMillan.

Evans, N., Campbell, D., and Stonehouse, G. (2003). *Strategic Management for Travel and Tourism*. London: Butterworth-Heinemann.

Fahey, L., and King, W. (1977). Environmental scanning in corporate planning. *Business Horizons, August*, 61–71.

Fahey, L., and Narayanan, V. K. (1986). *Macroenvironmental Analysis for Strategic Management*. St. Paul, MN: West Publishing.

Fahey, L., King, W. R., and Narayanan, V. K. (1983). Environmental scanning and forecasting in strategic planning—the state of the art. In D. E. Hussey (Ed.), *The Truth about Corporate Planning: International Research into the Practice of Planning* (pp. 495–509). Oxford: Pergamon Press.

Farh, J. L., Hoffman, R. C., and Hegarty, W. H. (1984). Assessing environmental scanning at the sub-unit level: A multitrait-multimethod analysis. *Decision Sciences*, 14(1), 197–220.

Garland, E. (2007). *Future Inc.: How Business can Anticipate and Profit from What's Next*. New York: AMACOM.

Gilbert, G. N. (1993). *Analyzing Tabular Data*. London: UCL Press.

Ginter, P., and Duncan, W. (1990). Macro-environmental analysis for strategic management. *Long Range Planning*, 23(6).

Hambrick, D. C. (1981). Specialization of environmental scanning activities among upper level executives. *Journal of Management Studies*, 18, 299–320.

Hambrick, D. C. (1982). Environmental scanning and organizational strategy. *Strategic Management Journal, 3,* 159–174.

Hoffman, R. C., and Hegarty, W. H. (1983). Cross-cultural research: A model for development of a data collection instrument. *Proceedings of the Annual Meeting of the Academy of Management,* Dallas, TX.

Jain, S. C. (1984). Environmental scanning in US corporations. *Long Range Planning, 17*(2), 117–128.

Jain, S. C. (1993). *Marketing Planning and Strategy.* Ohio: South-Western Publishing.

Johnson, G., Scholes, K., and Whittington, R. (2006). *Exploring Corporate Strategy: Text and Cases* (7th enhanced media ed.). London: Financial Times Press.

Keegan, W. J. (1974). Multinational scanning: A study of the information sources utilized by Headquarters' executives in multinational companies. *Administrative Science Quarterly, 19,* 411–421.

Kefalas, A., and Schoderbeck, P. P. (1973). Scanning the business environment. *Decision Sciences, 4,* 63–74.

Lenz, R. T., and Engledow, J. L. (1986). Environmental analysis and strategic decision making: A field study of selected "Leading-Edge" corporations. *Strategic Management Journal, 7*(1), 69–88.

Lorange, P. (1982). *Implementation of Strategic Planning.* Englewood Cliffs, NJ: Prentice-Hall.

Mazarr, M. (1999). *Global Trends 2005: An Owner's Manual for the Next Decade.* New York: St. Martin's Press.

McCaskey, M. (1982). *The Executive Challenge.* Boston, MA: Pitman.

Miller, D., and Friesen, P. H. (1983). Strategy making and environment: The third link. *Strategic Management Journal, 4,* 221–235.

Mintzberg, H. (1992). Five Ps for strategy. In H. Mintzberg and J. B. Quinn (Eds.), *The Strategy Process: Concepts and Contexts* (pp. 12–19). London: Prentice-Hall.

Mintzberg, H. (1994). *The Rise and Fall of Strategic Planning.* London: Prentice-Hall.

Mintzberg, H., Ahlstrand, B., and Lampel, J. (2005). *Strategy Bites Back.* London: FT-Prentice Hall.

Murphy, J. J. (1989). Identifying strategic issues. *Long Range Planning, 22*(2), 101–105.

Nanus, B., and Lundberg, C. (1988). Strategic planning. *Cornell Hotel and Restaurant Administration Quarterly, 29*(2), 18–23.

Narchal, R., Kittappa, K., and Bhattacharya, P. (1987). An environmental scanning system for business planning. *Long Range Planning, 20*(6), 96–105.

Okumus, F. (2004). Potential challenges of employing a formal environmental scanning approach in hospitality in hospitality organizations. *International Journal of Hospitality Management*, 23, 123–143.

Olsen, M., Murphy, B., and Teare, R. E. (1994). CEO Perspectives on scanning the global hotel business environment. *International Journal of Contemporary Hospitality Management*, 6(4), 3–9.

Olsen, M., and Roper, A. (1998). Research in strategic management in the hospitality industry. *International Journal of Hospitality Management*, 17, 111–124.

Olsen, M., Tse, E., and West, J. J. (1992). *Strategic Management in the Hospitality Industry*. London: International Thomson Publishing.

Post, J. (1973). Window to the world: A methodology for scanning the social environment. *Working Paper No. 175*. School of Management, Boston University, Boston, MA.

Preble, J. F. (1978). Corporate use of environmental scanning. *Michigan Business Review*, 30(5), 12–17.

Preble, J. F., Rau, P. A., and Reichel, A. (1988). The environmental scanning practices of US multinationals in the late 1980's. *Management International Review*, 28, 4–14.

Segev, E. (1977). How to use environmental analysis in strategy making. *Management Review*, 66, 4–13.

Shim, J. K., and McGlade, R. (1989). The use of corporate planning models: Past, present and future. In D. Asch and C. Bowman (Eds.), *Readings in Strategic Management*. London: Macmillan.

Slattery, P., and Olsen, M. D. (1984). Hospitality organizations and their environments. *International Journal of Hospitality Management*, 3(2), 55–61.

Steiner, G. (1979). *Strategic Planning*. New York: Macmillan.

Stoffels, J. (1994). *Strategic Issues Management: A Comprehensive Guide to Environmental Scanning*. Oxford: Pergamon.

Stoner, J. A., and Freeman, R. E. (1986). *Management* (5th ed.). New York: Prentice-Hall.

Stubbart, C. (1982). Are environmental scanning units effective? *Long Range Planning*, 15, 139–145.

Terry, P. T. (1977). Mechanisms for environmental scanning. *Long Range Planning*, 10, 2–9.

Thomas, P. S. (1974). Environmental analysis for corporate planning. *Business Horizons*, 17, 27–38.

Van Deusen, C., Williamson, S., and Babson, H. (2007). New York: Auerbach Publications.

Weick, K. (1979). *The Social Psychology of Organising* (2nd ed.). Reading, MA: Addison-Wesley.

West, J. J. (1988). *Strategy, Environmental Scanning and their Effect Upon Performance: An Exploration Study of the Foodservice Industry*. Unpublished Doctoral Dissertation, Department of Hotel, Restaurant and Institutional Management, Blacksburg, VA, Virginia Polytechnic Institute and State University.

West, J. J., and Anthony, W. P. (1990). Strategic group membership and environmental scanning: Their relationship to firm performance in the foodservice industry. *International Journal of Hospitality Management*, 9(3), 247–267.

West, J. J., and Olsen, M. (1989). Environmental scanning, industry structure and strategy making: Concepts and research in the hospitality industry. *International Journal of Hospitality Management*, 8(4), 283–298.

Wheelen, T., and Hunger, J. (1989). *Strategic Management*. Reading, MA: Addison-Wesley.

Wu, A., Costa, J., and Teare, R. (1998). Using environmental scanning for business expansion into China and Eastern European: The case of transnational hotel companies. *International Journal of Contemporary Hospitality Management*, 10(7), 257–263.

Young, R. (1981). A strategic overview of business information systems. *Managerial Planning*, 29, 28–37.

Part Two

Strategy as investments in competitiveness

The development of international hotel chains in Europe

Paul Slattery[1], Ian Gamse[1] and Angela Roper[2]

[1]Otus & Co. Advisory Ltd., London, UK
[2]Savoy Educational Trust Senior Lecturer in Hospitality Management, School of Management, University of Surrey, UK

Introduction

At the end of 2006, the 52 countries of Europe had around 5 million hotel rooms of which 1.5 million were affiliated to hotel chains. In total there were more than 400 companies that operated portfolios of hotels within which there were more than 500 hotel brands. Of these brands, 185 accounting for 1.1 million rooms were present in more than one country and thus were international in their supply profile. In the year 2000 the European hotel chain presence accounted for about 100 international brands with about 700,000 rooms. Over the period, international chains grew their room stock in Europe by 410,000, an annual average of 8% and an indicative capital value of €88 billion. Drawing on the Otus Hotel Brands Database (2007) we will illustrate patterns in the international development that occurred, we will explain why this burst of international hotel chain expansion occurred and we will identify how it occurred. Before we tackle these questions we will review the academic literature on the internationalization of hotel chains and we will conclude with more effective interpretations of the development of international hotel chains.

Literature review

Contractor *et al.* (2003) are of the view that there has been little research on the growth and internationalization of service firms. While it is not clear as to the criteria employed to justify this comment, Litteljohn *et al.* (2007), in their review of publications from 1996 to 2005 from academic, industry, and policy sources confirm that research in the area of hotel internationalization is growing. However, when compared with research into hotel marketing, operations, and customer satisfaction it is much smaller.

In hotel internationalization research there has been a fixation with studies into the modal choice decisions or market entry strategy of hotel chains, much of it described as relatively homogenous in nature by Litteljohn *et al.* (2007). Dunning's (1981) eclectic theory has been favoured as the theoretical foundation for much of this research, possibly due to its holistic approach to explain hotel internationalization (Litteljohn *et al.*, 2007). However, transaction cost theory has also been applied and over time the hotel literature has begun to integrate a range of theoretical positions.

Research studies (since 1996) into those factors that influence international expansion overall, and modal choice more specifically, are examined comparatively by Litteljohn *et al.* (2007); it is therefore our view that they do not require further review here. It is interesting to note though that the majority of these previous enquiries identify the importance of internal, firm-specific factors with the experience and extent of internationalization and perceptions of executives being the most prevalent aspects influencing international and modal choice decisions. This perhaps reflects the more internally focused research efforts as well as the employment of more qualitative in-depth methodologies by researchers than in the past. Over the years, the unit of analysis has changed to that of the multinational firm as opposed to earlier work where, although senior executives in international hotel chains were the sample, the focus was more on individual hotel location decisions rather than on the strategic advantage of multinationals.

This body of previous research offers no outcome that prioritizes particular areas or possesses significant predictive power. Indeed, in more recent research carried out by Jones *et al.* (2004), no consistent pattern to entry mode choice was found within or across a sample of 512 firms. New lines of enquiry however are developing in more recent research, which reflects more contemporary developments among international hotel chains. We summarize some of these below:

- O'Gorman and McTiernan (2000) concluded in their analysis of Irish SME hotel chains that investment in organizational capabilities was more important than international experience, reflecting the identification of the phenomenon of the resource-based view and organizational competencies in the mainstream internationalization literature (a move on from the predomination of internalization and eclectic theories). A similar line of enquiry was taken by Aung and Heeler (2001) who applied the core competency concept to Accor and its competitors in the Thai marketplace. Their work is particularly useful in reminding us that while there is still multi-pronged competition with chains based in North America, Europe, and Asia competing in most of world's largest markets (Whitla *et al.*, 2006) multinational hotel chains are also being forced much more to "share the same economic and competitive pie with small local firms" (Aung and Heeler, 2001, p. 638). The latter of course is even more the case in certain market segments, a point established next.
- Chen and Dimou (2005) identify the importance that market segmentation plays on modal choices, a factor that seems to have been wanting in previous studies perhaps due to the fact that early internationalization was "based on branded,

often North American branded, relatively up-market and business-travel oriented provision" (Litteljohn, 1997, p. 187). In terms of the extent of internationalization, up-market brands require substantial capital, average €280,000 per room, to create portfolio mass. It is budget and economy hotel portfolios that need most length, because they are in the mass market, but require significantly less capital, average €75,000 per room for economy hotels and €30,000 per room for budget hotels.

- While demand has often been identified as an important driver for hotel development (it is explicit in the location-specific advantage construct), access to capital has so far been insufficiently explored as a driver for decisions on where, what and how to develop hotel brands. Altinay and Altinay (2003) establish the importance of this factor in their paper, although one cannot generalize single case study findings. Doherty (2007) has similarly identified the issue of capital availability as a driver, but in the context of fashion retailers.

- Doherty (2007), although outside the hospitality area, also establishes the importance of the presence of strong franchiseable brands, which attract franchise partners and third party investors. There is a link between franchising and the availability of capital, given that it is a non-equity means of growth for hotel brands. The key to growth through franchising is the availability of potential (franchise) partners, which in turn depends on the availability of capital for single hotel assets. While all other factors maybe in place, the reality of the marketplace and its impact on the availability of franchise partners may make entering through franchising difficult. This is a line of argument not fully appreciated in the location-specific advantage construct and is linked to the accessibility of investment capital, as mentioned above. Connell (1997, p. 95) recommends that "Franchisors need to assess not only whether…strategy would work for customers but how departures from domestic formats will affect longer-term efficiency and effectiveness of the wider franchise network."

- More recent research by Dev *et al.* (2007) and Brown *et al.* (2003) is somewhat revolutionary in finally arguing that ownership and control dimensions of foreign market entry choices can be separated and that decisions relate to more than just production and distribution and include marketing and operations. Using an integrated theoretical framework they focus on three factors important to the entry strategy of their 124 hotel chain sample: namely, the firm's ability to transfer its know-how to the local market, the ability of potential local partners to absorb the know-how, and the availability of qualified and trustworthy investment partners in the local market (Dev *et al.*, 2007, p. 21). The authors conclude that the "interplay between the company's strengths and local resources drives the type of partnership or affiliation arrangement that the company uses to enter the foreign market" (Dev *et al.*, 2007, p. 13). This research reflects much more the state of play among hotel chains today and recognizes that at the hotel property a number of different parties may be involved in its ownership, management, and marketing.

- The preference of senior managers (often resulting from past experience and stakeholder needs) is a further interesting line of enquiry. Several authors (Altinay and Roper, 2005; Altinay, 2005) suggest that the influence is often strong of those key managers responsible for international franchise operations as they are driven, experienced people with very definite ideas as to why franchising is the best method to internationalize. The impact has also been felt at property level where hotel managers' relational skills and expertise has had to be extended due to the importance of mutually beneficial relationships between hotel chains and their property owners (Gannon, 2007). The research carried out by Groschl and Doherty (2006) also points to the fact that traditionally market entry modes used by companies were strongly influenced by national origins.

Limitations still exist among these more contemporary studies. The analyses by academics of the internationalization of hotel chains have tended to be empirically small, discrete, one-off analyses with a variety of methodologies from shallow surveys of managers to single case studies and offer conclusions that rarely progress beyond the commonplace. In contrast, the analysis that follows here draws on the continuous tracking of all hotel chains in all 52 countries of Europe, the continuous tracking of the economic structure of each country as well as the response by hotel chains to the specific sources and patterns of demand in each country and its sources of capital.

There are fundamental questions for hotel chains faced by the need or inclination to expand beyond their home country. The first is, which countries to expand into and within the selected countries, which regions, cities, and specific sites on which to concentrate and why. In parallel, the chains need to satisfy themselves about which of their hotel brands will be most effective for the available demand in the selected countries and which new brands will need to be developed and why. We start by providing an overview of the growth of international hotel chains in Europe between 2000 and 2006.

Overview of international hotel chains in Europe 2000–2006

As the table below illustrates, in the period since 2000 significant international development by hotel chains occurred in Europe (Table 3.1).

Of the 52 countries of Europe only Belarus, Liechtenstein, Moldova, San Marino, and Turkmenistan are without a presence of international hotel chains. This should not come as a surprise since they are also the only countries in which there is no hotel chain presence whatever. Of the 410,000 rooms added by international chains over the period, more than 60%, 256,000 with a capital value of €49 billion, were added in only four countries: Spain, UK, France, and Germany, which are among the largest, with a combined population of 243 million and structurally most developed economies. This translated to 950 citizens per international chain room and an average capital cost of €190,000 per room. The hotels added by international brands in these countries covered all market levels: deluxe, up-market, mid-market, economy, and budget, but three quarters were at mid-market, economy, and budget. They also covered all affiliations: owned, leased, management contract, and franchised.

A further nine countries: Albania, Armenia, Azerbaijan, Bosnia and Herzegovina, Georgia, Kyrgyzstan, Serbia and Montenegro, Ukraine, and Uzbekistan, which have a combined population of 110 million, are among the weakest and structurally most underdeveloped economies, which were the target for international chains to add only 2580 room additions with a capital value of only €1.4 billion. This translated to 43,000 citizens per international chain room and an average capital value of €530,000 per room. Three quarters of these rooms operated

---

Table 3.1 Total International Hotel Brand Development 2000–2006

Year	Brands	Countries	Rooms	Capital Value (€bn)
2006	185	47	1092 K	196
2000	100	40	682 K	108

Source: Otus & Co. Advisory Ltd.

at the up-market level, all hotels were affiliated to the brands by equity free management contract or franchise and none of the international chains invested capital in any of the hotels.

Estonia, Iceland, Latvia, Lithuania, Macedonia, Portugal, and Slovenia, which have a combined population of 22 million are stronger economies, but still are structurally weak, added only 2460 rooms with a capital value of only €1 billion. This translated to 8900 citizens per international chain room and an average capital value of €420,000 per room. The hotels covered a wider range of market levels and all of the affiliations. Gibraltar, Luxembourg, and Monaco, which have a combined population of only 510,000, but are among the strongest and structurally most developed economies, added only 800 rooms mainly mid-market, up-market, and deluxe at a capital value of €0.5 billion. This translated to 435 citizens per international chain room and an average capital value of €660,000 per room. In these countries, the chains invested more of their own capital. In the remaining 24 countries with a population of 486 million the international chains added 155,000 rooms, around 6500 in each country amounting to a capital value of €36 billion. This translated to 3130 citizens per international chain room and an average capital value of €230,000 per room.

All of the chain presence in 20 of the European countries is from international hotel chains—Albania, Armenia, Azerbaijan, Bosnia and Herzegovina, Georgia, Kazakhstan, Kyrgyzstan, Ukraine and Uzbekistan; Estonia, Latvia, Lithuania, Macedonia, Malta, Norway and Slovenia; Andorra, Gibraltar, Luxembourg, and Monaco. This list of countries very closely resembles the countries in which international chains added fewest hotels. The simple reason why all of the chain presence in these countries is by international chains is that there are no domestic hotel chains. The remaining 27 countries contain both international chain hotels and hotels that are in the portfolios of domestic hotel chains that do not operate in any other countries.

Just as there has been explicit patterns in the countries of Europe into which international hotel chains have expanded so also has there been explicit patterns in the choice of cities into which they have expanded. The two major hotel cities in Europe—those with more than 30,000 chain rooms—London and Paris, saw international chains add 20,000 and 11,000 rooms respectively. The 29 primary hotel cities—those with more than 6000 chain rooms, but less than 30,000 chain rooms—including: Madrid, Berlin, Barcelona, Amsterdam, Frankfurt, Munich, Vienna, Rome, Budapest, and Stockholm, saw international chains add 106,000 rooms, an average of 3650 per city. The remaining 273,000 rooms added by international chains are located in around 3000 conurbations, an average of less than 100 rooms per conurbation. A fundamental driver of the choices of countries and cities for expansion by international hotel chains is the expectation of superior demand growth and this is a function of the structure of the economies.

Economic structure and the growth of hotel brands in Europe

Economic activities have been classified and periodically revised by the United Nations Statistics Division (2006), International Standard Industrial Classifications into three groups:

- Primary industries such as cultivation of crops, livestock production, fishing, forestry, and hunting.
- Secondary industries such as construction, manufacturing, mining, quarrying, and utilities.
- Tertiary industries such as banking, bars, betting shops, bingo clubs, casinos, cinemas, communications, distribution, education services, finance, health services, hairdressers, hotels, insurance, logistics, personal services, professional services, public administration, restaurants, retailing, security services, sports clubs, storage, transport, travel, theatres, visitor attractions, and welfare services. Within each of these activities there are sub-divisions that extend tertiary activities throughout the lives of citizens of advanced economies and establishes the tertiary segment as the most diverse and complex of the three economic segments.

Employment in each economic segment is different. It requires different knowledge and skills and it involves different relationships with the land, with machines, with colleagues, and with the buyers of their output. As the balance of an economy ascends through the economic segments so its structure becomes more complex and diverse. It is what is meant when we talk of economic progress. At any one time within any economy some economic activities are in a period of growth, others are in decline and yet others have not emerged. There are skills and jobs that are in demand to deliver the economic output, others that are in decline and vanish, and others that have yet to emerge. As a result, the availability of products and services is not constant and their provision and consumption is not uniform. The economic activities and jobs within an economy are the building blocks of economic structure. As they change so do patterns of provision and consumption and vice versa.

Each European economy is involved in primary, secondary, and tertiary economic activities and the amount and types of activity in each segment determine its economic structure. Tertiary activities are different in kind from primary and secondary activities. At the core of the difference is that tertiary activities are concerned with the provision and distribution of services whereas primary and secondary activities produce durable and non-durable goods. Within primary activities the dominant work interaction is between the worker and the land. Within secondary activities the dominant interaction is between the worker and the machine. In tertiary services, the crucial relationship is between people. A wider range and frequency of operational interaction with colleagues is necessary for the provision and delivery of services as is the interaction between the providers of services and the consumers of the services. Reflecting this, services involve more mental work than the manual work that is characteristic of primary and secondary activities and consequently more white-collar work than blue-collar work.

The range of tertiary activities is too diverse to be of sufficient analytical value to explain the demand for services and they need to be classified into more homogeneous groups. The classification of tertiary services must accommodate two influences: one is the inherent features and functions of the services and the other is the influence of the political system of a country on its economy. The political influence is crucial. At one extreme, under Communism, the government controlled all services, whereas at the other extreme, in a free-market economy, many services are businesses with little control exerted by the government. The more that the supply of and demand for services within an economy are controlled by the government, then the weaker the structure, performance, and growth of the economy as a whole and services in particular. Accordingly, we present the tertiary economy in three stages: citizen services, market service businesses, and experience businesses (Pine and Gilmore, 1998).

Citizen services are controlled by governments. In Europe, access to many citizen services such as public education, public health care, and social services are available to all as a right of citizenship and most are free at the point of delivery. As a result, some citizen services such as public health and public education have grown to be among the largest employers in a country. As the structural balance of an economy becomes tertiary, citizen services expand. Education expands as childhood and adolescent education become mandatory and a higher proportion of the population have access to further education, higher education, continuing education, and pre-school education. Health care improves to sustain longer life expectancy and diversifies to include preventative as well as curative medicine. Community health grows and paramedic disciplines such as nutrition, physiotherapy, and holistic medicine advance and the prison service seeks to reform criminals in addition to their basic custodial role.

The extent to which the citizen services dominate the tertiary segment is both a political and an economic matter. Indeed the main theme in political economy throughout the 20th century in Europe and North America was about the most effective way to provide citizen services. Europe emphasized the moral responsibility of governments not only to provide citizen services, but also to ensure that all citizens had access to them. In contrast, the US approach emphasized the role of citizen choice in accessing many services and that when choice was involved a market was created. Thus, the US approach was to involve business in the provision of many citizen services. The distinction between Europe and the US in the role of the government in the provision of citizen services was at the core of the distinction throughout the century between the left wing and the right wing in politics. The more leftwing a government, the more its commitment to managing citizen services and the more it extends its management of the economy by taking control of key sectors including: coal, oil and gas, water, electricity, telephony, roads, rail, air transportation, and any other that it deems sufficiently important to national preservation. In these ways its commitment is to big government. The bigger the citizen services segment the more income the government needs to generate from other parts of the economy to fund the provision of citizen services. The result is that when the market service and experience segments are minor, a higher tax burden falls on the primary and secondary segments and the poorer the quality and scope of core citizen services such as health and education. The more rightwing an elected government the less it is committed to the encroachment of citizen services and the more it is committed to the development of market service and experience businesses. In these ways its commitment is to smaller government. The less pervasive the citizen services segment and the larger the market service and experience segments, the more business activities there are in the economy from which to generate government income to provide citizen services. The result is a lower tax burden on primary, secondary, market service, and experience businesses and the higher quality and scope of core citizen services such as health and education.

Market services include: banking, communications, distribution financial services, logistics, personal services, professional services, real estate management, retailing, and wholesaling. Unlike citizen services, market services are not administered by the state. They are businesses whose size, range, and performance are determined by prevailing conditions in the two markets that they serve, the corporate market and the personal market. As secondary activities mature, the growth in market services businesses is faster because of the growth of the personal markets in addition to the growth in corporate markets. The growth of personal demand in market service businesses requires their adaptation to meet the demands of the mass of the population.

As secondary economies grow and prosper there is increasing growth in the range of consumer goods produced and retailing emerges as a distinct skill to maximize the sale of goods. There is the recognition that manufactured goods do not sell themselves and that advertising, marketing, merchandising, and in-store facilities are necessary to sell more goods. Shops become larger and retail chains grow nationally. Buying consumer goods involves the transfer of ownership of the goods, but there are differences in the patterns of purchase and use of durable goods and non-durable goods. Consumer non-durables such as food and drink involve frequent repeat purchase because they have a high degree of perishability and once consumed cannot be re-used. Once consumer durables such as brown goods, white goods, cars, and houses have been acquired there can be continued gratification from their use and re-use. Repurchase of consumer durables depends on the goods wearing out, falling out of fashion, or becoming obsolete. Moreover, the consumption of many consumer durables, particularly brown and white goods, is private consumption, which occurs within the home.

The largest and fastest growing of the market services are financial services. As secondary economies grow and prosper so does the demand for financial services from both corporate and personal customers. The proportion of the population with bank accounts increases materially and financial services diversify. The access to personal credit is eased so that the volume of unsecured loans increases as does the supply and use of credit cards, which accelerates personal spending on both goods and services. There is also an expansion in savings through pension schemes, insurance policies, stock market investments, and other forms of saving. The provision of mortgages to enable citizens to own their home rises sharply and provides the widespread source of ownership of an appreciating asset. The communications industry was transformed by the inventions of the postal service, the telephone, radio, motion pictures, and television. In the late 20th century there was a further explosion in communications for both the corporate and the personal markets with the invention of mobile telephony, personal computers, and the Internet. Personal demand for domestic services such as housekeeping, home repairs, home maintenance, and gardening increases as do quasi-domestic services such as laundry, dry cleaning, and car maintenance. As an economy develops its tertiary sector so the range of asset classes increases. As well as land and industrial real estate, which are the preserve of the primary and secondary segments, domestic housing increases with population growth and the growth in prosperity. Citizen service expansion produces an increase in the number of schools and hospitals. Commercial real estate increases with the market service economy as a result to the greater need for offices, warehouses, and retail outlets. However, the widest diversity of real estate occurs as the experience segment of the economy grows. Experience activities occur in venues: hotels, restaurants, bars, nightclubs, sports clubs, health clubs, hairdressers, visitor attractions, cinemas, theatres, aircrafts, and cruise ships. As the experience segment grows to become a significant part of the economy so experience properties emerge to become a significant asset classes and real estate management becomes a specialist professional service.

In addition to its demand for banking and financial services, communications, and real estate management there are two other ways in which the corporate market accesses market services. First, distribution and wholesaling are the preserve of the corporate market and secondly, as well as professional services occurring in their own right there are professional services within corporations. Such jobs include white collar and professional jobs in accounting and finance; marketing and selling; human resource management; and other professional services. The larger the size of an organization the larger the corporate infrastructure and the more and wider the range of professional service jobs within companies, irrespective of the industry or service in which they operate. The development of larger industrial companies in the US than in the European countries meant that the US also developed larger professional services within these companies and at an earlier stage of economic development than in Europe.

The third tertiary segment relates to experience businesses that include hotels, restaurants, bars, nightclubs, casinos, bingo clubs, hairdressers, health clubs, and visitor attractions. They also include passenger air travel, sea travel, and rail travel; sports watching and sports playing; other out-of-home recreation activities such as theatres and cinemas as well as private health care, private education, and private custodial services. Experience businesses provide contexts in which their customers, students, patients, clients, passengers, prisoners, audience, players, and spectators are participants in events, which are designed for them to experience sensations such as enjoyment, knowledge, health, or remorse. The prime market for experience businesses is the personal market. Corporate demand for experience businesses is limited to business travel and the use of hotels, restaurants, and other experience venues for business entertaining. For the personal market there is a sequencing of demand between market services and experience businesses. The frequency of personal demand for a wide range of experience businesses accelerates when ownership or at least the access to the compass of household and personal consumer goods has been achieved. In contrast, there is less sequencing between market services and experience services for the corporate market, which accesses the services as required. As with the other classes of tertiary activity, the political influence on the experience segment is crucial. State involvement in the experience segment has shown itself to be the major depressant of personal experience businesses since they become prescribed by the state. The only economies in which personal markets for experience businesses have become economically significant are those in which government intervention has been slight.

There are six features of buying experience services, which differentiate them from other purchases:

1. Experience activities occur in specific venues such as hotels, casinos, and aeroplanes designed to deliver specific experiences.
2. Consumption in experience businesses occurs on site. Central to the management of experience businesses is the creation of the conditions for consumption in the venue and the management of the consumption process. This is different from market services such as retailing where consumption occurs away from the point of sale and outside the control of the retailer or service provider. Retailers do not manage the consumption of the products that they sell.
3. Consumption in experience businesses is both time and location specific. Thus, experience services cannot be stored. A hotel room, which is not rented for any night is business lost forever whereas consumer durables can be stored, sold, used, and re-used.
4. Buying experience services involves renting, but not transferring ownership of facilities and the relationship between the buyers and the providers of the experience services is a

crucial ingredient for the buyers to achieve their goals. Thus, jobs that involve direct contact with buyers of experience services are relationship intense.

5. Because the buyer of an experience service does not own the service, continued gratification can only be gained by buying again. After the experience of hospitality only the memory sustains gratification until repurchase. Enjoyment of an experience, for example, is a powerful motivator and the memory is short term in its capacity to sustain gratification without re-experience.

6. Consumption in experience businesses occurs out of home. They involve conspicuous public consumption, which defines status, standard of living, and lifestyle of the participants.

Economic performance and economic structure

Economies with low GDP/head in primary and secondary activities are not able to make an effective transition to tertiary under any political system because there is not enough government revenue to fund any more than basic citizen services and there is not enough corporate and personal income to generate demand for any more than the most basic market service and experience business. The prime condition for an economy to make the transition in structural balance from secondary to tertiary is a sufficiently high GDP/head in primary and secondary activities to generate enough government income to fund more extensive citizen services and to generate demand from the population and from corporates for mass-market service and experience businesses. In 2005, the Russian GDP/head had reached $4000. In the same year the US economy achieved $40,000, 10 times more and Britain achieved $36,000, nine times more. Also in 2005, Russian GDP/head in agriculture reached $200 at a time when the US achieved better than two and a half times more and Britain better than one and a half times more. In the same year, Russian secondary industries achieved GDP/head of $1400, while the US and Britain each achieved more than six times as much, but the sharpest differences were the tertiary segment. Russia delivered tertiary GDP/head of $2400, while the US bettered it by 13 times and Britain by 11 times.

The figure illustrates the diversity of economic structures in Europe and the US is added as a comparison (Figure 3.1).

The significance of economic structures for making sense of hotel demand and supply is that greater the proportion of GDP generated by the market service and experience segments, the greater the volume of hotel supply and the greater the level of

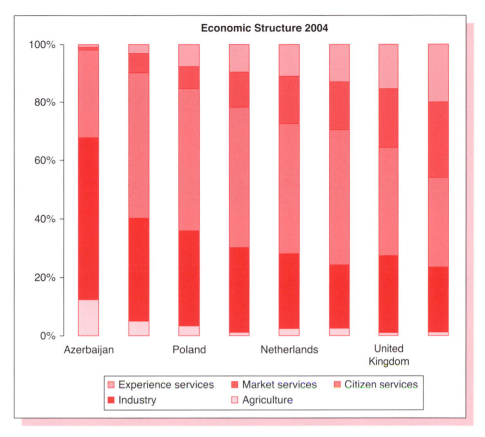

Figure 3.1
Economic structure in selected European countries (*Source*: World Bank and Otus & Co. Advisory Ltd.)

concentration in the hotel business as the figure below illustrates (Figure 3.2).

Many countries of Europe including: Austria, Belgium, Denmark, France, Germany, Ireland, Italy, Netherlands, Spain, Sweden, and Switzerland have reached the stage at which the structural balance of the economies is moving towards service businesses, which provide their most effective source of growth and employment. Britain has already passed this stage and now enjoys the benefits of being a full-blown service business economy. This group of countries account for 76% of the rooms and 56% of the total capital value added by international hotel chains since 2000, in spite of the recession, sluggish growth, and geo political atrocities suffered by many in the early years of the period. The economic policies being pursued by the governments of these economies are designed to grow market service and experience businesses and accordingly they present the

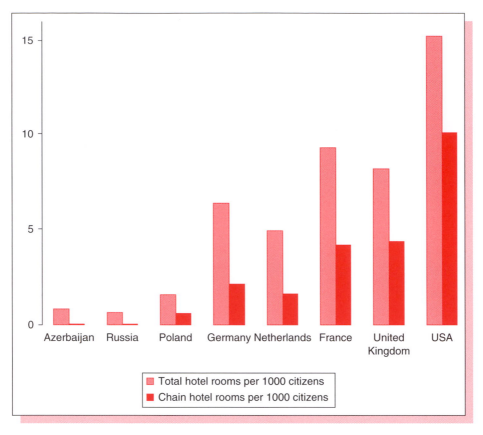

Figure 3.2
The supply of hotel rooms and chain rooms per thousand citizens (*Source*: Otus & Co. Advisory Ltd.)

prospect of strong future growth in hotel demand and are a continuing attraction to international hotel chains. Otus projects that, over the next 10 years in these economies, the agriculture and industrial segments will grow at sub-market levels, that citizen services will grow in line with the market, but that market service and experience business contribution to GDP will achieve real growth. As a result, the segments of the economies that are growing at the fastest rates are also the segments that provide most demand into hotels. Otus also projects that, over the next 10 years, hotel chains will need to add at least 1 million hotel rooms to service the projected demand growth. When this stage was reached in the US in the 1950s and 1960s there was a rocketing growth in hotel demand and an equivalent growth in hotel chains. For instance, from a standing start in 1952, Holiday Inn grew its portfolio to 100,000 rooms by 1960. At this period in the US, hotel chain growth was predominantly by domestic chains since few international chains existed and the US was not only the largest hotel market in the world, but also the fastest growing. Indeed, in 1964 Hilton Hotels Corporation (HHC) sold its international business to raise the capital necessary for it to participate vigorously in the growth of the US domestic hotel market. Similarly, in the 1980s when the UK economy reached this stage in the development of its economic structure, hotel demand escalated, as did the growth of hotel chains.

The greater the proportion of GDP generated by the market service and experience segments, the greater volume of hotel demand. It is for this reason that the US has the highest level of concentration in the hotel business and the highest ratio of hotel chain rooms per 1000 citizens. Within Europe, Britain has the most structurally developed economy and has the highest level of hotel concentration and the highest ration of chain hotel rooms per 1000 citizens. The diverse pattern of economic structures throughout Europe determines the diverse volume of demand for hotels. Agriculture is not only the smallest contributor to GDP in most economies, but most of its sales are in its local region and to wholesalers. Thus, the proportion of agricultural employees whose job requires business travel is microscopic as is the volume of agricultural business demand into hotels. Within the industrial sector the bulk of domestic business travellers are sales and marketing executives, who constitute a minor proportion of total employees. As the structure of economies develop and industrial activities decline as a proportion of GDP and of employment so also does the volume of sales and marketing executives and thus, the volume of hotel business demand that they generate. Within citizen services there are no measurable sales and marketing functions that involve regular business travel with hotel stays. The majority of the business travellers within citizen services are professionals in education, health, and social services whose roles involve only infrequent hotel-based business travel. Market service businesses and experience businesses require a high proportion of executives from the corporate structure to be involved in frequent business travel, because the very nature of service businesses entails that a greater proportion of executives interact with customers and with creating the conditions for customers to buy their services. Executives in sales and marketing, accounting, finance, human resources and development are all involved in business travel as part of the operational management of the companies. Consequently, when the market service and experience segments of an economy achieve real growth so the business demand into hotels grows significantly. It is not only domestic business travel that benefits from this pattern of economic development. Foreign business demand into an economy also grows because of the range of service businesses and expertise in many of these businesses is held in the most developed economies that expand into the emerging service economies.

Leisure demand into hotels also grows when an economy grows its service businesses since the transition entails a shift in consumer spending from consumer goods to consumer services. Both long and short holiday taking are direct beneficiaries of the transition to service businesses. Economies that make the transition to service businesses have increased the volume of citizens who take foreign holidays and simultaneously the economies develop industrial cities in ways that makes them more attractive to tourists. The changes over recent decades in cities such as Pittsburgh, Pennsylvania in the US and Glasgow, Liverpool, and Newcastle in Britain are examples.

Major global hotel companies and other international chains in Europe

There is a group of seven international hotel companies that have multiple hotel brands with a presence in the Americas, Europe, and Asia. In Europe these global majors—Accor, Carlson Hospitality, Choice Hotels International, HHC, Intercontinental Hotels Group (IHG), Marriott International, and Starwood Hotels and Resorts operate 39 hotel brands with 557,000 rooms representing a capital value of €100 billion. The global majors account for just more than half of the international chain presence in Europe having added, over the period, 168,000 rooms and introduced 12 new brands including Accor's Suitehotel, Carlson's Regent International and Park Inn as well as Marriott's Ritz-Carlton and JW Marriott brands. The indicative capital value of the global majors room additions was €40 billion, representing a two-thirds increase on the 2000 value.

Of the room stock added by the global majors, 44% was in the mid-market and was dominated by brands such as Accor's Mercure and Novotel, Carlson's Park Inn, IHG's Holiday Inn, and Courtyard by Marriott. The capital value of this mid-market growth was almost €14 billion. Up-market hotels accounted for 27% of their room additions driven by the Marriott brand with almost 10,000 rooms, Carlson's Radisson with 8000 rooms, Hilton with more than 7100, Choice's Clarion with more than 6500, Marriott's Renaissance with 2000, Starwood's Westin with 1400, and Accor's Sofitel with around 1000 room additions. However, the up-market segment was not all about additions. Three brands shrank their portfolios.

Intercontinental reduced its room stock by 2600 and Starwood reduced its Le Meridien Brand by 1000 rooms and Sheraton by 300 rooms. The portfolio reductions were due to management contracts coming to an end and not being renewed and also by an issue that was specific to this period when global majors were reducing their balance sheet exposure to hotels and this involved the sale and removal of the brand from several hotels notably the Intercontinental, Paris which became a Westin and the Waldorf, London which changed flag from Le Meridien to Hilton. Overall the capital value of the up-market additions by the global majors was €18 billion.

Nineteen percent of the global major room additions were in the economy segment and were accounted for almost entirely by two brands: Accor's Ibis, which added 18,700 rooms and IHG's Express by Holiday Inn, which added 13,600 rooms. IHG also lost 2200 rooms with the progressive winding down of the Holiday Inn Garden Court brand. The capital value of the economy lodging additions of the global majors was only €3 billion. Accor added 13,600 budget rooms mostly in its Etap brand, which added 12,000 rooms with the remainder in Formule 1, which has been replaced by Etap. The difference between Etap and Formule 1 is that all bedrooms in Etap have private bathrooms. The low capital cost of budget hotels limited the value of the additions to only €600 million. The last market segment in which the global majors expanded was deluxe, the most capital intense segment in which they added 4800 rooms at a capital value of €4 billion. Starwood's Luxury collection added 1700 rooms, Marriott's Ritz-Carlton added 1400 rooms, HHC's Conrad added 1300 rooms, and Carlson's Regent added 400 rooms.

The pattern of expansion by the other international brands in Europe was different from the global majors. In 2000, there were 73 other international brands and by 2006 this was doubled to 146 with the addition of 255,000 rooms at a total capital cost of €60 billion. In Europe these international brands are small with an average of 3700 rooms per brand compared with the global majors 14,300 rooms per brand. More than half of the added rooms of international brands, 123,000, were in the mid-market; 29%, 71,000 rooms were in economy lodging; 13%, 31,600 were at the up-market level; 4%, 9700 rooms were deluxe; and the final 3%, 6800 were at the budget level. The key difference between the global majors and the other international brands is the greater focus by the international brands on up-market hotels, while the main focus of the other international brands is on the mid-market. This difference is also evident in the location of the hotels. Up-market hotels have a greater exposure to capital and gateway cities, where much of the foreign business demand and a proportion of the foreign leisure demand are concentrated. Mid-market hotels have a greater exposure than up-market hotels to provincial conurbations where domestic demand is more prevalent. Although there is no data to prove the point, the logic is that with their greater exposure to the more significant conurbations the global majors will achieve a higher RevPAR than the other international chains at each market level. This is reinforced by the smaller brand size of the other international chains and the greater investment by the global majors in demand generating infrastructure.

Developments in the affiliation between hotel chains and their hotels

The burst of expansion by international hotel chains in Europe since 2000 has been accompanied by a shift in affiliation structures away from the brands owning and leasing their hotels and towards expansion by management contracts and franchises, which do not require the brands to invest capital in the hotels. It would be wrong to believe that the relationship between expansion by international hotel chains and the shift in affiliation was causal. There were three prime drivers of the change in affiliation. First, stock markets, particularly in the US and Britain reassessed the risk and return profiles of hotel chains and concluded that chains that owned and leased their hotels were exposed to higher economic risks and simultaneously achieved lower returns than those chains that were involved predominantly in management contracts and franchises. These chains needed less capital, achieved higher returns, and grew at faster rates. This triggered a bout of balance sheet restructuring by the global majors mostly in programmes of sale and management back, which reduced the risk and increased the returns. Over the period IHG sold around £3 billion of hotel assets converting mainly from ownership to management contracts. HHC, Starwood, and Marriott were also involved in this process. Accor, with different accounting policies from the US and British companies, embarked on a sale and lease back programme. Carlson and Choice hotels were already franchise chains and owned no real estate.

Secondly, and conveniently in parallel with the asset lightening by the global majors was the realization by real estate funds and private equity funds that they were underweight in their ownership of hotels. They became major buyers of the hotels being sold by the global majors and thus, the period was marked by the transfer of hotel ownership from stock market investors to primary real estate owners who had different risk and return criteria that could accommodate hotel ownership. Third, the rate of growth in and the size of the European hotel market are such that it is inconceivable that the global majors would be able to fund their expansion from internal equity resources. For instance, IHG's expansion in Europe alone over the period had a capital value of around €5.2 billion, which is broadly equivalent to the market capitalization of the company.

We illustrate some of the points made above by providing an evaluation of the development of international hotel chains in Russia.

The case of Russia and international hotel chains

Russia is the largest European country in terms of land mass and with a population of 144 million it is substantially larger than the next largest, Germany with 83 million. However, as far as the hotel business is concerned Russia is a backwater with only 95,000 hotel rooms, a ratio of 1520 citizens per room compared with Britain, which has 125 citizens per room. Not only that, but the chains have a paltry 12,000 rooms in Russia compared with 260,000 in Britain.

Since 1998 total Russian GDP growth has been impressive, exceeding 6% CAGR for the period 2000–2005 when many of the western European economies struggled close to recession. The growth in total Russian GDP provided growth in hotel demand, but this came largely from foreign visitors and largely in cities such as Moscow and St. Petersburg. Historically, the communists were dead against foreign visitors, but that is changing. Since 2000, the number of foreign overnight visitors has grown by more than a quarter to 9 million, significant for Russia, but minor in comparison with the 75 million who visited France. Domestic hotel demand did not grow much, which was not unexpected given the low GDP per citizen in Russia, now only $4000, while Britain achieves nine times as much. On a per capita basis Russia is a weak economy with little impetus to generate domestic hotel demand. More specifically, Russia's economic structure is not conducive to developing a large hotel business. Agriculture, which generates little domestic business demand into hotels, accounts for 5% of GDP, down from 6.4% in 2000, but still far higher than countries such as Britain with only around 1%. Secondary economic activities—manufacturing, mining, and utilities—accounted for 38% of GDP in 2000 and declined to 35% in 2004, still very high compared with western

Europe. Citizen services accounted for a high 46% of GDP in 2000 and rose to 49% in 2004. The market service and experience segments jointly amounted to only 10% of GDP in 2000 and rose to 11% by 2004, still extremely low compared with the western European economies. Domestic hotel demand is driven by the significance of the market service and experience segments of an economy and their very low levels in Russia cement the very low levels of domestic hotel demand and hotel supply.

Much of the economic growth in Russia over the past 5 years has been generated by natural resources such as gas, oil, metals, and timber, which collectively account for around 80% of exports. Importantly for the hotel business, these activities generate little more business demand into hotels than does agriculture. When it comes to manufacturing, Russia is a mess. Its productive capacity is outdated, very inefficient, and heavily underinvested. For Russian manufacturing to reach anything remotely like the productivity levels of western Europe, massive long-term capital investment in new plants and new products as well as the radical long-term development of domestic demand for consumer goods will be required. The first two do not look to be on the medium term horizon, and although consumer demand is growing strongly from very low levels, consumer access to capital is minor. The Russian banking and financial services sector is still suffering from the tribulations of the communist era when personal credit was not available, ownership of appreciating assets was out of the question, and savings was no more than a pipe dream for the mass of the population on subsistence living. The rest of the market service and experience segments are so insignificant that they hardly register.

The challenge for the Russian government is to find effective ways to use the income generated from the export of natural resources. The problem is that it has not yet embarked on an effective policy. Indeed, it has been going backward as a result of the expansion of direct state participation in sectors such as power generation, aviation, oil, and finance. In addition, spending on public services increased by 27% in 2005. No economy has been able to develop a significant hotel business when state control has been expanded in such ways.

The most attractive context for the Russian economy is that export demand for its natural resources remains high and that producers are able to exert the same vigorous pricing power as they are presently with gas. This will allow the government to buy time to invest in other sectors, notably manufacturing, to increase labour productivity, and to reduce the cost and time of production. In parallel, there needs to be a major expansion of the banking and financial services sector to enable Russian consumers to have access to credit to acquire goods such as household goods, clothes, and cars. These are higher priorities than developing demand for other market service businesses such as retailing, communications, wholesaling, and advertising, which are likely to follow after the higher priority developments.

The World Bank (2007) projects average annual economic growth of 3.1% for Russia over the next 10 years. When we translate this into the potential growth in the economic segments there is little to suggest any structural shift in the balance of the economy. Our mid-range projection is for market services to grow by 4.2% per year and experience businesses to grow by 4.9%, which looks impressive for the hotel business. However, between 2000 and 2005 market service and experience segments grew by 9.5 and 8.6% respectively and because they came from such a very low level their impact on domestic hotel demand, while positive, was not transforming. We estimate that domestic business and leisure demand accounts for around 7 million room nights in Russia compared with 75 million in Britain, a country with a population of only 40% that of Russia, but with a significantly more developed economic structure.

Domestic leisure demand in Russia is predominantly summer holiday demand in the southern resorts. As the cohort of middle class grows we expect this demand will continue to be for summer holidays into existing heavily seasonal hotels. The current level of short break demand is microscopic and is mainly into the larger cities. We expect domestic short breaks to remain minor in the first instance because the United Nations (2007) expects the population to decline to 137 million by 2018, shrinking almost 5%. Moreover, younger adults at an early stage in the family life cycle make up a significant proportion of the population and are in the forefront of buying consumer goods rather than staying in hotels at the weekend. Older adults at later stages of the family life cycle have little or no savings, receive a subsistence state pension and are not a market for short breaks. Most foreign visitors stay in hotels and are leisure travellers, predominantly to the main cities.

Hotel chain supply at end-2000 had been around 4500 rooms. At end-2006, chain hotel supply in Russia was approximately 12,000 rooms, a concentration of 13%. International chains account for 32 hotels in the country and only in four cities, 18 hotels in Moscow, 10 in St. Petersburg, 3 in Sochi, and 1 in Samara. Of the global hotel companies, Accor, Carlson, Intercontinental, Marriott, and Starwood had 24 hotels while Hilton and Choice had none. All the hotels were in the mid-market to deluxe range and none of the chains have invested capital in the hotels. Chain room stock in Russia is equivalent to that in Denmark with a population of only 5.4 million or The Czech Republic with a population of 10.2 million. As the Russian economy continues in its current economic structure there will be growth in hotel demand, but without significant change in economic policies the Russian hotel business will continue to lag behind those in western Europe. If hotel demand grows in line with the projected growth in the key sectors then around 50,000 hotel rooms will be added over the next 10 years, which will reduce the number of citizens per hotel room to 945, down from 1520 in 2006.

Most of the global majors have arrived in Russia and are seeking further exposure, but all of the international chains will be faced with several challenges in the years ahead. First, they are unwilling to risk their own capital in the face of questionable rule of law and questionable security of foreign investments, so significant local capital will need to be invested in hotels. The issue is the low proportion of local capital seeking hotel investments in the face of more pressing need for investment in other asset classes such as industrial, residential, and commercial, each producing higher volumes of development opportunity and greater political support. Secondly, the chain presence in Russia is located to capture foreign demand rather than domestic demand. As domestic demand grows it will spread to the cities where chains are not represented, but the chains have minimal brand infrastructure in the country and are not well organized to penetrate the domestic markets. We expect new hotel developments in the country to continue to be full feature and basic feature hotels rather than limited feature and room only because of the paucity of freestanding restaurants. This is before we get to the massive task and investment in training and education needed to provide an effective hotel workforce.

The volume and pattern of hotel demand in Russia is a function of its economic structure. The economy is weak and is particularly weak in those segments necessary to generate a meaningful level of domestic hotel demand. The recent economic history and current government economic policies do not hold out much hope of a dramatic increase in hotel demand or hotel supply to the levels common in western Europe. However, the current low level of total hotel provision and the token presence of hotel chains coupled with the economic developments and opening of the borders to foreign visitors means that there will be expansion by hotel chains. The problem is that many other European countries have more developed economies, with greater capacity to generate hotel demand, larger and faster growing hotel businesses and lower operating risks. For the hotel market in Russia to narrow the gap on western Europe will need sizeable change in government economic policy, secular shift in the structure of the economy, and monumental improvement in the standard of living and lifestyle of the Russian population. This is likely to take decades.

Conclusion

The chapter has shown the significance of Europe to the development of international hotel chains. Previous studies have failed to predict and explain the burst of hotel chain and international hotel chain development in the region. Perhaps this is because they have tended to focus on providing short and superficial answers to what hotel chains have done without attention to why they took the action that they did. Our analysis is that hotel chains grew by responding to developments in the structure of European economies that generated higher growth in hotel demand. Further, it is our conviction that it is necessary to give prominence to the economic context, which propels the developments of hotel companies, because to ignore this is to produce sterile analyses of hotel chains with no hope of explaining the actions on which they embark. Prior available analyses of the internationalization of hotel chains have been short and one-off analyses that have tried to shed some light on investment and management issues that were too big, too complex, and too changeable to tackle. Our solution is the incessant tracking of three activities: the economic structures of the countries, including the economic policies that influence the developments in economic structure; the sources of demand for hotels generated by developments in the economic structures; and the supply variables of all hotel chains. Only by investing in these activities are we able to identify the opportunities and threats to the hotel business and to have sufficient longitudinal data to explain why hotel chains develop as they do. Anything short of this fails to address the significance of the issues that are involved.

References

Altinay, L. (2005). Factors influencing entry mode choices: Empirical findings from an international hotel organization. *Journal of Hospitality and Leisure Marketing*, 12(3), 5–28.

Altinay, L., and Altinay, M. (2003). How will growth be financed by international hotel companies? *International Journal of Contemporary Hospitality Management*, 15(5), 274–282.

Altinay, L., and Roper, A. (2005). The entrepreneurial role of organizational members in the internationalisation of a franchise system. *International Journal of Entrepreneurial Behaviour and Research, 11*(3), 222–240.

Aung, M. (2000). The Accor multinational hotel chain in an emerging market: Through the lens of the core competency concept. *The Service Industries Journal, 20*(3), 43–60.

Aung, M., and Heeler, R. (2001). Core competencies of service firms: A framework for strategic decisions in international markets. *Journal of Marketing Management, 17*, 619–643.

Brown, J. R., Dev, C. S., and Zhou, Z. (2003). Broadening the foreign market entry mode decision: Separating ownership and control. *Journal of International Business Studies, 34*(5), 473–488.

Chen, J. J., and Dimou, I. (2005). Expansion strategy of international hotel firms. *Journal of Business Research, 58*(12), 1730–1740.

Connell, J. (1997). International hotel franchise relationships— UK franchisee perspectives. *International Journal of Contemporary Hospitality Management, 9*(5/6), 215–220.

Contractor, F. J., Kundu, S. K., and Hsu, C.-C. (2003). A three-stage theory of international expansion: The link between multinationality and performance in the service sector. *Journal of International Business Studies, 34*(1), 5–18.

Dev, C. S., Brown, J. R., and Zhou, K. Z. (2007). Global brand expansion: How to select a market entry strategy. *Cornell Hotel and Restaurant Administration Quarterly, 48*(1), 13–27.

Doherty, A. M. (2007). The internationalization of retailing: Factors influencing the choice of franchising as a market entry strategy. *International Journal of Service Industry Management, 18*(2), 184–205.

Dunning, J. H. (1981). *International Production and the Multinational Enterprise*. London: Allen and Unwin.

Gannon, J. M. (2007). *Strategic Human Resources and their Management: The Case of Unit General Managers in International Hotel Companies*. Unpublished doctoral dissertation, Oxford Brookes University, Oxford.

Groschl, S., and Doherty, L. (2006). The complexity of culture: Using the appraisal process to compare French and British managers in a UK-based international hotel organization. *International Journal of Hospitality Management, 25*(2), 313–335.

Jones, P., Song, H., and Hong, J. H. (2004). The relationship between generic theory and hospitality applied research: The case of international hotel development. *Journal of Hospitality and Tourism Management, 11*(2), 128–138.

Litteljohn, D. (1997). Internationalization in hotels: Current aspects and development. *International Journal of Contemporary Hospitality Management, 9*(5/6), 187–192.

Litteljohn, D., Roper, A., and Altinay, L. (2007). Territories still to find—the business of hotel internationalization. *International Journal of Service Industry Management*, *18*(2), 167–183.

O'Gorman, C., and McTiernan, L. (2000). Factors influencing the internationalization choices of small and medium-sized enterprises: The case of the Irish hotel industry. *Enterprise and Innovation Management Studies*, *1*(2), 141–151.

Otus Hotel Brands Database. (2007). Otus & Co. Advisory Ltd.

Pine, B. J., II, and Gilmore, J. H. (1998). Welcome to the experience economy. *Harvard Business Review, July/August 98*, *76*(4), 97–105.

The World Bank. (2007). Data and statistics, http://www.worldbank.org.

United Nations. (2007). Populations division, data and statistics, http://www.un.org.

United Nations Statistics Division. (2006). International Standard Industrial Classification of All Economic Activities, Revision 2.

Whitla, P., Walters, P. G. P., and Davies, H. (2006). Global strategies in the international hotel industry. *International Journal of Hospitality Management*, In Press, Completed Proof.

Industry critical success factors and their importance in strategy

Nicolas S. Graf

Conrad N. Hilton College of Hotel and Restaurant Management, University of Houston, Houston, TX 77204-3028

In kitchens, Chefs have the same pots and knives. However, some keep them cleaner and sharper than others. In the end, some dishes taste and look better than others.

Franco Fontebasso, Chef and Owner

Introduction

The fundamental tenet in strategy states that, in order to perform well, a firm must achieve a certain degree of alignment between environmentally driven imperatives and its competencies and capabilities. At a micro level, such alignment is achieved by matching the firm strengths to the critical success factors (CSFs) specific to the existing structure of the industry and segment it is competing in.

Early literature on CSFs focuses on reporting systems and data gathering, and is essentially driven by executives' needs for more relevant information. In this initial attempt to prioritize business issues, scholars and practitioners delved into those few areas in which results need to be satisfactory for the organization to ensure successful competitive performance. What emerged from these inquiries are lists of CSFs, organized by industries or functions.

Other works, more interested by the economic nature of CSFs, shed some light on the relationships between industry factors and firm-specific resources and capabilities. These efforts highlighted the dynamic relationships between organizations' strategic choices and the character of CSFs, which, in turn, influenced the performance potential and overall attractiveness of the industry.

While these efforts all stressed the importance of CSFs in strategy, the questions of what those CSFs are in the hospitality industry, and how they relate to the environment and firm performance remain unanswered. This manuscript provides an overview of past and current thinking about CSFs, their relationships to environmental forces and firm performance. In an attempt to synthesize the literature on the subject, both from the general management literature and, more specifically from the hospitality field of study, it offers a conceptual definition of CSFs, and, through industry examples, illustrates their importance to strategic management as applied to hospitality firms. Finally, a practical framework for the identification and management of CSFs is proposed.

Critical success factors and information needs

Strategic decision-making centres around two fundamental questions pertaining to domain definitional and navigational issues. At the corporate level, top-management teams are faced with the daunting task of domain selection and definition which determines in which industry the firm is to be in. Such undertaking aims at aligning the corporation with the major remote environmental forces driving change. The second issue, usually referred to as business strategy, is narrower in its scope as it is primarily concerned with the task environment. At this level, the navigational concerns call on managers to align their business units or firms to the forces shaping the task environment. In both cases, understanding the forces driving change requires managers to scan their environment and to cope with massive information flows.

Several frameworks have been provided by strategy management scholars and consultants to assist managers in their scanning duties. At the task level, Rockart (1979) suggested that companies could more effectively scan their environment by concentrating their information needs on those "limited number of areas in which results, if they are satisfactory, will ensure successful competitive performance for the organization" (p. 85). These key areas in which success is necessary are industry-wide CSFs. Together, they characterize the structure of the industry and how firms compete in it and respond to environmental forces. Rockart (1979) provided examples of CSFs for varying industries. For instance, styling, quality dealer system, cost control and meeting energy standards are typical CSFs shared by all automobile manufacturers. Rockart (1979) also posited that CSFs evolve over time and shape the boundaries of the industry.

Other authors have emphasized the importance of defining those areas that are critical to the long-term success of firms. Freund (1988) stressed the importance of monitoring CSFs to avoid business failure rather than to gain competitive advantage. To him, CSFs need to be defined for the overall organization, as well as for each business unit and function. Freund (1988) also pointed out that CSFs need to be generic enough to include means required to achieve strategic goals as opposed to specific and related only to performance indicators. He suggested that firms should identify CSFs using a top-down approach that would ensure the alignment of business units with the overall goals and objectives of the corporation. Freund (1988) proposed a 5-step approach to CSFs:

1. Identify the success factors necessary to the attainment of the overall corporate objectives;
2. Determine the related CSFs for each business unit's functional area. Only five to ten CSFs should be retained at each level;

3. Develop strategies that leverage strength and prevail over weaknesses in each CSF;
4. Develop lists of key performance indicators to monitor the performance on each CSF; and
5. Establish processes and procedures to monitor performance and provide timely feedback.

The use of CSFs as control or monitoring systems has been advocated by several other authors (Green and Welsh, 1988). This control approach suggests that CSFs are not only important areas to supervise during the strategy implementation phase, but also that they are detached from the strategy development stage and used primarily to manage exceptions or to detect early signs of failure. Other research however has shown that the CSFs approach is used more proactively by managers too. Simons (1991) for instance discussed the potential advantages of using CSFs in the strategy-making process. While the author recognized that CSFs do not necessarily help managers reduce the uncertainties pertaining to the future changes that can occur in their environment, he argued that they could be used as signalling tools providing information about how changes actually affect their firms. Accordingly, he suggested that top managers should use subset of control systems interactively while keeping the rest for diagnosis purposes. In his study of 16 large corporations, Simons (1991) found that executives using some control systems and CSFs interactively had a much clearer vision and sense of direction than those not doing so.

Critical success factors and industry structure

While information and control-system scholars looked as CSFs as being things executives need to pay attention to, other streams of research in strategy have looked at them from an industry structure perspective. The idea that industry structure is crucial to the enduring success of firms has been central to the development of the industrial organization's (IO) view of strategy. As suggested by Porter (1980), the attractiveness of an industry depends on its relationships with the external forces present in the task environment. Firms' strategic actions are responses to environmental changes with the aim of increasing their bargaining power over suppliers and buyers, or raising entry barriers to prevent potential new competitors to enter the industry. The concepts of entry barriers and bargaining power are powerful to explain what CSFs can be and why they are important to strategy. Table 4.1 provides examples of Porter's (1980) generic strategies. Principally conceptual and prescriptive, these generic

Table 4.1 Porter's Generic Strategies

Generic Strategy	Strategic Actions (Content)	Strategic Consequences
Overall low-cost leadership	Aggressive construction of efficient-scale facilities Cost reduction from experience (experience curve) Tight cost and overhead control Avoidance of marginal customer accounts Cost minimization in areas like R&D, service, sales force, etc.	Defend the firm against intense rivalry as still can earn returns after its competitors have competed away their profit. Decrease the bargaining power of buyers as they cannot drive down prices more than at the level of the next most efficient firm. Buffer the firm from actions taken by powerful suppliers as it provides flexibility to cope with cost increases. Reduce threat of new entrants as the position requires factors that raise entry barriers. Reduce threats from substitutes due to the relative advantage gained over the competitors.
Differentiation	Create a unique design or brand image Create a unique technology Create unique features Create unique customer service Create unique dealer network	Insulate the firm against rivalry through brand loyalty and lower price sensitivity from the buyers. Provides higher margins that mitigate the power of suppliers. Decrease the threats posed by potential new entrants and substitutes through customer loyalty.
Focus	Concentrate all efforts on a particular buyer group Serve the narrow strategic market more effectively and efficiently than competitors	Achieve the same advantages than low cost and differentiation strategies *vis-à-vis* its narrow target market, but not from the perspective of the market as a whole.

Source: Porter (1980).

strategies still suggest several propositions related to the relationships between structural factors of the industry, strategic choices made by firms and their strategic consequences.

For instance, firms following a differentiation strategy would attempt to develop their businesses by focusing on unique areas which would be difficult to imitate and thus raise entry barriers. Likewise, differentiators would prevent customers from selecting other alternatives by increasing their switching costs. In both cases, the actions taken by these firms to establish their position would alter the structure of the industry. These areas in which the differentiator creates its uniqueness then become CSFs. For example, a restaurant franchisor could try to differentiate itself by developing superior site selection capabilities. If successful, the strategic action would likely become a benchmark in the industry and change the way franchisors compete. The superior site selection capabilities would ultimately become industry-wide CSFs and need constant attention from management.

The concepts of bargaining power and entry barriers are to be understood in the context of the five forces shaping the task environment of firms (Porter, 1980). In the five forces framework, the relative bargaining power of the industry *vis-à-vis* its external forces, as well as the relative heights of the entry barriers, define the degree of rivalry among industry competitors. As industries and task environments evolve, different dynamics become apparent, and different CSFs emerge. These interactions have been described extensively from the perspective of the industry or market life cycle. For example, Wasson (1974) suggested that strategic focus changes depending on the stage of the life cycle. He argued that product development, pricing strategy, distribution policy, and intelligence focus varied depending on the type of competition at each stage of the cycle. For instance, at the market development stage, the distribution policy should concentrate on selected distributors and provide them with high margin so that they could heavily advertise. In contrast, at the maturity stage, distribution policy should include as many dealers as possible, and provide them with a well supplied but low-cost inventory.

Synthesizing the literature on strategy and industry life cycle, Hofer (1975) presented a list of organizational, environmental, and resource variables that were deemed as strategically significant at different stages of the cycle. While based on manufacturing industries, these variables are interesting as they illustrate the evolutionary nature of CSFs.

Table 4.2 presents some of the variables of Hofer (1975) that are closely related to CSFs. The evolutionary nature mentioned above is exemplified by the importance of the rate of

Table 4.2   Strategically Significant Variables at Different Stages of the Life Cycle

Life Cycle Stages	Industry Structure Variables	Organizational Characteristics and Resources
Introduction	Uniqueness of the product Rate of technological change in product design	Quality of products
Growth	Type of product Rate of technological change in product design No. of equal products Barriers to entry	Market share Quality of products Marketing intensity
Maturity	Type of product Rate of technological change in process design Degree of product differentiation No. of equal products Transportation and distribution costs Barriers to entry	Market share Quality of products Value added Degree of customer concentration Marketing intensity Discretionary cash flow/gross capital investment
Saturation	Degree of product differentiation Price/cost structure Experience curves Degree of integration Economies of scale	Market share Quality of products Length of the production cycle Newness of plant and equipment Relative wage rate Marketing intensity
Decline	Degree of products differentiation Price/cost structure Marginal plant size Transportation and distribution costs	Market share Quality of products Length of the production cycle Relative wage rate Degree of customer concentration

Source: Adapted from Hofer (1975).

technological change in product design at the introduction and growth stage, which evolved into the rate of change in process design at the maturity stage. As industries grow, new product development is a critical element to market share building and sales growth, while as growth slows down, business processes that produce or distribute products or services become more important to sustain operating margin and profit growth. It is also interesting to note that, as the industry (or market) matures, the number of critical variables increases; variables are more often added to the list than removed. Indeed, it appears that CSFs are cumulative rather than specific to stages in the life cycle. Consequently, it seems unlikely that firms actually gain a competitive advantage through CSFs, but rather avoid failure by considering them. This view is consistent with that of Simons (1991) and other information system scholars.

Another important notion put forth by Porter (1980) and IO students is the concept of strategic group and mobility barriers. Strategic group represent clusters of firms within an industry that follow essentially the same strategy. In this context, strategy is defined by the actual activities undertaken by firms at all level of the organization. These activities include functional-level, pricing, and positioning strategies among others things. The existence of such groups within industries rests on the assumption that firms not only attempt to raise entry barriers and leverage their bargaining power in relation to participants outside their industry, but also try to distinguish themselves from rivals by investing in mobility barriers (Caves and Porter, 1977). Much like industry entry and exit barriers, these mobility barriers can be tangible or intangible assets firms developed or acquired, such as a strong brand name, a loyal customer base or some distribution channels (Mascarenhas and Aaker, 1989). They can also be skills and capabilities, such as the ability to perform a task better than others or to design products or services that are reliable and inexpensive to produce or deliver.

Mobility barriers are principally assets and capabilities that delineate strategic groups, and because strategic groups have been viewed as key determinants to success, they appear to be closely related to the CSFs concept. In other words, firms that enjoy sustained high performance due to their group belonging would have to pay special attention to the determinants of their mobility barriers which are CSFs to them. From this perspective, CSFs are defined as being those resources (i.e., assets and capabilities) that help firms buffer themselves against external forces present in their task environment as well as from their competitors.

Critical success factors and the market for strategic resources and capabilities

While management scholars are still debating whether superior performance is mostly driven by industry- or firm-specific factors (Hawawini, Subramanian, and Verdin, 2003; McGahan and Porter, 1997; Schmalensee, 1985), it appears that both are important to strategy. Where IO researchers saw firms' resources as determinant of strategic groups and industry structure, students of the resource-based view (RBV) of the firm envisioned resources as firm-specific factors and key differentiating elements among companies or business units. Wernerfelt (1984) advocated the value of analysing firms from a resource perspective instead of the product-market side. He argued that, unlike the entry barrier concept of IO students, resources created position barriers that provide its owner an advantage over other industry members as long as it is not replicated by other competing firms or new entrants.

Similarly, Barney (1986a) argued that the creation of imperfectly competitive product markets (i.e., generic strategies) may not suffice to explain above normal economic performance. In his reasoning, abnormal economic performance can only exists when the cost of implementing product-market strategies (e.g., differentiation or cost leadership) is lower than the returns. According to economic theories, this can only be achieved when competition is not perfect. Barney (1986a) suggested that the imperfections are more likely to reside in the way resources are distributed among firms. In other words, the principal competitive market is not about positions in industries, but more a market for strategic factors in which firms attempt to control unique resources or to acquire resources of which the future value has not been well recognized by competitors.

Building on this resource approach, Prahalad and Hamel (1990) suggested that the roots of competitive advantage were not product market related, but entrenched in the core competencies of companies. Using historical examples of corporate successes and failures, they posited that "the real sources of advantage are to be found in management's ability to consolidate corporatewide technologies and production skills into competencies that empower individual businesses to adapt quickly to changing opportunities" (p. 81). They defined core competencies as "the collective learning in the organization, especially how to coordinate diverse production skills and integrate multiple streams of technologies" (p. 82). In terms of resource allocation, they distinguished between the traditional view of the firm, where capital is allocated to discrete business units, with a competence-based approach, where capital and talents are allocated to competencies and businesses at large.

In an attempt to formalize the RBV of the firm, Grant (1991) proposed a practical, 5-step framework to strategy analysis. Synthesizing the work of RBV proponents such as Wernerfelt (1984), Barney (1986a, 1986b), Shoemaker (1990), and Prahalad and Hamel (1990), as well as prior works of Penrose (1959),

Andrews (1971), and Thompson (1967); he suggested that firms should first analyse their resources, and appraise their strengths and weaknesses relative to their competitors, as well as identify opportunities to better utilize them. Then, firms should identify their capabilities (i.e., competencies) and understand what they do better than their competitors. They should gain an understanding on which resources are necessary to their capabilities. Next, firms should appraise the rent-generating potential of their resources and capabilities, and select their strategies on the basis of the best possible exploitation of their internal strength (i.e., resources and capabilities) relative to external opportunities. Finally, firms should identify any gap between the strategy pursued and their resources and capabilities endowment, and, if necessary, invest in refilling or maintaining their resource base. Grant (1991) concluded that "key to a resource-based approach to strategy formulation is understanding relationships between resources, capabilities, competitive advantage, and profitability—in particular, an understanding of the mechanisms through which competitive advantage can be sustained over time" (p. 133).

In an effort to integrate apparently contrasting views of strategy, Amit and Schoemaker (1993) developed theoretical propositions that linked the RBV and the industry analysis perspectives. Drawing on the concept of key success factors (Vasconcellos E Sa and Hambrick, 1989) and on the industrial economics notion of strategic factors (Ghemawat, 1991), they linked firms' resources and capabilities to the structure of the industry. Using Ghemawat's (1991) notion of sunk cost, they stated that "When the industry (or product market) is the unit of analysis, one may observe that, at a given time, certain *Resources* and *Capabilities* which are subject to market failure, have become the prime determinants of economic rents" (p. 36). Additionally, they argued that these *Resources* and *Capabilities*—labelled strategic industry factors—were characterized by their propensity to market failure and consequent asymmetric distribution over firms. In contrast, by focusing on the firm unit of analysis, unique bundles of resources and capabilities can be identified that enable the firm to earn economic rents. The authors labelled these firm-specific resources and capabilities strategic assets. Further, they argued that the rent-generating potential of these strategic assets was dependent on their applicability to a particular industry setting; "the overlap with the set of *Strategic Industry Factors*" (p. 40). The authors concluded that strategic analysis would gain from a more multidimensional approach, including both industry structure, defined by strategic industry factors and environmental forces, and firms-specific strategic

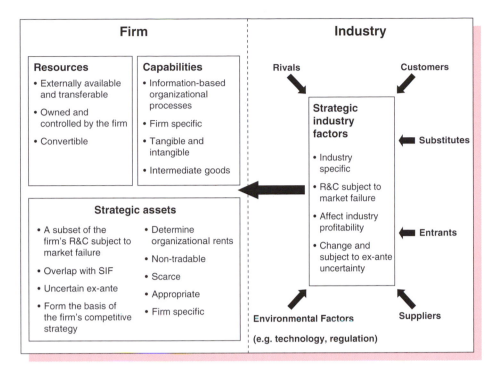

Figure 4.1
Strategic assets and strategic industry factors. (Reproduced with permission from Amit and Schoemaker, Strategic Management Journal. © 1993 by John Wiley & Sons Limited.)

assets that are asymmetrically distributed within the industry. These constructs and relationships are depicted in Figure 4.1.

In another attempt to theoretically synthesize and clarify the earlier works on the RBV, Peteraf (1993) proposed a model describing four conditions to gaining a sustainable advantage through resources. To her, all four conditions need to be met if firms want to generate superior rents on the long run (i.e., earnings in excess of the cost of capital). The first condition is that firms should be heterogeneous in a given industry and that superior resources exist in limited supply. These superior resources enable firms to produce at a lower average cost than competitors with inferior resources, and as they are limited in supply, efficient firms are able to sustain that competitive cost advantage. The second condition results from the need to maintain some degree of heterogeneity across firms. What the author coined as *ex post* limits to competition refer to forces that restrict competition for rents that have been gained by a firm. Some factors shaping these forces have been recognized in the RBV literature as resulting from imperfect imitability and imperfect substitutability. The third suggested condition is what Peteraf (1993) labelled imperfect mobility. This notion is related to Ghemawat's (1991) sunk costs and Shoemaker's (1990) idea of asset specificity. Resources that are imperfectly mobile are hard to trade as their use and value is firm specific. The fourth condition, *ex ante* limits to competition, refers to the importance of the cost of implementing strategies brought out by Barney (1986a). The argument is that the future potential value of resources needs to be perceived differently by competing firms so that one that perceives it as valuable can acquire it at a relatively low cost.

Whether taken from an industry structure perspective or from a firm's resource side, some resources and capabilities appear to be major determinants of financial and competitive success. Thompson and Strickland (1996) noted that "Key success factors point to the things a firm must concentrate on doing well, the specific kinds of skills and competences that are needed, and which aspects of the which internal operating activities at the most crucial and why" (p. 76). They also observed that these CSFs varied from industry-to-industry as well as from time-to-time. To them, because such factors have to be of utmost importance to the financial success of firms, CSFs are to be related to major value adding activities. Put differently, the way firms perform on these CSFs need to have a direct and major influence on its key value drivers, be them revenue or cost related. For example, in the beer industry, CSFs are the utilization of brewing capacity, the dealer distribution network, and the advertising effectiveness. In industries with high transportation costs, the location of production plants and the ability to sell products within an economical shipping distance are CSFs. The authors highlighted that the identification CSFs, while necessary to successful planning, was a difficult task that had to be performed regularly and at industry level.

Critical success factors in the hospitality industry

Several authors have discussed or studied CSFs in the context of the hospitality industry. Some research were carried toward the identification of industry-wide competitive methods (CMs) and CSFs. These efforts principally looked at the strategic actions taken by hospitality firms and how quickly they were copied. For instance, Olsen, West, and Tse (1998) defined strategy choice as being investments in CMs and CSFs, which are products and services that are bundled in a unique way and that attract customers from within the overall demand curve of the industry. The authors also made a distinction between CMs and CSFs. To them, competitive advantages, resulting from the investment in CMs, are rarely sustained for a long period of time as competitors, principally in the service sector, tend to quickly and successfully copy them. CMs that are copied become CSFs, and shape the boundaries of the industry as they develop into benchmarks. This idea is consistent with Porter's (1985) mobility barriers, where he argued that "firms, through their strategies, can influence the 5 forces" (p. 7). It is through the dynamic evolution of CMs and CSFs that those firms define their industry domain. Consequently, CSFs are defined as those things that are necessary for firms to invest in if they aspire to compete within an industry (Olsen *et al.*, 1998).

As shown in Olsen and Zhao (1997), distinguishing between CMs and CSFs can be a daunting task as CMs "frequently have very short life spans" (p. 57). Reporting on Olsen's (1995a) work, commissioned by the International Hotel and Restaurant Association (IH&RA), the authors also stated that "the leading or innovative firms were always the first to come up with a new or better method and they were then copied within a very short period of time" (p. 57). Thus, the primary distinguishing factor between CMs and CSFs appears to be time, where the leading firms take an advantage over the time period during which its CM is unique.

Olsen (1995a) and Olsen and Zhao (2000) researched the CMs used by international hotel firms during the 1985–1994 and 1995–1999 periods. Using content analysis techniques, information on 20 international hotel groups from 10 different countries were analysed and resulted in the identification of a number of CMs. These CMs are listed in Table 4.3.

Other scholars have also tried to uncover key CSFs in the hospitality industry. Geller (1985) interviewed 74 executives of 27 hotel companies and asked them to identify the most important CSFs to the performance of their firm, to which strategic goals they were related, and how they would track them. The most frequently cited were employee attitude, guest satisfaction (service), superior product (physical plant), superior location, maximization of revenue, and cost control.

Another attempt to identify those CSFs can be found in the explanatory study of Brotherton and Shaw (1996). Using mailed questionnaires, the authors initially attempted to identify corporate and unit level CSFs, yet they had to concentrate solely on unit level as they received only one response from corporate offices. In their study, they asked respondents to identify and rank CSFs, as well as to classify them according to functional areas.

Reporting on multiple studies performed on the U.S. lodging industry, Dubé and Renaghan (1999) described the best

Table 4.3 Competitive Methods in the International Hotel Industry: 1985–1999

Period	Category	Competitive Method
1985–1994	Customer products and services	Frequent guest programs
		Amenities
		In-room sales and entertainment
		Business services
	Technology development	Technology innovation
		Database management
		Computer reservation systems
	Market efforts	Branding
		Niche marketing and advertising
		Pricing tactics
		Direct to consumer marketing
	Market expansion	International expansion
		Strategic alliances
		Franchising and management fee
	Operation management	Cost containment
		Core business management
		Service quality management
		Travel agency valuation
		Employee as assets
		Conservation/ecology programs
1995–1999	Rapid information technology development	Customer-oriented technology
		Management-oriented technology
	International expansion and market cooperation	Mergers and acquisitions
		Management contracts
		Franchise agreements
		Joint ventures
		Strategic alliances
	Relationship management	Customer relationships
		Employee relationship
		Franchise relationship management
		Travel agency relationship management
	Customer-oriented products and services development	New segments, brand names, hotel room design and style
		Health awareness amenities
		Time-share programs
	Structural engineering	New presidents and CEOs
		New divisions
	New market initiatives and campaigns	Heavy advertising investment
		Co-promoting activities
		Brand and image marketing
		Competitive pricing tactics

(*Continued*)

Table 4.3   (Continued)

Period	Category	Competitive Method
	Quality control	Use of brand name products
		Renovation and modernization
		Quality performer rewards
		Employee as assets
		Training
	Social awareness and environmental protection	Social responsibility
		Responsible corporate citizenship
		Protecting the natural environment

Sources: Adapted from Olsen (1995a) and Olsen and Zhao (2000).

practices of "29 overall champions" (p. 16). While not labelling them CSFs, the authors established their ranking based on strategic actions commonly practiced in the industry. For instance, they classified Four Seasons as Deluxe-segment champion based on its leading performance in customer service that was attributed to investments in employees' training and selection. For Embassy Suites, the Upscale-segment champion, the deciding factors were the physical attributes, amenities and service, such as the size of the room, as well as quality service and breakfast quality.

In the foodservice industry, Olsen and Sharma (1998) offered a review of the CMs used by multinational companies between 1993 and 1998. Using the content analysis research method, the author summarized the key CMs described in trade journals and magazine, company and consultant reports as well as academic journals. Table 4.4 summarizes these CMs.

After more than two decades of applied research and theory development, it appears clear that CSFs are important to the enduring success of hospitality firms. What remains unclear, however, is what these CSFs really are. The next section provides a synthesis of the definitions provided for the concept as well as illustrative examples.

Defining critical success factors for hospitality strategy

The business and academic literature offers several definitions of CSFs. While it appears that there are as many definitions as

83

Table 4.4 Competitive Methods Multinational Foodservice Companies: 1993–1998

Competitive Method	Examples
Strategic expansion	Franchise/master franchise
	Management contract
	Strategic alliance/joint venture/partnership/co-branding
	Merger and acquisition
Technological development	Internet communication with target market
	Management information systems
	Production and service-oriented technology
	Training and development systems
Internal competency development	Quality management
	Employee training and retention
	Organization restructuring
New product/service development	Modifying the menu to adapt to local needs
	New product/concept/theme development
	Safety and cleanliness
	Chain and brand name domination
	Facility renovation
Target marketing	Heavy advertisement
	Internet advertising and promotion
	Database marketing
	Sponsorship, community service, and charity
	Environmental awareness
Pricing strategies	Price/value relationship
	Discounting war
	Coupons

Sources: Olsen and Sharma (1998).

articles or books published on the subject, several definitional attributes are commonly mentioned:

- CSFs are related to CMs and other strategic and tactical actions;
- CSFs are related to the cost structure of the industry (specifically, to sunk costs);
- CSFs are tangible or intangible assets that are developed over time through investments rather than acquired.

Similarly, authors' perspectives on what CSFs actually do to firm performance varied. Yet again, several similarities can be observed:

- CSFs help managers concentrate on the few elements that are necessary to compete successfully in a given industry;

- Sustained high performance on each CSFs is necessary for firms to sustain a positive performance;
- Failure to perform on CSFs is detrimental to the performance of firms;
- The nature and evolution of CSFs in relation to the task environment influences the performance potential of the industry or strategic group participants.

What emerges from these similarities is that the CSFs concept is complex and multidimensional. While some CSFs are related to the ability of firms to optimize the use of some resources, others are actual resources directly part of the production or service process. This distinction is consistent with what Hansen, Perry, and Reese (2004) termed administrative and productive resources. Administrative resources refer to the ability of managers to make the right decisions as to the use of the resources they possess. This ability is related to the extent to which managers recognize the value-generating potential of their resources or of resources available to them through their development or acquisition. This idea is closely related to the notion of peripheral competences discussed by Olsen *et al.* (1998) and to the concept of supporting activities in the value chain of Porter (1985). Examples of peripheral competences and support activities include human resources, environmental scanning, business development and financial systems, or procurement, and technology development activities, which facilitate the functioning of the core competencies of the firm and of its primary activities. For instance, firms with higher scanning capabilities are likely to make better investments in CMs as they can recognize opportunities and threats ahead of their competition. When companies fail to recognize important forces driving change, or fail to understand how these forces will influence their domain, their reactions tend to be delayed.

Such failure has been observed in the international hotel industry. While the industry recognized early that technology, and more specifically the Internet, represented a major environmental force, its participants fell short of understanding how that force would revolutionize the way hotel rooms were sold. The identification of technology as a major force was first documented by Olsen (1995b). Motivated by industry recognized needs, and with the support of the IH&RA, the author initiated a series of *visioning the future*© workshops. These workshops were held across the globe, bringing together diverse groups of participants in order to obtain a broader view on issues facing the industry. The author used nominal group techniques to monitor the sessions and to obtain consensus over the most central issues uncovered. The synthesis of the results of each workshop provided a global view of the forces driving change as reported by Olsen (1995b).

On industry request, this early work was taken a step further with the objective to provide more specific insights on each of the forces. A team of researchers, under the umbrella of the IH&RA, conducted another series of workshops entitled *Think Tanks*. The outcomes of those *Think Tanks* helped recognize the causal nature of those forces and resulted in several executive summaries published by the IH&RA. The initial efforts of Olsen (1995b) permitted the identification of five original forces, to which two other were later added: assets and capital, capacity control, new management, safety and security, technology, social responsibility, and sustainable development.

While the industry acknowledged the importance of technology advancements, its participants apparently did not understand that Internet-based distribution would become a major channel and would challenge their ability to control prices and room availability. Despite the development of their own websites, hotel chains started by early 2000 to massively sell large amounts of rooms to third-party websites. Faced with low occupancy rates driven by a rapidly declining economy (recession, Internet bubble, and 9/11), hoteliers perceived these third party websites as an opportunity to sell leftover inventory. By the end of 2002 and beginning of 2003, commentaries similar to the followings could be found in almost every industry trade magazine or business journals:

At first, hotel executives like Homestead Chief Executive Gary DeLapp viewed discount sites as a way to get a few hard-core bargain hunters into otherwise empty beds. Today, those executives hold a different view after watching the discount sites transform the way mainstream America buys travel. Instead of helping them, those sites have hurt the hotel firms' margins and made it difficult for the industry to rebound during tough economic times. Online discounters "are completely disrupting the pricing integrity of hotels," said Henry Harteveldt, analyst at Forrester Research.

(The Atlanta Journal, September 2002)

Observers say the burgeoning corps of online bargain hunters has helped to keep room rates below 2000 levels, and industry profits down 28 percent from that peak year. And hotel companies, in many cases, made it easy for them to do so. In their early forays into cyberspace, many hotel companies handed over too much control of inventory and pricing to third-party online travel agencies, observers say.

And now they are in the unenviable position of trying to take back the reins after early shopping patterns have been established.

(Chicago Tribune, January 2003)

"They found they were losing out on some of the direct consumer sales and allowing the Expedias and Hotel.coms to come in and take a direct role," she said. "The margins got bigger in terms of what they were making, and the rates were getting smaller. Once online penetration passed 10 percent, hotels realized, 'This is a real important channel to us.'" They also realized that they were losing control of their rates, Sileo said, which prompted hotel companies to launch new initiatives luring customers to book directly with the hotel, either through its own Web site or over the phone.

(Fort Worth Star-Telegram, July 2003)

Now that '03 is quickly coming to an end, let's make a resolution for '04 to do less whining about those big bad third-party suppliers that are ruining our average rates. As an industry, we chose to participate with them; we allocated rooms to them; and we gave them the low room rate ammunition to fire back at us. Let's face it; they do a better job than we do. They are in the primary search results for most major and secondary hotel-city searches. That doesn't happen by accident. Their sites are designed to lead people to make reservations, not to entertain users with fancy, but unnecessary flash animation. Few hotels make the extra effort and investment necessary to produce those results.

(Hotel-Online.com, December 2003)

What lead the industry into such a weak position? Could it have been avoided?

While the causes of the loss of capacity control are certainly many and complex, it is safe to argue that the industry's capabilities in scanning and technology development have been weaknesses rather than strengths when compared to the capabilities of third party websites and other distribution companies such as GDSs. These two types of capabilities are administrative CSFs, and clearly exhibit the characteristics discussed thus far. Indeed, when the performance on these CSFs is a relative weakness compared to the task environment, then the overall profit potential of the industry declines as the bargaining power shifts towards the upstream or downstream value chain participants.

When the unit of analysis is the firm, one can observe that some companies have been less negatively influenced by that loss of capacity control than others. For instance, Marriott International appears to have less suffered from the economic downturn and subsequent loss of capacity control than its peers. Over the 1998–2004 period, Marriott has consistently outperformed its direct rivals in both stock returns and operating margins. Although this performance is certainly the result of a variety of ingredients, it is worth noticing that Marriott has been leading the industry in terms of technology, with the initial development of its Marriott Automated Reservation System for Hotel Accommodation (MARSHA) in the early 1980s, and with its $70 million investment in a centralized e-business system in 1998. As a consequence, the leading position of Marriott on the technology development CSF enabled the company to outperform its competitors and avoid the performance failures observed for other hotel chain companies.

This example illustrates the importance of administrative CSFs and how firms with superior capabilities in administrative CSFs are better able to develop, acquire, and use resources related to productive CSFs. As introduced earlier, productive CSFs are associated with primary activities and core competences, and are directly related to the acquisition, and transformation of inputs into outputs. Examples of such productive CSFs include the operating system that organizes production and service activities, and marketing and sales systems. From a financial perspective, the use of most of these resources is translated into the statement of cash flows under operating, investing, and financing cash inflows and outflows. In every industry, a limited number of items in this statement have the most influence on the profitability of firms. For instance, in the fast-food segment of the restaurant industry, food and labour costs are critical to the ability of firms to generate operating margin that are sufficient to pay for non-operating costs and generate a profit. Any failure to manage these costs effectively has a dramatic influence on the firm's profit. In addition, as in most service-oriented industries, the aptitude of hotel and restaurant companies to constantly maximize the use of their perishable assets is of utmost importance. When one considers the drivers of most service firms' return on assets (ROA), the capability of continually generating a sufficient level of sales from the assets is paramount as most of the potential value from these assets is perishable and cannot be stocked in inventories. Consequently, the operation of these assets and the distribution of their capacity are productive CSFs.

The significance of these productive CSFs has been exemplified in the fast-food industry by the decline of McDonald's corporation in the mid-1990s and early 2000s, followed by the widely reported turnaround strategy led by its late CEO Jim Cantalupo. While the decline of McDonald's can be traced back to the early 1990s which witnessed a series of poor quality ratings and law suits, it really fully came into view in January 2003 when the company posted its first loss ever of

$343.8 million for the last quarter of 2002. According to Matt Paull, McDonald's CFO, *"The culture of the company was to produce more restaurants. That wasn't a healthy culture, given that the customers were shifting and we hadn't focused on it."* (Chicago Tribune, June 2004). This loss of focus was principally a lack of consideration of some productive CSFs such as production and service systems, which resulted in *"poor product and service quality"* (CNN Money, April 2004). While these two CSFs are well known in the foodservice industry (i.e., product and service quality), the failure of constantly monitoring the performance of the company on these two CSFs had immense consequences on the financial results of McDonald's. This again highlights the importance of CSFs to the conduct of a firm's strategy, and specifically, of performance evaluation of these CSFs. In the McDonald's case, the company's U.S. COO stated that *"McDonald's had abandoned many of the measurement methods that had led to its success. The company hadn't graded the performance of individual stores for 15 years. Store owners didn't have to worry about mystery diners, either, company employees who secretly visited restaurants and judged their performance."* (Chicago Tribune, June 2004).

The next section provides a framework of analysis for companies to incorporate CSFs into their strategic management practices and to develop performance metrics for monitoring their performance.

Critical success factors approach to strategy: a framework

As suggested earlier, the value chain (Porter, 1985) and the concepts of core and peripheral competences (Olsen *et al.,* 1998) provide some initial guidelines as to what firms need to consider when making strategic choices. Indeed, this chapter started by stressing the importance of aligning the firm's resources and competences to the environmental forces driving change. In order to do so, firms need only to develop innovative CMs which foster growth, but they also must continuously ensure a minimum performance on those administrative and productive CSFs that prevent them from failing. Even though CSFs are not necessarily sources of competitive advantage in themselves, they can become sources of superior performance when other firms in the industry fail to perform on them as illustrated by the case of the hotel industry and third party websites. Often, these CSFs are well known to industry participants. Yet, a number of examples exist that demonstrate the lack of focus of firms on CSFs and their subsequent poor performance. The following framework provides a systematic approach to the evaluation of CSFs in the context of strategic decision-making and performance review.

Identify value-preserving activities and assets

The initial step in the identification of CSFs is to develop a thorough understanding of the revenue and cost structure of the industry. At this stage, firms need to consider the drivers of both the demand and supply curves for the industry. The major issue at stake is about value-preservation. In other words, firms must identify the activities and assets that allow them to sustain a profit and maintain their margins. For the demand curve, the questions to answer are directed toward the comprehension of what helps the industry prevents potential new competitors or substitute, or other external forces from eroding the demand (or shifting the curve to the left—the doted green

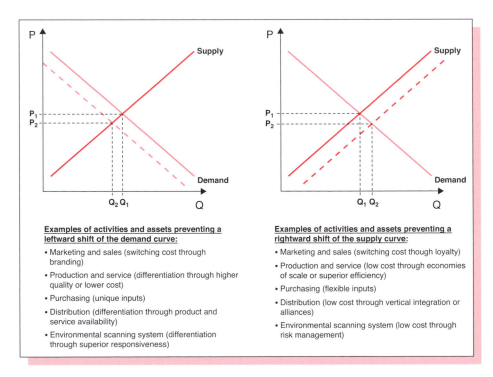

Examples of activities and assets preventing a leftward shift of the demand curve:

- Marketing and sales (switching cost through branding)
- Production and service (differentiation through higher quality or lower cost)
- Purchasing (unique inputs)
- Distribution (differentiation through product and service availability)
- Environmental scanning system (differentiation through superior responsiveness)

Examples of activities and assets preventing a rightward shift of the supply curve:

- Marketing and sales (switching cost though loyalty)
- Production and service (low cost through economies of scale or superior efficiency)
- Purchasing (flexible inputs)
- Distribution (low cost through vertical integration or alliances)
- Environmental scanning system (low cost through risk management)

Figure 4.2
Value-preserving activities.

line in Figure 4.2). For the supply curve, attention should be paid to the threats that could potentially make the curve shift rightward (the doted red line in Figure 4.2). Examples of such threats include an increasing bargaining power from some suppliers following a wave of mergers and acquisition in this tangent industry. Figure 4.2 illustrates the idea of preserving the supply and demand curve balance and raising barriers to buffer the industry from environmental threats.

In many situations, because these activities and assets are well recognized, one can rely on the analysis of trade journals, analyst reports or companies' annual reports to identify them. What is more difficult is to understand their relative importance; developing this understanding can be facilitated by completing the framework of analysis presented in Table 4.5.

This framework lists four steps—or questions—that can help clarifying the nature of the key value-preserving activities and assets. The first column asks for the identification of the key value-rich services, products, and processes. Value richness, in this context, refers principally to the importance of the service, product, or process to the revenues and expenses of the firm. The example provided in Table 4.5 uses purchasing as an important value-rich process in the restaurant industry. This process is deemed as important in terms of value potential because it is directly related to some of the major expenses found on income statements of restaurant firms, such as food and beverage costs. This process typically includes activities such as the selection of suppliers and the negotiation of purchase contracts, which are to be listed in the second column. In the third column, these activities or assets are detailed and their relationships with the supply and demand curves are explained. For instance, the negotiation of purchase contracts is directly related to the potential future price volatility of major food items such as beef or seafood. The sharp decline in stock price suffered by Darden Restaurants in the end of 2002 due to rising seafood prices is a good illustration of the value richness of such activity. Not all activities of a process, and not all assets used in delivering a service or a product share the same degree of value-richness. In the example in Table 4.5, storage and inventory-related decisions are not perceived as conveying as much value as other activities. While such activities can indeed help reduce part of the costs and volatility of important supplies, it is not considered as having as much influence on costs as other purchasing activities. The fourth column in the Table is designed to rate the relative importance of each activity. This rating will then be used in subsequent stages of

Table 4.5 Identification of Value-Preserving Activities and Assets: Example of the Restaurant Industry

Identify and Briefly Describe the Key Value-Adding Services, Products and Processes Existing in Your Industry Segment	Using Key Words, List the Activities and Assets Significant to the Delivery of These Services and Products, or Part of These Processes	Briefly Describe How These Activities and Assets Influence the Supply and Demand Curves	Using a 3-Point Scale (High Value, Moderate Value, Low Value), Assess How Much Value is Linked with the Activities or Assets
Purchasing: efficient, safe, and cost-effective purchasing processes	a. Suppliers' selection	a. A large number of suppliers offer more bargaining power as they will compete on price. Fewer suppliers may help develop a stronger relationship which could help shorten the lead time.	a. High value (cost)
	b. Supply chain control (including tracking and temperature control)	b. A strong control of the supply chain reduces potential defects and errors which lead to lower inventory levels and waste. The control of the temperature prevents waste and potential safety hazards.	b. High value (risk/cost)
	c. Financing, contract management	c. The management of contractual agreements and payment options reduces price volatility.	c. Moderate value (risk/cost)
	d. Storage and inventory management	d. Storage and inventory decisions affect the ability of dealing with changing prices.	d. Moderate value (risk/cost)

the analysis and permit the firm to prioritize its attention and focus more intensely on the most value-preserving CSFs.

Identify the administrative and productive CSFs (resources and competences) required to sustain a competitive performance in these activities and assets

The activities and assets identified in the previous stage are critical to the enduring success of firms and industries. The reason for performing well in these activities or maintaining the quality of these assets is to be found in the administrative and productive CSFs. For instance, if the relative age of the real-estate assets in a hotel or restaurant company is assumed to be a critical component of its sustained performance, managers need not only to acknowledge it, but they must also recognize the underlying causes to sustaining the quality of these assets at a competitive level. The ability to negotiate franchise agreements or management contracts that ensure the continued maintenance and preservation of the assets would then be an administrative CSF. Besides, the ability to operate the asset while preserving its original state would be a productive CSF.

As illustrated in the McDonald's case, firms may lose their focus on these CSFs. McDonald's strategy before the turnaround was to add value by growing its number of new restaurants at an exponential rate. Yet, the company witnessed its growth via expansion being offset by its decline in existing operations[1] as it failed to keep two crucial CSFs under control: the ability to control quality in its existing units (administrative CSF) and the ability to sustain quality in the delivery of its products and services (productive CSF). While it is always easier to discuss the past than to plan for the future, McDonald's could have avoided these pitfalls by answering the following question:

- What are the administrative and productive CSFs that must be kept under control in order to sustain the current performance on these critical value-preserving activities and assets?

The study and synthesis of the elements listed in Table 4.5 is a necessary step to answering this question. To achieve this synthesis, the concept mapping methodology is helpful as it permits to relate the activities of various processes as well as

---

[1] At some point, the decrease in McDonald's existing units' sales accounted for more than 100% of its increase in revenue from new units.

93

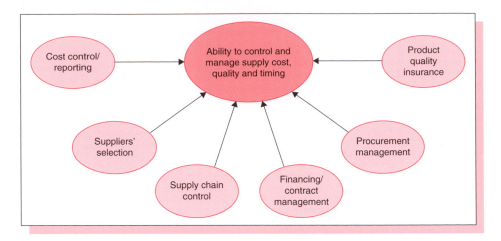

Figure 4.3
Identification of administrative and productive CSFs, example of the hotel industry.

diverse assets to identifiable abilities and competencies. Figure 4.3 provides an example of such concept map.

Identify the internal and external value drivers associated with these CSFs

Another chapter in this book discusses the notion of value drivers and their importance to strategy. Because these value drivers shed light on how and where value is created, they are necessary ingredients to the management of CSFs. The necessity of measuring and assessing how one performs on each CSF calls for firms to identify these value drivers that are associated with them. As in the case of capacity control in the hotel industry, firms can keep track of how well they control these critical activities and assets, and thus evaluate their performance on their CSFs. In this case, hotel chains could have tracked how much of their capacity they were controlling by measuring the number of rooms sold through owned channels versus intermediaries. In the McDonald's case, the lack of focus on service quality in its existing restaurants translated into the absence of measurement of key internal value drivers such as customer complaints or restaurant cleanliness and appearance. Assessing and evaluating the performance on CSFs requires firms to identify internal and external value drivers associated with their CSFs. Table 4.6 present a framework for listing and tracking these value drivers.

Table 4.6 CSFs and Value Drivers: Example of the Restaurant Industry

List and Briefly Describe Your Industry Segment CSFs	List the Key Internal Value Drivers Related to Each CSF, and Include Key Quantitative Measure	List the Key External Value Drivers Related to Each Internal Value Driver, and Include Key Quantitative Measure	Briefly Explain the Relationship Between the Internal and External Value Drivers

Ability to control and manage supply cost, quality, and timing	1. Food cost
	  1.1 Beef price (incl. volatility)
	  1.2 Seafood price (incl. volatility)
	  1.3 Average maturity of future contracts
	  1.4 Average payment period
	
	2. Food quality
	  2.1 Number of defect
	  2.2 Waste percentage
	  2.3 Percentage of items controlled throughout the supply chain
	
	3. Supply chain cycle
	  3.1 Average inventory turnover
	  3.2 Average days in cycle
	  3.3 Average lead time
		1. Food cost
		  1.1 Beef supply
		  1.2 Seafood supply
		  1.3 Number of suppliers
		  1.4 Tax rate and quota on imports
		
		2. Food quality
		  2.1 FDA quality standards
		  2.2 Number of suppliers in the supply chain
		  2.3 Number of food born illness cases
		
		3. Supply chain cycle
		  3.1 Average lead time
		  3.2 Transportation cost and efficiency
		  3.3 Average shipping distance
			1. The total domestic (incl. imports) supply of food items is directly related to the price level and volatility. The number of suppliers affects the bargaining power of the firm and influence prices. Tariffs and quotas imposed by the government on imports directly influences the available supply and overall price levels.
			2. The FDA standards and quality insurance programs influence the overall quality of food supply in the US. The number of suppliers in the supply chain makes quality control and tracking more or less difficult. The number of cases of food born illnesses is related to risks of pandemic or other illness proliferation.
			3. The lead time offered by suppliers is determined by their technological capabilities. This lead time influence directly the lead time of the firm, which influences the inventory turnover and average supply chain cycle.

95

Assess the competitive performance on these CSFs

Because performance is not only a function of how firms raise and maintain entry barriers to buffer themselves from external forces, but also an outcome of how firms perform relative to their peers, CSFs need to be looked at from a competitive perspective as well. As suggested by the introductory quote, some perform better than others because they simply are better at doing these things that are at the core of the business. When realtors appraise real-estate value in the hotel industry, they often conclude that the location, age of the assets, and distribution channels are crucial determinants of the competitive index as measured by RevPAR penetration. At this stage of the CSFs analysis, firms are required to understand how they perform on these CSFs relative to their competitors. This insight can be developed through a two-dimensional matrix analysis.

First, the performance of each firm on each CSF relative to the other firms within the industry must be evaluated. In Table 4.7, this evaluation is performed by the ranking of firms that appears in the lines. Firms that consistently rank better than others are expected to perform better and bear less risk of failing due to external changes. The second dimension relates to the relative strength of the industry as a whole relative to the industries in the task environment. For this second evaluation, the industry strength is evaluated as being stronger, neutral, or weaker than outside industries for each CSF. This analysis indicates the comparative bargaining power resulting from entry barriers for the entire industry. Categories in which the industry is weaker, and where the individual firm is weaker, indicate greater risk of failure.

Developing the ranking of firms on each CSF may be a daunting task and prone to too much subjectivism when

Table 4.7 CSFs Matrix Analysis

CSF	Comparative Industry Strength	Ranking			
		Firm No. 1	Firm No. 2	...	Firm No. N
CSF 1	Stronger	1	2	...	3
CSF 2	Weaker	1	4	...	2
CSF 3	Neutral	3	4	...	1
...	...	...	...	...	...
CSF N	Neutral	2	3	...	1

accomplished internally. While no explicit methodology exists, firms may take advantage of published ratings, rankings, or other awards. For instance, if the ability to consistently deliver high-quality service in the deluxe segment of the lodging industry is a CSF, then awards such as the Baldridge Award, or achievements in some kind of quality standards such as ISO and Six Sigma, provide a good sense of how firm actually perform on their quality promises. Another example could be the awards granted to firms offering the best loyalty programme, or customer ratings for restaurant companies.

Develop investment and maintenance budgets to achieve a minimum of competitive parity on these CSFs

When the relative strength and weaknesses of each CSF is assessed, firms need to take the necessary actions to correct or sustain their performance. As exemplified by McDonald's case, firms must ensure a minimum level of competitive parity or edge before they can attempt to develop new growth strategies without taking too much risk. Correcting or sustaining that level of performance requires the development of investment and maintenance budgets. Due to capital constraints, these budgets should be elaborated on the basis of urgency of the action. A recent example in the foodservice industry may help explain this point. In April 2006, Compass Group announced the sale of its station, airport, and roadside divisions (SSP and Moto) for about £3.2 billions. While the divisions were not performing poorly and showed good future potential, Compass recognized it had to concentrate on two CSFs that had been detected as being important weaknesses. Compass used part of the proceeds to (1) strengthen its balance sheet by paying back part of its huge debt, and (2) reduce its massive pension deficit. In other words, the company acknowledged the need to develop a budget to overcome two serious weaknesses that related to two CSFs: the ability to raise cheap capital and the ability to manage its HR practices and pension fund. While Compass would certainly have had other opportunities to spend the proceeds, the urgency of correcting these CSFs forced them to postpone other investments. When developing the investment and maintenance budgets for CSFs, companies need to consider the following questions:

- What are the risks associated with the current underperformance on these CSFs?
- How quickly can these risks materialize?

97

- How much investment is required?
- When are the investments required?

In order to answer these questions and properly allocate the necessary resources, a marginal investment analysis must be performed. Table 4.8 provides an example of such marginal analysis.

Develop an ongoing and systematic approach to CSFs analysis

The evolutionary nature of industries and CSFs mentioned earlier require firms to continuously apply the framework suggested. The CSFs approach to strategy involves an ongoing and systematic analysis of the industry value chain and of the firms' competences. Regular updates and reports on how the firm is performing on each CSF as well as on what new CSF has emerged should be an important source of information and subject of analysis and discussion for the top-management teams. As suggested by early studies on CSFs, firms should tailor their reporting systems in a way that facilitate the collection, storage, and dissemination of data related to CSFs. Figure 4.4 provides an overview of the system.

Concluding remarks

The quest for sustainable competitive advantage has often relegated the importance of other business practices to a second place. IO students have argued that firms should strive to find a position within their industry that allows them to gain a sustainable advantage. RBV authors, on the contrary, have claimed that firms should concentrate on some of their resources that were valuable, rare, inimitable, and that their organizations were using effectively. In this chapter, it has been contended that these sources of competitive advantage should only be sought after if the firm is already able to perform well on those CSFs that prevent it from failing. The CSFs approach to strategy implies that companies must do well the basic activities that are at the core of its business before it can successfully attempt to gain a competitive advantage. In their pursuit of infinite growth, firms may be tempted to tradeoff some of these principles, but as history shows, a lack of focus on CSFs inevitably ends with long-term performance failure.

Table 4.8 Marginal Investment Analysis: Example of the Restaurant Industry

	Year 0	Year 1	Year 2	Year 3	Year 4
Revenues with investment in CSF	–	105,000,000	105,000,000	105,000,000	105,000,000
Less revenues at current performance level on CSF	–	–105,000,000	–105,000,000	–105,000,000	–105,000,000
Less operating expenses with investment in CSF	–	–84,000,000	–84,000,000	–84,000,000	–84,000,000
Plus operating expenses at current performance level on CSF	–	+85,500,000	+85,500,000	+85,500,000	+85,500,000
Equals marginal EBIT	–	1,500,000	1,500,000	1,500,000	1,500,000
Less marginal interest expenses	–	–	–	–	–
Less marginal tax expenses	–	–250,000	–250,000	–250,000	–250,000
Less marginal working capital changes	–	–(–15,000)	–(–15,000)	–(–15,000)	–(–15,000)
Equals marginal operating cash flows to equity	–	1,265,000	1,265,000	1,265,000	1,265,000
Less marginal equity investment	–2,000,000	–100,000	–100,000	–100,000	–100,000
Equals net marginal cash flows to equity	–2,000,000	1,165,000	1,165,000	1,165,000	1,165,000

Net present value of the project at 15% discount rate:

$$NPV = CF_0 + \sum_{t=1}^{N} \frac{CF_t}{(1+i)^t} = -2,000,000 + \frac{1,165,000}{(1+0.15)^1} + \frac{1,165,000}{(1+0.15)^2} + \frac{1,165,000}{(1+0.15)^3} + \frac{1,165,000}{(1+0.15)^4} = 132,650$$

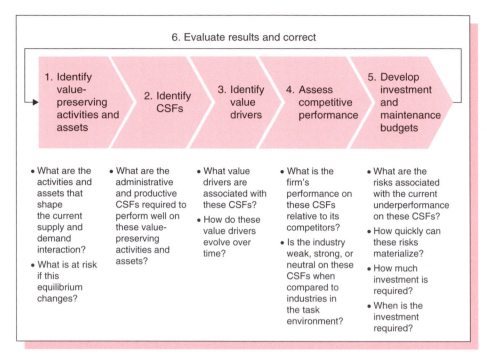

Figure 4.4
A systematic approach to CSFs analysis.

References

Amit, R., and Schoemaker, P. J. H. (1993). Strategic assets and organizational rent. *Strategic Management Journal*, *14*(1), 33–46.

Andrews, K. R. (1971). *The concept of corporate strategy*. Homewood, IL: Irwin.

Barney, J. B. (1986a). Strategic factor markets: Expectations, luck, and business strategy. *Management Science*, *32*(10), 1231–1241.

Barney, J. B. (1986b). Types of competition and the theory of strategy: Toward an integrative framework. *Academy of Management Review*, *11*(4), 791–800.

Brotherton, B., and Shaw, J. (1996). Toward an identification and classification of Critical Success Factors in UK Hotels Plc. *International Journal of Hospitality Management*, *15*(2), 113–135.

Caves, R., and Porter, M. E. (1977). From entry barriers to mobility barriers: Conjectural decisions and contrivers deterrence to new competition. *Quarterly Journal of Economics*, *91*(2), 241–261.

Dubé, L., and Renaghan, M. L. (1999). Strategic approaches to lodging excellence. *Cornell Hotel Restaurant Administration Quarterly, December,* 16–26.

Freund, Y. P. (1988). Planner's guide: Critical success factors. *Planning Review, 16*(4), 20–23.

Geller, A. N. (1985). Tracking critical success factors for hotel companies. *Cornell Hotel Restaurant Administration Quarterly, 25*(4), 76–81.

Ghemawat, P. (1991). *Commitment.* New York: The Free Press.

Grant, R. M. (1991). The resource-based theory of the competitive advantage: Implications for strategy formulation. *California Management Review, 33*(3), 114–136.

Green, S. G., and Welsh, M. A. (1988). Cybernetics and dependence: Reframing the control concept. *Academy of Management Review, 13*(2), 287–301.

Hansen, M. H., Perry, L. T., and Reese, C. S. (2004). A Bayesian operationalization of the resource-based view. *Strategic Management Journal, 25,* 1279–1295.

Hawawini, G., Subramanian, V., and Verdin, P. (2003). Is performance driven by industry- or firm-specific factors? A new look at the evidence. *Strategic Management Journal, 24*(1), 1–16.

Hofer, C. W. (1975). Toward a contingency theory of business strategy. *Academy of Management Journal, 18,* 784–810.

Mascarenhas, B., and Aaker, D. A. (1989). Mobility barriers and strategic groups. *Strategic Management Journal, 10*(5), 475–485.

McGahan, A. M., and Porter, M. E. (1997). How much does industry matter, really? *Strategic Management Journal, 18*(Summer Special Issue), 15–30.

Olsen, M. D. (1995a). Hotel industry performance and competitive methods: A decade in review 1985–1994. In *Into the New Millennium: A White Paper on the Global Hospitality Industry* (pp. 27–49). Paris: International Hotel and Restaurant Association.

Olsen, M. D. (1995b). Visioning the future. *Into the New Millennium: A White Paper on the Global Hospitality Industry* (pp. 51–70). Paris: International Hotel and Restaurant Association.

Olsen, M. D., and Sharma, A. (1998). *Forces Driving Change in the Casual Theme Restaurant Industry: A Global Perspective.* Paris: International Hotel and Restaurant Association.

Olsen, M. D., West, J., and Tse, E. (1998). *Strategic Management in the Hospitality Industry* (2nd ed.). New York: Wiley.

Olsen, M. D., and Zhao, J. L. (1997). New management practices in the international hotel industry. *Travel and Tourism Analyst, 1,* 53–74.

Olsen, M. D., and Zhao, J. L. (2000). *Competitive Methods of Multinational Hotel Companies: A Five Year Review, 1995–99*. Paris: International Hotel and Restaurant Association. pp. 31–45.

Penrose, E. T. (1959). *The Theory of Growth of the Firm*. London: Basil Blackwell.

Peteraf, M. A. (1993). The cornerstones of competitive advantage: A resource-based view. *Strategic Management Journal*, *14*(3), 179–191.

Porter, M. E. (1980). *Competitive Strategy: Techniques for Analyzing Industries and Competitors*. New York: Free Press.

Porter, M. E. (1985). *Competitive advantage*. New York: Free Press.

Prahalad, C. K., and Hamel, G. (1990). The core competence of the corporation. *Harvard Business Review*, *68*(3), 79–91.

Rockart, J. F. (1979). Chief executives define their own data needs. *Harvard Business Review*, *57*(2), 81–92.

Schmalensee, R. (1985). Do markets differ much? *American Economic Review*, *75*(3), 341–351.

Shoemaker, P. J. H. (1990). Strategy, complexity and economic rent. *Management Science*, *36*(10), 1178–1192.

Simons, R. (1991). Strategic orientation and top management attention to control systems. *Strategic Management Journal*, *12*(1), 49–62.

Thompson, J. (1967). *Organizations in Action: Social Sciences Bases of Administrative Theory*. New York: McGraw-Hill.

Thompson, A. A. J., and Strickland, A. J. I. (1996). *Strategic Management* (3rd ed.). Chicago, IL: Richard D. Irwin.

Vasconcellos E Sa, J. A. S., and Hambrick, D. C. (1989). Key success factors: Test of general theory in the mature industrial-product sector. *Strategic Management Journal*, *10*(4), 367–382.

Wasson, C. R. (1974). *Dynamic Competitive Strategy and Product Life Cycles*. St. Charles, IL: Challenge Books.

Wernerfelt, B. (1984). A resource-based view of the firm. *Strategic Management Journal*, *5*(2), 171–180.

Hotel investment risk: what are the chances?

Elie Younes and Russell Kett

HVS London, 7–10 Chandos Street, Cavendish Square, London W1G 9DQ

So, what is riskier: investment in a limited service hotel, full service hotel, serviced apartments/extended stay or shared ownership property? Should a mortgage of a limited service hotel be structured in a similar way to that of a full service hotel or other type of hotel asset, or should some distinctions be considered given the nature of each asset class?

By Elie Younes, Director and Russell Kett, Managing Director, HVS, October 2006

Hotel life cycle and risk components

In line with any type of real estate investment (and probably any investment!), a hotel's life cycle has three main phases: Development, Operation, and Exit.

It takes approximately 1–3 years to develop a hotel asset (depending on the type of property), and a typical investor would hold the asset for a period of between 5 and 25 years. At the end of the life cycle (or holding period), an investor would sell the property or redevelop it; a process that takes a minimum of 1 year and may, infrequently, never materialise.

Consequently, and as illustrated in Figure 5.1, a hotel investment inherits three categories of risk that are directly attributable to the main phases of its life cycle: development risk, operating risk, and obsolescence/exit risk.

Development risk

Development risk is the economic threat that a developer/investor is exposed to upon converting a vacant piece of land or an existing building into a fully operational hotel asset.

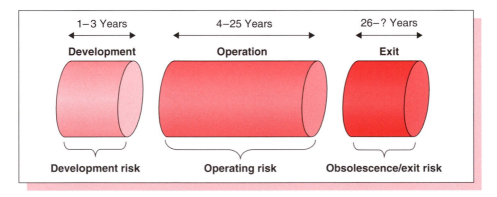

Figure 5.1
Hotel life cycle and investment risk factors.

Obviously, the more complicated the type of asset is, the higher the development risk would be. In other words, this risk is the probability that a setback takes place during the development process that has a negative effect on the development cost or any aspect that influences the future investment returns (location of the asset, positioning, type of operator, physical characteristics, construction and design, timing of completion, capital structuring, and so forth). There is sometimes a great difference between how a hotel asset should look and how it actually does when it is built!

Table 5.1 illustrates the main elements/steps (and hence the risk elements) that are required to develop a hotel asset. Developing hotels is highly capital-intensive and requires the ultimate harmony between all parties involved in order to secure an economically viable investment. Any setback during the development would severely impact the investment returns.

Full service and luxury hotels are, by nature, complicated hotels to develop, when compared to other hotel assets. Such properties require more time to develop, necessitate complicated space planning and design, are highly capital-intensive, and face high market expectations in terms of the physical product offering (which, again, makes it increasingly critical for the developer to ensure an appropriate end product). Therefore, such an asset class is exposed to a high level of development risk when compared to other hotel derivatives.

As with full service hotels, serviced apartments/extended stay units have different "grades" that span the budget, mid-market, and luxury sectors. In general, all can be said to

---

Table 5.1   Main Steps in Developing a Hotel Asset

Main Risk Elements of a Hotel Development

Location identification
Zoning and planning consents
Resort—very difficult
Feasibility and planning—decisions on asset positioning
Capital planning and structuring
Land acquisition
Construction and design partner selection
Land excavation
Construction and design; high rise vs. low rise
Extent of facilities
Timing and cost of capital

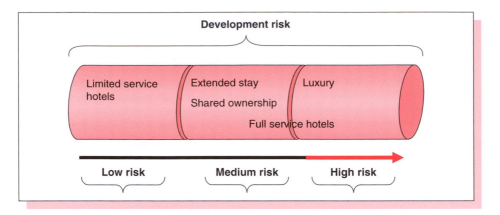

Figure 5.2
Development risk.

provide more spacious accommodation than traditional hotel rooms of a similar standard, with the benefit of kitchen facilities allowing for self-catering. While such an asset class is less complicated to develop than full service/luxury hotels, given its limited amount of public space, such properties (irrespective of their grade) are more complicated to develop when compared to limited service/budget hotels.

Shared ownership properties vary widely in terms of product offering, grade, and so forth. For example, products range from an up-market time-share development in a beach resort (hence requiring complicated designs, space planning, and so forth) to condominium units (second home/residential/investment) in a city (which are easier to develop). Therefore, the development risk associated with this asset class varies considerably. For the purpose of this article, we have assumed that this asset class is prone to a medium level of development risk, when compared to other hotel derivatives.

Figure 5.2 summarises the relative level of development risk of each asset class within the industry.

Ownership's operating risk

The total "holding period return" of any type of investment is the combination of the cash flow earned throughout the holding period as well as the capital appreciation (or depreciation) of the asset. Depending on the type of hotel property (and its holding period), the operating cash flow returns represent between 30 and 70% of the overall returns. Typically, the operating risk of a hotel

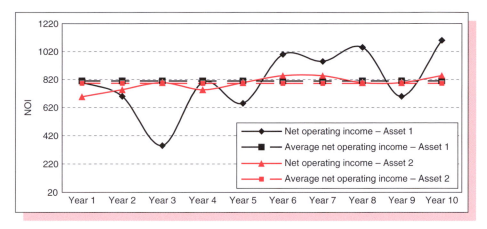

Figure 5.3
Illustration of operating risk (€000s).

asset is higher during the first years of operation of the property, when compared to the level of risk attributed to its operation once it reaches a stabilised level of trading performance.

The operating risk is simply the ability of the asset (and its management) to generate sufficient levels of cash flow in order to produce a certain level of financial returns to justify the investment and/or catalyse an exit.

Owners are significantly exposed to the operating risk in a hotel investment. Any fluctuation in the operating perform-ance of a hotel asset has a significant impact over the net operating income available to its owner to service the hotel mortgage/senior debt and secure a level of capital to justify a return on the investment. A severe economic downturn, for example, could potentially force the business (and its owner) into liquidation and result in a lender's step in, pulling the owner out of business. Obviously, the uplift is equally posi-tively rewarding.

The main operating risk factor in a hotel property is the vol-atility of its net operating income (EBITDA) throughout the holding period. The more the net operating income is likely to fluctuate over a specific period of time, the higher the operat-ing risk. As can be seen from Figure 5.3, while both Hotel Asset 1 and Hotel Asset 2 achieved an average annual net operat-ing income of approximately €800,000 over 10 years, Asset 2 achieved a more stable (and predictable) level of cash flow throughout this period. This implies that the operating risk of Asset 2 is lower than that of Asset 1.

Given the operating structure of a hotel asset, this risk can be attributed to two main characteristics: revenues and the fixed cost structure of the operation. Various dynamics and business characteristics, whether controllable or uncontrollable, impact on these operating risk factors.

There are fundamental operating differences between the various types of hotel asset. For example, while a conventional full service hotel typically requires a balanced and broadly based business mix (segmentation), an extended stay property is less dependent on such an operating dynamic. Furthermore, while the room inventory of a full service hotel is highly perishable (each room needs to be sold to different guests on a continuing basis), an extended stay unit inventory is less perishable given the long average length of stay of such an asset class (in both cases, however, you cannot sell yesterday's available room!). Other operating differences include the fact that the fixed cost structure of a full service hotel operation is greater than that of a limited service hotel or an extended stay property (due to food and beverage facilities, revenue mix, service quality expectations, and so forth). Moreover, our assessment of historical trading data of various hotel categories and classifications suggests that limited service hotels and extended stay units tend to be less vulnerable to economic shocks and external factors than full service and luxury hotels.

Some of the external factors that also impact the operating performance of a hotel asset include the demand and supply dynamics in a given market, as well as the barriers of entry for a specific asset class. An overly supplied market will undoubtedly hamper the trading performance of a hotel asset. Yet, barriers of entry such as scarcity of land, capital liquidity, zoning restrictions, planning regulations, bureaucracy, and so forth typically serve as a hedge against such a risk. While most hotel asset classes are equally exposed to this risk, one could argue that full service hotels tend to be, on occasions, hedged against that risk due to the barriers of entry associated with this asset class.

In terms of the shared ownership asset class, despite the cash flow volatility of such a business model, the operating risk of this type of hotel derivative is considerably reduced (to the original developer/investor), as the room inventory is typically sold before (or upon) completion of the development, which either transfers this risk to the individual owners of the units or significantly dilutes/eliminates this risk. The level of return associated with the operation of a shared ownership property is lower than that of other asset classes (between 10 and 20% of total holding period returns), given the initial inventory exit/sale of the units. Therefore, the operating risk of a shared ownership

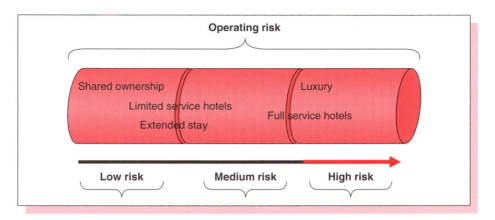

Figure 5.4
Operating risk.

development is minimal (unless the developer provides guaranteed returns), from the original developer's perspective.

Figure 5.4 summarises the relative level of operating risk of each asset class within the industry.

Obsolescence/exit risk

This risk impacts the ability of the owner of the hotel property to exit the investment or extend its economic life. This risk involves the potential decrease in a property's value as at the envisaged exit period. It is the uncertainty of the future value of the hotel asset.

Obsolescence is an incurable economic depreciation that has a considerable impact on the holding period returns of a hotel asset. There are various types of obsolescence that can impact hotel real estate but generally they are classified as either internal or external obsolescence (Figure 5.5).

Internal obsolescence ● ● ●

Typically this is functional obsolescence which occurs when a hotel no longer functions/operates the way it did when it was initially built; it is a change in the fitness for purpose. This includes the physical deterioration of the building, which can be either curable via repairs and capital expenditure or incurable if the basic structure of the building has been heavily damaged over time. While most types of physical deterioration

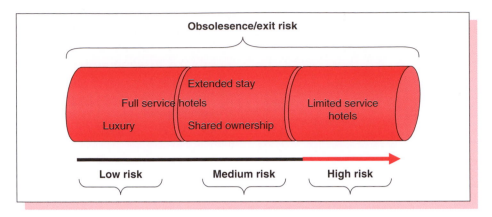

Figure 5.5
Obsolescence/exit risk.

of a hotel asset can be curable, sometimes it makes no economic sense to do so. For example, while the physical deterioration of the external appearance (exterior, public areas, and so forth) or the internal specifications (services, finishes, and so forth) can be cured, the property can become obsolete if the configuration of the building is no longer appropriate (style, plan layout, floor to ceiling heights, structural damages, and so forth). In general, most hotel assets are equally prone to this type of obsolescence; however, service/budget hotels are more exposed to this risk given the initial economical approach to the building and low-cost layout/structure.

External obsolescence ● ● ●

This is the loss in income and value resulting from external factors. Various economic, demographic, environmental, legal, and social factors may impact the economic viability of a hotel which may not be curable. For example, new legislation regarding safety may render a property obsolete if it impacts the layout of the hotel. A shift in the economic, demographic, or social gravity of the immediate area of the hotel can also render a property obsolete, especially if the hotel is located in a secondary location (as is usually the case with limited service and budget hotels with the aim to reduce the initial cost of land to boost economic viability) or if the area in which it was originally built migrates from primary to secondary over time.

Given the structural design, layout, building structure, style, and location of limited service hotels, they are exposed to the highest risk of internal and eternal obsolescence when compared to other types of hotel properties. Extended stay properties are less exposed to obsolescence risk than limited service hotels (given their typical locations, layout, and so forth), but are more exposed to this risk than full service and luxury hotel assets (especially from a "fitness for purpose" perspective).

The success of a shared ownership property investment depends heavily on the ability of the developer to sell the units during the development phase (or during the few years following the completion of the development). Therefore, this risk factor has a dual risk potential (in terms of its impact on investment returns) when compared to other asset classes: while the property itself may not become physically obsolete after a period of time, given the emerging nature of the shared ownership sector, the complexity of the exit process (heavy administrative and marketing overheads) and the heterogeneity of potential investors this asset class inherits a high level of exit risk. This exit risk occurs in two phases: initial exit of the units and exit upon transfer of ownership back to the developer in Year 20 or thereafter.

Synthesis and implications

Based on the previous analysis, Figure 5.6 summarises the relative levels of risk factors for the main types of hotel assets throughout their economic lives.

Various asset classes within the hotel sector have different risk profiles throughout their cycles. While full service and luxury hotels inherit higher levels of development and operating risks than limited service and extended stay properties, upscale hotel properties are less exposed to the obsolescence/ exit risk. Furthermore, while shared ownership developments have a lower operating risk than other hotel derivatives, this asset class probably inherits a high exit risk.

Therefore, the fundamental differences in the various asset classes have different implications for their investment evaluation, lending characteristics, and asset management.

Typically, when evaluating a hotel investment, one would project the property's cash flow over a specific period of time, and would then apply various financing parameters to assess the value of the investment in today's prices. Usually, a property yield is applied to those cash flows in order to compute the investment value of the asset at a specific date.

The property yield is usually the combination of the cost of capital as well as the potential property appreciation or

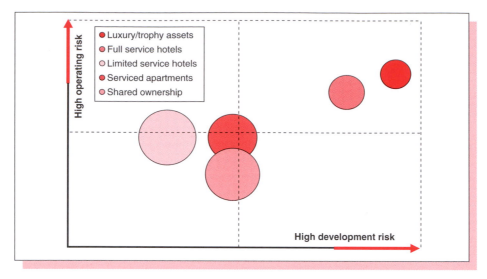

Figure 5.6
Risk matrix for the hotel industry (*Note*: The width of the sphere indicates the obsolescence risk).

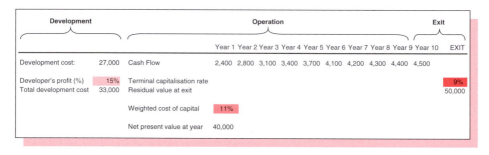

Development		Operation											Exit	
			Year 1	Year 2	Year 3	Year 4	Year 5	Year 6	Year 7	Year 8	Year 9	Year 10		EXIT
Development cost:	27,000	Cash Flow	2,400	2,800	3,100	3,400	3,700	4,100	4,200	4,300	4,400	4,500		
Developer's profit (%)	15%	Terminal capitalisation rate												9%
Total development cost	33,000	Residual value at exit												50,000
		Weighted cost of capital	11%											
		Net present value at year	40,000											

Figure 5.7
Illustrative hotel appraisal (€000s).

depreciation. Practically, the main variables that form the property yield include the cost of debt, the cost of equity, an optimum/market-specific financing structure, and a terminal capitalisation rate (the residual/reversionary value upon exit). These variables each impact the various time cycles in the cash flow differently, as can be seen in Figure 5.7.

The simplified illustration of an investment assessment, as shown in Figure 5.7, reflects the following.

● The developer's profit reflects the development risk associated with that phase; the higher the development risk, the greater the required profit percentage. Upon making investment decisions, the total development cost (including developer's profit—and taking into account the development risk) is then compared with the net present value of the cash flow (taking into account the time value of money);

- The cost of capital is typically applied to the operating cash flow during the holding period as well as upon discounting the exit/residual value of the investment to Year 1. This parameter reflects the operating risk (and other risks inherited from the development phase) of a hotel asset. A high operating risk would fuel the debt and equity yields and would therefore imply a higher weighted cost of capital;

- The terminal capitalisation rate reflects the value of a hotel property at exit, taking into account economic cycles as well as capital appreciation/depreciation. In a conventional valuation, this rate is usually the adjusted cost of capital less inflation. However, in practice the terminal capitalisation rate can fluctuate in order to reflect future capital appetite, yield compressions, cycles or, in some instances, obsolescence. A higher obsolescence risk in an asset class would therefore necessitate a higher terminal capitalisation rate (hence a lower exit value).

Assuming identical market and economic conditions and based on the preceding assessments, we make the following observations.

- A lower developer's profit (in percentage and quantum) could be applied to extended stay properties and limited service hotels, when compared to full service and luxury hotel assets, given their lower development risk;

- A lower cost of capital could be applied to extended stay and limited service hotel properties, when compared to full service and luxury hotel assets, in order to reflect their lower operating risk profile;

- Given the lower exit risk of five-star and luxury hotels, a lower terminal capitalisation rate should therefore be applied to this type of hotel property, when compared to limited service and extended stay properties;

- Due to the comparatively higher obsolescence risk of limited service/budget hotels, it should be no surprise when lenders resist long-term bullet/balloon financing for such an asset class;

- While the asset manager of a typical full service/luxury hotel continuously aims at maximising the value of the hotel asset and improving its operating cash flow, the asset management objective of limited service or extended stay properties should mainly focus on maximising the operating cash flow throughout the economic life cycle of the asset.

Unfortunately, no generalisation can be made or concluded in terms of what is the safest or least risky type of hotel property to invest in given the various risk profiles of the asset classes throughout their economic cycle. It is certain, however, that risk diversification can be achieved within the industry (from a portfolio perspective or by combining two or more asset classes within one development), which would enhance the risk-adjusted returns to the owners.

We would highlight that this approach of risk assessment is theoretical/fundamental, and that various market dynamics as well as characteristics and levels of investor appetite must always be considered upon appraising a hotel property. Capital markets can have diverse characteristics and risk profiles and would oftentimes view the risk of a hotel investment differently; a fact that must always be considered upon appraising an investment, as long as it represents the market participants. As in the theory of equity markets, the "market efficiency" of the hotel transaction sector is a debatable topic.

Finally, we emphasise that the specific risk associated with any individual hotel investment is determined by the characteristics of that investment, including location, property, ownership, management, and so forth.

Various hotel investors have different risk profiles, investment appetite and stimulants as well as perception of time. Once these are better understood the hotel asset classes and risks can then be chosen!

State-of-the-art cost of capital in hospitality strategic management

Melih Madanoglu

*Assistant Professor,
Davison of Resort and Hospitality Management,
Florida Gulf Coast University,
Ft. Myers, FL*

Introduction

Making well-informed and effective capital investment decisions lies at the heart of any successful business organization. However, prior to investing in a project, an executive/manager should make three key estimates to ensure the viability of a business project: economic useful life of the asset, future cash flows that the project will generate, and the discount rate that properly accounts for the time value of the capital invested and compensates the investors for the risk they bear by investing in that project (Olsen *et al.*, 1998). Although the first two items are fairly challenging to estimate, the last one is even more challenging. In their book related to cost of capital, Ogier *et al.* (2004) provided an excellent example which I would like to use to provide a practical introduction to this chapter. I take the liberty to modify the story in accordance with the needs of this chapter.

Imagine yourself at the edge of a river where your goal is to pass the river getting minimally wet in the least possible time. Before making your move you need to turn to a local inhabitant who knows which stepping stones are safe, what the velocity and the viscosity of the water are, what the turning moments are, and what the probability of loose stones on the stream bed is. This situation is similar to the world of today's business investments. That is, executives need to make informed decisions about their investments and find out the minimum acceptable rate of return their shareholders expect as a compensation for the risks investors undertake. In addition, when an investment consists of both debt and equity, then the executives need to estimate the total cost of capital employed in this project to be able to pay their debt holders. This chapter intends to serve as a field guide or handbook of the cost of capital estimation for hospitality executives and practitioners. However, before getting into the practical aspects of cost of capital, some relevant concepts will be discussed from a theoretical perspective to better understand the background of this important topic.

Risk

Prior to getting into the core of the subject of estimating cost of capital, it is useful to define what risk is and describe the role it plays in investment decisions. In the hospitality field, risk is often defined as the variation in returns (probable outcomes) over the life of an investment project (Choi, 1999; Olsen *et al.*, 1998). The concept of risk is at the foundation of every firm as it seeks to compete in its business environment. Financial theory states that shareholders face two types of risk: systematic and unsystematic. The examples of systematic risk could be changes in monetary and fiscal policies, the cost of energy, tax laws, and the demographics of the marketplace. Finance scholars refer to the variability of a firm's stock returns that moves in unison with these macroeconomic influences as systematic, or stockholder, risk (Lubatkin and Chatterjee, 1994). Stated differently, the level of a firm's systematic risk is determined by the degree of uncertainty associated with general economic forces and the responsiveness, or sensitivity, of a firm's returns to those forces (Helfat and Teece, 1987). In other words, these types of risk are external to the company and are outside of its control. However, a loss of a major customer as a result of its bankruptcy represents one source of unsystematic, or firm-specific risk (idiosyncratic or stakeholder risk). Other sources of unsystematic risk include the death of a high-ranking executive, a fire at a production facility, and the sudden obsolescence of a critical product technology (Lubatkin and Chatterjee, 1994). Unsystematic risk is a type of risk that can be eliminated by an individual investor by investing his/her funds in multiple companies' stocks. The same rule may not be applied by company executives, since the success of a single project determines their tenure within their firms.

Risk from financial management perspective • • •

The traditional financial theory looks at investment in securities from a portfolio perspective by assuming that investors are risk-averse and can eliminate the unsystematic risks (variance) associated with investing in any particular firm by holding a diversified portfolio of stocks (Markowitz, 1952, 1959). Markowitz pioneered the application of decision theory to investments by contending that portfolio optimization is characterized by a trade-off of the reward (expected return) of that individual security against portfolio risk. Since the key aspect to that theory is the notion that a security's risk is the contribution to portfolio risk, rather than its own risk, it presumes that the only risks that matter to investors are those that are systematically associated with market-wide variance in returns(Lubatkin and Schulze, 2003; Rosenberg, 1981). Investors, it argues, should only be concerned about the impact that an alternative investment might have on the risk-return properties of their portfolio. However, the capital asset pricing model (CAPM) (Lintner, 1965; Sharpe, 1964) (to be discussed in detail later) does not explicitly explain what criteria investors should use to select the alternative investments and how they should assess the risk features of these investments. Moreover, the CAPM assumes that because investors can eliminate the risks they do not wish to bear, at relatively low costs to them, through diversification and other financial strategies, there is little need, therefore, for managers to engage in risk-management activities (Lubatkin and Schulze, 2003).

Risk from strategic management perspective • • •

In contrast, the field of strategic management is based on the premise that to gain competitive advantage, firms must make strategic, or hard-to-reverse, investments in competitive methods (portfolios of products and services) that create value for their shareholders, employees, and customers in ways that rivals will have difficulty imitating (Olsen *et al.*, 1998). These investments enable the firms to protect their earnings from competitive pressure, and allow firms to increase the level of their future cash flow, while simultaneously reducing the uncertainty associated with them. The management of firm-specific risk lies at the heart of strategic management theories (Bettis, 1983; Lubatkin and Schulze, 2003), and, from this perspective, management must work hard at avoiding investments that create additional levels of risk for the firm. Bettis (1983) further affirms that the CAPM's emphasis on the equilibration of returns across firms (i.e., systematic risk) relegates to a secondary role strategy's central concern with managerial actions that seek to delay the calibration of returns (i.e., unsystematic risks). Thus, the claim that systematic risk is paramount to the firm is undermined by the two arguable assumptions from portfolio theory: stockholders are fully diversified, and the capital markets operate without such imperfections as transaction costs and taxes. Some stockholders, however, are not fully diversified, particularly the corporate managers, who have heavily invested, both financially and personally, in a single company (Vancil, 1987). Also, transaction costs, such as brokerage fees, act as a minor impediment, inhibiting other stockholders from completely eliminating unsystematic risk (Constantinides, 1986). Finally, taxes make all stockholders somewhat concerned with unsystematic risk (Amit and Wernerfelt, 1990; Hayn, 1989) because interest on debt financing is tax deductible, thereby allowing firms to pass a portion of the cost of capital from their stockholders to the government. Thus, firms can create value for their stockholders, within limits, by financing investments with debt rather than equity (Kaplan, 1989; Smith, 1990). The limits are determined in part by the amount a firm is allowed to borrow and the terms of such debt, both of which are contingent upon the unsystematic variation in the firm's income streams. Lubatkin and Chatterjee (1994) contend that the debt markets favour firms with low unsystematic risk because they are less likely to default on their loans (this is particularly the case of the hospitality industry firms). In summary, the discussion of partially diversified stockholders, transaction costs, and leverage suggests that some stockholders may be concerned with unsystematic risk and factor it along with market risk to determine the value of a firm's stock (Amit and Wernerfelt, 1990; Aron, 1988; Lubatkin and Schulze, 2003; Marshall *et al.*, 1984).

Cost of capital

Cost of capital is defined as the rate of return a firm must earn on its investment projects in order to maintain its market value and continue attracting needed funds for its operations (Fields and Kwansa, 1993; Gitman, 1991). Consequently, a firm adds shareholder wealth when it undertakes the projects that generate a return higher than the cost of capital of the project. Cost of capital is an anchor in firm valuation, project valuation, and capital investment decisions. Cost of capital is generally referred to as weighted average cost of capital (WACC):

$$\text{WACC} = \left(\frac{E}{V}\right) \times R_E + \left(\frac{D}{V}\right) \times R_D \times (1 - T_c)$$

where E is the market value of equity, D the market value of debt (and thus $V = E + D$), T_c the corporate tax rate, R_E the cost of equity, and R_D the cost of debt (Copeland *et al.*, 2000).

Both of these items (R_D and R_E) are difficult to estimate and require some careful deliberations. The cost of debt is relatively simpler to calculate when a hypothetical firm issues bonds that are rated by the major bond-rating agencies such as Standard & Poor's and Moody's. Thus, these ratings may be used as a guide in computing the cost of debt. In addition, an investor may use the bond's yield to maturity or the rate of return that is in congruence with the rating of a bond. Averaging the interest rates of long-term obligations of a firm is another method to calculate the cost of debt. The cost of debt estimation becomes difficult when a given firm has no bonds and no outstanding long-term debt.

The cost of equity is difficult to estimate in its own right. First, cost of equity is generally estimated using historical data, which may be confounded by business cycles and abnormal events affecting firm stock returns (e.g., fire in a hotel property) and industry returns (e.g., the terrorism events of 11 September 2001). Second, although several methods were developed in the last 40 years, there is not one single method that produces consistent and reliable estimates. Last, a hypothetical executive/entrepreneur will face greater challenges as he/she needs to estimate the required rate of a single restaurant/hotel unit. The next section covers some of the common methods that are used by practitioners in the fields of financial and strategic management.

Cost of equity

Cost of equity can be defined as the rate of return a firm must deliver to its shareholders who have foregone other investment opportunities and elected to invest in this particular company. However, cost of equity is a complex concept because firms do not promise paying a certain level of dividends and delivering a certain level of stock returns. Thus, since there is no contractual agreement between the shareholders and the firm, the expected rate of return on invested equity is extremely challenging to estimate. Fortunately, there are some models that can help us in tackling this challenging task. The next section will cover the major cost of equity models that gained prominence among practitioners and researchers in the last four decades.

Common cost of equity models

Dividend growth model • • •

One of the early forward-looking methodologies is the dividend growth model (DGM) originally developed by Gordon (1962). It offers a very parsimonious method for estimating discount rate and thus accounts for risk. The dividend growth approach to cost of equity states that

$$k_e = \frac{dps}{p} + g$$

where, k_e is the cost of common equity, dps the projected dividend per share, p the current market price per share, and g the projected dividend growth rate.

The model assumes that over time, successful reinvestment of the value received by retained earnings will lead to growth and growing dividends. The approach suffers from oversimplification because firms vary greatly in their rate of dividend payout

(Helfert, 2003). This is due to the fact that common stockholders are the residual owners of all earnings not reserved for other obligations, and dividends paid are usually only a portion of the earnings accruing to common shares. The other major difficulty in applying this model lies in determining the specific dividend growth rate, which is based on future performance tempered by past experience. Another key issue is that the model becomes unusable when a firm is not a dividend payer.

The capital asset pricing model • • •

The CAPM (Lintner, 1965; Sharpe, 1964) is based on the assumption of a positive risk-return trade-off and asserts that the expected return of an asset is determined by three variables: β (a function of the stock's responsiveness to the overall movements in the market), the risk-free rate of return, and the expected market return (Fama and French, 1992). The model assumes that investors are risk-averse and, when choosing among portfolios, they are only concerned about the mean and variance of their one-period investment return. This argument is, in essence, the cornerstone of the CAPM. The model can be stated as

$$E(R_i) = R_f + [\beta \times (R_m - R_f)]$$

where, R_m is the market return of stocks and securities, R_f the risk-free rate, β the coefficient that measures the covariance of the risky asset with the market portfolio, and $E(R_i)$ the expected return of i stock.

Although the CAPM is touted for its relatively simple application, several other studies (Lakonishok and Shapiro, 1986; Reinganum, 1981) present evidence that the positive relationship between β and returns could not be demonstrated for the period of 1963–1990. Particularly over the last two decades, even stronger evidence has been developed against the CAPM by Fama and French (1992, 1993, 1995, 1997), and Roll and Ross (1994). These researchers challenged the model by contending that it is difficult to find the right proxy for the market portfolio and that CAPM does not appear to accurately reflect the firm size in the cost of equity calculation, and that not all systematic risk factors are reflected in returns of the market portfolio.

From the strategic management perspective, business executives face the following issues. Implicit to the CAPM is the recommendation that managers should focus on managing their firm's overall market risk by focusing on β or the firm's systematic risk and not be concerned with what strategists may focus on: firm-specific (unsystematic) risk. Chatterjee *et al.* (1999) claim that herein lie two dilemmas: first, decreasing β requires managers to reduce investors' exposure to macroeconomic uncertainties at a cost lower than what investors could transact on their own by diversifying their own portfolio; and second, to downplay the importance of firm-specific risk that not only is contrary to the strategic management field but also tempts corporate bankruptcy (Bettis, 1983). Therefore, an executive of a given company has to take into account the total risk of the project because, unlike investors holding stocks of multiple companies, the executive may not be able to diversify the risk of his/her company's investment by investing in multiple projects.

Arbitrage pricing theory ● ● ●

Another prominent cost of equity model is the arbitrage pricing theory (APT) developed by Ross (1976). The model states that actors other than β affect the systematic risk.

The APT is based on the assumption that there are some major macroeconomic factors that influence security returns. The APT states that no matter how thoroughly investors diversify, they cannot avoid these factors. Thus, investors will "price" these factors precisely because they are sources of risk that cannot be diversified away. That is, they will demand compensation in terms of expected return for holding securities exposed to these risks (Goetzmann, 1996).

Although the model does not explicitly specify the risk factors, the APT depicts a world with many possible sources of risk and uncertainty, instead of seeking for equilibrium in which all investors hold the same portfolio. More formally, the APT is based on the assumption that there are some major macroeconomic factors that influence security returns. The APT states that no matter how thoroughly investors diversify, they cannot avoid these factors. Thus, investors will "price" these factors precisely because they are the sources of risk that cannot be diversified away. That is, they will demand compensation in terms of expected return for holding securities exposed to these risks. Just like the CAPM, this exposure is measured by a factor β (Goetzmann, 1996).

Chen *et al.* (1986) managed to identify five macroeconomic factors that, in their view, explain the expected asset returns: The Industrial Production Index, which is a measure of state of the economy based on the actual physical output; the short-term interest rate, measured by the difference between the yield on Treasury bills (TB) and the Consumer Price Index

(CPI); short-term inflation, measured by unexpected changes in CPI; long-term inflation, measured as the difference between the yield to maturity on long- and short-term U.S. government bonds; and default risk, measured by the difference between the yield to maturity on Aaa- and Baa-rated long-term corporate bonds (Chen *et al.*, 1986; Copeland *et al.*, 2000).

The APT describes a world in which investors behave intelligently by diversifying, but they may choose their own systematic profile of risk and return by selecting a portfolio with its own peculiar array of βs. The APT allows a world where occasional mispricings occur. Investors constantly seek information about these mispricings and exploit them as they find them. In other words, the APT somewhat realistically reflects the world in which we live (Goetzmann, 1996).

Although the APT provides the benefits explained above, these benefits come with some drawbacks. The APT demands that investors perceive the risk sources, and that they reasonably estimate factor sensitivities. In fact, even professionals and academics are yet to agree on the identity of the risk factors, and the more βs they have to estimate, the more statistical noise they have to put up with. Last, this model does not offer much guidance to business executives as it focuses primarily on investors.

The Fama–French three factor model ● ● ●

One of the major proponents of the CAPM Fama and French (1993) found that the relationship between average returns and β was flat and there was a strong size effect on stock returns. As a result, they developed a model that has gained popularity in recent years among the scholars and practitioners in the hospitality industry. The Fama–French (FF) model is a multifactor model that argues that factors other than the movement of the market and the risk-free rate impact security prices. The FF is a multiple regression model that incorporates both size and financial distress in the regression equation. The FF model is typically stated as

$$E(R_i) - R_f = (\beta_i \times (R_m - R_f) + (s \times \text{SMB}) + (h \times \text{HML})$$

where β is the coefficient that measures the covariance of the risky asset with the market portfolio, R_m the market return, R_f, the risk-free rate, s the slope coefficient, and small minus big (SMB) the difference between the returns on portfolios of small and big company stocks (below or above the NYSE median), h the slope coefficient, and high minus low (HML) the difference between the returns on portfolios of high- and low-BE/ME (book equity/market equity) stocks (above and below the 0.7 and 0.3 fractiles of BE/ME) (Fama and French, 1993).

The size factor is denoted as SMB premium where size is measured by market capitalization. SMB is the average return on three small portfolios minus the average return on three big portfolios as described by Fama and French (1993). HML is the average return on two value portfolios minus the average return on two growth portfolios (Fama and French, 1993). High BE/ME (value) stocks are associated with distress that produces persistently low earnings on book equity which result in low stock prices.

In practice, the FF model shows that investors holding stocks of small capitalization companies and firms with high book-to-market value ratios (Annin, 1997) need to be compensated for the additional risk they are bearing. The size argument is supported by Barad (2001) who reports that small stocks have outperformed their larger counterparts by an average of 5.4% over the last 75 years (1926–2000). However, Fama and French (1993) find that the book-to-market factor (HML) produces an average premium of 0.40% per month ($t = 2.91$) for the 1963–1990 period, which, in the authors' view, is large both in practical and statistical terms.

Cost of equity studies in hospitality and tourism

The starting point for selecting the best method for the estimation of the cost of equity can be achieved by reviewing the relevant studies undertaken in the fields of hospitality and tourism. Fields and Kwansa (1993) conducted the first study that directly looked into the cost of equity and suggested the use of pure-play technique for estimating the cost of equity for the divisions of a diversified firm. Later, several studies investigated how macroeconomic variables affect security returns in the hospitality industry (hotels and restaurants). The first study was conducted by Barrows and Naka (1994). Their study encompassed the 27-year period between 1965 and 1991 and employed five factors that were slightly different than the five factors of Chen *et al.* (1986). Barrows and Naka postulated that the return of the stocks is a function of the following five factors:

$$\text{Return} = f(\text{EINF, M1, CONN, TERM, IP}),$$

where EINF is the expected inflation, M1 the money supply, CONN the domestic consumption, TERM the term structure of interest rates, and IP the industrial production. The results revealed that none of the macroeconomic factors was significant in explaining the variance of U.S. hotel stocks at 0.05 level and the factors accounted for the 7.8% of the variance in the lodging stocks. However, EINF, M1, and CONN had significant effect on the variation of the stock returns in the U.S. restaurant industry. In terms of the signs of the β coefficients EINF had a negative whereas M1 and CONN had a positive relationship with the restaurant stock returns. The postulated model explained 12% of the variance in the restaurant stocks. The authors cautioned that the results should be interpreted with care due to the small sample size of both restaurant and hotel portfolios, which were represented by five and three stocks, respectively.

The second study was undertaken by Chen *et al.* (2005) who used hotel stocks listed on Taiwan Stock Exchange. The macroeconomic variables included in their study were IP, CPI, unemployment rate (UEP), money supply (M2), 10-year government bond yield (LGB), and 3-month TB rate. These variables were used in the following way: CPI was utilized to estimate EINF, and LGB, and TB were used for the computation of the yield spread (SPD). Based on the six time-series data the authors arrived at the common five macroeconomic variables which were predominantly used in the literature, namely, IP (change in IP), EINF $\in$ UEP (change in unemployment rate), M2 (change in money supply), and SPD (rate of the yield spread). These five variables explained merely 8% of the variation in hotel stock returns while only two of these variables were significant at the 0.05 level (M2 and UEP). The regression coefficient of change in money supply had a positive relationship with hotel stock returns, whereas the relationship between change in UEP and lodging returns was negative.

In Madanoglu and Olsen (2005) proposed a conceptual framework that called for the inclusion of some of the intangible variables into the cost of equity estimation in the lodging industry. Some of these variables were human capital, brand, technology, and safety and security. It is common knowledge that these variables were relevant for the lodging industry; however, there exists no time-series data to include them in the cost of equity estimations.

Shortcomings of the present models for the hospitality industry

Publicly traded multinational lodging companies tend to differ on some key points regarding how assets are treated on their balance sheets. Many of these companies do not actually own assets and produce their future cash flows from management contracts or franchise agreements. In many cases, they may also lease hotels or restaurants and the leases do not appear on their balance sheets. Instead, these firms hold an equity position in a different company that holds these leases. Therefore, it is almost unfeasible to properly assess the book value of the hospitality firms, which confounds the application of the FF model.

Sheel (1995) was the first researcher in the hospitality industry to point out that CAPM does not seem to meet the industry needs and called for further research into industry-specific factors. In the mainstream financial economics, Downe (2000) argued that in a world of increasing returns, risk cannot be considered a function of only systematic factors, and thus β. He pointed out that the position of the firm in the industry, as well as the nature of the industry itself become a risk factor. Thus, firms with a dominant position in the industry that succeed to adapt to the complexities of the business environment, will have a different risk profile than their competitors. This argument is particularly well fitting in the context of the hospitality industry where companies such as McDonald's and Marriott may demonstrate a different risk profile based on their market share in their segments.

As for FF factors, professionals in the lodging industry are sceptical about such measures as the book-to-market value ratio (HML). Some hospitality industry experts argue that HML is an inappropriate measure for the industry and attribute it to the fact that the difference between the firms whose value is captured by the assets they own and the firms whose value is derived from their intangible assets is not as distinct as in some manufacturing firms. While Jagannathan and Wang's study (1996) added a human capital variable to their cost of equity capital model, it measured human capital effects from the macroeconomic perspective as opposed to a micro level where most hotel firms operate. In other words, the overall labour index may not properly reflect the state of the human capital in the hospitality industry.

As Fama and French (1993) stated, their work (FF model) leaves many open questions. The most important missing piece of the puzzle is that Fama and French (1993) have not shown how the size and book-to-market factors in security returns are driven by the stochastic behaviour of firm earnings. This implies that it is not yet known how firm fundamentals such as profitability or growth produce common variation in returns associated with size and BE/ME factors and this variation is not captured by the market return itself. These authors further query whether specific fundamentals can be identified as state variables (variables that describe variation in the investment opportunity set) and these variables are independent of the market and carry a different premium than general market risk. This question is of utmost importance for lodging industry executives who are aiming to identify the major drivers of their companies' stock returns in their effort to create value for their stockholders.

In their current state, the cost of equity models are far from satisfying the needs of the hospitality industry. As Fama and French (1997) pointed out, the cost of equity estimates yielded by these models are distressingly imprecise. Standard errors of more than 3% per year were typical when the CAPM and FF models were used to estimate industry costs of equity in their study (Fama and French, 1997). They stated that large standard errors are driven primarily by uncertainty about true factor risk premiums. Since the hospitality industry is really the aggregate of individual units that all have their own unique business environments and return on equity structures, this means that the standard errors, and thus, cost of equity capital on a per-company, single-unit (a hotel property or a restaurant) basis, or for a new project will be even more imprecise. Therefore, the risk determinants of cost of equity and risk factor loadings for individual operating units will be even more difficult to estimate. Thus, it is very important to consider the purpose for which the cost of equity is estimated (e.g., a single project, business division, or an entire corporation). Particularly, in the case of single project cost of equity estimations there might be several factors that need to be considered before arriving at the proper discount rate of the project. These factors might be location of the project, local/regional competition, political risk, credit risk, and other risk idiosyncratic to a given project. Consequently, as Ogier *et al.* (2004) suggest when estimating a cost of equity for a given project the risk of the project will be much more important than the risk level of the corporation making the investment. In other words, when Marriott Corporation makes a capital investment decision in Nairobi, Kenya, the Marriott Corporation executives will be much more concerned with the risks surrounding that project.

Cost of debt

Unlike cost of equity, cost of debt does not require the use of sophisticated theoretical models. Rather, cost of debt is simply the rate at which a given company can borrow capital from a lender (e.g., bank) or the rate at which the aforementioned company can issue bonds. Some experts caution that the promised and the expected yields of debt are two different concepts. In other words, when a firm makes contracted debt payments on time it meets "the promised yield" to its lender. However, in reality, there is always a possibility for default and thus the difference between the promised yield and the probability for default equals the expected yield. The expected yield can be regarded as true cost of debt since it is more realistic. Although many textbooks calculate the cost of debt as promised yield, it should be noted that expected yield is more meaningful since it includes not only the systematic risk of the market but also the firm-specific risk of a given firm.

Another challenge for calculating the cost of debt might occur when a firm uses multiple debt instruments (e.g., bank loans, commercial papers, bonds). In this case, it may be fruitful to average the rate of these instruments based on their weight in the debt portfolio. However, an easier and more simplistic approach would be to use the "generic long-term debt" rate which can be calculated from the current rate of a company's bond or current rate at which the company can borrow a long-term loan (Ogier *et al.*, 2004). Last, to estimate the cost of debt, the issue of tax shield should be given a close consideration. For instance, although the majority of the finance textbooks use 35 or 40% as an average for corporate tax rate in the United States, it is common occurrence to observe companies whose effective corporate tax rate is often lower than the statutory rate. Here, an executive should assess the situation and decide whether the effective tax rate trend is expected to continue to be below the statutory corporate tax rate in the long term. If that is the case, then he/she should use the effective tax rate in calculating the cost of debt. However, if a low effective tax rate is a short-term occurrence, then a given firm should use the statutory corporate tax rate instead (Ogier *et al.*, 2004).

Other cost of capital factors in the hospitality industry

Human capital

Hospitality industry is part of the overall service sector and is dependent on human capital in order to maintain and grow its operations. In an increasingly competitive environment, the human factor becomes one of the keys in creating sustainable competitive advantage. Therefore, Murphy (2003) stated that the hospitality industry should learn to view its employees from a new paradigm that human capital is a strategic intangible asset (knowledge, experience, skills, etc.). This implies that, like other assets, it is an important determinant of firm value.

However, studies have concluded that "the research of human resources expenditures" is in its infancy and is seriously hampered by the absence of publicly disclosed corporate data on human resources (Lev, 2001).

Caroll and Sikich (1999) argued that keeping track of at least a 3-year history of labour costs would serve to identify the dollar value of "premium" labour-related costs, which could be thought of as all labour/benefit costs above federally mandated minimum wage. Other techniques proposed by the authors were (1) to design a scoring system that illustrates productivity versus both baseline and premium labour/benefit costs by departments, and (2) to establish metrics to determine a productivity level for guest experience standards, facilities standards, and targeted revenue improvements on a department-by-department basis.

Bloxham (2003) advocated adjustments to certain human resource expenditures to capitalize them over the time of the investment. In that approach, one-time human resources costs are amortized and capitalized in the value creation equation in an effort to demonstrate that human capital investments go beyond being a cost item in the firms' operations. These costs can include recruiting, interviewing, and hiring costs; one-time hiring bonuses and relocation expenses; and training costs. The costs are capitalized and amortized over the average employee tenure with the company. In this case, if employee turnover is high, these costs would be amortized over a shorter time period (thus the costs will be higher), whereas the longer tenure of the workforce will enable the firm to spread the costs over a longer period of time.

Kalafut and Low (2001) reported that in a study of the airline industry conducted by Cap Gemini Ernst & Young's Center for Business Innovation (CBI), the employee category was the single greatest value driver that had an impact on the firm's market value. The employee factor had a positive correlation of 0.68 with the firm value. Thus, Kalafut and Low (2001) conclude that in the aggregate, quality and the talent of the workforce, quality of labour management relations, and diversity are critically important in the value creation process of the airline companies.

The arguments above can be justified on the grounds that higher-quality human resources decrease labour turnover and increase employee productivity. This results in better organizational performance that results in stabilization of cash flows which in turn decreases the uncertainty of firms' stock returns. Therefore, one would expect that hospitality firms that have institutionalized quality human resource management practices would achieve a more realistic cost of equity estimates that reflect the lower risk associated with these practices.

Brand value

Although definitions of the concept of brand differ across the professional and trade literature, the underlying notion is that of a distinctive name with which the customer has a higher level of awareness and a willingness to pay a higher-than-otherwise average price or make a higher-than-otherwise purchase frequency (Barth *et al.*, 1998). A brand is the product or service of a particular supplier which is differentiated by its name and perceived expectations on the part of the consumer. Brands are important and valuable because they provide a "certainty" as to future cash flows (Murphy, 1990). However, since the task of estimating brand value is yet an improbable one, its value is not specifically reflected on the company's balance sheet. Yet, the lodging industry has made much of the importance of the value of the brand but has not been able to unequivocally substantiate the role of the brand in reducing the variance in firm cash flows, and thus contributing to lower cost of capital for the firm.

Srivastava *et al.* (1998) provided an analytical example of how successful market-based assets (the term authors use in lieu of intangibles) lower costs by building superior relationships with customers, enable firms to attain price premiums, and generate competitive barriers (via customer loyalty and switching costs). All these factors lead to the conclusion that a strong brand reduces the uncertainty pertaining to the future cash flows which in turn decreases the required return by the investors for the risk they bear by investing in a particular firm.

In attempts to value the brand in the manufacturing industries, the use of the following methods has been cited by Murphy (1990):

- Valuation based on the aggregate cost of all marketing, advertising, and research and development expenditures devoted to the brand over a stipulated period.
- Valuation based on premium pricing of a branded product over a non-branded product.
- Valuation at market value.
- Valuation based on various consumer-related factors such as esteem, recognition, or awareness.
- Valuation based on future earning potential discounted to present-day value.

In further analysis, the investigators rejected these methods because, if indeed, brand values were the function of its cost of development, then failed brands would be attributed high values. In addition, brand valuation based solely on the consumer esteem or awareness factor would bear no relationship to commercial reality (Murphy, 1990).

In an effort to link the firm's security returns with brand value, Simon and Sullivan (1993) proposed a technique to estimate the firm's brand equity based on its value. This was done by estimating the cost of tangible assets and then subtracting it from the market capitalization of the firm to obtain the value of intangible assets. As a second step, the researchers tried to break down the intangible assets into brand value and non-brand value components. The authors utilized the Aaker and Jacobson (1994) EquiTrend brand quality measure to evaluate the quality of 100 major brands. They examined associations between measures of brand quality and stock returns and reported that the relationship is positive.

According to Murphy (1990), the only logical and consistent way to develop a multiple for brand profit was through the brand strength concept. Brand strength is a composite of six weighted factors: leadership, stability, market, trend, support, and protection. The brand is scored on each of these factors according to different weightings and the resultant total known as "brand strength score." A further addition to the brand strength concept came from Prasad and Dev (2000) who developed a hypothetical brand equity index via customer ratings of the brand using five key brand attributes in two sets of indicators—brand performance and brand awareness. Brand performance was measured by overall satisfaction with the product or service, return intent, price-value perception, and brand preference, while brand awareness was measured as top-of-mind brand recall. Olsen (1996) proposed brand-related value drivers specific to the lodging industry such as brand dilution and brand sincerity ratio. Brand dilution is related to the question of how many new corporate sub-brands must be introduced in order to maintain growth, whereas, brand duration deals with what percentage of hotels in the portfolio currently meet the brand standards or promise. As a result, it is argued that hospitality companies that possess higher-brand strength will be able to achieve a lower cost of equity capital.

Technology investment and utilization

According to Connolly (1999), one of the greatest issues plaguing the advancement of technology in the hospitality industry is the difficulty of calculating return on investment. Until recently, most technology investment decisions have been considered using a support or utility mentality that stems from a manufacturing paradigm. Current policies rely more on faith than on a rational business assessment. As a result, the hotel industry is perceived to be lagging behind the rival industries in the use of technology (Sangster, 2001). In part, this is attributed to the fragmented nature of the hotel business itself; however, it is also believed to be closely related to hoteliers' lack of experience and understanding in technology investments (Sangster, 2001).

Connolly further argued that "Today's financial models are inadequate for estimating the financial benefits for most of the technology projects under consideration. While the hospitality industry has disciplined models and sufficient history to determine the financial gains or success of opening a new property in a given city, it lacks the same rigorous models and historical data for technology, especially since each technology projects are unique. Although this problem is not specific to the hospitality industry, it is particularly problematic since the industry tends to be technologically conservative and unwilling to adopt new technology applications based on the promises of their long-term merits especially if it cannot quantify the results and calculate a defined payback period. When uncertainty surrounds the investment, when the timing of the cash flows is unpredictable, and when the investment is perceived as risky, owners and investors will most likely channel their investment capital to projects with more certain returns and minimal risk. Thus, under this thinking, technology will always take a back seat to other organizational priorities and initiatives. Efforts must be made to change this thinking and to develop financial models that can accurately predict and capture the financial benefits derived from technology (Connolly, 1999; p. iii)."

Although there are no hard and fast rules to facilitate the valuations of technology investments, it is common knowledge that technology is transforming the way business is conducted in the lodging industry. Particularly the surge in Internet usage in the early years of the new millennium brought about the issue of capacity control for hotel room inventory holders. Therefore, firms that are more adaptive to utilize technology to market and sell their perishable product (hotel rooms) may accomplish a lower variation in their future cash flows, since they are able to retain greater control over pricing.

The author would like to acknowledge the fact that the body of literature does not offer a direct causal relationship between the cost of equity capital and the technology utilization. However, based on the arguments discussed above, the author contends that firms that invest in technology wisely may achieve a higher average daily rate or REVPAR in their properties which in turn will lead to a decrease in the variance in firm's cash flows. Thus, better utilization of information technology can possibly reduce the uncertainty surrounding the future earnings of the firm. As a result, capital markets will assign a lower risk premium to hospitality firms that successfully utilize and deploy technology into their operations.

Safety and security

Guest safety and security topics in the lodging industry can vary from building safety codes and bacterial contamination of hotel whirlpools to restaurant food safety and hotel crime statistics (Olsen and Merna, 1991). The need for greater commitment to safety and security for the hospitality industry became evident in 1990 after the San Francisco earthquake and Hurricane Hugo occurred (Olsen and Merna, 1991). The culmination of these events and all the other events sparked an effort by the hotel industry to manage the risk and liability related to guest safety and security.

Ray Ellis, the director of risk management and operations in the American Hotel & Motel Association (at that time in 1991), contended that after the end of the Gulf War the benefits of increased security for the industry go far beyond intangibles such as peace of mind (Jesitus, 1991). Ellis stressed that improved safety and security will significantly decrease the insurance premiums of the properties, and thus enable the companies to have more resources to invest in their operations. Although Ellis said that chances of terrorist attacks on the United States post Gulf War were fairly remote, he warned that the hotels, particularly those serving international markets, be most wary of arson and bomb threats.

The International Hotel and Restaurant Association in 1995 identified safety and security as one of the major forces driving change in the global hospitality industry (Olsen, 1995). With the destruction of the World Trade Center in 2001, and subsequent terrorist attacks in Bali and Kenya, it is clear that force has emerged now as a major risk factor for all tourism-related enterprises. In February 2003, the Federal Bureau of Investigation (FBI) alerted its law enforcement partners that "soft targets," such as hotels, can be subject to terrorist attacks (Arena et al., 2003). This report simply reaffirms the argument proposed by Olsen (1995, 2000) that lodging properties which are situated in an area exposed to terrorist attacks, should factor that risk into their cost of capital estimates. Therefore, lodging property executives should apply this risk factor into their future capital investment decisions.

In addition, outbreaks related to food-borne diseases, infectious bacteria occurrences on cruise ships, increased crime, and the growing threats of human immunodeficiency virus (HIV), and other viral infections such as severe acute respiratory syndrome (SARS) have created a significant challenge for hospitality managers worldwide. These must be considered as important risk variables that will no doubt have an impact on the estimates of cost of capital.

Although the factors mentioned above are critical in estimating the cost of capital of a given project, there are no methods that can quantify these factors and apply them to the cost of equity models. However, executives are advised to consider these industry-specific risk factors before making a capital investment decision.

Global/multinational projects

The models covered thus far do not provide any guidance for estimating the cost of equity in a global setting or multinational projects. In order to fill this void, academics and practitioners developed adjustment models to account for differences in cost of equity among markets in developing and emerging countries. The adjustment models are primarily concerned with whether the emerging markets are segmented or integrated with the world markets. That is, in a completely segmented market, assets will be priced based on local market return. The local expected return is a product of the local β times and the local market risk premium (MRP) (Bekaert and Harvey, 2002).

Bekaert and Harvey (2002) developed a modified model after researching 18 emerging markets for the pre-1990 and post-1990 periods and reported that the correlation of the emerging markets with the Morgan Stanley Capital International (MSCI) World Index increased noticeably. For instance, Turkey is one of the countries whose market correlation with MSCI World Index increased from less than 0.10 to more than 0.35. Based on this, Turkey may be considered an integrated capital market where the expected return is determined by the β with respect to the world market portfolio multiplied by the world risk premium. This is the core argument of the Bekaert–Harvey Mixture model (Bekaert and Harvey, 2002).

In cases when integrated markets assumption does not apply, investment banks and business advisory firms use a method called "the Sovereign Spread Model (Goldman Model)." This is conducted by regressing an individual stock against the Standard & Poor's 500 stock price index returns to obtain the risk premium. Then, an additional "factor" is added which is called the "sovereign spread" (SS). This spread between respective country's LGB for bonds denominated in U.S. dollars and the U.S. Treasury bond yield is "added in." The bond spread serves as a tool to increase an "unreasonably low" country risk premium (Harvey, 2005).

Practical example for estimating WACC

This section offers a practical example for managers to estimate the WACC of their projects. In addition, this section breaks down the WACC into its respective components in order to assist executives in the capital investment decisions. The major components of the WACC estimations are a firm's stock return, market return, risk-free rate, regression coefficients (β, s, and h), SMB, HML and equity market risk premium (EMRP) (which is $R_m - R_f$), capital structure (proportion of debt and equity), corporate tax rate, and cost of borrowed debt.

Estimating cost of equity

If you are an executive of a company that is not publicly traded, you have two options to estimate the cost of equity. You can either use the industry average for cost of equity or locate two or three comparable firms that compete in the same line of business and estimate their cost of equity. However, even if you are an executive of a large restaurant corporation that is traded publicly, it is still recommended that you estimate the cost of equity for the entire restaurant industry because the standard error of regression coefficients for a single firm is fairly high, which decreases the reliability of these coefficients. My past research experience has showed me that at times using a single firm may create a situation in which cost of equity cannot be even estimated. More often than not, I obtained distressing results when running a regression for small- or medium-size hospitality firms. As a result, in the practical example, I will estimate the restaurant industry's cost of equity. Since the cost of equity calculation process may be a fairly complex process for someone who is not familiar with data analysis, I will offer a step-by-step procedure, which should better clarify this process:

Step 1: obtaining a 5-year monthly stock return for your company/industry and the market • • •

Ideally, you need 5 years of monthly stock return data for your firm and the 5-year market return. The issue of selecting the best index of all traded assets in the world is a very challenging and sometimes a controversial issue. Based on seminal studies in financial management, the market index that yields most reliable results in the United States is Center of Research in Security Prices Value Weight (CRSPVW) Index housed at the University of Chicago. Both your company's stock and market return should be used as excess return (i.e., return less risk-free rate which is 1-month TB rate) in order to measure the cost of equity in real units (i.e., after accounting for inflation). For reasons mentioned before, I will be estimating the U.S. restaurant industry's cost of equity and leave the decision to restaurant industry executives to adjust this value to their specific projects at hand. In order to be able to observe the accuracy of cost of equity models, we estimate the restaurant industry cost of equity by using the CAPM and FF model. The observation period of this example is between 2000 and 2004. The reason for not selecting a longer observation period is that the values of β and other variables become unstable over extended periods. The sample is developed from the Nation's Restaurant News (NRN) Index, which entails 81 restaurant firms. In cases when executives are not familiar with building stock portfolios, they can alternatively use monthly returns of hospitality indices for lodging and restaurant industries from data providers such as Yahoo! Finance, Wall Street Journal, or industry publications such as NRN.

Step 2: estimating β and Fama–French factor coefficients • • •

The CAPM's β can be computed by regressing excess stock return of a firm over the excess market return. The monthly returns for FF factors (SMB and HML) can be retrieved from Eventus Database housed in the Wharton School at the University of Pennsylvania or from Kenneth French's website at Dartmouth College. By regressing monthly SMB and HML returns on market returns you can obtain "s" and "h" coefficients that can later be inserted into the equation to estimate the cost of equity.

In our practical example, the results indicate that the FF model explains more than half (51.8%) of the variation in the returns of the NRN Index. In addition, the FF model results in a significant R^2 change over the CAPM, which showed that the two FF variables (SMB and HML) explained some extra variance over and above the CAPM which accounted for 19.6% of the variation in the restaurant industry stock returns.

The analysis at the variable level indicates that the market index variable (β) and the HML are significant at 0.01 level (see Table 6.1). However, the SMB was not significant at the

Table 6.1 Regression Coefficients and Explained Variation

Model	Variable	B	SE	T
CAPM	β	0.538	0.137	3.923**
FF	β	0.913	0.123	7.400**
	SMB	−0.147	0.129	−1.136
	HML	0.721	0.163	4.431**

Notes: SMB = size variable, HML = distress variable, B = regression coefficient, SE = standard error.

** Denotes significance at 0.01 level.

0.05 level, which means that the size factor does not affect the restaurant industry stock returns while controlling for β and HML. In practice, this means that restaurant industry portfolio behaves as a large company stock, and therefore there is no size premium when considering the overall cost of equity for the restaurant industry. It should be remembered that if you are an executive of a small restaurant company there is a high possibility that your stock returns will have a size premium.

Step 3: the risk-free rate, market, size and distress premiums • • •

There are certain rules of thumb that executives should be aware of before inserting the regression coefficients into the cost of equity calculation. First, it should be pointed out that there are two risk-free rates (R_f) in the CAPM and FF models. The first R_f is used in order to demonstrate the level of risk-free rate that a firm needs to exceed to compensate its investors for the risk they undertake. The second R_f should ideally match the life of an asset. In other words, if the asset in this project is expected to last at least 10 years, then a given investor/executive should use a 10-year government bond as its risk-free rate to obtain the MRP $(R_m - R_f)$.

Another important issue is calculating market, size and distress premiums. Executives/investors may often face challenges when the 5-year MRP (which equals $R_m - R_f$) is negative or extremely low, or when size premium (SMB) and distress premium (HML) figures are negative. In these cases, I would recommend that executives/investors use the long-term equity premium $(R_m - R_f)$ figure of 5% (Siegel, 1998) and use SMB and HML figures that capture at least a 10-year period. I calculated MRP, SMB, and HML premiums since 1992 by using 10-year rolling periods (e.g., 1992–2001, 1993–2002, 1994–2003, and so on) until 2006 and verified that in all instances SMB, and HML premiums were positive.

Step 4: solving cost of equity equation • • •

Since the market index (VWCRSP) has a very low return (0.21%) for the 5-year period, I will use the long-term equity premium of 5% (Siegel, 1998). Next, by using the obtained regression coefficients in Table 6.1, the regression equations provide the following results:

$$Ke(CAPM) = 3.2 + 0.538 \times (5.00) = 3.20 + 2.69 = 5.89\%$$

$$Ke(FF) = 3.2 + 0.913 \times (5.00) + 0.721 \times 14.78 = 18.42\%$$

As it can be seen from the results above, the restaurant industry cost of equity is considerably higher when estimated by using the FF model. In basic terms, this means that a hypothetical investor will expect a return of 18% from the U.S. restaurant industry in order to invest his/her funds in the U.S. restaurant portfolio. However, if a restaurant executive believes that 18% is a fairly high rate of return and his/her restaurant company does not have the same risk profile as the overall U.S. restaurant industry, he/she may elect to use the average of the CAPM and FF estimates, which is around 12%.

Next, a restaurant executive may adjust the rate of his/her firm's project by considering whether the project will be riskier than the restaurant industry's expected return. Here one should consider factors such as competition, life of the project, and the events that may have an impact on the risk of the project by influencing forces driving change in firm's external (e.g., economic, political, technological) and internal (e.g., industry, local) environment.

Cost of debt

The next step in estimating the cost of capital is to estimate the cost of debt. Unlike cost of equity, cost of debt does not require consideration of the average cost of debt for the hospitality industry. This is because in simple terms, cost of debt denotes an interest rate at which a given company can borrow. Therefore, a given company can calculate the cost of debt for a given project in a relatively simple manner. The situation is little more complex in cases when a corporation has multiple projects to invest in and has to estimate its corporate cost of debt. This is because some of the projects may be expansion projects that are already financed by loans obtained in the past. Consequently, executives need to average out the interest rate of the outstanding debt related to this project and also consider the interest rate at which the company can borrow new funds.

In this particular example, we will assume that a hypothetical company plans to issue bonds which mature in 10 years and will also secure a 10-year loan to finance a portion of the project. In this scenario, we assume that both the bond issuance and the loan will have equal contribution to the funding of the project (e.g., 50% each). Let us assume that the hypothetical company in this example issues 10-year bonds whose expected yield-to-maturity is 8%. This rate is assumed based on the present bond rating of this company. We also assume that the rate of a 10-year bank loan is 7% and the corporate tax rate 38%. Thus, the cost of debt can be calculated as follows:

$$Kd = \left[\frac{(8+7)}{2}\right] \times (1 - 0.38) = 7.5 \times 0.62 = 4.65\%$$

Cost of capital calculation

Before entering the values from previous sections we assume that the current project will be financed with 60% equity and 40% debt. We use the average cost of equity estimate (12.25%) and the cost of debt (4.65%) we obtained before. Consequently, the weighted cost of capital for this project can be calculated as follows:

$$WACC = (12.25\% \times 0.6) + (4.65 \times 0.4) = 7.5 + 2.16 = 9.68\%$$

It should be noted that the executive of this hypothetical firm needs to make adjustments to this project if the project carries any specific risk such as political risk, divisional risk (if the firm has multiple divisions), risk of early termination, stiff competition, and so on.

International cost of equity example

This section considers a case when the cost of equity needs to be estimated for an international project. Here I use a hypothetical scenario where a Thai investor plans to make a hotel investment in Turkey in 2006. In this case, the hotel property is expected to be managed by a North American Company (Four Seasons Hotels and Resorts). At this point, an investor faces the following two challenges: First, what market data should he/she use in estimating the cost of equity? Should stock market data be Thai, Turkish, or North American? Second, how should he/she apply the country risk premium or exchange risk premium to his/her cost of equity estimates?

To answer these questions, in this example I use two different samples. The first sample is represented by a single company—the Four Seasons Hotels and Resorts and is listed on New York Stock Exchange in 2006. The second sample is the Tourism Index (composed of seven tourism stocks) of the Istanbul Stock Exchange (ISE). The observation period in this study is the 5-year period between 2001 and 2005. Stock data is obtained from the Center of Research in Security Prices (CRSP) at the University of Chicago and brokerage houses in Turkey.

In line with the suggestions made by Annin (1997), and Barad and McDowell (2002), a minimum of 36 months' stock market trading is the criterion for a hospitality firm to be included in the Turkish Tourism Index. In addition, CRSPWV Index is used as a market portfolio index for the United States. This is in congruence with the previous seminal studies related to asset pricing models (Fama and French, 1992, 1993, 1997; Jaganathan and Wang, 1996). However, IMKB Ulusal 100 Index is utilized as a market portfolio for Turkey.

β is computed by regressing excess return of the Four Seasons and Turkish Tourism Index over the excess market return; therefore, both variables are analysed in real units (e.g., after subtracting inflation). Excess market return (MRP) for the United States is computed by subtracting 1-month TB rate from the monthly VWCRSP Index return. The MRP for Turkey is calculated by subtracting the Turkish Government's TB from the monthly ISE Ulusal 100 Index return.

The data for the five APT variables are obtained from Global Insight Database. The APT variables are calculated as in Chen *et al.* (1986). EINF is estimated following the method of Fama and Gibbons (1984). Country risk premium is adapted from Aswath Damodaran at New York University. Damodaran (2006) explains the estimation procedure as "To estimate the long term country risk premium, I start with the country rating (from Moody's: www.moodys.com) and estimate the default spread for that rating (US corporate and country bonds) over the treasury bond rate. This becomes a measure of the added country risk premium for that country. I add this default spread to the historical risk premium for a mature equity market (estimated from US historical data) to estimate the total risk premium."

Both direct and indirect approaches are used to estimate the expected return (indirect and direct) of an investment.

Indirect approach

In this method, I first compute the expected rate of return for the U.S. stock (in this case Four Seasons) by using the average estimates for the CAPM and APT. Then I adjust for country risks of Turkey and Thailand based on Moody's country risk ratings as reported by Damodaran (2006).

This method assumes that the Turkish Stock Market is integrated and thus using the U.S. market indices to estimate the cost of equity for Four Seasons is equivalent to using Ulusal 100 Market Index for the Turkish Tourism portfolio. First, I run a regression of the monthly returns of Four Seasons over the CRSPVW return for the 2001–2005 period. The results show that the β for Four Seasons is 1.6. Next, the 5-year annualized return for the CRSP was calculated in order to estimate the MRP. The 5-year historical return for CRSP was 4.3%. The risk-free rate for the 2001–2005 period was 2.16%. As a result, the cost of equity estimate based on the CAPM for Four Seasons is as follows:

$$E(R_i) = 2.1 + 1.6 \times (4.3 - 2.1) = 5.4\%$$

In an effort to have less biased estimates, I also use the five APT variables (Chen et al., 1986) to calculate the expected return for Four Seasons. The results reveal that, among the five APT variables, only the default risk variable (UPR) is significant at the 0.05 level. However, it is not feasible to use this variable to estimate the expected return because the regression coefficient for UPR is a negative number. As a result, the Four Seasons is likely to have a negative expected return based on the APT. As a consequence, I elect not to use the APT results in the final stage of the direct approach, since the results of the APT are in conflict with the contemporary financial theories.

Therefore, I use the CAPM's estimate of 5.4% and adjust this estimate with the country risk of Turkey and Thailand. According to Damodaran (2006), the historical risk premium for the United States is 4.80%. Turkey's country risk premium is 5.60% above the United States value and that for Thailand is 1.65% above the risk premium for the United States. This denotes that Turkey's country risk premium is 3.95% over that of Thailand. These figures result in an expected return of 9.35% (5.4 + 3.95%) for the Thai entrepreneur who is undertaking an equity investment in a hotel in Turkey.

Direct approach

In the direct approach, I estimate the nominal required rate of return for the portfolio of Turkish tourism and hospitality stocks. As a next step, I adjust for the sovereign spreads of Turkey and Thailand as it is assumed that the Thai investor will repatriate the returns from an investment to his/her home country.

In this method, I regress the monthly return of the Turkish Tourism Index over the return of the ISE. The β for the Tourism Index was merely 0.17. The 5-year average for the risk-free rate (Turkish government's TB) for the 2001–2005 period was 46.4%. The annualized return of the market index (ISE) for the 2001–2005 period was 37.7%. The expected return for the tourism portfolio was calculated by applying the CAPM and it provided the following results:

$$E(R_i) = 37.7 + 0.17 \times (46.4 - 37.7) = 37.7 + 1.5 = 39.2\%$$

The next step entails the addition of the sovereign spread between Thailand and Turkey to arrive at the estimate for the cost of equity capital for the Thai investor. The sovereign spreads are obtained from Fuentes and Godoy (2005). The spread for Turkey was 11.875% and that of Thailand 7.750%. Based on these figures, the cost of equity for the direct approach was 43.3% (39.2 + 4.1%).

Discussion and conclusion

As it can be seen from both the examples of cost of equity estimation (the United States and international), the expected returns (costs of equity) varied widely. In the example of United States, the use of the CAPM resulted in a cost of equity that was fairly low (less than 6%). It is worth asking, would a given investor invest in a U.S. restaurant portfolio of stocks for less than 6% a year? The answer would probably be "no." However, if one elects to use FF as its main cost of equity model then the possibility of obtaining more relevant results is likely to increase. As it can be seen in this example, the cost of equity by using the FF model yielded a fairly logical return which far exceeds the historical equity premium for the United States.

For the international example, one of the main reasons for the stark difference in cost of equity estimates using the two approaches (direct and indirect) is the high historical inflation in Turkey. This is demonstrated by the gap in the TB rates for this country (82.3% for 2001 and 16.3% for 2005). Hence, if a hypothetical investor elects to use the "going-rate (16.3%) in 2005 then the new expected return for the Turkish Tourism portfolio would be at least twice lower than the original estimate of 43.3%. Another challenge in the direct approach for international cost of equity estimations is the low β estimate for the Turkish Tourism portfolio (0.17). Does this mean that the tourism portfolio is five times less risky than the overall ISE Index? What if the real risk of tourism stocks is twice higher than that of the market? (This is quite likely as the β for Four Seasons in the United States was 1.6.) If that is the case, then the Thai investor needs to require a rate of return that is more than 50% in Thai currency. How can the investor hedge his investments against the large swings in the cost of equity estimates?

As the results indicated thus far, cost of equity estimations for hospitality investments in emerging and developed markets are beset with uncertainty. The main shortcomings stem from the challenge of applying the seminal models such as the CAPM, FF, and the APT. The second set of challenges arises when countries such as Turkey tend to have high historical rates of inflation but now are entering a more stabilized period of fiscal reforms. Thus, should an investor use the historical data or try to forecast the future interest rates in Turkey? Although the practical examples provided some answers to these questions, few more questions are left for future research. Hence, I suggest two interim solutions for this cost of equity conundrum in the emerging markets: (1) the investors and academics should either solely focus on future cash flows of the project, or (2) use simulations such as Monte Carlo in order to create multiple scenarios that approximate the investment realities of the emerging markets. Otherwise, the expected return remains to be a "gut feeling" estimate for foreign investors in emerging markets.

References

Aaker, D. A., and Jacobson, R. (1994). The financial information content of perceived quality. *Journal of Marketing Research*, *31*(2), 191–201.

Amit, R., and Wernerfelt, B. (1990). Why do firms reduce business risk? *Academy of Management Journal*, *33*(1), 99–110.

Annin, M. (March, 1997). Fama-French and small company cost of equity calculations. *Business Valuation Review*. Retrieved July 15, 2003, from http://ibbotson.com/content/kc_published_research_search.asp?catalog=Article&category=Cost%20of%20Capital&prodID=ARTC41220026

Arena, K., Meserve, J., Ensor, D., and Candiotti, S. (2003). Preparations for possible attacks gear up: New flight restrictions planned around Washington. Retrieved February 12, 2003, from http://www.cnn.com/2003/US/02/08/threat.level/index.html

Aron, D. J. (1988). Ability, moral hazard, firm size, and diversification. *RAND Journal of Economics*, 19, 72–87.

Barad, M.W. (September 2001). Technical analysis of the size premium. *Business Valuation Alert*. Retrieved December 16, 2002, from http://www.ibbotson.com/content/kc_published_research_search.asp?catalog=Article&category=Cost%20of%20Capital&prodID=ARTC61920021

Barad, M. W., and McDowell, T. (August 2002). Capturing industry risk in a buildup model. *Business Valuation Alert*. Retrieved December 16, 2003, from http://www.ibbotson.com/content/kc_published_research_search.asp?catalog=Article&category=Cost%20of%20Capital&prodID=ARTC82120021

Barrows, C. W., and Naka, A. (1994). Use of macroeconomic variables to evaluate selected hospitality stock returns in the U.S. *International Journal of Hospitality Management*, 13(2), 119–128.

Barth, M. E., Clement, M. B., Foster, G., and Kasznik, R. (1998). Brand values and capital market valuation. *Review of Accounting Studies*, 3(1/2), 41–68.

Bekaert, G., and Harvey, C. R. (2002). *Research in emerging markets finance: looking into the future*. Working Paper, Duke University, Durham, NC.

Bettis, R. (1983). Modern financial theory, corporate strategy and public policy: Three conundrums. *Academy of Management Review*, 8, 406–414.

Bloxham, E. (2003). *Economic Value Management: Applications and Techniques*. Hoboken, NJ: Wiley.

Caroll, C., and Sikich, F. J. P. (1999). What is your IRR on human capital? *Bottomline*, 14(10), 8–12.

Chatterjee, S., Lubatkin, M., and Schulze, W. (1999). Towards a strategic theory of risk premium: Moving beyond CAPM. *Academy of Management Review*, 24(3), 556–567.

Chen, M. H., Kim, W. G., and Kim, H. J. (2005). The impact of macroeconomic and non-macroeconomic forces on hotel stock returns. *International Journal of Hospitality Management*, 24(2), 243–258.

Chen, N., Roll, R., and Ross, S. A. (1986). Economic forces and the stock market. *Journal of Business, 59*(3), 383–403.

Choi, J. G. (1999). The *Restaurant Industry, Business Cycles, Strategies, Financial Practices, Economic Indicators, and Forecasting.* Unpublished Dissertation, Virginia Polytechnic Institute and State University, Blacksburg, VA.

Connolly, D. (1999). *Understanding Information Technology Investment Decision Making in the Context of Hotel Global Distribution Systems: A Multiple-case Study.* Unpublished Dissertation, Virginia Polytechnic Institute and State University, Blacksburg, VA.

Constantinides, G. M. (1986). Capital market equilibrium with transaction costs. *Journal of Political Economy, 94*, 842–862.

Copeland, T., Koller, T., and Murrin, J. (2000). *Valuation: Measuring and Managing the Value of Companies* (3rd ed.). New York: Wiley.

Damodaran, A. (2006). Country default spreads and risk premiums, New York University. Retrieved January 25, 2006, from http://pages.stern.nyu.edu/~adamodar/New_Home_Page/datafile/ctryprem.html

Downe, E. A. (2000). Increasing returns: A theoretical explanation for the demise of beta. *American Business Review, 18*(1), 86–89.

Fama, E., and French, K. (1992). The cross section of expected stock returns. *Journal of Finance, 47*(2), 427–465.

Fama, E., and French, K. (1993). Common risk factors in the returns on stocks and bonds. *Journal of Financial Economics, 33*(1), 3–56.

Fama, E., and French, K. (1995). Size and book-to-market factors in earnings and returns. *Journal of Finance, 50*(1), 131–155.

Fama, E., and French, K. (1997). Industry costs of equity. *Journal of Financial Economics, 43*(2), 153–193.

Fama, E., and MacBeth, J. D. (1973). Risk, return and equilibrium: empirical tests. *Journal of Political Economy, 81*(3), 607–636.

Fama, E. F., and Gibbons, M. R. (1984). A comparison of inflation forecasts. *Journal of Monetary Economics, 13*, 327–348.

Fields, B. J., and Kwansa, F. A. (1993). Analysis of pure play technique in the hospitality industry. *International Journal of Hospitality Management, 12*(3), 271–287.

Fuentes, M., and Godoy, S. (2005). *Sovereign Spreads in Emerging Markets: A Principal Components Analysis*, Working Paper No. 333, Central Bank of Chile, Chile.

Gitman, L. J. (1991). *Principles of Managerial Finance.* New York: Harper Collins.

Goetzmann, W. N. (1996). *Introduction to Investment Theory* (Hyper Textbook). Retrieved October 30, 2003, from http://viking.som.yale.edu/will/finman540/classnotes/notes.html

Gordon, M. (1962). *The Investment, Financing, and Valuation of the Corporation*. Homewood, IL: RD Irwin.

Graham, J. R., and Harvey, C. R. (2001). The theory and practice of corporate finance: Evidence from the field. *Journal of Financial Economics*, 60(2), 187–243.

Harvey, G. (2005). *Twelve Ways to Calculate the International Cost of Capital*. Working Paper, Duke University, Durham, NC.

Hayn, C. (1989). Tax attributes as determinants of shareholder gains in corporate acquisitions. *Journal of Financial Economics*, 23, 121–153.

Helfat, C., and Teece, D. J. (1987). Vertical integration and risk reduction. *Journal of Law, Economics, and Organization*, 3(1), 47–67.

Helfert, E. A. (2003). *Techniques of Financial Analysis: A Guide to Value Creation* (11th ed.). New York: McGraw-Hill/Irvin.

Jagannathan, R., and Wang, Z. (1996). Conditional CAPM and cross section of expected returns. *Journal of Finance*, 51(1), 3–53.

James, M., and Koller, T. M. (2000). Valuation in emerging markets. *McKinsey Quarterly*, 4, 78–85.

Jesitus, J. (1991). March 11. Safety and security: Risk management, threat of terrorism top hoteliers' concerns in 1991. *Hotel Motel Management*, 206(4), 35–36.

Kalafut, P. C., and Low, J. (2001). The value creation index: Quantifying intangible value. *Strategic Leadership*, 29(5), 9–15.

Kaplan, S. (1989). The effects of management buyouts on operations and value. *Journal of Financial Economics*, 24, 217–254.

Lakonishok, J., and Shapiro, A. C. (1986). Systematic risk, total risk and size as determinants of stock market returns. *Journal of Banking and Finance*, 10(1), 115–132.

Lev, B. (2001). *Intangibles: Management, Measurement, and Reporting*. Washington, DC: The Brookings Institution Press.

Lintner, J. (1965). The valuation of risk assets and the selection of risky investments in stock portfolios and capital budgets. *Review of Economics and Statistics*, 47(1), 13–37.

Lubatkin, M. H., and Chatterjee, S. (1994). Extending modern portfolio theory into the domain of corporate diversification: Does it apply? *Academy of Management Journal*, 37(1), 109–137.

Lubatkin, M. H., and Schulze, W. S. (2003). Risk, strategy, and finance: Unifying two world views (Editorial). *Long Range Planning*, 36(1), 7–8.

Madanoglu, M., and Olsen, M. D. (2005). Cost of equity conundrum in the lodging industry: A conceptual framework. *International Journal of Hospitality Management*, 24(4), 493–515.

Markowitz, H. M. (1952). Portfolio selection. *Journal of Finance*, 7(1), 71–91.

Markowitz, H. M. (1959). *Portfolio Selection: Efficient Diversification of Investments*. New York: Wiley.

Marshall, W., Yawitz, J., and Greenberg, E. (1984). Incentives for diversification and the structure of the conglomerate firm. *Southern Economic Journal*, 51, 1–23.

Murphy, J. (1990). Assessing the value of brands. *Long Range Planning*, 23(3), 23–29.

Murphy, K. (2003). *A Proposed Structure for Obtaining Human Resource Intangible Value in Restaurant Organizations Using Economic Value Added*. In the Proceedings of Annual Symposium of Council on Hospitality, Restaurant and Institutional Education, August 6–9, (pp. 301–305). Palm Springs, CA.

Ogier, T., Rugman, J., and Spicer, L. (2004). *The Real Cost of Capital: A Business Field Guide to Better Financial Decisions*. London: Prentice Hall.

Olsen, M. D. (1995). *Into the New Millennium: The IHA White Paper on the Global Hospitality Industry: Events Shaping the Future of the Industry*. Paris: International Hotel Association.

Olsen, M. D. (Conference chair and presenter). (1996). *Global Hotel Finance—The Future*. One-day program co-sponsored by Hong Kong Shanghai Bank Corporation, Deloitte & Touche Consulting Group and Richard Ellis International Property Consultants, October. London, England.

Olsen, M. D. (2000). *Leading Hospitality into the Age of Excellence: Competition and Vision in the Multinational Hotel Industry 1995–2005*. Paris: International Hotel Association.

Olsen, M. D., and Merna, K. M. (1991). March 11. Trends in safety & security. *Hotel and Motel Management*, 206(4), 35–36.

Olsen, M. D., West, J. J., and Tse, E. C. (1998). *Strategic Management in the Hospitality Industry* (2nd ed.). New York: Wiley.

Prasad, K., and Dev, C. (2000). Managing brand equity: A customer-centric framework for assessing performance. *Cornell Hotel and Restaurant Administration Quarterly*, 41(3), 22–31.

Prasad, K., and Dev, C. (2002). Model estimates financial impact of guest satisfaction efforts. *Hotel Motel Management*, 217(14), 23.

Pratt, P. S. (1998). *Cost of Capital: Estimation and Applications*. New York: Wiley.

Reinganum, M. R. (1981). A new empirical perspective on the CAPM. *Journal of Financial and Quantitative Analysis, 16*(4), 439–462.

Roll, R. R., and Ross, S. A. (1994). On the cross-sectional relation between expected returns and betas. *Journal of Finance, 49*(1), 101–121.

Rosenberg, B. (1981). The capital asset pricing model and the market model. *Journal of Portfolio Management, 7*(2), 5–16.

Rosenberg, B., Reid, K., and Lanstein, R. (1985). Persuasive evidence of market inefficiency. *Journal of Portfolio Management, 11*(1), 9–17.

Ross, S. A. (1976). The arbitrage theory of capital asset pricing. *Journal of Economic Theory, 13*(3), 341–360.

Sangster, A. (2001). Technology: The importance of technology in the hotel industry. *Travel and Tourism Analyst, 3*, 43–56.

Sharpe, W. F. (1964). Capital asset prices: A theory of market equilibrium under conditions of risk. *Journal of Finance, 19*(3), 425–442.

Sheel, A. (1995). An empirical analysis of anomalies in the relationship between earnings' yield and returns of common stocks: The case of lodging and hotel firms. *Hospitality Research Journal, 19*(1), 13–24.

Siegel, J. J. (1998). *Stocks for the long run* (2nd ed.). New York: McGraw-Hill.

Simon, C. J., and Sullivan, M. W. (1993). The measurement and determinants of brand equity: A financial approach. *Marketing Science, 12*(1), 28–52.

Smith, A. (1990). Corporate ownership structure and performance: The case of management buyouts. *Journal of Financial Economics, 27*, 143–164.

Srivastava, R. K., Shervani, T. A., and Fahey, L. (1998). Market-based assets and shareholder value: A framework for analysis. *Journal of Marketing, 62*(1), 2–18.

Vancil, R. F. (1987). *Passing the Baton: Managing the Process of CEO Succession*. Boston, MA: Harvard Business School Press.

Competitive methods of multinational hotel companies in the new millennium (2000–2007)

Jinlin Zhao[1] and Wei He[2]

[1]Associate Professor,
School of Hospitality and Tourism Management,
Florida International University, USA
[2]School of Hospitality and Tourism Management,
Florida International University, USA

Introduction

Entering the new millennium, multinational hotel companies have been tremendously challenged by a very complex business environment. Consequently, they have been increasingly relying on a variety of competitive methods to compete with their global rivals. An in-depth review and summary of those competitive methods is likely to reveal the most recent changes occurring in the global hotel industry and indicate how the international industrial leaders react in an efficient way to gain sustainable competitive advantage. It is hoped that the results unveiled not only shed some light on the practical issues concerning industrial practitioners, but also provide useful contextual information that can be further examined by future researchers.

This chapter starts by reviewing literature relevant to several important concepts and explaining how they are interrelated, especially in the context of the international hotel industry. The second part of this chapter consists of a comprehensive in-depth content analysis and summary of major competitive methods employed by multinational hotel firms between 2000 and 2007. The chapter concludes with a brief comparison between the summarized results and the competitive methods used in the period 1995–1999 (Zhao, 2000). The relevant implications are also discussed.

Strategy and competitive strategy

Defining strategy

Since the 1960s numerous researchers have attempted to define "strategy." Chandler (1962) described strategy as the process of determining the organization's long-term goals and objectives as well as the process of adopting a course of action and allocating sufficient resources. Later scholars, such as Mintzberg and Waters (1985), contended that strategy was more a pattern of action resulting from whatever intended (deliberate) or unintended (emergent) strategies were realized, thus indicating that strategy could be something more than an explicit plan of action (Mintzberg, 1978). Incorporating both the intended and apparent manifestations of strategy in a dynamic and responsive sense and embracing a broad range of participants, Kerin *et al.* (1990) defined strategy as a fundamental pattern of present and planned objectives, resource deployments, as well as organizational interactions with relevant markets, competitors, and other environmental forces. Over a 40-year span of re-examination and redefinition, strategy has been regarded as the pivotal construct of the business-planning process and the critical mechanism used to align firms with their environments (Hitt and Ireland, 1985). The current literature on strategy is able to provide at least 10 separate schools of thought and a variety of definitions focusing on divergent perspectives (Fréry, 2006).

Overview of competitive strategy

Nowadays, firms throughout the world are being challenged by both domestic and global competitors. Thus competition is at the core of a firm's success or failure, and competitive strategy is at the heart of a firm's performance in the competitive environment. Competitive strategy is a firm's search for a favourable competitive position in an industry, and its objective is to establish a profitable and sustainable position against the forces that determine industry competition (Porter, 1985). The most significant theoretical foundation of competitive strategy was contributed by Michael Porter, who defined three generic strategies—Cost Leadership, Differentiation, and Focus—which are theoretically thought of as a means of establishing strategic group membership at the business level.

According to Porter (1980, 1985), cost leadership indicates that cost reduction becomes the major theme running throughout strategy. The emphasis of this strategy is efficiency. The firms using this strategy hope to take advantage of economies of scale by conducting continuous search for cost reductions in all aspects of the business. By using a differentiation strategy, a firm tries to be unique in its industry along some dimensions that are widely valued by buyers (Porter, 1985). The firm that hopes to maintain differentiation strategy needs to have strong R&D, marketing, and creativity skills as well as good communication with distribution channels and other business alliances. Quality, delivery, flexibility, and innovativeness are all operational objectives that are consistent or fit with differentiation-oriented strategies (Devaraj *et al.*, 2004). The focus strategy is different from cost leadership and differentiation in that it relies on choosing a narrow competitive scope within an industry (Porter, 1985). Firms using this strategy typically seek to gain a competitive advantage through effectiveness rather than efficiency. Porter (1985) also pointed out the two variants of focus strategy. In differentiation focus, firms' base focus on differentiation, targeting a specific segment of the market with unique needs not met by others in the industry, while in cost focus, firms have access to specialized production and operations equipment to save costs from smaller production lots or runs. Focus strategy can be used by a wide range of companies and is most effective when consumers have distinct preferences or competitors overlook the niche (David, 2002).

Despite initially having been given strong empirical support (Dess and Davis, 1984; Hawes and Crittendon, 1984; Miller and Friesen, 1986; Robinson and Pearce, 1988), Porter's generic competitive strategies were later challenged by a number of studies (White, 1986; Buzzell and Gale, 1987; Wright, 1987; Hill, 1988; Murray, 1988; Parnell, 1997; Proff, 2000). These researchers argued that the generic strategies lack specificity, lack flexibility, are limited. The particular conceptual limitations proposed by those researchers include the following: generic strategies are not mutually exclusive (Wright, 1987; Hill, 1988); generic strategies are not collectively exhaustive and thus are unable to describe the strategies adequately (Wright, 1987; Chrisman *et al.*, 1988); and the appropriateness of Porter's simple notions of low cost and differentiation in the current corporate environment characterized by increased global competition and technological change is questionable (Mintzberg, 1988).

Evolution of competitive strategy theory

To address some of the above criticisms, researchers started to make efforts in developing alternative typologies of generic strategies. A very useful one was proposed by Mintzberg (1988), who distinguished *focus* from *differentiation* and *cost leadership*. He pointed out that the focus strategy defined the scope of a market domain based on the resource held by the firm, whereas the other two generic strategies reflected how a firm competes in the relevant market domain. He further argued that cost leadership did not provide an advantage by itself but had to result in below-average market prices to be a competitive advantage and hence had to be regarded as differentiation by price. Specifically, Mintzberg (1988) disaggregated Porter's differentiation strategy into differentiation by marketing image, product design, quality, support, and undifferentiation. Mintzberg's arguments were empirical supported by Kotha and Vadlamani (1995).

In response to the criticisms of generic strategies, the proponents of the combination strategy approach based their arguments not only on broad economic relationships but also on the evidence demonstrating how individual firms have identified such relationships unique to one or a small group of firms in an industry (Parnell, 2006). Following this logic, Bowman and

Faulkner (1997) noted the importance of value activity competitive strategies since buyers see price and not cost. They argued that sustainable competitive advantage is achieved by offering products or services that are perceived by customers to be better than those of the competition regardless of price, or to be equal to the competition but at a lower price, or to be better and cheaper.

Following the strategy-performance approach, Parnell (2006) presented a refined conceptualization of competitive strategy by integrating research founded on the resource-based view (RBV) of the firm and proposing value and market control as the two prominent overarching factors in business strategies. The refined market control-value framework includes five conceptual anchors: emphasis on value, emphasis on market control, moderate market control and value emphasis, strong market control and value emphasis, and lack of emphasis on either value or market control. The typology developed by Parnell (2006) incorporates Porter's original framework, follows the logic of the RBV, and is sensitive to recent changes in the competitive environment. Hence it represents a balance between the generalizability and parsimony typically associated with strategic group models and the specificity and completeness sought by proponents of the RBV.

Competitive strategy in the hotel industry in the new millennium

Practical challenges and academic studies

Although Porter's (1980) typology of competitive strategy is one of the theories most widely cited by academics and practitioners, it is debatable whether a single strategy will lead to sustainable competitive advantage (Helms *et al.*, 1997). This is particularly true for the international hotel industry in the new millennium. The complexity of forming and implementing competitive strategy has continued to increase. To a large extent this has resulted from the intensive competition in the international lodging market and the tremendous changes taking place in the global business environment in this period of time. Multinational hotel firms are challenged by the rapid development of information technology; changing demands from lodging consumers with various economic, cultural, and educational backgrounds; higher returns required by investors; increasing necessity for foreign expansion; and dramatic changes in global security and natural environment. In responding to these challenges, multinational hotel firms have applied a variety of competitive strategies, which have been recorded, analysed, and extended in the research works of contemporary lodging scholars.

A brief review of relevant literature reveals that beginning with the new millennium, a large amount of research has been conducted within the field of lodging competitive strategy, while extensive studies have focused on the areas of effective and efficient application of information technology, especially the Internet and data mining technology (Sigala *et al.*, 2001; Magnini *et al.*, 2003; Martin, 2004; Law and Jogaratnam, 2005); strategic human resource management (Tracey, 2003; Knox and Walsh, 2005; Wilton, 2006); service quality management (Keating and Harrington, 2003; Candido, 2005; Presbury *et al.*, 2005); strategic relationship marketing, branding, and pricing as well as hotel revenue management (Yelkur and DaCosta, 2001; Lai and Ng, 2003; Cai and Hobson, 2004; Jain and Jain, 2005; Holverson and Revaz, 2006), and so on. Other studies are closely related to exploring the ownership patterns of the hotel industry (Dimou *et al.*, 2003) or examining the application of a specific overall competitive strategy in the hotel industry (Crook *et al.*, 2003). More recent studies are particularly concerned with the relationship between strategic behaviours and business performance. For instance, aiming to analyse the predictive validity of strategic groups and to determine which strategic behaviours have the most positive impact on hotel performance, Claver-Cortés *et al.* (2006) conducted a principal components factor analysis and found that if hotels are to achieve higher performance levels, they should preferably be medium or large sized, belong to a chain, increase their category, and base their competitive strategy on improvement and dimension. These studies have revealed significant insights into the contemporary competitive strategies employed in the hotel industry from both practical and academic perspectives. However, most of the studies confined the research domain at one functional level or within a specific geographic region; more comprehensive studies remain to be taken that can effectively upgrade the research generalizability and offer management implications from the overall industrial level.

Competitive strategy, competitive methods, and critical success factor

Before proceeding to the next section, it is paramount to compare and specify three important and interrelated concepts—competitive strategy, competitive method, and critical success factor (CSF).

Although strategic management literature does not provide a specific comparison of definitions between competitive strategy and competitive method, a slight difference does exist between these two concepts. While competitive strategy is a more comprehensive and academically oriented term that reflects the policies, rules, and methods firms employ to establish a profitable and sustainable position against the competitors in the industry, competitive methods are concrete actions taken or special resources used in the overall strategy development process in order to increase firm performance (Porter, 1980, 1985; Day and Wensley, 1988; Bharadwaj *et al.*, 1993; Campbell-Hunt, 2000).

Another important concept that is closely related to competitive strategy and competitive method is the CSF. CSFs refer to the factors that must be achieved if a firm's overall goals are to be attained (Brotherton, 2004). Brotherton and Shaw (1996) further noted that CSFs are combinations of activities and processes designed to support the achievement of desired outcomes specified by the company's objectives and goals, and CSFs are supposed to be actionable, measurable, and controllable by management. CSFs may be derived from the features of a company's internal environment and reflect the company's core capabilities and competencies (Berry *et al.*, 1997). At the same time they are determined by the nature of a company's external environment (Boardman and Vining, 1996).

In the context of the hospitality industry, several scholars have contributed valuable works in comparing and distinguishing competitive method and CSFs. For instance, Olsen *et al.* (1998) proposed that strategy choices are invested in competitive methods and CSFs, while competitive advantages, as outcomes of investment in competitive methods, are not likely to be sustainable for a relatively long period of time since competitors tend to efficiently copy them, especially in the hospitality industry. Once the competitive methods are copied they evolve into CSFs and become the industrial benchmarks. From this evolutionary perspective, CSFs are defined as things that are necessary for hospitality firms to invest in if they aspire to compete within the industry (Olsen *et al.*, 1998). These insights indicate that time in this case appears to be the most important factor distinguishing competitive methods and CSFs as innovative firms merely take advantage within the time period during which its competitive method is unique in the overall industry.

Competitive methods in the international hotel industry

In this section, the competitive methods employed by 15 multinational hotel firms (listed in Table 7.1) between 2000 and

Table 7.1 Major Multinational Hotel Chains Analysed in this Research

Corporate Chains	Rooms in 2006	Hotels in 2006
InterContinental Hotels Group	556,246	3741
Wyndham Hotel Group	543,234	6473
Marriott International	513,832	2832
Hilton Hotels Corp.	501,478	2935
Accor	486,512	4121
Choice Hotels International	435,000	5376
Best Western International	315,401	4164
Starwood Hotels & Resorts Worldwide	265,600	871
Global Hyatt Corp	140,416	749
TUI AG/TUI Hotels & Resorts	82,111	279
Sol Meliá SA	80,856	407
LQ Management LLC[a]	64,856	582
Interstate Hotels & Resorts	50,199	223
MGM Mirage	43,785	18
Shangri-La Hotels & Resorts	23,956	49

Source: Hotels (2007) Hotel's corporate 300 ranking. Hotels magazine. Available from: http://www.scribd.com/doc/210143/Hotels-corporate-300-ranking. Accessed on July 15, 2007.
[a] This was La Quinta Corp.

2007 are summarized and categorized through an in-depth content analysis research method. Information for the analysis of these companies was collected from Internet databases and e-magazines such as *Hospitalitynet.org*, *Hotelnewsresource.com*, and *Hotel-online.com*, as well as news and reports published on the companies' own websites. A total of 13,000 articles were collected, categorized, and analysed. This section concludes with a comparison of the similarities and differences between the competitive methods employed in the new millennium era with those methods used in the period 1995–1999.

Continuing information technology deployment

The rapid development of information technology has radically reshaped the basic structure of the overall hospitality industry by effectively transforming the nature of products, processes, companies, industries, and competitions in the industry (Cho and Olsen, 1998). Beginning with the new millennium, multinational hotel companies have been continually and increasingly using this driving force of change as the means of creating competitive advantage. Several key technological deployment areas are summarized as follows.

Customer-service oriented technology • • •

Online Reservations   From the middle of the 1990s major multinational hotel firms started to rush into the online era as the Internet was becoming one of the most important information sources and communication channels for international travellers (Hueng, 2003). The most significant symbols for this included the rapid application and improvement of online reservation service, the initial provision of in-room high speed Internet, and the inclusion of web-based entertainment programmes.

Beginning at the new millennium, all major multinational hotel firms had established advanced online reservation service either on their own website or through more centralized online travel agencies, such as Travelocity or Expedia. More efforts were put into system upgrading and feature adding. Several hotel chains developed enhanced personalized booking processes supported by the most updated technologies. Beginning in 2002, customers could request driving directions and locate 2200 Marriott International hotels along the route on the company's website. By the summer of that year, Marriott.com visitors had already used the maps and driving directions more than 13.5 million times, an average of 2.2 million times per month. In the same year, Marriott.com became the first hotel website to provide customers with simultaneous searching of availability and rates across an inventory of more than 2400 hotels. In 2003, InterContinental Hotels Group launched industry—leading website enhancement, enabling its Priority Club Rewards members to make reservations online by significantly reducing the number of steps it took to book a room, and by adding customer-directed features. In 2004, InterContinental launched its fully integrated Holiday Inn Chinese language website, allowing guaranteed reservations on the website even if the customer did not use a credit card. The improved web-based reservation system offered multinational hotel companies tremendous economic benefits. For instance, in the summer of 2005 revenues generated via Choice Hotels International's proprietary website, choicehotels.com, were up a total of 17% year-to-date over the same period in 2004.

Wireless Communication and Application   With the beginning of the new millennium, the most rapid technological development taking place in the international hotel industry was closely related to wireless communication and wireless network development. Mobile computing and communication devices such as wirelessly connected laptops, personal digital assistants (PDAs), web-enabled cell phones, and MP3 players have been used widely in organizations of all types worldwide (Gayeski and Petrillose, 2005). The adoption of wireless technology in the hotel industry dramatically enriched the service domain that can be provided to a variety of hotel customer groups and meanwhile enhance management efficiency.

Entering into the new millennium, multinational hotel firms increasingly have been launching their wireless-based applications and services. Five years after being the first hotel company to offer real-time access to its reservation system via the Internet in 1995, Choice Hotels International achieved reservations via the Palm VII and Palm VIIx handheld computers with wireless Palm.NetÂ® service at its Comfort, Quality, Clarion, Sleep, Econo Lodge, Rodeway Inn, and MainStay Suites brand hotels. In 2001, Bass Hotels & Resorts, a major brand of InterContinental Hotels Group, also launched comprehensive wireless services for locating hotels and making room reservations by working with Air2Web Inc. Before the end of 2001, Best Western entered the mobile commerce arena by launching the first phase of its wireless capabilities, allowing users of web-enabled phones, pagers, and PDAs to access Best Western information. In 2002 MGM Mirage became the first U.S. gaming company to offer wireless Internet access to several of its resort-casino websites, thereby allowing customers to book room reservations at six of the company's Las Vegas resorts, as well as access information about gaming, entertainment, dining, spas, golf, and other hotel services all via wireless devices, including web-enabled cell phones and PDAs. In 2004 the world's first wireless minibar network, an E-fridges wireless system with independent IP address that can avoid the cost and disruption of hard wiring, was installed in the Washington Willard InterContinental Hotel. In 2005 Global Hyatt Corp. launched its plan to make Hyatt the first company to offer a wireless solution in all of its guestrooms in the United States, Canada, and the Caribbean. By the year 2005, most major multinational hotel companies have been able to provide wireless Internet access and other wireless-based service to different customers.

Deployment of Entertainment Technology Adoption of modern technology for upgrading entertainment facilities has become a key strategy employed by different multinational hotel firms to attract both leisure and business travellers. In 2002, Choice Hotels International and On Command signed a 3-year agreement to market On Command's in-room video-on-demand, pay-per-view system to Choice Hotels' franchisees, which enables those small and middle Choice hotels to build revenue by providing a service that millions of guests enjoy in larger mid-scale and luxury hotel properties through On Command's MiniMate solution. Four years later, similar actions were taken between Hilton Hotels Corporation and global fitness equipment leader Precor for launching dynamic Fitness by Precor facilities at full-service Hilton, Doubletree(R), and Embassy Suites Hotels(R) in North America and at the Waldorf-Astoria in New York City. More recently, industrial attention has been focused on the development of the in-room digital high definition TV system. A pioneer practitioner is Marriott, which started in 2005 to roll out 50,000 sets of digital HDTV manufactured by LG Electronics over the next 4 years. The critical device that is connected with the television will be a connectivity panel, which offers ample power outlets to enable guests to connect laptops, PDAs, and personal entertainment devices, including DVD players, MP3 players, camcorders, and video games into the television.

Additionally, Plasma TV, integrated DVD playing systems, video games, and wireless pre-view systems have been widely established in the properties of primary multinational hotel firms to extensively enrich the entertainment experience of hotel customers.

Self-Service Facilities The most popular technology in this area is self check-in and check-out kiosks, which have been widely installed in the properties of Hilton, Starwood, and Hyatt. From the fourth quarter of 2004, Hilton began to provide web-based check-in for Gold and Diamond Hilton HHonors members. These password-protected online accounts permit guests to check into their hotel rooms in advance of arrival, regardless of how they made their reservation. Other hotel chains, such as InterContinental and Choice, also started the test procedures of the self-service facilities in their properties from 2005.

E-commerce Technology The continuing development of the Internet and relevant network technology enables multinational hotel firms to establish their own e-commerce platforms, not only for general hotel customers but also for internal customers and other stakeholders. For instance, Choice Hotels International developed a productive e-procurement system—ChoiceBuys.com—realizing $5 million in purchases in 2001—up from $700,000 in 2000. The system effectively enables more than 2800 Choice franchisees now using the system to purchase over 250,000 products available through the Internet. Beginning in 2000, Hilton worked with SkyMall to develop a "virtual mall" on Hilton's corporate website, allowing customers to make purchases from a wide array of SkyMall's premier merchandise. Both Hilton and SkyMall would promote the travellers' e-shop programme through newsletters and brochures, e-mails, direct mail campaigns, and other targeted communications to their respective customers. In 2004, InterContinental successfully integrated three dedicated Japanese language websites with its global hotel network, allowing for personalized end-to-end online transactions in Japanese.

Management and decision-making support technology ● ● ●

The advanced technology was not only deployed in the customer service direction, but also widely used by multinational hotel companies in management and strategic decision-making processes to improve operation efficiency, cost control, and marketing analysis, as well as add value. Several key technology deployments in management and administrative areas are summarized as follows.

Customer Relationship Management System (CRM) In 2001, Starwood Hotels & Resorts Worldwide increased investment in the CRM project of Unica's Affinium to seamlessly integrate with other CRM systems and to provide its worldwide marketing team with an easy-to-use tool for creating targeted campaigns that can be customized as needed. Others, like Shangri-La, integrated its CRM solutions in the facilities of a regional reservation centre in Asia. In the new millennium era, a variety of CRM solutions are employed in the major multinational hotel companies at both the operational and business level functioning as key instruments for gaining competitive advantages.

Improvement of Property Management System The property management system (PMS) is not a new application in the hotel industry. However, the most up-to-date features of the PMS, including its ability to be tuned with other systems on the local properties, have become critical for creating competitive advantage. Several multinational hotel companies have taken the steps. In 2001, Choice completed the roll out of a "last room" sell function at more than 2400 hotels, allowing synchronization of the hotel's PMS with the Choice 2001 central reservations system. In 2004, Multi-Systems Inc. (MSI) and Best Western International Inc. implemented the two-way interface based on the Open Travel Alliance (OTA) specifications, which enabled MSI's WinPM PMS and the Best Western Central Reservation Systems to integrate and establish seamless connectivity. A year later, Holiday Inn started to test a reception kiosk that has a real-time interface to the MICROS

OPERA PMS using MICROS OPERA Web Services as the communication tool.

Database Marketing and Data Mining Database marketing is the act of applying databases to the marketing paradigm (Baker and Baker, 1995; Fairlie, 1995), thereby contributing to customer profiling in market segmentation and new customer prospect identification (Mayer and Lapidus, 1998). In the new millennium, multinational hotel companies have increased their investment to develop a more comprehensive database system that can effectively integrate both an online interface with a database management system on an enterprise-wide platform.

A more advanced relationship-management-oriented technology is data mining, which is a largely automated process that uses statistical analyses to sift through massive data sets to detect useful, non-obvious, and previously unknown patterns or data trends (Magnini *et al.*, 2003). Several multinational hotel practitioners, including Wyndham, Choice, and InterContinental, have worked with industrial technology partners to develop relevant solutions.

Revenue Management System According to the study results revealed at the fourth Hospitality Sales & Marketing Association International (HSMAI) Revenue Management Strategy Conference held in June 2007, 43% of the hotel respondents used an automated revenue management system and 75% were satisfied or very satisfied with their systems. In 2002, Six Continents Hotels launched an integrated technology solution— HIRO—as the new revenue management system, replacing arcane coding with a Windows/Internet look and feel via a graphical user interface that makes it faster and simpler to use. Marriott's One Yield revenue management system helps over 1700 Marriott hotels maximize top-line revenue and enhance inventory decision-making processes.

Yield Management and Cost Control System In addition to a revenue management system, Starwood implemented the new company-wide yield management system in 2001. Similar technological solutions, which focused on capacity control for short-term and medium term, can be found in Interstate Hotels & Resorts and Wyndham Hotel Group.

International expansion and market occupation

In order to increase the overall market share, since entering into the new millennium, multinational hotel firms have taken tremendous steps to continue their global expansion plans. Best Western International announced that it would offer more than 4000 hotels around the globe in 2000. While Homewood Suites by Hilton invested in property development in North America, another mid-priced brand of Hilton, Hilton Garden Inn, continued to introduce new properties in European countries such as Germany and Italy in 2006. Other industrial practitioners, such as InterContinental, Marriott, Choice, and Starwood, all exclusively made their own expansion and growth plans. Specifically, four primary competitive methods were employed: mergers and acquisitions, management contract and franchise, joint ventures with strategic partners in emerging markets, and strategic alliances or partnerships.

Merger and acquisition

Over the past 7 years, major mergers and acquisition transactions in the billions took placed in the international hotel marketplaces, as illustrated in Table 7.2.

To fulfil the expanding plan, multinational hotel firms have been increasingly including special business divisions in their targets of acquisition. For instance, in 2005 TUI AG acquired CP Ship to seek business synergy. In 2006 Cendant purchased Orbitz for $1.2 billion. In 2007 Wyndham Vacation Ownership acquired the sales and marketing business and the physical assets and contractual rights associated with privately held Activities-4-Less, a Maui-based vacation ownership sales and marketing operation in Hawaii.

Table 7.2 International Hotel Industry Mergers and Acquisitions 2000–2007

Year	Company Acquiring	Company Acquired	Value
2000	MGM Grand	Mirage Resorts	$4.4 billion
2005	MGM Mirage	Mandalay Resort Group	$7.9 billion
2005	The Blackstone Group	Wyndham International	$3.24 billion
2005	TUI AG	CP Ships Limited	$2 billion
2005	Marriott International	CTF Holding Ltd.	$1.452 billion
2005	Hilton Hotel Corporation	Hilton International	GBP 3.3 billion
2006	The Blackstone Group	La Quinta Corporation	$3.4 billion
2006	Host Marriott Corporation	Starwood Hotel Portfolio	$4.23 billion
2006	Royal Bank of Scotland Plc	JV of Marriott with Whitbread	$1.69 billion
2007	The Blackstone Group	Hilton Hotels Corporation	$26 billion

Management contract and franchise • • •

The management contract is still a popular means of business expansion widely employed by multinational hotel firms over the past 7 years. It was also a widely used entry mode for penetrating emerging markets. For instance, in 2004 InterContinental signed nine management contracts with Chinese industrial practitioners at one time. Marriott has planned to increase its hotel portfolio in India to 21 properties by 2010, all of which will be run under long-term management contracts. The franchise is another popular method applied by multinational hotel firms to expanding business. However, more firms such as Starwood focus on value creation rather than increasing new franchising contracts. Marriott substantiated its strategy for processing new franchise programmes: "growing selectively with the best operators is more important than growing fast."

Joint venture with strategic partner • • •

Since the beginning of the new millennium, multinational hotel firms have been increasingly forming joint ventures with strategic partners to employ their location-bound assets and mature service and production resources, especially in the emerging markets, such as China, India, and Russia. In 2006, Hilton Hotels Corporation started to create a joint venture company in India with DLF Limited, one of India's leading real estate developers. The project would eventually develop and own 75 hotels and service apartments over the next 7 years. In 2004, TUI entered into the Russian market by forming a joint venture with Mostravel, one of Russia's leading tour operators for trips to Turkey and Egypt.

Strategic alliance • • •

In the new millennium, multinational hotel companies use strategic alliance as an important method to gain competitive advantage. A variety of strategic goals for forming strategic alliances include acquisition of new technology, such as Bass Hotels & Resorts with Lastminute.com; supporting a cross-industry marketing programme, such as InterContinental with AeroMexico Airlines, Japan Airlines, South African Airways, Arabian Airlines, and Air China; enjoying the benefits of business integration across different locations, such as Le Meridien with Nikko Hotels; developing long-term projects, such as MGM Mirage with Peel Holdings PLC, and MGM Mirage with

163 • • •

Pequot Tribal Nation; creating special services to stakeholders, such as Ritz-Carlton Club with The African Collection Choice and with the accounting management consulting firm Grant Thornton LLP; and creating special function for environmental protection, such as Choice with Green Seal.

In light of expanding business in the new market, apart from forming joint venture with important local practitioners—multinational hotel firms also took steps in creating strategic alliance with other investors to penetrate emerging markets. For instance, in 2001 Best Western entered into a strategic alliance with the Korean Group, Business Group for Hospitality, to develop hotels in South Korea. In 2006 Hilton, RREEF, and private equity firm H&Q Asia Pacific together created the alliance intending to introduce more than 20 focused service hotels across China.

Stakeholder relationship management

In order to successfully compete in the international hotel industry, multinational hotel firms have been increasingly allocating resources in relationship management with critical stakeholders—customers, employees, and business partners.

Customer relationship management • • •

Supported by enhanced technology, hotel firms developed and modified a variety of customer loyalty and customer retention programmes. For instance, Six Continents Hotels Inc. competed for increased customer loyalty by continually enhancing and modifying its Priority Club Rewards programme as well as bringing in strong industrial partners for strategic planning and redesigning all of Priority Club Worldwide collateral. In 2004 this programme became the world's largest hotel loyalty programme for the overall InterContinental Hotels Group. Similar point-based guest loyalty programmes can also be found in Marriott, Choice, Hyatt, and many other hotel chains.

Employee relationship management • • •

Apart from a variety of training and development programmes carried out in the hotel industry, multinational hotel companies have launched a range of employee incentive and employee care programmes to improve management–employee relationships as well as boost employee morale and productivity.

For instance, the central management rules of Choice Hotels are to institute policies and practices that can help employees reach their personal goals. Choice has found that incorporating work-life initiatives into organizations is a valuable talent recruitment and retention tool. Choice's interesting work, good benefits, collegial staff, stability, employee development, and community involvement make it a very attractive place to work. Marriott continually received honours for its diversity efforts, especially its support for black workers. Six Continents has continually increased the investment in employee incentive schemes since 2001.

Business partner relationship management ● ● ●

Multinational hotel firms paid special attention to developing a positive relationship with their franchisees, alliances, and associated travel agencies. Choice introduced an incentive for development of the brand that netted a potential $130,000 rebate for Sleep brand franchisees in 2000 and launched a new fee structure greatly enhancing ease of entry into the Rodeway Inn system in 2005. In 2001 Choice launched a corporate realignment project designed to provide sharper strategic focus on delivering value-added services to franchisees. MGM Mirage and Mashantucket Pequot Tribal Nation (MPTN) entered into a strategic alliance agreement in 2006 that was more focused on long-term collaboration, a wide range of technology support and cross-marketing opportunities, enabling the foundation of a substantial alliance relationship. To enhance the relationship with travel agencies, Best Western hotels in cities throughout the U.S. sponsored the evening sessions as well as provided refreshments for Town Hall Meetings for U.S. travel agency owners in 2001. Supported by the modern web technology, Hilton started to offer exceptional Travel Agency Commission Processing and an online resource for agencies to track their incoming and outgoing commissions as well as process future meeting-planner commissions, at www.tacsnet.com from 2006.

Development of new product and services

New products and services deployment ● ● ●

Offering new products and services has always been a competitive strategy in the international hotel industry. A wide range of creative hospitality products and services were developed over the past 7 years. In 2002 Six Continents Hotels made available

21-Day Advance Purchase Rates and last-minute travel deals through Weekend WebSavers. Marriott launched the new service "PrintMe Networks," enabling guests to print from a guest room to a hotel printer via their personal PCs. Holiday Inn developed the "Best Breaks" rate as a complement to its award-winning "Best-4-Breakfast" menu in 2003 and introduced low-carb breakfast "Low-Carb InspirationsTM" in 2004. The "Total Trip Pricing" service was launched by Marriott in 2006, allowing potential guests to calculate room rate plus applicable taxes, surcharges, and any fees before guests completed reservations.

Innovation in service concept • • •

In response to intensive competition, multinational hotel firms have been increasingly focused on offering new and innovative features to customers so as to establish competitive advantages. In 2000 Sheraton started to create the "home style" hotel rooms particularly for business travellers in the properties across the U.S. The new "Grand Bed" debut in 2004 provided guests staying in Hyatt hotels with more luxurious, comfortable, and novel experiences. Hyatt Place hotels also feature the Gallery, an innovative welcoming arrival area where guests are personally greeted by the Gallery Host, a dynamic new position in the hospitality industry that encompasses everything from guest check-in to giving personal tours of the hotel. In 2007, Hilton launched two new hotels in the U.K., reflecting the company's move towards "new look" contemporary and design-led lifestyle.

Engaging in research practice • • •

In order to provide substantiated support for service and product innovation, some multinational hotel firms have taken the initiative of organizing or sponsoring business-related research and studies. As part of a strategy to better meet the needs of the growing ranks of women business travellers, InterContinental and Crowne Plaza Hotels and Resorts in 2000 formed a Travel Advisory Council under the aegis of the Project Future initiative to bring together female business leaders to address gender-specific issues as they relate to the travel experience, and to help recommend possible new products and service offerings. Best Western combined the customer research function with its powerful online applications. La Quinta also based its new Return Guest loyalty programme on comprehensive research regarding programme members, hotel guests, and general managers. In order to identify how guests combine work and leisure activities while travelling, Hilton Garden Inn conducted extensive research which led to the new hotel concept of "personal business."

Change of business structure

In order to catch up or even play the leading role in the fast-paced and frequently changing business environment, an increasing number of multinational hotel firms conducted business re-engineering and restructuring.

Spin-offs of peripheral assets • • •

To enhance the operation efficiency and financial return on asset, many hotel companies continued to spin off their non-core strategic assets. In 2000, Starwood announced the agreement to sell the Desert Inn for $270 million. In the same year, to reduce debt incurred from acquisition, MGM Grand Inc. sold approximately $13 million in assets that consisted predominately of paintings from the collection at the former Bellagio Gallery of Fine Art. As part of the continuation of its strategy of continuing to grow its management and franchise businesses and reduce asset ownership, InterContinental Hotels Group disposed of approximately £500 million of hotel assets in 2004. Marriott also made efforts to sell its senior living services. Similar spin-off strategy was also applied by Starwood, Hilton, etc.

Reshaping organization structure • • •

Shaping organization structure is another strategy widely used by multinational hotel firms for improving management and operation efficiency. Creation of a new business division, decentralization, and integration took place in many hotel enterprises.

In 2000, La Quinta Inn decentralized its operation organization and Starwood established Starwood Vacation Ownership to further integrate its vacation ownership subsidiary and further capitalize on the synergies between Starwood and its vacation ownership division. Aiming to improve efficiency and streamline cost, InterContinental Hotels Group unveiled the shape of the new organization in Asia Pacific in 2003. This included an integrated sales and marketing focus, to extend brand leadership across the region and consistently drive revenue, demand

and system delivery across IHG's hotels portfolio. In order to make the production and marketing of holidays more efficient, TUI moved the holiday production of the airtours brand from Frankfurt to Hanover and merged its tour operation and distribution activities into a single powerful marketing entity in 2006.

Naming critical personnel • • •

To improve management operation and working team productivity over the past 7 years, multinational hotel firms frequently named new core management personnel or changed personnel. The concerned positions were concentrated on functions such as IT, marketing, and strategic management. New chief management positions were also added in accordance with the specific company's strategy. For instance, 10 new Regional Vice Presidents of operations were added in La Quinta Inn in 2000.

Marketing initiatives and campaigns

To successfully compete in the fast-moving business environment and effectively communicate with the target market and customer, multinational hotel firms applied a variety of marketing strategies.

Special promotion programme • • •

Many multinational hotel firms launched different promotion campaigns aimed at targeting specific customer groups. Best Western's "Summer Adventure," Choice's "Fee Gas" campaign, and Holiday Inn's "Big Sale" were all successful cases of special sales promotions that took place in the hotel industry. To promote the brand image as an ideal upscale hotel choice for small-to mid-sized business meetings, Crowne Plaza rolled out the logo "The Place To Meet," combining three key components and representing a completely unique and powerful positioning for Crowne Plaza in the meetings segment. Shangri-La Hotels & Resorts launched a Female Executive Traveler Program in 2003, with the aim of providing the female business traveller with further convenience and comfort during her stay.

Co-promoting with marketing partner • • •

Multinational hotel companies have increasingly taken advantage of co-promoting supported by strategic business partnerships. For instance, partnering with Diners Club International, InterContinental launched the Diners Club Double Weekend Options promotion across 20 InterContinental Hotels and Resorts in 14 countries in Asia Pacific in 2003. In the summer of 2006, Embassy Suites Hotels worked as the official hotel partner of Build-A-Bear Workshop to support the Find-A-Bear ID Program.

Brand repositioning ● ● ●

Brand repositioning is the strategy taken by multinationals to alter or maintain the brand image portrayed to consumers. This involves manipulating the marketing programme and organizational processes to maintain or improve the equity of a brand (Aaker, 1991). It has been a widely used competitive method in the international hotel industry in the new millennium. In 2004, Cendant Corporation's Hotel Group launched a multimillion-dollar repositioning of its Ramada brand aimed at improving overall product quality, guest experience, and value. This action was designed to ensure its future growth and competitiveness in the mid-market segment. Staring in 2002, Starwood has put a comprehensive plan into force to upgrade the Sheraton brand. This has included a number of key elements—better beds, new room design, renovation of flagship, new prototype, tougher standards, and brand clean-up. The re-ignition of the Hilton brand flagship programme has effectively enhanced the profile and customer loyalty to the company.

Image advertising campaign ● ● ●

Multinational hotel firms have increasingly focused on using concentrated advertising campaigns as means of promoting company image. Choice's "Thanks for Travelling" advertising programme in 2001 significantly promoted its image, especially after the "9–11" attack. In 2004, Hilton launched its "Take Me To The Hilton" image campaign aimed at positioning Hilton as the number one solution to some of the most commonly voiced concerns among modern-day travellers. It combined fresh imagery with straightforward text. In the summer of 2006, in order to increase its visibility in emerging markets around the globe, Hyatt launched an ambitious TV and print advertising campaign that included an image-building television commercial and a series of three print ads that accentuated the versatility of Hyatt properties catering to high-end meetings business.

Internet marketing • • •

The Internet was also increasingly used by multinational hotel firms as an important marketing channel. Hiltonjourneys. com, the online element of the new Hilton campaign, received international accolades from two sites honouring the best in creative content on the Internet, especially for its great role in the campaign of "Travel Should Take You Places" launched by Hilton Hotels Corporation in 2006. Both Best Western and InterContinental reported strong Internet marketing outcomes and improved functioning of their Internet marketing team. Marriott won the 2006 Internet Advertising Competition judged by the panel of The Web Marketing Association.

Effective pricing • • •

Although discount pricing is not an innovative strategy for gaining competitive advantage, it was still widely used by many multinational hotel firms. In order to effectively target the baby boomer group, Choice launched a promotion programme in 2000, allowing travellers 50 years of age and older to receive a 10% discount at all Choice hotels and travellers 60 years of age and over to receive a 20–30% discount at participating hotels. Beginning in 2002, All AAA members received a minimum 10% discount off regularly published room rates at Best Western hotels due to the joint marketing agreement between Best Western and AAA. In 2005, franchisees of Travelodge were deeply encouraged to tap into discount pricing, rebate opportunities, and the potential for free equipment in the company-wide "ultimate value equation" programme.

Quality consistency and improvement

Being a repeat business, hotel service requires a high level of quality consistency. Therefore, pursuing continuous quality improvement can help multinational hotel firms achieve customer satisfaction, gain advantages over competitors, and increase profitability. Several competitive methods were employed by multinational hotel firms centring on maintaining quality consistency and achieving quality improvement.

Investing in human assets • • •

The investment in human assets centred on a series of education, training and career development programmes launched in the hotel industry. Since 2002 MGM Mirage has employed a diversity education programme as a key factor in helping create a unified company vision and a culture of shared values between its employees from different backgrounds. By 2005 more than 1200 employees had completed Diversity Champion workshops—an industry-training first that fused leadership, diversity, and professional development during intense classroom instruction. Also, in 2005, Best Western International launched its Best Western Certified Manager Program and Best Western Learning Series for the owners and managers of its North American hotels. Shangri-La Hotels and Resorts, China's largest luxury hotel group, opened Shangri-La Academy to centralize employee training near Beijing. It features progressive training methods that focus on critical thinking, problem-solving and empowerment.

Property renovation ● ● ●

Many multinational hotel firms continued their property innovation projects in the new millennium to enhance brand image and to meet changed customer requirements. Sheraton started its $350 million, 2-year renovation programme in order to make the brand consistent and friendlier to families and business travellers. InterContinental started to invest $1 billion refurbishing major InterContinental properties around the world in 2002. Since the beginning of the new millennium, large renovation projects have also taken place in the individual properties of Choice, La Quinta, Best Western, and Marriott, etc.

Upgrading service standards ● ● ●

Many multinational hotel firms also upgraded their service standards to match increased customer needs and changed competitive environment. For instance, Best Western launched the new quality initiatives concentrating on the establishment of parallel-service-standards enhancement with a simplified design-evaluation process worldwide. To successfully implement the standards, the organization of Best Western assembled a special team of quality assurance experts to visit and review the quality of Best Western property and assist owners in enhancing quality and guest satisfaction as well as profitability.

Quality performance rewards and evaluation ● ● ●

Multinational hotel firms also applied relevant rewards and evaluation protocol as tools to encourage internal properties and franchisees to maintain quality consistency. For instance, in 2005, Doubletree launched its newly designed "Most Improved Quality Award." Intensively focusing on results of guest surveys, the new quality assessment programme, supported by the most updated Guest Endorsement System, was introduced at InterContinental in 2003. The programme uses three criteria that compose the hotel's quality score: performance on physical product-related questions, performance on service-related questions, and the average of responses on key questions designed to determine the guest's intent to return to that hotel.

Social awareness and environmental sensation

Showing concern for social issues and practicing for natural environment protection have been regarded as important corporate norms for multinational firms. Multinational hotel firms have increasingly allocated resources to community development projects, natural disaster assistance programmes, and environmental protection programmes to improve brand image as well as gain economic benefits.

Partnership for community development • • •

In 2000, Starwood launched a new community service programme, StarCare for the Community, which encouraged Starwood employees to donate 8h per year to volunteer activities within their communities. To assist the programme, Starwood partnered with America's Promise and City Cares, which have the capability of matching Starwood volunteers with non-profit organizations and community service events in cities across the U.S. MGM Mirage entered into a partnership agreement with Jeanco Realty Development to form a joint venture. The purpose of this partnership master plan is a mixed-use development of an undeveloped site and the creation of a community featuring residential, commercial, and retail elements in addition to a new hotel casino.

Aid programme for regions wrecked by natural disaster • • •

Some multinational hotel firms provided regions that were wrecked by natural disasters with economic aid as the means for improving company image and brand awareness. For instance, TUI AG set up a long-term aid programme for the crisis region in Southeast Asia that was destroyed by the tsunami, and carried out a total of €1.25 million for the measures in 2005.

Environmental protection practice • • •

Because of the increasing global concern over changing natural environment, more and more multinational hotel firms have correspondingly developed management rules or conducted operation practices to fulfil the initiatives of environmental protection and meanwhile to achieve economic benefits or improve brand awareness. Open in 2003, the Best Western Agnes Water Beach Club, Australia's most impressive and technologically advanced, environmentally sensitive, fully self-sustainable resort, achieved the designed goal of creating a new benchmark for ecotourism and self-sustained development. Starwood set up special management leadership to reduce greenhouse gas emission. In 2005, TUI AG was certified in accordance with international environmental standard DIN EN ISO 14001, indicating that both its in-house system as well as the group-wide environmental management system gained the worldwide recognized certification stamp for environmental standards. In 2006, Marriott was recognized for saving more than 83 million kilowatt-hours (kwh) of electric energy consumption, the equivalent of lighting Washington, DC, for 3 months; and reducing greenhouse gas emissions by 68,000 tons annually, the equivalent of removing 15,000 cars from the road or planting 1,500,000 trees per year.

Summary

Comparison of the competitive methods between the New Millennium and the period 1995–1999

The competitive methods contributed by Zhao (2000) are categorized into eight categories. They are: rapid information technological development; international expansion and market cooperation; relationship management; customer-oriented products and services development; structure re-engineering; new marketing initiatives and campaigns; quality control; and social awareness and environmental protection. The conformity between the overall categorical structure used in this research and that used for the last period indicates a high level of realistic prediction in the previous research with respect to the evolution of the international hotel industry over the last decade. However, comparison between the corresponding categories from the two periods still reveals some differences. The specific differences as well as similarities are summarized as follows:

- The fast development of information technology still works as the most significant driving force for influencing multinational hotel companies to create their competitive methods. Advanced technologies have brought a wide range of options that can help hotel firms gain competitive advantages. Hotel firms have been increasingly invested in this area, thus intensive competition is inevitable. Although the majority of IT-related competitive methods in the new millennium are similar to those of the last period, there has been a significant evolution of technology to an improved mature level. More features and functions have been created, and most of the technologies have been upgraded to a new level. More powerful, cost-effective, and easy-to-use technologies have won the competition. It is expected that tremendous change will take place in the near future in this field. However, when comparing the competitive methods of the two periods, the wide adoption of wireless technology and related applications seems to be the most remarkable difference.

- Mergers and acquisitions are still important ways for multinational hotel firms to implement international expansion strategy. Cross-industry and cross-sector mergers and acquisitions have reached a greater level. This was not so salient in the earlier period. These indicated multinational hotel companies have been increasingly concentrated on achieving competitive advantages by integrating business divisions and implementing economies of scale. In terms of applying joint venture and strategic alliance as expansion methods, more attention has been paid to finding a critical strategic partner, especially in the emerging market.

- The importance of strategic stakeholder relationship management has been widely recognized in the international hotel industry. Many relevant programmes have been launched, and application of new information technology has become a critical way to process the relationship-related management.

- Innovation has become a key competitive method used by multinational hotel firms. Compared to those of the last period, the new product and service development in the new millennium is more concerned with concept design and innovation. Direct investment and resource allocation in research activities is a star point found in this research.

- Spinning off non-core strategic assets, reshaping organizational structure, and naming critical personnel are still critical competitive methods in terms of structure change. More significantly, division and function integration across a large geographical scope has attracted increasing concerns from the strategic decision makers of multinational hotel firms.

- In terms of market campaigns and initiatives, some traditional methods, such as co-promotion, special sales promotion, and discounted price still play important roles in the overall portfolio of competitive methods. However, this research reveals that instead of specific service packages or products, the overall company brand and image have become the main promoting targets of marketing campaigns.
- In order to maintain consistent service quality, multinational hotel firms have increasingly focused on human asset development. The most useful way is to improve employee education, training, and personal development. Service standard management and upgrading has been a particular concern of multinational hotel firms. This topic was not as extensively researched in the earlier period.
- With respect to social awareness and environmental protection practices, strategic partnerships for community development and aid projects for regions wrecked by natural disasters are two new methods which were not emphasized in previous studies.

Conclusion and implication

In this chapter a total of 36 competitive methods adopted by multinational hotel companies over the last 7 years have been reported. The overall conformity between the results of the two research studies at categorical level implies that the international hotel industry is experiencing a special period in which the function of critical influencing factors is being accumulated. The relatively slight differences existing in each category indicate the complexity of the competitive environment. In the meantime this also implies that time has become a critical factor for judging the business environment, as increased previous competitive methods are being increasing transferred into CSFs at the overall industrial level. Multinational hotel firms must be able to examine the business environment in which they locate and determine appropriate strategy to balance resource between different strategic choices.

More importantly, multinational hotel firms must understand the environmental driving force that is likely to have a profound influence on their business. For example, this research revealed that private equity firms such as Blackstone have become the most powerful investor and intervener in the international hotel industry. But how to create a relevant competitive method supported by this kind of investor and intervener remains unclear. Further research focused on such issues should be conducted by both industrial practitioners and academic scholars.

References

Aaker, D. A. (1991). *Managing Brand Equity*. New York: The Free Press.

Baker, S., and Baker, K. (1995). *Desktop Direct Marketing—How to use up-to-the-minute Technologies to Find and Reach New Customers*. New York: McGraw-Hill.

Berry, L. L., Seiders, K., and Gresham, L. G. (1997). For love and money: The common traits of successful retailers. *Managing Service Quality*, 26(2), 7–23.

Bharadwaj, S. G., Varadarajan, P. R., and Fahy, J. (1993). Sustainable competitive advantage in service industries: A conceptual model and research propositions. *Journal of Marketing*, 57(October), 83–99.

Boardman, A. E., and Vining, A. R. (1996). Defining your business using product-customer matrices. *Long Range Planning*, 29(1), 38–48.

Bowman, C., and Faulkner, D. (1997). *Competitive and Corporate Strategy*. London: Irwin.

Brotherton, B. (2004). Critical success factors in UK corporate hotels. *The Service Industries Journal*, 24(3), 19–43.

Brotherton, B., and Shaw, J. (1996). Towards an identification and classification of critical success factors in UK hotels Plc. *International Journal of Hospitality Management*, 15(2), 113–135.

Buzzell, R. D., and Gale, B. T. (1987). *The PIMS Principles*. New York, NY: Free Press.

Cai, L. A., and Hobson, J. S. P. (2004). Making hotel brands work in a competitive environment. *Journal of Vacation Marketing*, 10(3), 197–208.

Campbell-Hunt, C. (2000). What have we learned about generic competitive strategy? A meta-analysis. *Strategic Management Journal*, 21(2), 127–154.

Candido, C. J. F. (2005). Service quality strategy implementation: A model and the case of the Algarve hotel industry. *Total Quality Management and Business Excellence*, 16(1), 3–14.

Chandler, A. (1962). *Strategy and Structure: Chapters in the History of American Enterprise*. Cambridge, MA: MIT Press.

Cho, W., and Olsen, M. D. (1998). A case study approach to understanding the impact of information technology on competitive advantage in the lodging industry. *Journal of Hospitality and Tourism Research*, *22*(4), 376–394.

Chrisman, J. J., Hofer, C. W., and Boulton, W. R. (1988). Toward a system of classifying business strategies. *Academy of Management Review*, *13*(3), 413–428.

Claver-Cortés, E., Molina-Azorín, J. F., and Pereira-Moliner, J. (2006). The impact of strategic behaviors on hotel performance. *International Journal of Contemporary Hospitality Management*, *19*(1), 6–20.

Crook, T. R., Ketchen, Jr, D. J., and Snow, C. C. (2003). Competitive edge: A strategic management model. *Cornell Hotel and Restaurant Administration Quarterly*, *44*(3), 44–53.

David, F. (2002). *Strategic Management: Concepts* (9th ed.). Upper Saddle River, NJ: Prentice-Hall.

Day, G. S., and Wensley, R. (1988). Assessing advantage: A framework for diagnosing competitive superiority. *Journal of Marketing*, *52*(April), 1–20.

Dess, G. G., and Davis, P. S. (1984). Porter's generic strategies as determinants of strategic group membership and performance. *Academy of Management Journal*, *26*(3), 467–488.

Devaraj, S., Hollingworth, D. G., and Schroeder, R. G. (2004). Generic manufacturing strategies and plant performance. *Journal of Operations Management*, *22*(3), 313–333.

Dimou, I., Chen, J., and Archer, S. (2003). The choice between management contracts and franchise agreements in the corporate development of international hotel firms. *Journal of Marketing Channels*, *10*(3,4), 33–52.

Fairlie, R. (1995). *Database Marketing and Direct Mail: A Practical Guide to the Techniques and Applications*. Herts: Kogan Page.

Fréry, F. (2006). The fundamental dimensions of strategy. *MIT Sloan Management Review*, *48*(1), 71–78.

Gayeski, D. M., and Petrillose, M. J. (2005). No strings attached: How the gaming and hospitality industry uses mobile devices to engineer performance. *Performance Improvement*, *44*(2), 25–31.

Hawes, J. M., and Crittendon, W. F. (1984). A taxonomy of competitive retailing strategies. *Strategic Management Journal*, *5*(2), 275–287.

Helms, M. M., Dibrell, C., and Wright, P. (1997). Competitive strategies and business performance: Evidence from the adhesives and sealants industry. *Management Decision*, *35*(9), 678–692.

Hill, C. W. L. (1988). Differentiation versus low cost or differentiation and low cost? A contingency framework. *Academy of Management Review*, *13*(3), 401–412.

Hitt, M. A., and Ireland, D. R. (1985). Corporate distinctive competence, strategy, industry and performance. *Strategic Management Journal*, *6*(3), 273–293.

Holverson, S., and Revaz, F. (2006). Perceptions of European independent hoteliers: Hard and soft branding choices. *International Journal of Contemporary Hospitality Management*, *18*(5), 398–413.

Hueng, V. C. S. (2003). Internet usage by international travelers: Reasons and barriers. *International Journal of Contemporary Hospitality Management*, *15*(7), 370–378.

Jain, R., and Jain, S. (2005). Towards relational exchange in services marketing: Insights from hospitality industry. *Journal of Services Research*, *5*(2), 139–150.

Keating, M., and Harrington, D. (2003). The challenges of implementing quality in the Irish hotel industry. *Journal of European Industrial Training*, *27*(8/9), 441–453.

Kerin, R. A., Mahajan, V., and Varadarajan, P. R. (1990). *Contemporary Perspectives on Strategic Market Planning*. Boston, MA: Allyn and Bacon.

Knox, A., and Walsh, J. (2005). Organizational flexibility and HRM in the hotel industry: Evidence from Australia. *Human Resource Management Journal*, *15*(1), 57–75.

Kotha, S., and Vadlamani, B. L. (1995). Assessing generic strategies: An empirical investigation of two competing typologies in discrete manufacturing industries. *Strategic Management Journal*, *16*(1), 75–83.

Lai, K. K., and Ng, W. L. (2003). A stochastic approach to hotel revenue optimization. *Computers and Operations Research*, *32*(5), 1059–1072.

Law, R., and Jogaratnam, G. (2005). A study of hotel information technology applications. *International Journal of Contemporary Hospitality Management*, *17*(2/3), 170–180.

Magnini, V. P., Honeycutt, E. D., Jr., and Hodge, S. K. (2003). Data mining for hotel firms: Use and limitations. *Cornell Hotel and Restaurant Administration Quarterly*, *44*(2), 94–105.

Martin, L. M. (2004). E-innovation: Internet impacts on small UK hospitality firms. *International Journal of Contemporary Hospitality Management*, *16*(2), 82–90.

Mayer, K. J., and Lapidus, R. S. (1998). Database marketing: A potent tool for hospitality marketers. *FIU Hospitality Review*, *16*(1), 45–57.

Miller, D., and Friesen, P. H. (1986). Porter's generic strategies and performance: An empirical examination with American data. *Organization Studies*, *7*(1), 37–55.

Mintzberg, H. (1978). Patterns in strategy formation. *Management Science*, *24*(9), 934–948.

Mintzberg, H. (1988). Generic strategies toward a comprehensive framework. *Advances in Strategic Management*, *5*, 1–67.

Mintzberg, H., and Waters, J. A. (1985). Of strategies deliberate and emergent. *Strategic Management Journal*, *6*(3), 57–72.

Murray, A. I. (1988). A contingency view of Porter's 'generic strategies'. *Academy of Management Review*, *13*(3), 390–400.

Olsen, M. D., West, J., and Tse, E. (1998). *Strategic Management in the Hospitality Industry* (2nd ed.). New York: Wiley.

Parnell, J. A. (1997). New evidence in the generic strategy and business performance debate: A research note. *British Journal of Management*, *8*(2), 175–181.

Parnell, J. A. (2006). Generic strategies after two decades: A reconceptualization of competitive strategy. *Management Decision*, *44*(8), 1139–1154.

Porter, M. E. (1980). *Competitive strategy*. New York: Free Press.

Porter, M. E. (1981). The contributions of industrial organization to strategic management. *Academy of Management Review*, *6*(4), 609–620.

Porter, M. E. (1985). *Competitive Advantage: Creating ands Sustaining Superior Performance*. New York: The Free Press.

Presbury, R., Fitzgerald, A., and Chapman, R. (2005). Impediments to improvements in service quality in luxury hotels. *Managing Service Quality*, *15*(4), 357–373.

Proff, H. (2000). Hybrid strategies as a strategic challenge: The case of the German automotive industry. *Omega*, *28*(5), 541.

Robinson, R. B., and Pearce, J. A. (1988). Planned patterns of strategic behavior and their relationship to business unit performance. *Strategic Management Journal*, *9*(1), 43–60.

Sigala, M., Lockwood, A., and Jones, P. (2001). Strategic implementation and IT: Gaining competitive advantage from the hotel reservations process. *International Journal of Contemporary Hospitality Management*, *13*(7), 364–371.

Tracey, J. B. (2003). Human resources roundtable 2003: Current issues and future developments. *Cornell Hotel and Restaurant Administration Quarterly*, *45*(4), 373–375.

White, R. E. (1986). Generic business strategies, organizational context and performance: An empirical investigation. *Strategic Management Journal*, *7*(2), 217–231.

Wilton, N. (2006). Strategic choice and organizational context in HRM in the UK hotel sector. *The Service Industries Journal*, *26*(8), 903–919.

Wright, P. (1987). A refinement of Porter's strategies. *Strategic Management Journal*, *8*(1), 93–101.

Yelkur, R., and DaCosta, M. M. N. (2001). Differential pricing and segmentation on the Internet: The case of hotels. *Management Decision*, *39*(4), 252–261.

Zhao, J. L. (2000). Competitive methods of multinational hotel companies—A five-year review, 1995–99. In Hamilin, H. (Ed.), *Leading Hospitality into the Age of Excellence, Expansion, Competition and Vision in the Multinational Hotel Industry 1995–2005*, International Hotel & Restaurant Association White Paper, Paris 2000.

CHAPTER 8

The importance of intangible assets: trends and patterns

Francis A. Kwansa[1], Cynthia Mayo[2] and Tevfik Demirciftci[3]

*[1]Associate Chair, HRIM Department,
University of Delaware, Newark, DE
[2]Program Director, Hospitality Management,
Delaware State University, Dover, DE
[3]HRIM Department, University of Delaware,
Newark, DE*

Introduction

Business environment in the United States, along with the rest of the industrialized world, has changed tremendously over the last two decades. For example, many of the things for which companies used to charge a fee are now given away to customers and clients for free and the support services which used to be free now attract a fee. The current business reality in most industrialized countries is that their economies are dominated by outputs that are mainly services or experiences. About two-thirds of U.S. GDP is created by services or what is termed intangibles "products."

Today there are relatively fewer investments in tangible assets such as factories, machinery and equipment, buildings, land, and other primary resources. These assets, such as property, plant and equipment, are still considered significant elements for manufacturing and service companies; however, they have lost their importance. Intangible assets significantly define the way business is conducted, how revenues are generated, and how enterprise value is created.

Intangible assets are defined as non-physical factors that contribute to or are used in producing goods or providing services that are expected to generate future economic benefits for the individuals or firms that control their use. Examples of these include:

- Ideas
- Mailing lists
- Databases
- Business and operating processes
- Relevant repertoire of business experiences
- Service reputation
- Customer relationships
- Vendor/supplier relationships
- Loyalty programmes
- Human capital
- Intellectual capital

Their possession and use of the assets enable businesses to achieve results that they would otherwise not have been able to achieve. Thus, such assets create value for the enterprise just as tangible assets. Today some industries, such as the software industry, are highly dependent on intellectual assets to achieve a healthy bottom-line profit (Kapardis and Thomas, 2006). The labour-intensive hospitality industry is another example of an industry whose success is dependent on human capital. There are several characteristics of intangible assets that make them unique:

1. Intangible assets are difficult to quantify and measure directly. It is easier to answer the question, "What was your average daily rate yesterday?" than to answer the question, "How satisfied were your customers last night?"
2. Generally these assets do not appear on corporate balance sheets. Thus they cannot be directly reflected in the company's net worth.
3. The assets are expensed on the corporate income statement rather than capitalized.
4. If identified and properly utilized, they can represent a source of competitive advantage to the business that owns them.
5. Often the value they create depends on investments in complementary intangible assets.
6. Intangible assets, unless copyrighted or patented, are often not protected from competitors. They are easily duplicated.
7. They must be harnessed. Simply having such assets without a deliberate attempt and effort to utilize them will yield no benefit to the business.
8. Many intangible assets tend to be out of the control of management, consequently they can be very difficult to manage.

The above characteristics underscore the challenges faced by accounting and finance professionals in fully embracing the call to compute and reflect these valuable assets in the book values of companies.

Traditionally, the book value of a company is calculated as the difference between its assets and liabilities at historical cost less the value of preferred stock (if any). The market value of the company represents what investors are willing to pay for the business considering its future growth opportunities, its ability to generate profits, and remain profitable in the future. This market value fully reflects all available public information about the company, particularly those that will yield future economic benefits. Investors are motivated, first, by the chance to receive dividends today and the growth in dividends in the future. This dividend growth is directly influenced by the growth in a company's profits and cash flows. Second, they are motivated by stock price appreciation which is driven by the company's financial and operating performance along with prospects for growth in the future. So the company's market value is determined by multiplying the closing stock price by the number of common stock outstanding. The business intangible value represents the difference between the book value of the net assets (i.e., assets minus liabilities) and the market value. This difference has been growing larger and larger in the last decade due to increased corporate investments in intangible assets.

Intellectual capital is an example of an intangible asset that has received a great deal of attention in the trade press. Brooking (1996) defined it as "the term given to the combined intangible assets which enable the company to function." Stewart (1997) defined intellectual capital as "packaged useful knowledge." Stewart (1997) also added that organizational processes, technologies, patents, employee's skills, and information about customers, suppliers, and stakeholders are all considered part of this definition. The next section will focus some attention on intellectual capital.

The components of intellectual capital

Edvinson and Malone (1997) identified three types of intellectual capital. These are human capital, structural capital, and customer capital. Human capital comprises of knowledge, skills, and abilities of employees. Human capital is specific to the people and does not belong to the organization. In addition, human capital also includes how effectively an organization utilizes its employee in terms of creativity and innovation. Structural capital is everything used to assist employees in their work. Structural capital is regarded as the supportive infrastructure that helps employees work effectively and efficiently. Structural capital does belong to the organization. Traditional things such as buildings, hardware, software, processes, patents, and trademark are considered as the components of structural capital. Organization's image, organizational structure, information systems, and databases can also be part of structural capital (Bhartesh and Bandyopadhyay, 2005). Edvinson and Malone (1997) broadened the classification of structural capital further into organizational, process, and innovation capital. Organizational capital deals with the organization's philosophy and systems. Process capital includes the techniques, procedures, and programmes that improve and develop the delivery of goods and services. Intellectual properties, such as copyrights, patents, and trademarks, which protect the commercial rights of the owners, are considered examples of innovation capital. Customer capital is related to the strength and loyalty of the company's customer relations. Customer satisfaction, repeat business, financial well-being, and price sensitivity are the components of customer capital (Bhartesh and Bandyopadhyay, 2005).

Intangible assets and their usage by various industries

Intangible assets enable companies to gain competitive advantage. According to the 2000 report of the European Commission's High Level Expert Group, a firm's intangible assets are seen as the main element in its competitiveness. More and more, the capacity to unite external and internal sources of knowledge to take advantage of commercial opportunities has transformed this capacity into a distinctive competency (Eustace, 2000). Intangibles also allow companies to analyse and predict future business performance. For example, Sears Roebuck and Company (now Sears Inc.) created a tool to measure employee satisfaction, and monitor the relationship between this metric, customer loyalty, and financial performance. The company discovered that a 5-unit increase in employee attitude provided a 1.3-unit increase in customer impression and consequently revenue increased by 0.5% (Low and Kalafut, 2002). In another example, Southwest Airlines invested significantly in their human resources department in order to hire people who can adapt to their corporate culture. In 1998, 140,000 people applied to work for Southwest Airlines; 90,000 were interviewed; and only 4200 were hired by the airline. The hiring process was very expensive; however, it created impressive results for Southwest Airlines. At the end of September 2001, Southwest's price to sales ratio had climbed to 2.10 compared to an industry average of 1.35 (Low and Kalafut, 2002).

Intangibles that drive corporate business performance

In their book, *The Invisible Advantage*, Low and Kalafut (2002) identified 12 intangible assets that have continued to widen the gap between the book and market values of today's corporations. This section will discuss the intangibles.

Leadership

Corporate CEOs were unknown to the public 20–30 years ago, they stayed behind the scenes to direct and manage their companies. Today, CEOs have become the spokespersons for their company's products and many have been successful at it. Examples include the late Dave Thomas of Wendy's, Michael Eisner formerly of Disney, Lee Iacocca formerly of Chrysler, Donald Trump, Bill Gates, and Charles Schwab of Schwab and Company. Some of today's CEOs are like rock stars in their popularity (e.g., Sir Richard Branson of Virgin Group). In a

1977 survey the results showed that 77% of investors are likely to purchase stock based on the reputation of the CEO. Thus it matters who leads the company and the leadership qualities he/she possesses. In a study by Mayo and Nohria, (2005), the author compiled data on 860 leading U.S. business figures in the past 100 years that generated outstanding shareholder value over a 15-year period to their companies. The most common trait among these business figures that made them successful was "contextual intelligence"—the ability to understand and capitalize on the sweeping trends influencing the marketplace of their time. Therefore, a company with the right CEO will enjoy a price premium on the stock market.

Strategy execution

Corporate strategy describes the roadmap that sets a company on the path to achieve its mission. Most corporations have a strategy; however, the more successful companies are the ones that are able to effectively execute the strategy. Strategy execution is a company's ability to do what it says it will do. This ability is challenged daily due to the high level of competition that exists in all industries today. The competition is both domestic and global making it quite difficult to sustain competitive advantage. Those companies that deliver effectively on their promises to customers are able to prevail over the competition and therefore are very attractive on the stock market to potential shareholders. Such companies enjoy a premium on the stock market due to their superior ability to execute their corporate strategy. For example, Wal-Mart has become one of the most successful global companies because it attracts and retains its customers by offering good quality products at low prices consistently. Its mission is to give ordinary people the chance to buy the same things as rich people, and through its efficient supply-chain management system, utilizing technology, and reducing employee turnover Wal-Mart has been successful in delivering on its promise to customers worldwide.

Communication and transparency

Information today is readily available, thanks to the ubiquitous internet. Consequently people are better informed, and when they seek information they expect it to be readily available. Therefore, except in very specific cases, there is little value in companies holding back information from shareholders and the public at large. The more forthcoming a company is about its financial and operating results the more trustworthy its management is perceived. As a result, the more information a company provides the more attractive it will become to potential investors, creditors, suppliers, and customers. Today lodging and foodservice companies routinely measure customer satisfaction index, employee satisfaction index, the impact of community involvement activities, brand strength, and many more. Such data are now made available to operational managers and employees to enable them to perform effectively and to be accountable.

Another trend that is forcing public corporations to be more transparent and communicative is the rise of activist shareholders. In the past shareholders tended to defer to management and the board of directors to make decisions on their behalf and trusted that these agents would make choices that would be in the best interest of shareholders. With the unprecedented failures of WorldCom, Enron, Global Crossing, Tyco, and many more, shareholder trust and confidence in management and directors have dropped leading to an erosion of the traditional deference (Anonymous, 2007). Representatives of institutional investors and individual shareholder activist now sit on corporate boards to ensure that transparency prevails. Public companies that are transparent tend to enjoy transparency capital which contributes to their intangible value on the market.

Brand equity

Brand represents a cluster of attributes and emotions that customers associate with a product or service. When the U.S. marines declare that they "are looking for a few good men" it is clear in the public's mind the type of person the marines recruit. There is a definite perception of confidence and success that the public has about business leaders such as Donald Trump and Richard Branson and this perception carries over into the enterprises in which they are involved. If this image and perception of a brand is strong enough it has the ability to deliver positive sustainable financial performance over the long term. Well managed brands yield higher profit margins with lower risk and those which do not invest in their brands and manage them strategically often experience declines in financial performance and shareholder value over time.

Reputation

This describes how a company is viewed by the public at large, including customers, suppliers, investors, employees, other businesses, regulators, and the community at large. This view that the public has of a company, favourable or unfavourable, can be enduring. Companies spend years to carefully cultivate their reputations of trust, innovativeness (e.g., 3 M), responsiveness, customer service (e.g., Nordstrom), social responsibility (e.g., The Body Shop), fun (e.g., Virgin Group), and many more. Yet in today's environment of consumer empowerment coupled with easy access to the internet it is easy to destroy a company's reputation that took years to build by carefully placed unfavourable information about the company. Another phenomenon that has gained currency over the last two decades is that consumers, in a cooperative manner, can reward or punish companies by giving or withholding patronage. The Adams Mark Hotel chain and the Denny's Restaurant chain are examples of corporations whose businesses have suffered from the boycotts by African-American consumers due to evidence of discriminatory practices towards Blacks. Therefore it is imperative for a company to monitor its reputation in the public domain and to manage it strategically such that it enhances the corporate image and adds to its market value.

Networks and alliances

In today's competitive environment it is impossible for a company to be all to its customers and to be able to do everything by itself. Thus partnerships have become a necessary component of doing business. For example, the top 500 global corporations average about 60 major strategic alliances (Dyer *et al.*, 2001). Some alliances and partnerships are obvious, such as car rental, hotel, and lodging companies. Since airlines cannot cover every route and yet they need to meet their customers' need for air transportation from their home to their destination, airlines have created strategic alliances such as One World and Star Alliance. This enables, for example, USAir to carry a Lufthansa passenger during a time of day that Lufthansa would not have aircraft flying from Philadelphia to Frankfurt. By code sharing airlines are able to maximize their yield and not lose potential business. Another example is Avendra LLC, a company founded in 2001 by ClubCorp, Hyatt Hotels, InterContinental Hotels Group, Fairmont Hotels and Resorts, and Marriott International, to provide volume purchasing of product and services at below-market prices. Such strategic partnerships have the effect of expanding a company's market reach, providing flexibility to customers, cost savings, and efficient delivery of products and services.

Technology and processes

Technology's impact on businesses today cannot be overstated. In the hospitality industry investment in technology has led to increases in employee productivity, process efficiencies, and cost savings, and has enabled hoteliers and restaurateurs to meet guest needs. It must be noted that technology equipment, such as computers, represents tangible assets; however, the source of intangible value are the complementary things that allow the technology to do what it is intended to do. For example, it is not enough to have a state-of-the-art property management system if the system is constantly failing or crashing. System reliability, which requires adequate system monitoring by well-trained technicians, is what is key in providing intangible value to the company. There is anecdotal evidence that companies that invest in information technology also invariably invest heavily in greater employee training.

Human capital

The hospitality industry is simultaneously capital and labour-intensive. The buildings, furniture, fixtures, and equipment require upfront capital investment before customers and guests interface with the business. However, without well-trained and skilled talent a well-capitalized hotel or restaurant cannot be successful. Thus the hospitality business, like all other service businesses and unlike manufacturing, is dependent on human skills. Often it is the people that work for a lodging company that distinguishes it from its competitive set because the hospitality enterprise is about delivering service and an experience and it takes people to accomplish that. Those companies that have a good track record of recruiting dynamic service-oriented employees, have proven employee training and development programmes, have better-than-market compensation programmes, and have defined career development paths for their employees, will consistently out-perform their competitors. Indeed, institutional investors, for example, observe, investigate, and consider companies' compensation practices in their investment decisions. Many have identified human capital as one of the top three value drivers in all companies today.

For companies to be attractive to potential shareholders and for their value to grow requires a dedicated focus on managing human capital. This requires successful and strategic recruitment strategies, training strategies relevant to the skills required in the industry, a workplace environment that celebrates diversity and is family-friendly, empowerment of employees, and leadership that is able to attract and develop an effective management team. The management of human capital in today's hyper-competitive environment has made the job of a manager or CEO more challenging and complex. To be a very successful manager today, it is less about being the best chef, the best player, the smartest instructor, the best designer. It is more about understanding how the pieces of the business all fit together, understanding the opportunities in the marketplace, knowing what the company's strengths are, knowing the sources of value in the company, and deploying competent employees to capitalize on all of these. The companies that do this well enjoy a market premium.

Workplace organization and culture

There are national rankings today of the best family-friendly places to work, the best companies for ethnic minorities, the best companies for women, and many more. These developments are testament to the importance of the workplace environment in contributing to highly productive employees. Many companies ignore the fact that the workplace constitutes a social system and many of the accommodations that are made in the larger society must also exist in the workplace to facilitate employee effectiveness. Although all workplaces are different, a productive workplace has four key elements: employee empowerment, open communication, performance measurement, and passion and commitment. The more successful companies are able to develop and integrate these elements into the culture of the companies such that it creates a competitive advantage for them.

Innovation

Innovation is the process of making improvements by making something new. Economists typically view innovation as a central driver to economic development. The more successful companies constantly innovate across many fronts of the business enterprise. For example, the pay-what-you-like restaurants in the UK do not provide patrons with a check at the end of their meal. Rather patrons are encouraged to pay what they believe the meal and dining experience is worth. Invariably patrons, on the average, have ended up paying more than the cost of the meal; average check at these restaurants is higher than at comparable restaurants that provide a bill at the end of a meal. Companies can and must innovate in their service delivery, business model, organizational structure, internal processes, alliances, marketing, and customer relations. Contemporary management practices such as Six Sigma have been adopted by many larger corporations such as Starwood Hotels; however, other companies have found new ways of applying the original method. Research and new product development is the key to sustaining company growth, and those companies that invest significantly in this area are the successful innovators.

Intellectual capital

There is tremendous value in having "thinkers" in an organization because they tend to be the sources of ideas and ideas represent intellectual capital. Some companies have the distinctive ability to merge external and internal sources of knowledge in order to exploit business opportunities that exist in their environment. The stories of how Indian IT services companies like Infosys, Tata Consultancy Services, and Wipro have emerged to become powerful players in the business services and IT industry, is legendary. The pool of talented young professionals that exist in India have been harnessed by these companies to create an information technology power centre in southeast Asia that is unprecedented.

The key for companies is to recognize that intellectual capital exists in the organization, encourage employees to experiment with new ideas, and thereby add value to the organization. Failure to recognize and harness intellectual capital causes employees to lose enthusiasm and excitement in the company.

Adaptability

Organizations by necessity must change or die because change is inevitable. As the domestic and global business environments have changed dramatically over the last two to three decades, companies have been forced to respond effectively or have died. In September of 2006 same-store sales of KFC in the U.S. declined by 2% due to the saturation of the domestic market as well as the impact of concerns about obesity in the country. On October 11, KFC's domestic sales declined by 7% while its reported earnings rose by less than 1%. Yet the stock price of Yum Brands, KFCs parent company, was trading on the stock market at a price close to an all-time high. The explanation for this seeming paradox is that worldwide earnings of KFC rose by about 14% due almost exclusively to growth in China where the company opens a new restaurant every 22 hours (Arndt and Roberts, 2006). Its sales rose by 28% with reported profit growth of 26%. McDonalds, though in China also, has not had the same success as KFC, its profit growth has been modest in single digits. Part of the reason is attributable to PepsiCo's (KFC's former parent company) foresight in adapting to the changing quick service restaurant environment and opening its first store in 1987 in Beijing, 3 years before McDonalds entered that market.

Therefore, companies that continuously scan the environment, understand, and anticipate the changes that are on the horizon, and strategically adapt the organization in order to sustain their operating and financial performance enjoy a premium on the market and continue to widen the gap between their market and book values.

Intangible value in the lodging industry: trends and patterns

Ten lodging companies were chosen and the size of their intangible values was tracked over a 5-year period to illustrate the widening gap between market and book values. The market values calculated by multiplying the end-of-year closing stock price of a company by the number of common shares outstanding. Then, annual total assets of the ten lodging companies were obtained from each company's annual 10-K reports. The size of each company's intangible value was estimated for each year by subtracting total assets from the total market value. The annual percentage of intangible value of each company was found. The data covers the period 2002–2006. The annual pattern for each company is presented in graphical form below.

Marriott international

Marriott International has the highest market value in the lodging industry (Figure 8.1). In 2002, the size of intangible value as a percentage of total market value was −6.99%. This period was the aftermath of the September 11 terrorist attacks that hit the stock market and the lodging industry. From 2002 to 2004 there was a steep climb in the size of intangible value. In 2004 the percentage had risen to 39.05% and 38.14% in 2005. In 2006, 44.14% of its total market capitalization was intangible. There has been a clear upward trend in the size of Marriott's intangible value over the 5-year period.

The company has had a reputation for being responsive to employees' welfare. In recent years, Marriott has been on the list of Fortune's "100 Best Companies To Work For." In addition to this, Marriott was selected as the best workplace for women

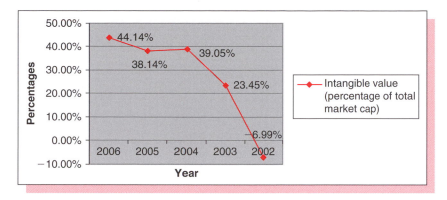

Figure 8.1
Marriott International.

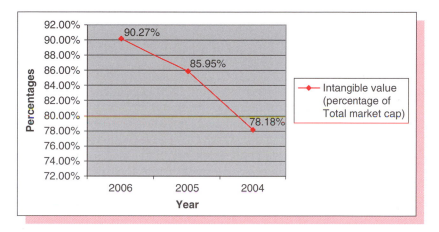

Figure 8.2
Choice Hotel Corporation.

by Working Mother Magazine. Its human capital is highly diversified: 80 different languages are spoken system-wide in Marriott International (Fischer *et al.*, 2003). Marriott has also invested on customer relationship technology in order to maintain long-term relationship with its customers. In order to optimize the revenue management applications, Marriott installed One Yield revenue management system. This system enabled Marriott International to save $9 billion in 1 year thereby giving the company a competitive advantage (Overby, 2005).

Choice hotel international

In 2004 Choice's intangible value was at 78.18% and it rose steadily to 85.95% in 2005 and 90.27% in 2006 (Figure 8.2). Again, the

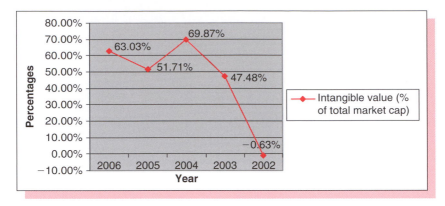

Figure 8.3
Four Seasons Hotel Corporation.

upward trend is clear even without 2002 and 2003 data. Choice Hotels is a management company with no ownership of lodging properties; consequently it reduces the level of business risk that it could potentially confront. In the absence of lodging revenues and operating expenses, the company's cash flows are relatively more predictable and sustainable. This is one of the reasons for the relatively large size of Choice Hotel International's intangible value. The company's investment in e-procurement technologies has also provided additional revenue stream. For example, in 2000 Choicebuys.com generated $400 million in e-procurement business alone (Wolff and Brennan, 2001). Additionally, Choice Hotels signed a strategic partnership agreement with the American Automobile Association. This strategic agreement has generated $200 million revenues for the company.

Four seasons

Lodging companies' earnings were seriously damaged in 2002 because of the SARS epidemic and September 11th and as a result lodging stocks did not do well on the stock market (Figure 8.3). The percentage of intangible value was −0.63%. However, in 2003 this figure rose to 47.48% and in 2004 it climbed to 69.07%. There was a slight drop in 2005 to 51.71% and later rising in 2006 to 63.03%. Overall, the size of intangible values is very high in Four Seasons. Several reasons may account for this high intangible value. One factor is that Four Seasons enjoys a competitive advantage in the area of human capital among its competitors. Four Seasons' employee selection process is very rigorous and competitive. For instance,

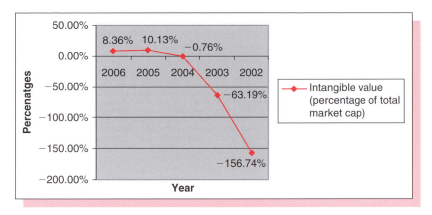

Figure 8.4
Starwood Hotels and Resorts Worldwide Inc.

before the opening of the Four Seasons New York, 30,000 people applied for positions. 3000 applicants out of 30,000 were called for interviews, and only 400 people were hired.

Starwood hotels and resorts worldwide

In 2002, the size of Starwood's intangible was very negative and very high at −156.74% (Figure 8.4). The figure improved after that year to −63.19% in 2003 and −0.76% in 2004. Since 2004, Starwood's intangible value has been positive and rising. By 2006, 8.36% of total market capitalization is intangible value. A factor contributing to Starwood's intangibles is its Starwood's Preferred Guest Programme. It was the first frequent guest programme in the hotel industry. Brand Strength is also another competitive advantage of Starwood. Their global distribution system helped Starwood maintain good relationship with its current and prospective customers.

Hilton international

The figure in 2002 and 2003 were −75.62 and −26.38%, respectively (Figure 8.5). Like other hotels during this period, Hilton was affected by the SARS epidemic and the September 11th terrorist event. 2004 and 2005 showed positive intangible value of 5.61 and 5.32%, respectively. These figures although positive are relatively very small compared to the other hotel chains like Marriott, Choice, and Four Seasons. Nonetheless the upward trend is evident.

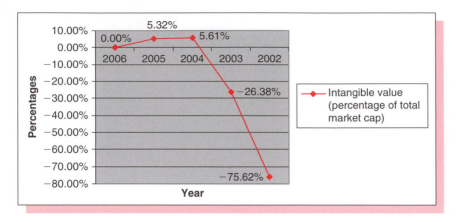

Figure 8.5
Hilton Hotel Corporation.

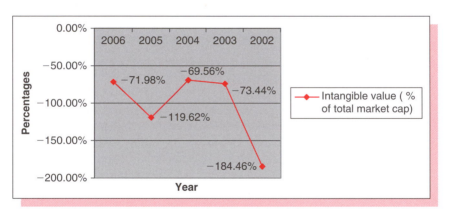

Figure 8.6
Interstate Hotels and Resorts.

Interstate hotels and resorts

Interstate Hotels exhibits the general upward trend of intangible value it is clear that during this period between 2002 and 2006 investors were neither impressed with the company's performance nor its future growth opportunities (Figure 8.6). For those 5 years the market value of Interstate was consistently below its book value. In 2002 the size of intangible value was −184.46%, increasing to −73.44% and −9.50% in 2003 and 2004, respectively. In 2005 the value declined to −119.62% and later rising to −71.98% in 2006.

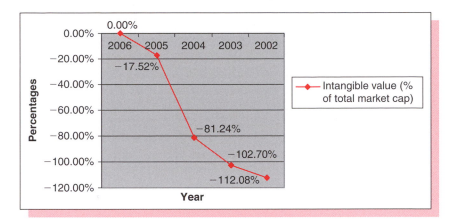

Figure 8.7
Orient Express Hotel Ltd.

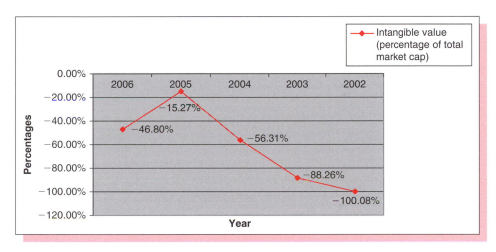

Figure 8.8
Marcus Corporation.

Orient express

Similar to Interstate Hotels the Orient Express showed negative intangible value during the 5-year period under review (Figure 8.7). In 2002 the value was −112.08% and it rose in each of the following years to −102.70, −81.24, −17.52, and 0.00%. The upward trend remained consistent with this company.

Marcus corporation

Marcus Hotel Corporation exhibits negative intangibles values for the 5-year period (Figure 8.8). It is obvious that investors

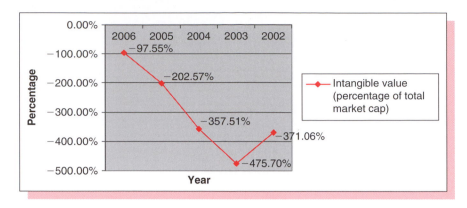

Figure 8.9
Red Lion Hotel.

have little confidence in the performance of the company at this time. In 2002 the intangible value was −100.08% and it rose to −88.26% in 2003. There was a further increase to −56.31% in 2004 and −15.27% in 2005. There was a setback in 2006 when the value dropped to −46.80%. Overall the upward trend of the intangible value is present.

Red lion hotel

Like Marcus Corporation and Orient Express, Red Lion had consistently negative intangible value over the study period; nonetheless the annual trend was increasing (Figure 8.9). It is evident that although companies like Marriott and Four Seasons rebounded relatively quickly from the devastating effects of SARS and September 11th, several hotel companies took longer to recover. The intangible value was −371.06% in 2002 then dropped to −475.70% the following year. Then the value began to increase from 2003 to −357.51% in 2004, 202.57% in 2005, and −97.55% in 2006.

Sonesta international

Sonesta International's intangible value was also negative from 2004 to 2006 (Figure 8.10). The negative value was as high as −469.63% in 2004 and declined dramatically to −17.82% in 2005 and −35.40% in 2006.

Measuring intangibles: is it possible?

Measuring intangibles using traditional accounting methods is a challenge in the emerging new knowledge economy. It

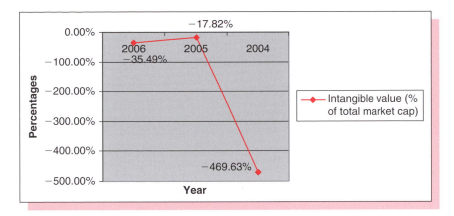

Figure 8.10
Sonesta International.

becomes a challenge because the value of intangibles is different for different people. Tangible assets have exact number values and there is no level of uncertainty in calculating results. Yet it is known that intangibles, especially intellectual capital, contribute to the bottom line. One standard of measurement has been proposed by Kaplan and Norton (1992, 1996) known as the "Balanced Scorecard." The authors identified three elements for assessment, (1) companies need to know how customers perceive them and what is needed to excel, (2) companies need to know how they can improve and create value, and (3) they need to know how they are perceived by their shareholders. Not all of the Balanced Scorecard components, however, are quantifiable relative to traditional accounting processes.

Measuring intangibles in dollar value is the real challenge. In March 1997, the *Montague Institute Review Journal* published 12 techniques that may be used to assess the value of intangible assets. Of the 12 techniques described, 4 are quantitative, and 8 are qualitative. The four quantitative techniques include *business process auditing, knowledge banks, calculated intangible value, and colourized reporting.*

Business process auditing measures show how information improves value related to a specific business process, such as production, marketing, or accounting. What is the reduced cost of production or completing accounting functions? Dollar value can be placed on reducing costs, because an intangible asset was determined by estimating the cost reduction associated with the use of new information utilized.

Knowledge bank techniques treat capital spending as an expense, rather than as an asset, and treat a portion of salaries as an asset, since capital spending creates future cash flows. *Calculated intangible value* compares the return on assets with a published average ROA for the industry. The ROA is assessed relative to industry standards.

Percentage comparisons between actual performance and industry standards can be completed and used as goal-setting targets for improvement.

Colourized reporting was suggested by SEC commissioner Steven Wallman. He suggested that traditional financial statements are to be supplemented with additional information such as brand values, customer satisfaction measures, and the dollar value of having a trained workforce (http://www. montague.com, Anonymous). Such information will add "colour" to the traditional financial reporting.

Additionally, valuation analytical methods include three broad categories, which include Cost, Income, and Market Approaches. The recommended techniques for Cost Approach Methods include determining replacement and reproduction costs of intangible assets. The costs should be based on the acquisition cost, projected with an inflation and growth percentage. The Income Approach Methods include costing direct and yield capitalization, along with identifying income measures associated with each intangible asset. The Market Approach Methods include sales comparison transactions, license comparison transactions, and royalty rates. The rates may be amortized over the life of the asset (http://intelegen. com, Measuring intangibles and intellectual capital: An emerging first standard).

Foster *et al.* (2003) recommended several practices for accounting for intangible assets. Their suggestions included allocating the purchase price of an acquired entity to the assets acquired and liabilities. It is also recommended that:

- An intangible asset may be recognized as an asset apart from goodwill if it arises from contractual or other legal rights and it is transferable or separable from the acquired entity. Some examples include: trademarks, internet domain names, customer lists, etc. If is not recognized as contractual, then it must be capable of being divided and sold, transferred or rented, regardless of the intent to do so. (http://www.nysscpa.org/cpajournal/2003).
- Other intangible assets would be amortized over its useful life, using a method that indicates how benefits of the asset are consumed. The straight-line method is the most common method used.

Conclusion

Companies create intangible value from many sources; these include innovation, human capital, leadership, strategy execution, and many more. Companies that recognize, harness, and leverage these intangible assets are rewarded by investors on the stock market. These assets help companies maintain competitive advantage as well as sustain their revenues and earnings stream for the future. Some intangible assets exist in all companies while others are created. The current hyper-competitive nature of the lodging industry requires that companies look beyond the traditional bricks and mortar and identify the sources of intangible value within the company and invest in them. What is clear from the ten examples of lodging companies is that the rising trend in intangible value is obvious although the size is negative for some of the companies. It is also clear that the companies that have exhibited negative values over the 5-year period have a lot to do to impress the stock market. The devastating effects of an epidemic such as SARS and September 11th impacted all the lodging stocks; however, some stocks recovered more quickly than others.

References

Anonymous. (2007). *Hail, Shareholder!* The Economist, June 2, pp. 65–66.

Anonymous. *Measuring Intellectual Assets*. http://www.montague.com

Arndt, M., and Roberts, D. (2006). *A Finger-Licking' Good Time in China*. Business Week, October 30, p. 50.

Bhartesh, K. R., and Bandyopadhyay, A. K. (2005). *Intellectual Capital: Concept and its Measurement*. Finance India, April 19, pp. 1365–1375.

Brooking, A. (1996). *Intellectual Capital: Core Assets for the Third Millennium Enterprise*. London, United Kingdom: Thomas Business Press.

Choice Hotel Thanks AAA for Business. (2006). Retrieved from http://www.choicehotels.com/ires/en-US/html/Press Release?pr=20060407a&sid=TAgJg.8uYnigjW$.8

Dyer, J. H., Kale, P., and Singh, H. (2001). How to make strategic alliances work. *Sloan Management Review*, 42(4), 37–43.

Edvinson, L., and Malone, M. S. (1997). Intellectual capital: Realizing your company's true value by finding its hidden brain power. New York: Harper Business.

Eustace, C. (2000). *The Intangible Economy: Impact and Policy Issues*. Report of the European High Level Expert Group on the Intangible Economy, European Commission.

Fischer, K., Gross, S. E., and Friedman, H. M. (2003). Marriott makes the business case for an innovative total rewards strategy. *Journal of Organizational Excellence, Spring*(22/2), 19–24.

Foster, B. P., Fletcher, R., and Stout, W. D. (2003). Valuing intangible assets. *The CPA Journal*, http://www.nysscpa.org/cpajournal/2003.

Kapardis, M. K., and Thomas, A. (2006). Hospitality industry in Cyprus: The significance of intangibles. *International Journal of Contemporary Hospitality Management, 18/1*, 6–24.

Kaplan, R. S., and Norton, D. P. (1992). *The Balanced Scorecard: Measures that Drive Performance*. Harvard Business Review, Jan–Feb, pp. 71–80.

Kaplan, R. S., and Norton, D. (1996). *The Balance Scorecard: Translating Strategy into Action*. MA: Harvard Press.

Low, J., and Kalafut, P. C. (2002). *Invisible Advantage. How Intangibles are Driving Business Performance* (1st ed.). Perseus Publishing.

Mayo, A., and Nohria, N. (2005). *In their Time: The Greatest Business Leaders of the 20th Century*. Boston, MA: Harvard Press.

McConnell, C., and Brue, S. L. (2005). *Economics: Principles, Problems and Policies*. New York: McGraw-Hill Irwin.

Measuring intangibles and intellectual capital: An emerging first standard. http://intelegen.com

Overby, S. (2005). *The Price is Always Right: Marriott Applied its Business Wisdom to Building an IT System that has Successfully Tackled its Greatest Challenge-maximizing Revenue*. CIO, Framingham, September 18, p. 1.

Stewart, T. A. (1997). *Intellectual Capital: The New Wealth of Organizations*. New York: Doubleday/Currency.

Wolff, C., and Brennan, K. (2001). Enjoy the ride. *Lodging Hospitality, 57*(1), 35–40.

Recent findings regarding hotel brand and strategy

John O'Neill[1] and Anna Mattila[2]

[1]Associate Professor,
School of Hospitality Management,
The Pennsylvania State University,
University Park, PA
[2]Professor of Services Marketing,
The Pennsylvania State University,
School of Hospitality Management,
University Park, PA

Introduction: overview of the chapter

As hotel management and development organizations formulate strategies and programmes regarding existing and future hotel facilities, services, and positioning, a question that naturally arises is, what factors actually drive hotel's profitability? (O'Neill and Mattila, 2006). One such factor is branding.

To maximize brand equity, most hotel mega-companies have developed multiple brands to serve multiple markets (Jiang *et al.*, 2002; O'Neill and Mattila, 2004). The value of a brand is based on the awareness of the brand, its quality perception, and overall customer satisfaction (Aaker, 1996; O'Neill and Mattila, 2004). Lodging operators have turned their attention to guest satisfaction and branding because brand name operates as a "shorthand" for quality by giving the guest important information about the product/service, sight unseen (Brucks *et al.*, 2000; Jacoby *et al.*, 1977; O'Neill and Mattila, 2004).

A recent annual brand report in *Hotels* magazine listed 285 lodging brands worldwide (Hotels, July 2005; O'Neill and Xiao, 2006). Some companies, such as Marriott International, include the corporate name in most of their brands, while others, such as Wyndham, employ a house-of-brands strategy, i.e., individual brand names for each segment (O'Neill and Mattila, 2006).

Branding is particularly critical in service industries such as the hotel business (Onkvisit and Shaw, 1989). The recognized goal of hotel branding is to provide added value to both guests and hotel companies by building brand loyalty (Cai and Hobson, 2004; O'Neill and Xiao, 2006). The notion that a hotel's brand contributes significantly to the property's market value is supported by an analysis of over 1000 hotel sales transactions over the past 15 years (O'Neill and Xiao, 2006). From a corporate strategy viewpoint, well-managed hotel brands tend to gain increasing market share (O'Neill and Mattila, 2004).

What is a brand?

The American Marketing Association defines brand as a "name, term, sign, symbol, or design, or combination of them intended to identify the goods and services of one seller or group of sellers and to differentiate them from those of competition" (http://www.ama.org). As brand represents the company itself, it should always be very consistent in the market. Though there are cases when companies change their positioning or strategies, corporate colours, and even their logos and typeface, very few companies ever change their brand names (Vaid, 2003).

Brand is a logo and trademark and identifies the goods or services of one specific seller, but more importantly, a brand is the source of a promise to consumers. A brand promises a product's services and an organization's distinctive identity that differentiates it from the identity of its competitors. Those identities indicate the source(s) of that promise to consumers. Its differentiated identity should provide benefits in any form to the consumer and it is an organization's goal to enhance and maximize those benefits to deliver the promise.

Brand relates to consumer emotions. Gobé (2001) explains that the biggest misconception in branding strategies is people tend to believe branding is about market share, but it is really about mind and emotion share. Of course, superficial aspects of branding are ubiquity, visibility, and function, but the major significance is to remain in the mind as something that is emotionally relatable. There are several reasons why people become emotionally connected to a brand. Brands are supposed to be intense and vibrant, and to connect on multiple levels of the senses. Brands are unique and should be admirable because a brand is a promise to consumers. It consistently interacts with them and should not disappoint the consumer by any reasons that break the promise. A brand is something for consumers to feel good about (Vaid, 2003).

In sum, a hotel brand is a relationship with people. Getting to know a brand, whether it is by consumer intention or not, using, evaluating, and continuing to use a product and/or service, are all parts of the process of building a relationship between a brand and a consumer. Developing this relationship is the real purpose of brand and branding. The promise to the consumer and the products and services should be unique to the identity of the brand and should be strong in peoples' minds. Ultimately, the brand represents the consumer's experience with its organization.

Brand power

How to measure value of a hotel brand

A number of factors have been shown to be correlated with a hotel property's market value. Net operating income (NOI), average daily rate (ADR), occupancy rate, and number of guest rooms have proven to be significant predictors of a hotel's value (O'Neill and Lloyd-Jones, 2001). Some brands consistently have stronger bottom lines, i.e., NOIs, than do others (O'Neill and Mattila, 2006), although ADR (an indicator of a hotel's "top line") is a better predictor of a hotels' market value than its NOI (an indicator of a hotel's "bottom line") (O'Neill and Mattila, 2006), and some brands have consistently stronger ADRs than others. More recent research has shown that hotel brand effects hotel market value, and it does so above and beyond the effect of NOI, ADR, occupancy rate, and number of guest rooms (O'Neill and Xiao, 2006).

Brand affiliation is an important factor affecting hotel revenue. The branding literature has demonstrated that consumers use brand name as an important quality cue. Moreover, consumers are typically willing to pay a price premium for brands they view as high in quality (O'Neill and Mattila, 2006). Brand affiliation, name recognition, and reputation for high-quality service together can contribute as much as 20–25% of the going concern value of a successfully operating hotel (Kinnard *et al.*, 2001; O'Neill and Xiao, 2006).

Brand as a value creator

In general, brand power represented as a name, logo, or symbol in the market might be expressed as brand equity (Mahajan *et al.*, 1994). Brand equity results from benefits of marketing efficiency and enhanced performance associated with that brand and long-term brand effect based on customer loyalty. Brand equity results in the potential to expand the brand in a variety of markets (Mahajan *et al.*, 1994).

Brand equity is created when firms deliver quality products, and strong brand associations are created when firms conduct appropriate communications and advertising strategies (Aaker, 1991; Rao *et al.*, 2004). Brand equity, as well as brand, can represent the relationship between the firm and its customers, and the positive relationship may enhance cash flows and reduce risk of the firm as a whole, and it may have a positive effect on value of the firm (Rao *et al.*, 2004). When correctly and objectively measured, brand equity can be the proper metric for estimating the long-term impact of marketing decisions (Rao *et al.*, 2004).

The level of brand equity is positively related to a hotel company's financial performance, e.g., revenue per available room (Kim *et al.*, 2003; O'Neill and Xiao, 2006). Realizing that a brand's strength ultimately drives stock price and shareholder value, the lodging industry has been recognized as a "brand-equity business" (Morgan Stanley Report, 1997; O'Neill and Xiao, 2006).

Well-established brands create financial value due to their ability to generate cash flows via relatively higher margins (Aaker and Jacobson, 1994; O'Neill and Mattila, 2006).

In general, major contributors of generating cash flows are high margins, customer loyalty, brand extension including licensing opportunities, and enhanced marketing efficiency (Rao *et al.*, 2004).

Hotel executives recognize brand quality as an important company asset and as a potential source of strategic advantage (Damonte *et al.*, 1997; O'Neill and Mattila, 2004). Brand is generally categorized as an intangible asset. Intangible assets are earned cash flows of a firm in excess of the return on tangible assets. In other words, intangible assets boost the earning power of the firm's tangible assets. Patents, trademarks, R&D, and franchises are examples of intangible assets as well as brand equity (Simon and Sullivan, 1993).

Not only is it generally recognized that brands create value for both consumers and companies (Aaker, 1991; O'Neill and Xiao, 2006), but consumers use brands as cues to infer certain product attributes, such as quality (O'Neill and Mattila, 2004; O'Neill and Xiao, 2006). The value of a brand chiefly resides in the minds of customers and is based primarily on customers' brand awareness, their perceptions of its quality, and their brand loyalty (Aaker, 1991; O'Neill and Xiao, 2006).

Hotel guests rely on brand names to reduce the risks associated with staying at an otherwise unknown property (Bharadwaj *et al.*, 1993; O'Neill and Xiao, 2006). In that regard, strong brands enable hotel chains to be part of and to differentiate themselves in the minds of customers (Prasad and Dev, 2000; O'Neill and Xiao, 2006).

Brands first create value for customers by helping to assure them of a uniform level of quality (Keller and Lehmann, 2003; O'Neill and Xiao, 2006). After customers become loyal to a brand, the brand owner can capitalize on the brand's value through price premiums, decreased price elasticity, increased market share, and more rapid brand expansion. Finally, companies with successful brands benefit in the financial marketplace by improving shareholders' value (Ambler *et al.*, 2002; O'Neill and Xiao, 2006).

Although it is important for hotel owners to be able to recognize the effects of a brand on hotel market value, other benefits associated with a brand, such as guest satisfaction and loyalty, should be considered to fully assess the brand's total value (O'Neill and Xiao, 2006).

Brand and satisfaction

Due to increased attention to a customer focus, brand managers use satisfaction as a measure of operational success of their overall branding strategies (Shocker *et al.*, 1994; O'Neill and Mattila, 2004).

The strategic management of satisfaction is of utmost importance in today's crowded marketplace, where customers are overwhelmed with lodging choices (O'Neill and Mattila, 2004). Satisfaction is believed to lead to repeat purchases (Oh, 1999; Mattila and O'Neill, 2003), favourable word-of-mouth behaviour (Gundersen *et al.*, 1996; Mattila and O'Neill, 2003), and loyalty (Dube and Renaghan, 2000).

Satisfaction in the lodging industry is composed of several factors, including guest room cleanliness, hotel maintenance, employee friendliness, and knowledgeable employees (Oh, 1999; Mattila and O'Neill, 2003), as well as the hotel's physical environment (Mattila, 1999; Mattila and O'Neill, 2003). Brands with higher levels of guest satisfaction achieve not only higher ADRs, but these brands achieve significantly greater percentage increases in their ADRs over time (O'Neill and Mattila, 2004).

Brand extension

In many industries, including the hospitality business, marketing new products and services as extensions of the original brand name has been a popular strategy for many reasons (Lane and Jacobson, 1995). Hilton, Hyatt, InterContinental, Marriott, Starwood, and Wyndham have all grown through brand extensions. Major reasons why consumers depend on trusted brands are to economize on time and search costs (Lane and Jacobson, 1995). Consumers immediately conceive brands' extensions' attributes and benefits through established brand names. The favourable, strong, and unique brand associations are stored in memory when the consumer possesses familiarity with a brand (Lane and Jacobson, 1995).

Consideration sets are "a set of alternatives that the consumer evaluates in making a decision" (Peter and Olson, 2005). Consumers choose products and services that are familiar to them more often than those with which they are unfamiliar. Therefore, the extensions of familiar brand names are in consideration sets, and are highly likely to be chosen by consumers using peripheral cues (Lane and Jacobson, 1995). This situation happens more in cases when consumers are without specific product knowledge in the purchase situation, and serves as a heuristic to guide product choice (Lane and Jacobson, 1995).

The advantages of brand extension provide firms with not only higher revenues, but with savings in marketing expenditures, as well (Lane and Jacobson, 1995). In addition, more highly familiar brands tend to generate greater future revenues because of opportunities in expanding markets (Lane and Jacobson, 1995).

Despite the advantages of brand extensions, there are negative points to be noted, as well. First, a brand which possesses a rather unfavourable image may negatively affect consumer choice. If a brand is familiar but not preferred by consumers, it could suffer in its brand extensions relative to brands that are more preferred (Lane and Jacobson, 1995). Second, although a firm has maintained a positive image, dilution or confusion about the brand image can happen via inconsistent brand extensions (Lane and Jacobson, 1995). Third, dilution of the core image of the original brand can be possible when the brand image loses consumer conception of exclusivity or status appeal (Lane and Jacobson, 1995) and can lead to reduction of demand for the original product or service (Lane and Jacobson, 1995). Fourth, brand extensions have a greater risk of cannibalizing the firm's other products than actual new brands (Lane and Jacobson, 1995). In this regard, brand extensions can create but also destroy a firm's stock market equity by increasing or decreasing future economic earnings (Lane and Jacobson, 1995). Therefore, when a firm is to launch a new product or service connected to its original brand, the strategic decisions are critical regarding the types of branding strategies it adopts (Rao *et al.*, 2004).

Branding and franchising

Protecting reputation for guest satisfaction at a brand level has become a key issue, both in terms of consumer perceptions and franchisee willingness to sign and/or stay with a particular hotel brand (Prasad and Dev, 2000; O'Neill and Mattila, 2004). Since today's hotel franchisees are quick to change their brand loyalty, it may be more important than ever for hotel brand executives to maintain consistent brand quality (O'Neill and Mattila, 2004).

Since chain affiliation is incorporated in lenders' tight underwriting formulas, obtaining financing for an independent hotel is generally more difficult than for a branded one (O'Neill and Xiao, 2006). Potential franchisees need to examine the parent firm's brand portfolio because hotel companies differ in their choice of branding strategies (O'Neill and Mattila, 2006).

Different hotel brands deliver different levels of profitability. Hotel owners have figured out this situation based on their prior brand relationships and they have become less hesitant to seek brands that are in closer conformance to their financial goals (O'Neill and Mattila, 2006).

For hotel owners, whose goal is to maximize the market value of their asset, recognizing the role of brand name in hotel market value is beneficial for positioning and flagging decisions. For hotel companies' brand-management teams, effectively assessing brands' effects on hotel market values can strengthen the overall value of the brands and possibly improve the brands' franchise sales. Such rational analysis can signal weaknesses and assist with the development of re-imaging, retrenchment, or remedial brand strategies, when necessary. Furthermore, such analysis can assist corporate brand managers in evaluating whether their intended brand strategies are being achieved (O'Neill and Xiao, 2006).

Growth via franchising might have an adverse effect on quality (Michael, 2000; O'Neill and Mattila, 2004). The percentage of franchised units within a hotel brand has been shown to be negatively correlated with both guest satisfaction and occupancy percentage (O'Neill and Mattila, 2004).

As hotel brand executives continue to focus their growth strategies to a greater extent on franchising and brand management rather than actual property management, the issue of guest satisfaction could become an increasingly important factor in determining the ultimate revenue success of hotel brands (O'Neill and Mattila, 2004). One study investigated a total of 26 hotel brands between 2000 and 2003 (O'Neill et al., 2006). It is interesting to note that 23 out of 26 brands studied achieved guest satisfaction improvements while at the same time many of them were experiencing ADR and occupancy decreases. In fact, 18 brands suffered from ADR decreases during the recessionary study period. Apparently, ADR may serve different strategic goals for brands in different market environments. After September 11, 2001, it is more likely that some hotel operators and brand managers voluntarily chose to reduce their ADRs to maintain or enhance the level of guest satisfaction. It is possible that lower prices might increase customers' value perceptions, thus having a positive effect on satisfaction. For example, Marriott and Wyndham were among the brands that experienced most dramatic drops in ADR (−14.0 and −13.7%, respectively); on the other hand, they also significantly improved their guest satisfaction during the same period of time (2.5 and 4.0%, respectively) (O'Neill et al., 2006).

Among the brands studied by O'Neill *et al.* (2006), several specific cases further clarify the possible effect of franchising on guest satisfaction. For instance, La Quinta Inn & Suites was virtually a franchise-free brand in 2000, but by 2003, 25.8% of its hotels were franchised. Unfortunately, such a growth strategy correlated with a decrease in guest satisfaction at La Quinta (−2.6%) during the course of the study period. As another example, Hampton Inn & Suites increased its room inventory by 16.1% during the study period, with 99.3% of its properties being franchised in 2003. Despite this rapid growth, Hampton Inn & Suites experienced improvements in occupancy (3.7%), ADR (6.6%), and guest satisfaction (2.5%) during the same period. Such overall success suggests a healthy balance among Hampton Inn's branding, franchising, and service and quality strategies. Westin increased its percentage of franchised properties (9.6% increase) with minimal decreases in ADR (−0.5% change) and occupancy rate (−4.4% change). Its widely touted "Heavenly Bed" programme, which it implemented during the course of the study period, may have contributed to enhanced guest satisfaction (up by 6.4% between 2000 and 2003), which in turn probably acted as a buffer to downward ADR and occupancy pressure (O'Neill *et al.*, 2006).

Concluding remarks

In spite of the agreed upon enormous value of hotel brands, there is a widespread sentiment that brands are often being mismanaged (Aaker, 1991; Simon and Sullivan, 1993). Some have argued that too much emphasis is being placed on short-term performance rather than the long-term value of brand equity (Simon and Sullivan, 1993). The recent research presented here could be of assistance to corporate brand management teams seeking guidance regarding the long-term strategic direction of the brands they guide.

References

Aaker, D. (1991). *Managing Brand Equity: Capitalizing on the Value of a Brand Name*. New York: Free Press.

Aaker, D. (1996). *Building Strong Brands*. New York: Free Press.

Aaker, D., and Jacobson, R. (1994). The financial information content of perceived quality. *Journal of Marketing, 58*, 191–201.

Ambler, T., Bhattacharya, C. B., Edell, J., Keller, K. L., Lemon, K. N., and Mittal, V. (2002). Relating brand and customer perspectives on marketing management. *Journal of Service Research, 5*(1), 13–25.

Bharadwaj, S. G., Varadarajan, R. P., and Fahy, J. (1993). Sustainable competitive advantage in service industries: A conceptual model and research propositions. *Journal of Marketing*, *57*, 83–99.

Brucks, M., Zeithaml, V., and Naylor, G. (2000). Price and brand name as indicators of quality dimensions for consumer durables. *Journal of the Academy of Marketing Science*, *28*(3), 359–374.

Cai, L. A., and Hobson, J. S. P. (2004). Making hotel brands work in a competitive environment. *Journal of Vacation Marketing*, *10*(3), 197–208.

Damonte, T., Rompf, P., Bahl, R., and Domke, D. (1997). Brand affiliation and property size effects on measures of performance in lodging properties. *Journal of Hospitality Research*, *20*(3), 1–16.

Dube, L., and Renaghan, L. (2000). Creating visible customer value: How customers view best-practice champions. *The Cornell Hotel and Restaurant Administration Quarterly*, *41*(1), 62–72.

Gobé, M. (2001). *Emotional Branding: The New Paradigm for Connecting Brands to People*. New York: Allworth Press.

Gundersen, M., Heide, M., and Olsson, U. (1996). Hotel guest satisfaction among business travelers. *Cornell Hotel and Restaurant Administration Quarterly*, *37*(2), 72–81.

Hotels. (July 2005). The largest hotel brands. p. 50.

Jacoby, J., Szybillo, G., and Busato-Schach, J. (1977). Information acquisition behavior in brand choice situations. *Journal of Consumer Research*, *3*, 209–215.

Jiang, W., Dev, C., and Rao, V. (2002). Brand extension and customer loyalty: Evidence from the lodging industry. *The Cornell Hotel and Restaurant Administration Quarterly*, *43*(4), 5–16.

Keller, K. L., and Lehmann, D. R. (2003). How do brands create value? *Marketing Management*, *12*(3), 26–40.

Kim, H. B., Kim, W. G., and An, J. A. (2003). The effect of consumer-based brand equity on firms' financial performance. *Journal of Consumer Marketing*, *20*(4), 335–351.

Kinnard, W. N., Worzala, E. M., and Swango, D. L. (2001). Intangible assets in an operating first-class downtown hotel. *Appraisal Journal*, *69*(1), 68–83.

Lane, V., and Jacobson, R. (1995). Stock market reactions to brand extension announcements. *Journal of Marketing*, *59*, 63–77.

Mahajan, V. V., Rao, V. R., and Srivastava, R. (1994). An approach to assess the importance of brand equity in acquisition decisions. *Journal of Product Innovation Management*, *11*, 221–235.

Mattila, A. S. (1999). Consumers' value judgments. *Cornell Hotel and Restaurant Administration Quarterly*, *40*(1), 40–46.

Mattila, A. S., and O'Neill, J. W. (2003). Relationships between hotel room pricing, occupancy, and guest satisfaction: A longitudinal case of a midscale hotel in the United States. *Journal of Hospitality and Tourism Research*, *27*(3), 328–341.

Michael, S. (2000). The effect of organizational form on quality: The case of franchising. *Journal of Economic Behavior and Organization*, *43*(3), 295–318.

Morgan Stanley Report. (May 5, 1997). "Globalization: The next phase in lodging", as cited in Jiang, W., Chekitan, D. S., and Rao, V. R. (2002). Brand extension and customer loyalty: Evidence from the lodging industry. *Cornell Hotel and Restaurant Administration Quarterly*, *43*(5), 5.

Oh, H. (1999). Service quality, customer satisfaction, and customer value: A holistic perspective. *International Journal of Hospitality Management*, *18*, 67–82.

O'Neill, J. W., and Lloyd-Jones, A. R. (2001). Hotel values in the aftermath of September 11, 2001. *Cornell Hotel and Restaurant Administration Quarterly*, *42*(6), 10–21.

O'Neill, J. W., and Mattila, A. S. (2004). Hotel branding strategy: Its relationship to guest satisfaction and room revenue. *Journal of Hospitality and Tourism Research*, *28*(2), 156–165.

O'Neill, J. W., and Mattila, A. S. (2006). Strategic hotel development and positioning: The effect of revenue drivers on profitability. *Cornell Hotel and Restaurant Administration Quarterly*, *47*(2), 146–154.

O'Neill, J. W., Mattila, A. S., and Xiao, Q. (2006). Hotel guest satisfaction and brand performance: The effect of franchising strategy. *Journal of Quality Assurance in Hospitality and Tourism*, *7*(3), 25–39.

O'Neill, J. W., and Xiao, Q. (2006). The role of brand affiliation in hotel market value. *Cornell Hotel and Restaurant Administration Quarterly*, *47*(3), 210–223.

Onkvisit, S., and Shaw, J. J. (1989). Service marketing: Image, branding, and competition. *Business Horizons*, *32*, 13–18.

Peter, J. P., and Olson, J. C. (2005). *Consumer Behavior and Marketing Strategy*. New York: Mcgraw-Hill/Irwin.

Prasad, K., and Dev, C. (2000). Measuring hotel brand equity: A customer-centric framework for assessing performance. *Cornell Hotel and Restaurant Administration Quarterly*, *41*(3), 22–31.

Rao, V. R., Agrawal, M., and Dahlhoff, D. (2004). How is manifested branding strategy related to the intangible value of a corporation? *Journal of Marketing*, *68*, 126–141.

Shocker, S., Srivastava, R., and Ruekert, R. (1994). Challenges and opportunities facing brand management: An introduction to the special issue. *Journal of Marketing Research*, *31*, 149–158.

Simon, C., and Sullivan, M. (1993). The measurement and determinants of brand equity: A financial approach. *Marketing Science*, *12*, 28–52.

Vaid, H. (2003). *Branding: Brand Strategy, Design, and Implementation of Corporate and Product Identity*. New York: Watson-Guptill.

CHAPTER 10

Strategic alliances in the hospitality industry

Prakash K. Chathoth

School of Hotel and Tourism Management,
The Hong Kong Polytechnic University,
Hung Hom, Kowloon, Hong Kong

Introduction

Strategic alliances have been increasingly used by firms over the past three decades as a key source of competitive advantage (Chathoth and Olsen, 2003; Hagedoorn, 1996). Cooperative strategies have grown in importance as firms expand and innovate (Insch and Steensma, 2006). Firms have used the networking strategy to sustain their competitiveness and address the challenges they confront in their business environment. In order to address the business risks associated with investments, firms need to identify appropriate strategies to manage these risks and ensure that the strategies they implement result in long-term returns. This is even more the case in an international setting when the risk exposure of firms is higher. This is why alliances with international firms provide a basis to mitigate such risks.

An alliance as a strategy is viewed from the perspective of reduction of a firm's risk exposure in terms of environmental uncertainty (Burgers *et al.*, 1993; Dickson and Weaver, 1997). Networking can be seen as a strategy that helps companies share costs of risky projects (Harrigan, 1985) and at the same time, equip them to respond to environmental uncertainties (Burgers *et al.*, 1993). Moreover, alliances are effective in countering the effects of mature, low growth markets. In fact, it can be viewed as an organizational survival strategy (Staber, 1996) that can help firms reestablish themselves in their competitive domain.

Firms have realized the importance of using alliances as a key component of the competitive strategy development and implementation process. Environment scanning is also more effective through the use of alliances as a result of the access firms have to information. Since value-adding resources are scarce, firms have taken steps towards building strengths and addressing weaknesses through alliances. Networks with competitors, suppliers, and customers, have provided firms with the required strengths to compete more effectively (Lewis, 1990). Value addition through alliances is more viable as this strategy provides firms with the ability to address weaknesses and counter threats with a low-cost commitment.

Given that researchers and practitioners alike have viewed the alliance strategy as a key source of value addition to the firm, it becomes imperative to delve into this source of competitive advantage in more depth. With this as the precursor, this chapter aims at reviewing the conceptual underpinnings of strategic alliance with the overall objective of bringing together the concepts researched and proposed by numerous researchers. The aim is to provide insight into the alliance strategy to highlight the sources of competitive advantage that can be drawn from it so as to address the challenges faced by industries/firms. Specifically, the focus of this chapter is to highlight the use of alliances in the hospitality industry from a strategic management perspective.

Strategic alliances: definitions

Strategic alliances are vehicles of growth and learning that allying firms use to accomplish joint and individual objectives (Iyer, 2002). Alliance partners use each others' resources and competencies for joint accomplishment of their objectives (Gulati, 1995). In an alliance, the parties remain independent to the alliance being created, but jointly govern the activities related to the alliance. The partners pool-in co-specialized assets that are used to generate relational rents (Dyer and Singh, 1998). These co-specialized assets could be in functional areas such as marketing, technology, research and development, and production. Alliances become a viable option when the cost of resources and capabilities is more when acquiring them through the market or creating them internally (Gulati and Singh, 1998). Moreover, in an external environment that is uncertain and turbulent, firms would need to have the flexibility related to investments in core technology and competencies. Since alliances provide greater flexibility in dealing with external environment conditions, they are preferred as a vehicle to address such factors.

The growth of alliances seen over the past three decades has been from various perspectives. In the seventies, firms predominantly used alliances from a product perspective for market reach as well as raw material procurement. In the eighties, the use of alliances evolved to building economies of scale and scope, and in the nineties, firms developed alliances in developing core competencies through innovation in technology and capabilities.

Objectives and characteristics of strategic alliances

The objectives of strategic alliances can be summarized per Contractor and Lorange (1988), which include:

- Risk reduction
- Achieving economies of scale
- Technological exchanges
- Creating barriers to entry/blocking competition
- Overcoming government-mandated trade or investment barriers

217

- Facilitating international expansion of inexperienced firms
- Vertical quasi-integration of linking the complementary contributions of partners in a value chain.

Other objectives that align with the above objectives include: access to co-specialized resources and capabilities, cost reduction, sharing information, reacting to market opportunities faster, and sharing and enhancing firm-specific knowledge and learning.

The characteristics of strategic alliances can be summarized as:

- Independence of partnering firms is retained.
- Most forms of strategic alliances are non-equity based alliances.
- A separate entity is not created in an alliance, which distinguishes such alliances from joint ventures.
- Firms use their strengths (competencies) to create co-specialized assets to tap market opportunities.
- Alliances can be formed by firms across industries (airline, hotels, and car rentals) or between competitors within a given industry (e.g., Marriott, Hilton, Hyatt, and Starwood).

Advantages and disadvantages of the alliance strategy

Strategic alliances lead to competitive advantage for the firms that participate in the alliance. Key advantages that alliances provide to incumbent firms include:

- Respond to environment uncertainties and turbulence
- Deal with the risk exposure in domestic and international markets
- Create avenues for growth in mature and new markets
- Be able to put the core resources and competencies to productive use
- Develop new competencies through interorganizational learning

Although alliances are a source of competitive advantage, there are certain disadvantages of strategic alliances that need to be highlighted. They include:

- Difficulty in identifying strategic partners
- Compatibility among partners
- Resources and time commitment required in getting partnering firms to agree to each other's terms and conditions
- Opportunism and potential for entering into conflict

- Evolving internal and external factors that lead to a change in firms' objectives related to the alliance strategy
- Barriers to terminating the alliance including cost
- Governance costs and mechanisms especially during the initial phase of the alliance
- Coordination costs and mechanisms related to alliance activities

Alliance networks

The alliance network theory has evolved during the past two to three decades of research work ranging from network theory in multinational corporations to present day interorganizational network theory. From a network theory perspective, strategic alliances are a source of revenue addition and value creation (Dyer and Singh, 1998). This result when allying firms are able to optimally combine alliance-specific assets to tap market opportunities. Since firms are constantly looking to tap market opportunities within a short time period, acquiring and developing resources, and capabilities may be a more costly option. Hence, firms pursue alliances to manage the costs of input factors so that the value addition is optimized when the combined resources and capabilities of allying firms lead to rent maximization. This provides the basis for firms to create networks that involve one or more firms as part of the alliance strategy.

According to Amit and Schoemaker (1993), asset specialization is an integral part of the value-creation process. Since acquiring specialized assets from the market or developing them internally would require time, strategic alliances provide firms with the option of achieving their objectives faster and more efficiently. For an alliance to succeed, it is imperative that allying partners are able to combine their resources to create co-specialized, alliance-specific assets (Dyer and Singh, 1998). It must be noted that allying firms are able to create relational profits and advantage if they combine specialized assets effectively (Dyer and Singh, 1998; Teece, 1987). Dyer and Singh (1998) point out that "relational rents" come about only when firms combine assets in a way that leads to effective leveraging of complementary resources.

The exchange relation is at the core of interorganizational theories, which is defined as consisting of transactions involving the transfer of resources between two or more actors for mutual benefit (Cook, 1977). Several perspectives exist that define the formation and development of strategic alliances. Foundations for the development of alliances have been based on economic theories such as market power theory (MPT) and transaction cost economics (TCE) (Child and Faulkner, 1998), as well as resource-based view (RBV), industry structure view, and the relational view (Dyer and Singh, 1998).

MPT is developed on the underpinning that firms succeed if they are in a stronger competitive position. Cooperative strategies play an integral role in strengthening the competitive position of the firm. Hymer (1972) was among the first researchers to apply MPT to cooperative strategies in his emphasis of the difference between offensive and defensive coalitions. The intended strategy of firms using offensive coalition according to Child and Faulkner (1998) is to attain competitive advantage by increasing market share at a faster rate as compared to competition or by increasing their production and marketing-related costs.

However, defensive coalitions are those that are used to create/enhance barriers to entry with the objective of securing the firms' market position and/or to stabilize the industry to increase profits. The MPT also emphasizes on the economies of scope through sharing of strategic resources, sharing and transferring knowledge, rationalizing capacity, and/or sharing risks (Child and Faulkner, 1998). The key underpinnings of this theory is that firms can be successful by choosing to ally with other firms that have complementary resources enabling partnering firms to gain competitive advantage in terms of time (faster) and cost (cheaper).

This is similar to the industry structure view suggested by Dyer and Singh (1998), which attributes the mechanism of preserving profits to industry entry barriers that stresses on government regulations and production economies/sunk costs. The RBV on the other hand identifies scarce physical resources, human resources, technological resources, financial resources, and intangible resources as the source of supernormal profits, which is similar to the value chain underpinnings of cooperative strategies suggested by Child and Faulkner (1998).

The relational view purported by Dyer and Singh (1998) is based on the complementarity of the pooled-in assets of allying firms. From such a perspective, the primary sources of supernormal profit returns are relation-specific investments, interfirm knowledge sharing routines, complementary resource endowments, and effective governance. The mechanisms that preserve profits in the case of relational view is because of dyadic/network barriers to imitation, causal ambiguity, time compression diseconomies, interorganizational asset stock interconnectedness, partner scarcity, resource indivisibility, and institutional environment (Dyer and Singh, 1998). The uniqueness of the combined resources may be a source of sustained competitive advantage as compared to individually owned set of resources. Firms will enter into such relationships if and only if the period of sustained competitive advantage generates rents that can cover the payback period (Dyer and Singh, 1998). In other words, the sum of the cost of entering into such relationships and the cost of owning resources should be lower than the returns that the firms will benefit by entering into the relationship.

However, TCE delves into the costs related to market transactions (Williamson, 1975). The essence of TCE lies in the governance mechanism that alliance partners use to transact across markets that lead to the cost optimization related to managing and governing alliance-specific transactions. Opportunism is considered to be a cost-enhancing factor that firm's entering into alliances should protect themselves from (Williamson, 1985). This factor leads to added costs in terms of governing the transactions between partners.

There are limitations associated with TCE. It does not take into consideration that tacit relationship could exist between partnering firms that is informal in nature. In other words, according to TCE all transactions are explicit in terms of their mode of governance/organization, supporting the concept that markets and hierarchies are the only two forms of governance mechanisms. Furthermore, the theory supports the view that opportunism may be a source of concern when two or more contracting parties seek to benefit from transactions. According to TCE, the opportunistic behaviour of contracting parties can be controlled through: (a) formal contracts that explicitly defines the role each contracting partner in the transaction and (b) governance mechanisms that controls the actions of parties involved in the transaction. Yet, the growth of collaboration as opposed to equity alliances (joint ventures) is an indication of how informal contracts/arrangements are a source of advantage to firms. Although opportunism is a concern between allying firms, it decreases as trust develops between partnering firms and the relationship between networking firms mature (Chathoth and Heiman, 2004). To understand and interpret the alliance concept in a better way, it is essential to study the different types of alliances.

Types of strategic alliances

There are two basic types of strategic alliances that include formal and informal arrangements of cooperation. The two modes used by firms include equity participation and non-equity based cooperation, which define the nature of the relationship between partnering firms. Formal relationships are seen in joint ventures wherein two firms come together to create a new entity, in which equity participation from both parties take place. Therefore, joint decision-making in the new venture becomes the basis of effective management in such an alliance. Non-equity mode of alliance formation leads to cooperative arrangements which result in collaboration entailing informal relationships rather than the use of formal governance methods.

Child and Faulkner (1998) proposed a taxonomy of alliance forms, which entails three factors that influence alliance formation. They are: scope, size, and entity. Scope is determined by the motive of the partnering firms to form the alliance. It is a function of the type of resources the partnering firms decide to combine to achieve their objectives. The scope of the alliance could range between two extremes, that is, focused set of objectives and activities to complex set of objectives entailing a wide range of activities.

The size of the alliance can range from two to several partners. An alliance that involves more than two partners is called a consortium, which is effective when more than two firms' resources are required to create competitive advantage. The alliance entity ranges from joint ventures to collaborations depending on how the alliance partners seek to manage the networking relationship between them.

Collaboration is appropriate when task uncertainty exists between the partnering firms of the cooperative venture, flexibility between the partners is essential to maintain the effectiveness of the collaboration, and there are no distinct boundaries between the collaborating firms (Child and Faulkner, 1998). An important element of collaborations is that they are based on trust between partnering firms. This results from the awareness that both firms are better of trusting each other in the partnership. The opportunistic behaviour of partnering firms does not come into play in their relationship, as this may be an impediment to the realization of individual firm's objectives. Moreover, collaborations are a result of matured relationship between firms with a clear understanding of each other's long-term objectives, behaviour, and culture. Hence, firms with little understanding of each other's way of functioning will not seek to use collaborations.

Contractor and Kundu (1998) in their study of global hotel firms highlight the difference between joint ventures and collaborations. While studying various entry modes into international markets ranging from joint ventures to non-equity contracts, the authors found that non-equity contracts or collaborations have low transaction cost with a potential for higher rent generation. Such alliances use revenues to calculate firms' returns. However, joint ventures use bottom-line profits to assess the firm' returns. While explaining this further, Chathoth and Olsen (2003) point out that Contractor and Kundu's (1998) study provide a basis to understand the difference between collaborations and joint ventures in terms of measuring the rent/profit generating process. They point out that "collaborations are measured by the revenue it generates, as the marginal cost associated with it is not significant; while joint ventures are measured by the profit it generates because the allying partners create a new entity which has a significant cost component attached to it" (p. 423).

Alliances are categorized based on vertical and horizontal collaborative arrangements. Ghemewat *et al.* (1986) categorized alliances as either "x" or "y" based on such arrangements. Vertical collaborations are "x" alliances, in which allying partners specialized in different functions, whereas, horizontal alliances are "y" alliances, in which the alliance partners specialized in similar functions. Vertical or x collaborations are seen in alliances between buyer and seller firms, while competitor alliances depict horizontal or y type collaborations. Other categorizations are based on functional arrangements between partners. For instance, Pucik (1988) categorized alliances on technological relationships, co-production agreements, sales and distribution networks, product development ventures, and joint ventures.

The strategic alliance process

The development of an alliance entails a process that involves several stages. As stated previously, the fundamental principle of the alliance concept is based on the fact that distinctive resource(s) of one company when held in combination with that of another creates a set or bundle of resources that add more value than when the resources where held in isolation. This raises the barriers to imitation and is a source of competitive advantage for the alliance partners. The strategic positioning as a result of combined resources is the key to the value-creation process for alliance partners. The alliance process stems from firm needs that can be met through various alternatives. The firm's decision to use alliance as a strategy is the first step to the alliance formation.

Child and Faulkner (1998) state that the alliance decision should be based on the firm's strategic orientation even if it does not have the capabilities to carry the strategy forward.

This is why pursuing alliances with firms that have capabilities to accomplish the goals would be beneficial to the firm. The ability in terms of scale (assets), technology, market access, and other factors that lead to competitive advantage are essential components of screening while selecting partners (Porter and Fuller, 1986). Hence, screening becomes an important factor in the pre-alliance phase. Criteria identified as essential while selecting partners include strategic and cultural fit (Child and Faulkner, 1998). Strategic fit is the value creation resulting from combining resources, and the synergistic effects ought to be superior to the competition. Cultural fit, on the other hand, is the ability of partners to cope with each other's cultural differences. The key to such a fit lies in the willingness of alliance partners to compromise when they differ in orientation and action related to the joint activities undertaken.

Organizational screening results in a clear understanding of where synergies among partners exist, and which partner would be able to contribute more to the overall objectives of the alliance. The step following screening is organizational complementarity (Dyer and Singh, 1998). This step forms the basis of identifying the mechanisms of access to each other's resources and the benefits related to the resource complementarity. According to Dyer and Singh, the degree of compatibility among partnering firms related to systems, processes, and culture impact the value-creation process. Research in this domain suggests that decision process, operating systems, and culture are important factors in developing organizational complementarity. Strategic complementarity is related to the potential combinations of resources to tap future opportunities while revealed complementarity reflects the outcome related to joint activities undertaken in the past (Doz, 1996). It should be noted that identifying complementarity among prospective partners' resources forms an essential part in the partner selection phase of the alliance.

Governance mechanisms sought during the inception and development phase of the alliance will impact the rate at which the alliance moves forward. Opportunism could be an impeding factor in the progress of the alliance at the outset. Firms may choose a formal governance structure to closely monitor the actions of its partners. A more informal structure might develop as the alliance matures resulting from the development of trust (Chathoth and Heiman, 2004). This may lead to the development of informal contractual relationships among partnering firms.

It must be noted that organizational cultural similarities influences the type of contract employed in the alliance.

Firms that have similar cultural characteristics tend to use equity joint ventures (EJVs) as compared to contractual joint venture (CJV) and vice versa (Tallman and Shenkar, 1994). Furthermore, the use of EJVs over CJVs is more likely when: (a) the parent firms involved in the alliance are from more individualistic national cultures as compared to collectivist national cultures, and (b) there is greater scope for sharing organizational skills than specific technologies. CJVs could be used in alliances wherein trust becomes the basis of developing the relationship, and when partnering firms use lower level of control to monitor each other's actions.

Dyer and Singh (1998) summarize the benefits of governance mechanisms in an alliance, which they point out is best when informal governance modes are used to manage alliance-specific transactions. This is attributable to: (1) lower marginal costs, and (2) difficulty of imitation. On the other hand, the limitations of such a structure are that they take considerable time to develop and that the partnering firms are exposed to the risk of opportunism that may potentially emanate if safeguards to protect themselves from partner's opportunistic behaviour are low. However, it is essential to note that the development of trust between partners forms the key to alliance success on the long run (Chathoth and Heiman, 2004).

The alliance creation process is summarized in Figure 10.1. As depicted in the figure, the alliance creation process starts with the decision to pursue alliance as a strategy. Once this decision is made, the alliance creation process could then proceed to the next step, which pertains to developing a plan that identifies the long-term objectives of pursuing the alliance strategy with a given partner. The search criteria could be specified subsequently that pertain to the business objectives related to the alliance strategy.

The process of finding suitable alliance partners could begin once the above aspects of alliance formation are in place. Similarity theory suggests that firms with similar strategic focus form alliances with each other (Insch and Steensma, 2006). This is possible if information is available for decision-making related to alliance partner selection. For this to happen, firms seeking an alliance should use various sources to obtain information. Once a suitable partner is identified, the negotiation and contract development phase (if applicable) could be initiated. During this phase, firms discuss the governance structure and control mechanisms related to the alliance. It should be noted that alliances that succeed in the long term are able to combine both formal and informal control mechanisms as part of the governance structure.

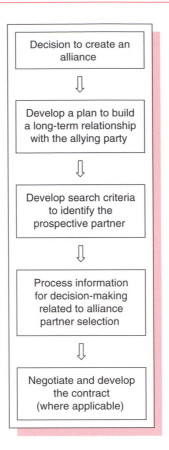

Figure 10.1
The alliance creation process.

Alliances in the hospitality industry

Alliances in the hospitality industry have grown from contract-based equity alliances to non-contract based relational alliances (Chathoth and Olsen, 2003). Many examples of alliances exist within the hospitality industry to support this. Contract-based alliances could be seen in a management contract or franchising wherein one partner allies with another partner while combining strategic resources. Examples include management contracts developed by Hilton Hotels and franchising contracts developed by Holiday Inn, subsequently emulated by competing firms that include leading hotel and restaurant firms such as Marriott, Hyatt, Accor, Intercontinental Hotels, Best Western, McDonald's, KFC, and others. These firms have pursued management and/or franchising contracts as vehicles for growth globally.

Alliances have been used as vehicles for market access by companies in matured as well as growing markets. For instance, a marketing alliance within the Asian context includes The Taj Group of Hotels and Raffles International. The main objective of this alliance was to create access to market for both firms where they do not have a good enough presence (Tata.com). A similar alliance was established between the Oberoi Group and the Hilton International as well as the ITC-Welcomgroup (Indian Tobacco Company) and Starwood Hotels. Other examples of marketing alliances in the hospitality industry include the alliance between Starwood Hotels and Vacation.com. This alliance was created to provide Vacation.com's members with access to Starwood Hotels products, which, according to the President and CEO of Vacation.com, provides "initiatives and incentives for our member agencies to promote and sell more hotel accommodations" (m-travel.com).

Other examples of marketing alliances include Le Meridian and Nikko Hotels. These hotel firms initiated a marketing alliance strategy with the focus on improving their booking system so that the customers could be provided with a worldwide "one-stop" option (Chathoth and Olsen, 2003). Yet another example of a marketing alliance that uses technology to create synergy is the Global Hotel Alliance. The objective of this alliance is to offer a "greater choice and enhanced recognition to customers in a growing collection of hotels, managed by individual, regional brands, which are respected in their home markets for reflecting and respecting local traditions and culture through their hotels' products and services" (globalalliance.com). This alliance has brought together seven prominent hotel brands that include Dusit Hotels & Resorts; Kempinski Hotels; Landis Hotels & Resorts; Marco Polo Hotels; Omni Hotels; Pan Pacific Hotels and Resorts; and The Leela Palaces and Resorts. This also provide the allying firms with a more global access to markets while at the same time providing customers with a one-stop internet site that provides customers and travel agents with attractive prices and access to all member hotels' products, while providing them access to airline products as well. Some of the member hotels have also recognize each other's guest recognition programs, which provides customers with the convenience of accumulating points and using them across these hotels.

A similar example that compares to the Global Hotel Alliance in terms of strategy is the Luxury Alliance. This alliance although similar to the Global Hotel Alliance in terms of strategy differs in scope as it brings together hotel, rail, and cruise companies in this technology-based marketing alliance to provide customers with a wide range of travel options in the luxury hospitality product segment. The companies participating in this alliance include The Leading Hotels of the World, Relais & Châteaux, and the Orient-Express Hotels, Trains and Cruises (Luxuryalliance.com).

The alliance between Cendant, Marriott, Hyatt, and Starwood that came into being in the late nineties is an example of a consortia-like agreement. This agreement brought about a reservation system to compete with on-line travel intermediaries such as Expedia and Travelocity (Cline, 2000).

Co-branding has been used by hotel and restaurant companies as an alliance strategy. Some examples include the alliance between Doubletree Hotel Corporation and the New York Restaurant Group as well as the alliance between Four Seasons Hotels and the Bice Ristorante (Strate and Rappole, 1997). Other examples of co-branding include the Renaissance Hotels and Starbucks, Hilton and Neutrogena, and W. Hotels and Bliss.

From a historical perspective, alliances have been used as vehicles to address labour shortage issues. As seen in the 1996 Hospitality Business Alliance between the Educational Foundation of the National Restaurant Association and the Educational Institute of the American Hotel & Motel Association to address the US hospitality workforce development. Such examples provide support to the thesis that alliances are effective in addressing issues in all domains and functions of business.

Implications and conclusion

Strategic alliances are considered as vehicles of growth that provide partners with access to each other's resources and capabilities so that they could address their weaknesses and threats. In today's global economy, it is essential that hospitality firms use alliances to access markets globally. Acquiring resources or developing them internally may be a more costly option which could be done away with if alliances are pursued.

As discussed in the preceding section, more and more alliances are being formed that have made it easier for the customer and the provider alike to create a customized and complete travel experience. Through the effective use of alliances, providers are able to understand and take care of customer needs better while at the same time being able to reduce costs and manage their business in a better way.

For hospitality firms to be able to use this vehicle of growth in a more efficient and effective way, core concepts related to how alliances are created and maintained over a prolonged period of time is of the essence. Due to a high failure rate of strategic alliances observed by scholars in the business field, it is imperative that hospitality firms are able to create alliances by identifying the right partners in the first place by using good selection criteria and at the same time managing the alliance process in an effective manner by using a governance structure that bring together the allying parties instead of alienating them. Examples of failed alliances suggest that opportunism is detrimental to the success of alliances. To make sure opportunism does not creep into the alliance at an early stage, it is imperative that allying partners take step towards each other to build trust as the alliance evolves. This would have an impact on the governance costs and mechanisms as well as the costs associated with managing the alliance.

Future research in the hospitality alliance domain should focus on the evolution of hospitality alliances. Researchers could delve into the alliance structure and governance mechanisms from an evolutionary perspective and the role of trust in an evolving alliance. This will provide industry practitioners with evidence of why alliances should be pursued as a long-term strategy. More research is needed in this domain as this strategy has been used by an increasing number of hospitality firms during the past decade.

References

Amit, R., and Schoemaker, P. (1993). Strategic assets and organizational rent. *Strategic Management Journal*, *14*, 33–46.

Burgers, W. P., Hill, C., and Kim, C. (1993). A theory of global strategic alliances: The case of the global auto industry. *Strategic Management Journal*, *14*(6), 419–432.

Chathoth, P. K., and Heiman, B. (2004). *Governance Cost in Alliances: Combining the Evolutionary and Transaction Cost Economics Views*, Jan 8–11, 2004, Proceedings of the International Business and Economy Conference, San Francisco, CA.

Chathoth, P. K., and Olsen, M. D. (2003). Strategic alliances: A hospitality industry perspective. *International Journal of Hospitality Management*, *22*, 419–433.

Child, J., and Faulkner, D. (1998). *Strategies of Cooperation: Managing Alliances, Networks, and Joint Ventures*. New York: Oxford University Press.

Cline, R. S. (2000). E-commerce: The pace picks up. *Hotels*, *34*, 71.

Contractor, F. J., and Kundu, S. K. (1998). Franchising versus company-run operations: Modal choice in the global hotel sector. *Journal of International Marketing*, *6*(2), 28–53.

Contractor, F. J., and Lorange, P. (1988). "Why should firms cooperate?" The strategy and economics basis for cooperative ventures. In F. J. Contractor and P. Lorange (Eds.),

Cooperative Strategies in International Business (pp. 3–28). New York: Lexington Books.

Cook, K. S. (1977). Exchange and power in networks of interorganizational relations. *The Sociological Quarterly, 18*, 62–82.

Devlin, G., and Bleackley, M. (1988). Strategic alliances: Guidelines for success. *Long Range Planning, 21*(5), 18–23.

Dickson, P. H., and Weaver, K. M. (1997). Environmental determinants and individual-level moderators of alliance use. *The Academy of Management Journal (Special Research Forum on Alliances and Networks), 40*(2), 404–425.

Doz, Y. L. (1996). The evolution of cooperation in strategic alliances: Initial conditions, or learning processes? *Strategic Management Journal, Summer Special Issue, 17*, 55–83.

Dyer, J. H., and Singh, H. (1998). Relational view: Cooperative strategy and sources of interorganizational competitive advantage. *Academy of Management Review, 23*(4), 660–679.

Ghemewat, P., Porter, M. E., and Rowlinson, A. (1986). Patters of international coalition activities. In M. E. Porter (Ed.), *Competition in Global Industries*. Boston, MA: Harvard Business School Press.

Globalalliance.com. Obtained from globalalliance.com, http://www.globalhotelalliance.com/About/Whoweare/Whoweare/LG-EN/Content.aspx

Gulati, R. (1995). Does familiarity breed trust? The implication of repeated ties for contractual choice in alliances. *Academy of Management Journal, 38*, 85–112.

Gulati, R., and Singh, H. (1998). The architecture of cooperation: Managing coordination costs and appropriation concerns in strategic alliances. *Administrative Science Quarterly, 43*(4), 781–814.

Hagedoorn, J. (1996). Trends and patterns in strategic technology partnering since the early seventies. *Review of Industrial Organization, 11*, 601–616.

Harrigan, K. R. (1985). *Strategies for Joint Ventures*. Lexington, MA: Lexington Books.

Hymer, S. H. (1972). The multinational corporation and the law of uneven development. In N. Bhagwati (Ed.), *Economics and World Order*. London: Macmillan.

Insch, G. S., and Steensma, K. (2006). The relationship between firm strategic profile and alliance partners' characteristics. *Journal of Managerial Issues, 18*(3), 321–339.

Iyer, K. (2002). *Learning in Strategic Alliances: An Evolutionary Perspective*. Academy of Marketing Science Review, p. 10, html version available at http://www.amsreview.org/articles/iyer10-2002.pdf

Lewis, J. D. (1990). *Partnerships and Profit*. New York: Free Press.

Luxuryalliance.com. Obtained from http://www.luxury-alliance.com/

m-travel.com. Obtained from http://www.m-travel.com/news/2007/07/starwood-and-va.html

Porter, M., and Fuller, M. (1986). Coalitions and global strategy. In M. Porter (Ed.), *Competition in Global Industries*. Boston, MA: Harvard Business School Press, 315–344.

Pucik, V. (1988). Strategic alliances, organizational learning and competitive advantage: The HRM agenda. *Human Resources Management*, 27(1), 77–93.

Staber, U. H. (1996). The social embeddedness of industrial district networks. In U. H. Staber, N. V. Schaefer, and B. Sharma (Eds.), *Business Networks: Prospects for Regional Development* (pp. 148–174). Berlin: de Gruyter.

Strate, R. W., and Rappole, C. L. (1997). Strategic alliances between hotels and restaurants. *Cornell Hotel and Restaurant Administration Quarterly*, 38(3), 50–61.

Tallman, S. B., and Shenkar, O. (1994). A managerial decision model of international cooperative venture formation. *Journal of International Business Studies*, 25(1), 91–113.

Tata.com. Obtained from http://tata.com/indian_hotels/media/20040820.htm

Teece, D. J. (1987). Profiting from technological innovation: Implications for integration, collaboration, licensing and public policy. *The Competitive Challenge: Strategies for Industrial Innovation and Renewal* (pp. 185–219). Cambridge, MA: Ballinger.

Williamson, O. E. (1975). *Markets and Hierarchies: Analysis and Antitrust Implications*. New York: Free Press.

Williamson, O. E. (1985). *The Economic Institutions of Capitalism*. New York: Free Press.

Part Three

Core competencies

Resource allocation decisions and organizational structure

Robert J. Harrington[1] and Michael Ottenbacher[2]

[1]Hospitality and Restaurant Management Program, University of Arkansas, Fayetteville, AR 72701
[2]School of Hospitality & Tourism Management, San Diego State University, San Diego, CA 92182

Introduction

Resource allocation decisions are tactical methods to implement organizational goals and objectives. These allocations are tied to firm action plans and policies that impact organizational structure, and, ultimately, performance. The basic concepts of resource allocation decisions and organizational structure are at the heart of an ongoing debate fundamental to management theory. Resource allocation decisions represent the strategic choice perspective. Central to the strategic choice perspective is the notion that management has a substantial amount of latitude in making strategic decisions about the future direction of the organization and its structure including how to respond to a variety of environmental pressures, changes, and other influences (Child, 1972; Pennings, 1975).

The influence of organizational structure has a connection to the roots of organizational theory. Initial work in this area emphasized the imperative of bringing together human and physical resources in a profitable manner (Wren, 1994). Early arguments support the notion of a structural–environmental determination of strategy. Apart from strategy, this school of thought proposes that organizational structure is a complex play of variables including culture, values, the past and present functioning of the organization, and an organization's history of success and failure (Hall and Saias, 1980). These central arguments have fuelled an academic debate over strategy versus structure in the strategic management literature for more than four decades (Amburgey and Dacin, 1994; Chandler, 1962; McWilliams and Smart, 1993; Miller, 1986).

The question of how to structure an organization along with the causes and consequences has been studied from individual, group, departmental, unit, and organizational perspectives. Early studies point to the idea that organizational structure provides both a limiting factor for organizations (i.e., there are limits to our ability to successfully implement strategy due to our structure) and its impact in relation to strategic choice (i.e., strategic leaders' ability to design structure to adapt to strategic needs).

While issues relating to resource allocation decisions and organizational structure are many, this chapter provides a discussion of its application for firms in the hospitality industry. First, we provide an overview of the current thinking regarding resource allocation decisions and organizational structure in the general and hospitality literatures. The application section considers resource allocation decisions and organizational structure issues for entry into a fast-growing foodservice business segment. Specifically, the emerging trend of channel blurring between retail and foodservice will be discussed in order to demonstrate the impact of level of control considerations, resource availability, and demand uncertainty on structural decisions. This example highlights issues of key resource allocation decision for this strategic option. The example also provides a glimpse at factors influencing structural decisions such as vertical integration and ownership forms.

Literature review

The review of the literature focuses on the impetus behind the strategy–structure debate, early findings related to the environment, and more recent studies on resource allocation decisions and the relationship with organizational structure.

Traditional strategy–structure debate

The age-old question in this debate is: Which comes first—strategy or structure? While at first glance this argument may seem entirely academic, the underlying issue is tied to a central concern for practitioners, namely, do we make resource allocation decisions based solely on achieving what we have defined as our strategic ends (with the assumption that it will be possible to achieve the necessary structure to achieve these ends)? Or, as decision makers, are we severely limited in what we can actually achieve based on the current organizational structure and a limited ability to change this structure given the environment we operate in?

An early study by Chandler (1962) provided a rallying cry for the influence of strategy and strategic choice on the organizational structure of the firm. While the idea that structure follows strategy was christened many times by fellow theorists in the area (Andrews, 1971; Ansoff, 1965; Schendel and Hofer, 1979), a counter-argument developed out of sociology and organizational theory suggesting that strategy follows structure (Amburgey and Dacin, 1994; Hall and Saias, 1980). This perspective argued that strategy grows out of structure, which in turn leads to the modification of structure. Both arguments are not without merit; the "structure follows strategy" concept supports the idea that leaders' actions and planning matter. The central concept here is that (1) managers interpret environment events, (2) they allocate resources to adapt the organizational structure in a fashion that addresses the need for change, and (3) this change makes efficient and effective use of the firm's resources. In so doing, organizations are able to successfully execute its defined competitive methods and achieve desired performance (Olsen *et al.*, 1998; Porter, 1980).

This idea sounds logical, but as the contingency-determinism arguments spotlight, structure is a complex mix of variables that are likely to have substantial effects on possible strategies, the ability to achieve structural change, and resulting inefficiencies. For instance, Hall and Saias (1980) indicate issues such as organizational culture pose a structural constraint on strategic choice as well as a suggestion that structural characteristics filter incoming information used to make resource allocation decisions by delaying or expediting the transmission of some types of information over others. As the authors state: "Once an organization begins to operate, the nature of its structure limits its perception—both of itself and its environment" (Hall and Saias, 1980, p. 157).

This basic concept seems to be akin to an organizational-level version of "bounded rationality" (Simon, 1945) from the decision-making literature. A strictly rational approach to decision making has been criticized due to the assumptions of the "perfectly rational man": information can be gathered without cost, the decision maker can be perfectly informed, the decision maker is perfectly logical, and the one criterion is economic gain. As Simon (1945) pointed out, managers use bounded rather than perfect rationality due to a number of personal, emotional, and contextual factors. Following the ideas of Hall and Saias (1980), this concept applies to the organizational level with limits to the type, amount, and use of information in the resource allocation decision process as well as having multiple performance interests rather than strictly an economic incentive.

By using both sides of the strategy–structure argument, logic would indicate that each side is partially right. Resource allocation decisions that are tied to achieving strategic objectives are likely to be derived through a complex interaction of variables based on environment events, physical organizational structure, and intangible structural elements such as culture, values, and history. This integrated approach seems to suggest a fit between external and internal needs as well as the need of management to consider both context and process in determining and implementing resource allocation decisions.

While this debate is an interesting one from an academic point of view, the resolution of this debate in the near future is unlikely. For practitioners, a helpful outcome of this debate is an integration of the concepts of contingency theory and the resource-based view of the firm applied to a hospitality service environment. Therefore, the following sections discuss contingency theory and applicable elements of resource-based approaches to allocation and structure decisions.

Contingency theory and the impact of the environment on structure

The basis of contingency theory is the idea that there is "no one best way" to organize (Scott, 1998) and that efficient and effective resource allocation decisions require creating a "fit" among the environment in which the firm finds itself, internal concerns and capabilities, and organizational structure (Harrington, 2004b; Olsen *et al.*, 1998; Scott, 1998).

The position of contingency theory is not one of contingency determinism but instead one of structural adjustment. In other words, the basic proposition by most modern advocates of a contingency approach is a structural–functionalist position where structural adjustment to regain fit (SARFIT) is sought after an acknowledgement of substandard performance. While misfits among strategy, environment, and structure have been shown to impact performance (Burns and Stalker, 1961; Geiger *et al.*, 2006; Harrington, 2004b; Harrington *et al.*, 2004; Lawrence and Lorsch, 1967), there is little support for the idea that structural change is an automatic response. This concept rejects the sole reliance on contingency determinism and strategic choice but instead defends the complex interplay between strategy–structure and the context in which the firm operates (Amburgey and Dacin, 1994; Harrington, 2004b; Hill and Hoskisson, 1987). For instance, Harrington (2004b) found a relationship among the external complexity, internal complexity, and firm performance. This finding indicated a tacit response by many executives across 18 industries to match the internal complexity with the external one (Ashmos *et al.*, 2002). By so doing, firms were able to achieve above-normal returns—a key objective of strategic management (Harrington, 2004b).

A related concept from the hospitality literature is the co-alignment principle (Olsen *et al.*, 1998). Olsen and colleagues describe this principle as an all-encompassing underpinning of strategic management. The basic idea is that environmental forces drive change in the firm's environment. Leaders chose competitive methods to take advantage of these forces (representing opportunities or threats for the firm). These choices require resource allocation decisions that impact organizational structure; ultimately, these changes and choices impact firm performance. If these choices co-align with environmental change and firm structure, the results will provide the firm with a sustainable competitive advantage (Olsen *et al.*, 1998).

At first glance, this overview appears to imply that strategic choice advocates and contingent determinists are talking in circles. In reality, the concepts of the co-alignment principle and the structural-functionalist arguments may be two sides of the same coin. Thus, while the explanation of the co-alignment principle is presented from a strategic choice perspective and the structural-functionalist view from a contingency and organizational theory perspective, both arrive at similar conclusions regarding a process of fit and readjustment based on balancing external and internal needs for determining what will be achieved, how it will be implemented, and the complex interplay involved.

Resource-based theory and intangible elements

The resource-based view provides useful concepts because it moves the strategic choice and structural arguments from being primarily physical resources and manufacturing based to greater acknowledgment of intangible elements and the business-unit level of analysis (Barney, 1986, 1991), both of which appear more applicable to a service-based environment such as hospitality. For instance, the unique characteristics of hospitality and other high-contact service firms indicate potential differences from the normative descriptions of what "should be" as described in the strategy literature. Contextual and situational issues such as geographic distribution of units (Harrington, 2005), size (Byers and Slack, 2001), type of ownership (Bradach, 1997; Roberts, 1997), greater difficulty in predicting the demand curve, and key characteristics that distinguish services from products (intangibility, heterogeneity, perishability, and inseparability) (Olsen *et al.*, 1998) have implications on the general assumptions developed in the resource allocation decision and organizational structure literatures.

The greater acknowledgement of intangible resources and activities in the resource-based approach is directly applicable to the hospitality total experience concept (Harrington, 2004a; Olsen *et al.*, 1998). Each hospitality experience can be thought of as a bundle of tangible and intangible products and services provided to the consumer. The total experience evolves from the bundle of resources and capabilities that create a total "product" or experience that is part of a product-service continuum (Olsen *et al.*, 1998). Given that much of the service provided is intangible in nature, firms allocate resources to create value for the customer and, hopefully, creating a service experience that is difficult to imitate (Harrington, 2004a).

Barriers to imitation ● ● ●

In a hospitality business environment, ideas can generally be quickly copied and imitated by competitors (Olsen *et al.*, 1998). One reason for this situation is that individual innovations in hospitality are generally transparent in nature and the resources (whether tangible or intangible) to create these products or services are readily available in the marketplace. Two methods of creating barriers to imitation established in the literature relate directly to the creation of barriers in hospitality: asymmetric information (Barney, 1986; Williamson, 1985) and causal ambiguity (Reed and DeFillippi, 1990).

Asymmetric information is described as competitors having difficulty in obtaining information on costs or other areas of expertise in the marketplace. Hence, if competitors (or network members in the branded foodservice product example) are able to obtain complete information, they will quickly understand where and how any competitive advantage arises. Reed and DeFillippi (1990) described a causal relationship among tacitness, complexity, and human asset specificity with causal ambiguity. Tacitness is defined as know-how that is achieved through experience and a learning-by-doing approach. Complexity arises from increases in the number and heterogeneity of technologies, organizational routines, and experiences in the organizational environment. Thus, imitation through observation by rivals is limited, and increased complexity safeguards firm information from being expropriated as rivals recruit employees. Human asset specificity is the specific deployment of firm resources in obtaining and developing human resources with specific knowledge and capabilities. Tacitness, complexity, and human asset specificity are proposed to have both direct and interaction effects on ambiguity. Therefore, all three of these elements should create higher ambiguity in relationships and ultimately heighten barriers to imitation by industry competitors (Harrington, 2004a).

From a marketing perspective, causal ambiguity appears to be a key driver of intangible concepts such as brand equity derived through an ongoing, internal tacit process as well as an ongoing process that impacts customers' perceptions of quality and image of a firm's products and services. Aaker (2004) classifies brand equity assets as brand loyalty, name awareness, perceived quality, brand associations in addition to perceived quality, and other proprietary brand assets (e.g., patents, trademarks, channel relationships, and so on).

Examples of foodservice products that have substantial brand equity assets include McDonald's (The Big Mac), Burger King

241 ● ● ●

(The Whopper), The Outback Steakhouse (Bloomin' Onion), and Dairy Queen (The Blizzard). In these cases, the product name is a brand on its own. However, it also automatically recalls to the consumer the brand of the operation relating to the entire bundle of tangible and intangible elements. In a recent interview, McDonald's former president supported the notion and importance of branding relating to both tangible and intangible concepts. Accordingly, a number of elements inherent in a branded item, such as the Egg McMuffin, protect it from direct duplication. These include supplier relationships, the implementation process, location factors, and price–volume relationships.

The strategic process, decisions, and structure

Strategic process • • •

A key consideration in strategy is how the process of strategy making is formulated, implemented, and evaluated. This question is particularly relevant at the point of resource allocation decisions and the impact on organizational structure. Resource allocation decisions are at the point of deciding how strategic ends will be implemented. Several key features are pointed out in the literature as important to the process and ultimately the decision outcomes. These features include how the process takes place and who is involved in the process (Ashmos *et al.*, 2002; Brews and Hunt, 1999; Harrington, 2004b, 2005; Mintzberg *et al.*, 1998; Okumus and Roper, 1999).

The importance of this area of study is the situational connection among external environmental characteristics, the internal context, and the impact of the process on desired outcomes. Thus, a key factor for decision makers in the area of resource allocations includes decisions on designing a strategic process that enhances the likelihood of achieving desired outcomes and performance. As pointed out in this and other studies, this decision includes an understanding of the impact of external factors (such as uncertainty, volatility, hostility, and complexity) (Harrington, 2004a; Jogaratnam and Tse, 2006) and internal factors (structure [size and ownership], culture, values, etc.) (Bradach, 1997; Okumus, 2004; Parsa, 1999; Ritchie and Riley, 2004; Schmelzer and Olsen, 1994) in hospitality industries.

Strategic decision making • • •

Most studies in the strategic decision-making arena are tied to the notion of a strategic or management choice perspective

(Child, 1972; Hambrick and Mason, 1984; Olsen *et al.*, 1998). This notion indicates that organizational structure and processes are, in part, a reflection of management's cognitive interpretation of contextual variables (both internal and external), thus driving decisions for the allocation of resources in process issues such as the complexity of the internal structure (Ashmos *et al.*, 2002).

Roberts (1997) determined that the choice to franchise in the hotel industry placed limits on managerial discretion and impacted strategic decision making. Byers and Slack (2001) studied the strategic decision-making processes used by owners of small firms in the leisure industry. The study determined that firms in this business sector used adaptive and reactive decision making. The reasons given for this approach included time constraints, an unwillingness to relinquish control, and the unique constraint by owners in this sector to "pursue their hobby while simultaneously operating their businesses" (Byers and Slack, 2001, p. 121). Harrington and Kendall (2006a) found that two main tactics were used by organizations: middle-up-down and top-down approaches. In many cases, middle managers in foodservice firms appeared to serve as boundary spanners synthesizing information up and down the organization. This approach was particularly prevalent in an environment of high uncertainty and when using multiple ownership forms. An autocratic and top-down management approach was also used frequently across the foodservice industry (85% of the time in this sample). Overall, the study provided support for a relationship among management structure needs based on ownership type (franchise, sole-proprietor, and wholly corporate owned), number of units, and the task environment.

Because a fit between managerial discretion and the aim of decision making is generally a desired characteristic, these findings relate to the need (and ability) to achieve strategic objectives with the appropriate structure. Overall, the studies on decision making point to the importance of context on the decision and the decision process. Specifically, issues such as uncertainty, complexity, and instability are important factors to consider when delegating to a resource allocation team or designing the decision-making process in general.

Organizational structure and service excellence in hospitality

Firms in many service industries understand the importance of service excellence and its relationship with a competitive advantage. Service quality can be defined by the customer, and a variety of industry segments have reputations for providing service excellence. For instance, McDonald's restaurants and Ritz-Carlton Hotels are two organizations with a reputation for service quality but the structure and approach at achieving it are very different. McDonald's utilizes a very standardized approach where everything from layout, equipment, and staff behaviours is tied to standard operating procedures and training systems. In contrast, Ritz-Carlton Hotels, twice a winner of the Baldridge Award for quality, use a process that emphasizes empowering all employees to do whatever it takes to exceed hotel guests' expectations. While two companies' approaches to delivering service excellence are quite different, so are the organizational structures that are designed to ensure customers' expectations are met.

Traditional structural characteristics ● ● ●

While every organization is unique in how it is structured, basic structural characteristics consider vertical and horizontal decisions on the division of labour and coordination of firm activities. Issues such as span of control, flat or tall organization, formalization of tasks, and centralization or decentralization of activities are key structural decisions for any organization. A key factor tied to a contingency approach discussed earlier is mechanistic versus organic organizational structures. Mechanistic structures are characterized be tallness, high specialization, centralization, and formality across the firm. Organic structures are characterized by flatness (few hierarchical levels), low specialization of labour, informality, and a decentralized process. Studies in this area suggest that firms in a more complex and uncertain environment perform better when using a predominantly organic structure and firms in a less complex and stable environment achieve better results using a mechanistic structure (Burns and Stalker, 1961; Lawrence and Lorsch, 1967; Harrington, 2004b).

Plural forms and other arrangements ● ● ●

Several studies in the hospitality literature have suggested that there is value in designing organizations utilizing multiple forms at different levels of the organization. Ritchie and Riley (2004) found the communication role of the multi-unit manager to balance an organic frontline structure that allowed employees to deal with operational contingencies while maintaining a more stable environment at the higher organizational levels to allow a formal and a more mechanistic structure for top-down communication of strategies.

Harrington (2005) used the quick service restaurant (QSR) segment as an example of the multiple structural form model. Earlier research indicates that the QSR environment lends itself to achieving greater efficiency by utilizing a deliberate and fairly individualistic (top-down) approach. This segment of the restaurant industry is more homogenous and, at the segment level, has been less uncertain. Theoretically, the nature of the organizational form in this segment indicates that a top-down, mechanistic approach can be successful. The franchise form should allow a top-down approach from the corporate level to individual units specifying product specifications, service levels, and marketing campaigns. This general proposition is supported by earlier research findings. Parsa (1999) determined that increased levels of profits for franchises in the QSR segment were associated with the use of Bourgeois and Brodwin's (1984) change model; this model was described as a predominately top-down strategy-making approach. Bradach (1997) found that QSR firms use a plural form to manage the restaurant chain and strategy-making processes. While the literature portrays the corporate-franchise structure as one of bureaucratic managers versus local owner-operators, Bradach (1997) found the arrangement to be generally a "large monolithic hierarchy (a company arrangement)" and "a federation of semi-autonomous small hierarchies (a franchise arrangement)" (p. 285). Therefore, a use of multiple models appears to enable firms to leverage company strengths of controlling and providing overriding directions for the firm. The strengths of franchise units are in understanding the needs of local markets and having a willingness to champion ideas up the chain to top management (Bradach, 1997). This finding supports the value of multiple ownership structures with implications on resource allocation decisions and processes.

In addition to a variety of ownership structures and traditional organizational forms, several other contemporary organizational structures have emerged due to changes in national borders, technology, and demographic shifts. Key contemporary organizational structures are described as network—virtual and modular. A network organization is a structure that facilitates the sharing of assets necessary to deliver the finished product or service that lie within the various members of the network rather than within one firm. A virtual organization is also a network but one that is a constantly changing independent group that shares the skills, knowledge, costs, and access to each other's markets (Johns and Saks, 2005; Miles and Snow, 1992). A modular organizational structure is one that performs a small number of core functions internally and outsources any non-core functions to other specialists and suppliers (Karim,

2006). While the nature of network and virtual organizations require that they give up much of their control, the modular organization maintains complete control over strategy and objectives (Dess *et al.*, 1995).

Summary

A synthesis of the literature instils several prominent points. First, the overwhelming evidence appears to support the concept of achieving a fit or co-alignment among firm strategic ends, resource allocations, and organizational structure. This fit does not appear to happen automatically but instead appears to be a tacit skill developed through experience. Ultimately, a co-alignment among these elements provides firms with higher performance. This enhanced performance is due to two main areas: (1) greater likelihood of successful implementation through the use of specific knowledge and an understanding of organizational culture, values, and history effects and (2) the utilization of organizational forms that adapt to the needs of an uncertain environment across and within the organization.

Practitioners and researchers should consider relationships at a variety of levels to appropriately operationalize the resource allocation process across the firm. For instance, due to the aforementioned characteristics in hospitality (i.e., a combination of multi-unit firms and independent operators, a variety of ownership structures, widely varying organizational sizes, and geographically dispersed business units), it seems likely that firms will utilize multiple models of the strategy-making process simultaneously based on the context and organizational level. Ritchie and Riley (2004) found that lower levels of the hierarchy in multi-unit service firms was where organizations coped with uncertainty in the environment, shielding the uncertainty from higher levels of the organization. Bradach (1997) found that QSR chains utilized multiple forms of management in the strategic process to simultaneously balance a need for control and adaptability. This finding illustrates the need to utilize a more adaptive approach at the unit level to maintain flexibility and use a more traditional, top-down approach at the corporate level of a firm to maintain control and linear strategic direction (Harrington, 2005).

To illustrate these points, resource allocation decisions on the restructuring of McDonald's over the past few years have been driven by many of these factors. First, in regards to ownership structure, McDonald's leadership wrestled with the fit and balance between a franchised and corporate-owned restaurant mix. In the U.S. market, McDonald's typically has an 80/20 (80% franchised and 20% company owned) ownership structure. Internationally, the structure is about 40/60 (40% franchised and 60% company owned). As stated by the recent president of McDonald's "I began strategically to say that in my opinion internationally we should have more of our operators run our restaurants because the presence of an on-premise owner operator is the most effective way to build the brand in that community. This is difficult because the profitability to the company [McDonald's]—if the restaurants are run well—the profit is greater when we own it. So, when I went to our team and said here is an idea, there were a lot of raised eyebrows." To evaluate this potential restructuring decision, the leadership at McDonald's followed a strategic decision-making process of

1. Analysis—(a) communicate with operators; (b) evaluate capabilities of operators; (c) analyse the market; (d) determine who is capable of running more units; (e) determine a price for each unit that would be competitive, enable them to do well, and yet provide the company with a good return; and (f) question employees and suppliers.
2. Financial considerations—implications to the company, operators, and shareholders.
3. Development of a plan of action.
4. Execution of the plan.

Part of this restructuring evaluation and implementation process included utilizing information from operators, managers, employees, and suppliers as well as assessing the company and asking questions to determine "what is working" and "what would you change." The McDonald's experience underlines the importance of involvement across the organization and the time commitment in seeing such an endeavour to fruition: spending time in restaurants, time to develop a gut feeling based on experience from visits, training, mentorship and history working with operators. Much of the process involved in this turnaround related to building trust and commitment from all members of the organization. This process provided greater turnaround success by breaking down barriers to implementation and avoiding costly mistakes prior to resource allocation decisions.

In a nutshell, earlier literature and the McDonald's example indicate a need in the resource allocation decision process to balance external and internal factors. Further, findings support the notion that there is no best way to do things and leaders need to be aware of options. These options include the various business options to consider but also process options on who to include in the process and how much adaptability is required. Organizational options include traditional organic and mechanistic forms as well as a variety of ownership forms to consider (Sorenson and Sorensen, 2001). New organizational forms of network, modular and other hybrid arrangements, provide potential opportunities to simultaneously increase service quality and organizational capabilities and lower costs.

Application: key resource allocation factors

In this section, we focus on key resource allocation factors that may impact decisions for internal or external implementation of strategic plans (i.e., structural arrangements). We present the discussion in the context of decisions related to possible entry into the branded foodservice product sector of retail. Specifically, we consider key resource allocation decision factors for entry in general and then factors that impact organizational structure decisions.

Restaurant branded products in a food retail environment

The separation between restaurant and grocery store food has slowly dissolved over the past two decades. With the advent of the ready-to-eat, prepared food counters in most full-service grocery stores and retail super-centres, the retail industry has made inroads into the foodservice market. A report on global pricing trends described this non-traditional strategy as "channel blurring" (Ernst and Young, 2004). In this discussion, restaurant-branded products are defined as food products that are tied to a specific restaurant brand and are made available in a food retail (grocery) environment, in other words foods using restaurant brands that have transitioned from foodservice establishment to grocers' retail shelves. Very little research has been published on this contemporary food topic. Thus, the purpose of the discussion in this chapter is to consider the resource allocation implications for foodservice firms entering the retail arena.

Figure 11.1 provides a framework of key issues to consider when making resource allocation decisions in this area. The framework is based on our research on this topic drawing on earlier studies and in-depth interviews of knowledgeable executives involved with this segment of the foodservice industry. In evaluating the resource allocation options in this area, restaurant operators need to evaluate intangible resources such as their firm's branding, brand equity, and brand awareness to

Figure 11.1
Key issues in the branded foodservice product decision.

determine the value added of their branded products (Aaker (2004)). Additional issues directly related to determining resource allocations include retail viability, internal versus external implementation issues, and barriers to entry (costs and process).

Resource allocation decision—step 1: evaluating a fit with strategic ends and brand equity • • •

As foodservice operators consider entering the branded foodservice product market (retail), it appears imperative to consider the strategic ends of the organization as well as the realistic value of its brand, brand equity, and brand awareness prior to entry to determine whether benefits of a brand extension are probable. Aaker (2004) describes brand extension benefits as having five main characteristics:

1. Enhancing the brand's visibility and image. Placing the brand in another setting can be a more effective and efficient brand-building approach than spending money on advertising.
2. Changing a brand image. If a brand needs to broaden or shift its associations in order to support strategic initiatives, moving the brand into a new area may be the most convincing way to do that.
3. Providing a way to maintain relevance by creating competitive entries in emerging product markets that would be difficult or impossible to enter without an existing brand asset.

4. Inhibiting a competitor from gaining or exploiting a foothold in the market. Thus, an extension can be strategically defensive and be worthwhile even though it might struggle.
5. Providing a source of energy for a brand, especially a brand that is established and a bit tired.

By using the built-up, intangible equity in a brand, a foodservice operator should be able to leverage this equity to create more opportunity and, possibly, more revenue. This type of leverage is not dissimilar to the use of tangible assets such as cash, equipment, or property. The extension of the brand is one way to leverage the consumer awareness and loyalty into new or existing markets in which the firm may not currently be competing. If the brand equity is strong enough, the idea is that consumers who are loyal to the brand, or at least aware, should follow into this new market. The idea of "channel blurring" is a direct result of brand extension. The practice of private label branding and an extension of the branded foodservice retail product provide an opportunity for many operators to extend the value of their brand. To determine the potential benefits of this strategy, foodservice operators need to consider a variety of issues based on the tangible and intangible resources they have at their disposal.

Many companies have determined not to enter this area and focus on their foodservice operations exclusively. In the case of McDonald's, the leadership has decided not to enter the branded foodservice retail market while many of their quick service competitors have (e.g., Taco Bell). McDonald's explains the decision based on alignment and accountability issues. They believe everyone's focus should be on "improving the customer experiences" of their more than 33,000 restaurants. The McDonald's brand strategy is to focus on things such as clean restrooms, relevant building design, new food offerings, and friendlier service rather than external products tied to its brand equity. Of course, the purchase of Boston Market by the company has provided a strong foothold in the branded foodservice product arena—but it is a brand clearly separated from McDonald's (interestingly, Boston Market branded foodservice products are achieving more success than the restaurant concept on which the brand was founded).

Therefore, leaders in the foodservice industry considering entering this area should answer the following questions: What is the strength of our brand equity? Will branded foodservice retail products provide a viable brand extension for the firm? What are the potential benefits? Further, in attempting to answer these questions, leaders should first determine who should be involved in this decision process based on knowledge, insights, and expertise, then design the resource allocation decision process integrating the desired involvement levels to increase the likelihood of achieving the best solution, successful implementation, and organizational support (Butler, 1997; Harrington and Kendall, 2006; Nutt, 1989).

Resource allocation decision—step 2: retail viability • • •

In order to fully comprehend the retail food market and determine retail viability of a restaurant food product, the current competition between national- and private-label food products needs to be considered. Based on the interviews of grocery executives and operators, food retailers appear to view all products as either a national brand or a private label. One interviewee, director of operations for a large retail food group, indicated that the creation of private labels in the late 1970s and early 1980s gave more control to the retailers in the area of product mix and allowed them to respond to consumers' needs. This branding paradigm shift nearly two decades ago created a situation where retailers could offer a wide range of products and product lines at competitive prices rather than having product development, pricing, and product mix dictated by a handful of large multinational manufacturers.

For retailers, one apparent advantage is the store brand; the store brand carries with it a substantial amount of brand equity as many consumers develop loyalty to a particular grocery chain. The residual effect of this increased loyalty is less competition based solely on price and an increase to the bottom line for the grocery chains. Interviewees indicated that the margin on private-label products is more favourable than that on national brands due to much lower marketing costs. This consensus was supported in the study by De Wulf *et al.* (2005). In the study, the researchers compared consumer perceptions of national brands versus private-label products. Their study confirmed that, "the common belief that private label products can offer the same or better quality than national brands, but a lower price …" and that "store patronage has an influence on perceived brand equity of store versus national brands (De Wulf *et al.*, 2005, p. 223).

Interviews indicated that food retail professionals consider branded restaurant food products to be a part of the private label group because the margins of these products are, typically, greater than the national brands. This appears to be due to the fact that many of the branded foodservice products are not totally controlled by the traditional manufacturers but instead can be joint ventures between product development consultants and the foodservice operator. However, retailers suggested that each foodservice branded product might be different in regards to manufacture, control, and profitability. In the case of the United States-based Carlson Restaurants' casual foodservice chain (TGI Friday's), the retail products that bare their name and logo are manufactured by several large multi-nationals including Heinz and Diageo; in this particular situation, consumer response and relations are also handled by these organizations. Therefore, the ability for Friday's to control the customer experience is limited using this format.

According to a large chain restaurant media representative, the company has some latitude with regards to product development but, for the most part, the arrangement with manufacturers is a royalty payment for use of the restaurant concept name and logo. This limits the chain's liability and resource output to zero—making any revenues derived from royalties a positive cash flow. Access to information due to confidentiality makes it impossible to understand the total relationship between this restaurant group and the manufacturers. However, if the control of these retail products rests with these large national brand producers, the likelihood of these products being considered private label would be greatly decreased. Therefore, the determination of whether a branded foodservice retail product is considered a private label depends on the relationship struck by the stakeholders involved: foodservice operators, product development consultants, R&D team, and manufacturers.

The relationship between McDonald's and Newman's Own provides an interesting twist to this retail viability scenario. In this case, McDonald's co-branding with Newman's Own assisted in creating brand equity for their salad products by bringing in a well-known name from the retail grocery sector. McDonald's implemented a new product line of foodservice salads in their restaurants originally called "salad shakers." They had done extensive research to determine a number of elements that were being done correctly but there were still several issues that were limiting the success of this new product line (issues with the price point, packaging, and disbursement of the salad dressing for greater eating quality). While McDonald's has longstanding equity in products such as McMuffins and French fries, until the not-too-distant past, it had little equity in the salad business. To address this issue, the leadership created a co-brand with Newman's who have a strong reputation as salad dressing experts using natural ingredients and sustainable practices. They hoped a relationship with Newman's would allow them to utilize the brand equity from Newman's millions in sales in the retail market and create a personality for the McDonald's salad. This "channel blurring" in its reverse form has made McDonald's the largest produce seller in the restaurant world.

This discussion highlights three main issues for retail viability consideration. First, from a retailer's perspective (particularly with small-to-medium-sized restaurant organizations), the viability of a branded foodservice product depends on whether the product can be viewed as a private label, providing greater profitability for the retailer. Second, from a foodservice operator's perspective, there is a need to determine whether a substantive level of brand equity has been established to warrant any value added to the consumer. Third, the channel blurring process can be utilized by taking foodservice products into the retail sector as well as bringing retail brands into the foodservice sector. While value added for the consumer can result from a variety of tangible or intangible attributes, in the case of a branded foodservice item, the value is likely to take the form of brand awareness tied to perceived quality. Thus, it provides an increase in pre-purchase consumer confidence and decreases pre-purchase anxiety (Locander and Herman, 1979).

Resource allocation decision—step 3: internal versus external implementation issues ● ● ●

This section points out several issues for consideration once retail viability is determined. Some of these issues include maintenance of production and marketing control, structural arrangements, internal knowledge, and a confirmation on whether the firm has the resources needed to execute. These resource allocation issues relate directly to decisions on ownership and organizational structure options.

There appears to be a wide range of opportunities for different types of foodservice operations to be involved in the branding for a retail food product. Based on a review of available products and interview responses, it makes little difference whether the development of the product is from a quick service concept, fine-dining, or casual operation. One interviewee, director of a large food product development company, supported the idea that one of the most important aspects to be considered is the equity of the brand and the weight it carries in the marketplace. But, a second consideration is the nature of the actual product to be produced, how it fits the brand it will be labelled with, and how it will ultimately be produced.

The Toronto-based product development company works with foodservice operators to develop retail food products and has worked with many foodservice firms in the past including Mr. Greek Restaurants, Kernels Popcorn, Pizza Pizza, Golden Griddle Family Restaurants, and New York Fries. In the case of product development firms, they attempt to tailor their relationship to fit the foodservice operator as well as provide services such as product development, retail services, and outsourcing production. A key factor of success in this process is ensuring that the type of product is consistent with the brand. For instance, if the consumer cannot associate the type of product to the brand it is labelled with, then the extension does not work. This situation will not provide the consumer with pre-purchase cues of product quality associated with the brand.

The emergence of R&D and product development companies working with foodservice organizations provides an example of contemporary organic organizational forms such as network and modular organizations. In this situation, foodservice firm leaders make organizational structure decisions based on who can do functions and activities most effectively and economically rather than fixed organizational ties in a traditional organizational chart (Miles and Snow, 1992). This new structure may take the form of a virtual organization (an alliance of partners concentrating on what they do best) or modular arrangements (outsourcing non-core activities to specialists) (Dess *et al.*, 1995).

Our interviews indicated different levels of involvement in product development, manufacturing, marketing, and retailing. For example, firms such as TGI Friday's may decide to have minimal resources allocated to implementation and rely on the strength of their brand recognition to provide retail demand. However, many firms (such as Salsateria [a small, independent Ontario firm]), are responsible for not only bringing the food product to the market but also its distribution. In case of firms such as LeBiftheque and Montana's Cookhouse (causal dining chain operations), distribution control may be maintained internally while the scale-up, manufacturing, and packaging of the final product may be outsourced to food development and manufacturing firms.

What are the reasons for differences in type of involvement? Our interviewees pointed to several issues that are supported in literature on macro and micro issues in management, organizational structure, marketing, and innovation (Barkema and Vermeulen, 1998; Ottenbacher and Gnoth, 2005; Harrington, 2004b).

Figure 11.2 highlights some of the key factors impacting resource decisions on implementation and structure decisions ranging from exclusively internally derived, to some sort of joint venture arrangement (ranging from a traditional JV

Figure 11.2
Key factors impacting decisions for internal or external implementation.

of two separate firms joining together to create a separate entity to a mix of internal and external implementation elements [e.g., internal product development and external manufacture]), to exclusively externally derived (e.g., licensing of the brand name and logo). These organizational structure factors are based on the resource allocation decisions of the foodservice operator and include issues on level of control, resources and resource commitments, dissemination of information, and demand uncertainty.

Level of control • • •

The need for control and a fear of dissemination of information (i.e., formulas, recipes, or process issues) over the product and its distribution may, in part, drive decisions to license the brand, create a joint venture, or create a wholly owned division to develop, manufacture, and distribute a branded foodservice product line. When there is a high need in one or more of these areas, foodservice operators are more likely to consider internal implementation in the areas of product development, manufacture, and distribution.

This control issue is, in part, related to the resource-based view of barriers to imitation. In the branded foodservice product arena, brand image and equity are key factors driving barriers to imitation by competitors, alliance partners, or retail chains copying products in the marketplace. Sustainability of brand equity is related to the idea of causal ambiguity and stems from concepts such as tacitness, complexity, and human asset specificity. Given the intangible aspects of brand equity, it stands to reason that these concepts are important in heightening barriers to imitation in foodservice operations as well as branded foodservice products. One interviewee pointed out the importance of control and managing everything from product size, ingredients, packaging, and positioning during the product development testing and implementation phases.

Therefore, organizational structure decisions should be influenced by not only the level of control over tangible elements of the branded foodservice product but also more intangible elements such as tacit processes and human asset specificity that may provide sustainable brand equity and ultimately a competitive advantage. As pointed out by one McDonald's executive, organizational structure and control is "a constant yin-yang, a constant process of giving and taking, a constant working together, sacrificing for the good of the whole." Hence, these decisions may need to be dynamic and adaptable over time.

Available resources • • •

A second issue in this decision is whether or not the firm has the resources to commit this venture (e.g., knowledge, know-how, facilities, network, access to distribution channels, time, and finance). As with level of control and information dissemination, when a foodservice firm has a high (or low) level of available resources and the knowledge and capabilities to implement (or if available in the marketplace), firms are more (or less) likely to use primarily internal avenues to implement a branded foodservice product.

In addition to internal limitation considerations, the firm should consider existing or potential relationships that could be utilized to maximize the benefits for all parties in rolling out branded foodservice products. These relationships can be with suppliers, education facilities, agricultural research centres, or other entities that can be utilized for sharing a variety of resources or capabilities. In some cases, even competitors can evolve into networks for resource sharing. For example, competing firms might share staff members with expertise for special events or projects and may form cooperative agreements for purchasing or marketing purposes (Harrington, 2004a).

Demand uncertainty • • •

A final area presented in Figure 11.2 to consider is the uncertainty in the demand for the branded product. This issue appears to be an important element to consider with its ultimate implications on risk versus return relationships (Barkema and Vermeulen, 1998; Buckley, 1983). Many foodservice firms have developed elaborate "test sell model" or similar processes that simultaneously work out the bugs of implementing new products along with determining demand levels once fully rolled out. As one executive indicated, new products have to go through a rigorous process that averages about 8 months in length. This process reduces the enormous risk involved. Managerial responsibilities of foodservice leaders in the product development area evolve into a "constant lifecycle of managing opportunity and managing risk."

In order to ensure a stable level of demand, a key consideration in the distribution in a food retail environment is getting the product on the store shelf and in front of the consumer. For many operations, the cost of getting the product to the store shelf can be prohibitive. Depending on the agreement with the specific retailer, a fee may be required just to get the product on the retail shelf. Our interviewees indicated that this fee can range from $25,000 to $50,000 for shelf space, assuming there is store space available. In North America, the average-size grocery store carries somewhere between 8000 and 10,000 different products at any given time. The shelf space is designated for products of large multinationals such as Kraft and Nestle. Therefore, our interviews revealed the difficulty of independent foodservice operators obtaining the shelf or freezer space to display branded foodservice products. Furthermore, not only it is challenging to place the restaurant food items on the store shelf but the specific location within the shelves is also very critical for high sales. For this reason (in addition to stakeholders for development and manufacture), interviewees emphasized the importance of utilizing a manufacturer or consulting company with a network and connections to successfully transfer a branded foodservice product to the retail setting.

Thus, the level of vertical integration (both forward and backward in the supply chain) by a firm involved in the process of bringing a branded foodservice product to the market will depend on the product and situation. In some cases, such as Salsateria, the vertical integration of all aspects from concept to final distribution will be appropriate for the consumer and the firm. However, if the foodservice operator intends to distribute the product on a larger scale, all elements of the process are open for outsourcing or integrating within the firm.

Resource allocation decision—step 4: barriers to entry • • •

Barriers to imitation have been discussed above but traditional barriers to entry ideas are relevant in the branded foodservice product decision. The barriers to entry for a foodservice operator can be divided into two categories: costs and process. In terms of cost barriers, cost issues are multifaceted. In addition to the costs described above in getting a product on the shelf, there are a variety of costs associated with development and manufacturing that can be substantial.

One critical issue pointed out in our interviews in bringing foodservice products into the retail market is addressing government regulations. The amount of regulation depends on the scope of the production and the area that the products will service. For instance, if the production is limited to an individual state or province, the state, province, or municipality will regulate the process. An example is a state health department or provincial ministry of health. However, if the goal is to distribute nationally, federal agencies will become involved in everything from inspection and food safety enforcement to nutritional labelling. In the United States, food safety and inspection issues may cross several organizational boundaries including the U.S. Department of Agriculture (USDA) and the Food and Drug Administration (FDA), whereas in Canada, the primary agency is the Canadian Food Inspection Agency (CFIA). Therefore, an additional barrier to entry for nationwide distribution is expertise in these issues.

According to one manager of product development, the cost of recipe and process development can run $25,000 or more. However, for large international endeavours, this cost can reach several hundred thousand to several million dollars. There are further major costs for those operators who decide to handle production themselves. First is the cost of setting up and running a separate line, specifically for the production of retail products. The production of these products is fundamentally different from a typical foodservice environment. One of the main differences is the use of fresh ingredients. While fresh ingredients are a recognized standard in most restaurant kitchens, shelf life and recipe modification take centre stage in creating most branded foodservice products. Recipe modification requires different equipment than that normally used in restaurants such as packaging, quick cool down, and large-scale production equipment. Other cost factors include storage for raw and finished goods inventories as well as the extra staff required to produce these products. Because most foodservice operators are not equipped (either financially or with expertise) in these areas, most enter into agreements with other companies who specialize in developing and producing retail food products.

Challenges and benefits ● ● ●

One of the challenges alluded to earlier is the loss of control that a foodservice operator may have to concede to get a product to the retail market. Ultimately, any quality problems will reflect badly on the entire foodservice brand—not just to the retail product. For instance, if the company produces a branded foodservice product for an operator and the consumers become ill, the outcome would affect the foodservice operation without much recourse in regards to brand equity.

Foodservice operators need to weigh the financial and control risks with the potential benefits. As Aaker (2004) indicated, many benefits in his explanation of extending a brand into a new product market include increasing the brand's visibility, providing energy for the brand, and broadening the brand into consumer areas that may not have been achievable previously.

A good example of the implementation and realization of these benefits is the placing of Lick's Homeburger products in the Metro Group grocery stores across Ontario. While Lick's is strictly a Toronto regional restaurant chain, the branded foodservice product offerings provide exposure across the province and give Lick's a platform for potential future growth with an already-established branded product line. A second benefit utilized by Lick's is marketing the brand across both retail and foodservice products. In the case of Lick's retail products, a coupon is included in most of the packaging to drive business to the foodservice locations. An added benefit of this marketing campaigning is that it allows Lick's to track the crossover between the retail and foodservice operations. Of course, the final benefit is the potential for revenue and profits. In many cases, much of the financial risk can be absorbed by the manufacturers and processors of the products with a foodservice operator receiving royalties for the use of its brand if the organizational structure is set up in this fashion. The implicit benefit to this process, in addition to revenues from the retail product line, is the increased advertising in the form of keeping the foodservice name in front of the retail consumer on an ongoing basis.

Conclusion

Resource allocation decisions provide the answer to "how" strategic goals and objectives become implemented. Resource allocation decisions and organizational structure are at the heart of the strategic choice perspective with implications on the future direction of the firm. For practitioners, a helpful outcome of this debate is an integration of the concepts of contingency theory and the resource-based view of the firm applied to a hospitality service environment. Thus, regardless of which side of the strategy–structure argument you might fall into, logic and a synthesis of the research indicate that successful allocation decisions are more likely to be fully implemented when the complex interaction of variables (e.g., environment events, physical organizational structure, and intangible structural elements such as culture, values, and history) are considered. This integrated approach reveals the need for a fit between external and internal factors as well as the need of leadership to consider both context and process in determining and implementing resource allocation decisions.

We argue that concepts such as the co-alignment principle and the structural-functionalist arguments are two sides of the same coin. A close reading of both perspectives imply a dynamic and adaptable process of fit and readjustment based on balancing external and internal needs for determining what will be achieved, how it will be implemented, and what will be the complex interplay involved. This dynamic component is particularly relevant given the turbulent, complex, and fast-paced nature of today's hospitality business environment.

The application section reveals the evolving and competitive nature of the retail food market. Manufacturers and retailers are continuously looking for ways to gain competitive advantage with the practice of using foodservice operations' brands as one method of achieving this goal. This business model creates an alternative paradigm of bringing foodservice products to the market. Instead of the traditional process of large companies spending substantial amounts on R&D to launch a product and then even more marketing it, this business model creates a more collaborative approach utilizing existing know-how and brand equity.

Based on our interviews, the typical business model involves the foodservice operator developing a menu item in the kitchen of its operation, testing it on restaurant guests to verify the food quality and its popularity. At the same time, the operator builds the brand of the operation through reliable quality, establishing the item as a signature dish. The retail product consultant or manufacturer then takes this popular signature menu item and develops it for the retail market. Once the product is ready for market, the product expert uses established connections within the retail industry to gain access to limited shelf space and sell the product in retail stores. A key benefit of this process for the product expert and retailer is a reduced need to promote the new product as a brand as the product benefits from existing brand equity of the foodservice operation. In many cases, this provides the retailer with an increased profit margin over typical national brands. By leveraging the capabilities of these three main stakeholders (foodservice operator, product expert, and retailer), this business model and collaboration benefits everyone involved including the retail consumer, who has less uncertainty and anxiety about the initial purchase of the food product.

The emerging trend of channel blurring between retail and foodservice demonstrates key resource allocation decision issues for this strategic option as well as the impact of level of control considerations, resource availability, and demand uncertainty on structural decisions. Organizational structure options in this example highlight a range of possibilities including organic and mechanistic forms, a variety of ownership forms to consider, and new organizational forms such as network, modular, and other hybrid arrangements.

References

Aaker, D. (2004). *Brand Portfolio Strategy: Creating Relevance, Differentiation, Energy, Leverage, and Clarity*. New York: Simon & Schuster, Inc.

Amburgey, T. L., and Dacin, T. (1994). As the left foot follows the right? The dynamics of strategic and structural change. *Academy of Management Review, 37*(6), 1427–1452.

Andrews, K. R. (1971). *The Concept of Corporate Strategy*. Homewood, IL: Dow Jones Irwin.

Ansoff, H. I. (1965). *Corporate Strategy*. New York: McGraw-Hill Book Co.

Ashmos, D. P., Duchon, D., McDaniel, R. R., Jr., and Huonker, J. W. (2002). What a mess! Participation as a simple managerial rule to complexify organizations. *Journal of Management Studies, 39*, 189–206.

Barkema, H. G., and Vermeulen, F. (1998). International expansion through start-up or acquisition: A learning perspective. *Academy of Management Journal, 41*, 7–26.

Barney, J. B. (1986). Strategic factor markets: Expectations, luck and business strategy. *Management Science, 32*, 1231–1241.

Barney, J. B. (1991). Firm resources and sustained competitive advantage. *Journal of Management, 17*, 99–120.

Bonn, I., and Rundle-Thiele, S. (2007). Do or die—Strategic decision-making following a shock event. *Tourism Management, 28*(2), 615–620.

Bourgeois III, L. J., and Brodwin, D. R. (1984). Strategic implementation: Five approaches to an elusive phenomenon. *Strategic Management Journal, 5*, 241–264.

Bradach, J. L. (1997). Using the plural form in the management of restaurant chains. *Administrative Science Quarterly, 42*(2), 276–303.

Brews, P. J., and Hunt, M. R. (1999). Learning to plan and planning to learn: Resolving the planning school/learning school debate. *Strategic Management Journal*, 20, 889–913.

Buckley, P. J. (1983). New theories of international business: Some unresolved issues. In M. Casson (Ed.), *The Growth of International Business*. London: George Allen and Unwin.

Burns, T., and Stalker, G. M. (1961). *The Management of Innovation*. London: Tavistock Publications Limited.

Butler, R. J. (1997). Designing organizations: A decision-making perspective. In A. Sorge and M. Warner (Eds.), *The IEBM Handbook of Organizational Behavior* (pp. 308–329). London: International Thomson Business Press.

Byers, T., and Slack, T. (2001). Strategic decision-making in small businesses within the leisure industry. *Journal of Leisure Research*, 33(2), 121–136.

Chandler, A. (1962). *Strategy and Structure*. Cambridge, MA: MIT Press.

Child, J. (1972). Organizational structure, environment and performance: The role of strategic choice. *Sociology*, 6(1), 2–22.

Dess, G. G., Rasheed, A. M. A., McLaughlin, K. J., and Priem, R. L. (1995). The new corporate architecture. *Academy of Management Executive, August*, 7–20.

De Wulf, K., Odekerken-Schroder, G., Goedertier, F., and Van Ossel, G. (2005). Consumer perceptions of store brands versus national brands. *The Journal of Consumer Marketing*, 4(5), 223–232.

Ernst and Young (2004). Consumer products. Retrieved August 2006 at http://www.ey.com/global/.

Geiger, S. W., Ritchie, W. J., and Marlin, D. (2006). Strategy/structure fit and firm performance. *Organization Development Journal*, 24(2), 10–22.

Hall, D. J., and Saias, M. A. (1980). Strategy follows structure! *Strategic Management Journal*, 1, 149–163.

Hambrick, D. C., and Mason, P. A. (1984). Upper echelons: The organization as a reflection of its top managers. *Academy of Management Review*, 9, 193–206.

Harrington, R. J. (2004a). Part I: The culinary innovation process, a barrier to imitation. *Journal of Foodservice Business Research*, 7(3), 35–57.

Harrington, R. J. (2004b). The environment, involvement, and performance: Implications for the strategic process of food service firms. *International Journal of Hospitality Management*, 23(4), 317–341.

Harrington, R. J. (2005). The how and who of strategy-making: Models and appropriateness for firms in hospitality and tourism industries. *Journal of Hospitality & Tourism Research*, *29*(3), 372–395.

Harrington, R. J., and Kendall, K. W. (2006). Middle-up-down and top-down approaches: Strategy implementation, uncertainty, structure, and foodservice segment. *Tourism: The International Interdisciplinary Journal*, *54*(4), 385–395.

Harrington, R. J., Lemak, D., Reed, R., and Kendall, K. W. (2004). A question of fit: The links among environment, strategy formulation and performance. *Journal of Business and Management*, *10*(1), 15–38.

Hill, C. W. L., and Hoskisson, R. E. (1987). Strategy and structure in the multiproduct firm. *Academy of Management Review*, *12*(2), 331–341.

Jogaratnam, G., and Tse, E. C.-Y. (2006). Entrepreneurial orientation and the structuring of organizations: Performance evidence from the Asian hotel industry. *International Journal of Contemporary Hospitality Management*, *18*(6), 454–468.

Johns, G., and Saks, A. M. (2005). *Organizational Behaviour* (6th ed.). Toronto: Pearson Education Canada, Inc.

Karim, S. (2006). Modularity in organizational structure: The reconfiguration of internally developed and acquired business units. *Strategic Management Journal*, *27*(9), 5.

Lawrence, P. R., and Lorsch, J. W. (1967). *Organization and Environment Managing Differentiation and Integration*. Boston, MA: Harvard University.

Locander, W., and Herman, P. (1979). The effect of self-confidence and anxiety on information seeking in consumer risk reduction. *Journal of Marketing Research*, *16*(May), 268–274.

McWilliams, A., and Smart, D. L. (1993). Efficiency vs. structure-conduct-performance: Implications for strategy research and practice. *Journal of Management*, *19*, 63–78.

Miles, R. E., and Snow, C. C. (1992). Causes of failure in network organizations. *California Management Review*, *Summer*, 53–72.

Miller, D. (1986). Configurations of strategy and structure: Towards a synthesis. *Strategic Management Journal*, *7*, 233–249.

Mintzberg, H., Ahlstrand, B., and Lampel, J. (1998). *Strategic Safari*. New York: The Free Press.

Nutt, P. C. (1989). Selecting tactics to implement strategic plans. *Strategic Management Journal*, *10*, 145–161.

Okumus, F. (2004). Potential challenges of employing a formal environmental scanning approach in hospitality organizations. *International Journal of Hospitality Management*, *23*, 123–143.

Okumus, F., and Roper, A. (1999). A review of disparate approaches to strategy implementation in hospitality firms. *Journal of Hospitality & Tourism Research*, 23, 21–39.

Olsen, M. D., West, J., and Tse, E. C. (1998). *Strategic Management in the Hospitality Industry* (2nd ed.). New York: Wiley.

Ottenbacher, M., and Gnoth, J. (2005). How to develop successful hospitality innovation. *Cornell Hotel and Restaurant Administration Quarterly*, 46(2), 205–222.

Parsa, H. G. (1999). Interaction of strategy implementation and power perceptions in franchise systems: An empirical investigation. *Journal of Business Research*, 45, 173–185.

Pennings, J. (1975). The relevance of the structural-contingency model for organizational effectiveness. *Administrative Science Quarterly*, 30, 393–410.

Porter, M. E. (1980). *Competitive Strategy*. New York: The Free Press.

Reed, R., and DeFillippi, R. J. (1990). Causal ambiguity, barriers to imitation, and sustainable competitive advantage. *Academy of Management Review*, 15, 88–102.

Ritchie, B., and Riley, M. (2004). The role of the multi-unit manager within the strategy and structure relationship: Evidence from the unexpected. *International Journal of Hospitality Management*, 23(2), 145–161.

Roberts, C. (1997). Franchising and strategic decision making. *Journal of Hospitality & Tourism Research*, 21(1), 160–178.

Schendel, D. E., and Hofer, C. W. (1979). *Strategic Management: A New View of Business Policy and Planning*. Boston, MA: Little, Brown & Co.

Schmelzer, C. D., and Olsen, M. D. (1994). A data based strategy implementation framework for companies in the restaurant industry. *International Journal of Hospitality Management*, 13, 347–359.

Scott, W. R. (1998). *Organizations: Rational, Natural, and Open Systems* (4th ed.). Upper Saddle River, NJ: Prentice-Hall, Inc.

Simon, H. A. (1945). *Administrative Behavior*. New York: The Free Press.

Sorenson, O., and Sorensen, J. B. (2001). Finding the right mix: Franchising, organizational learning, and chain performance. *Strategic Management Journal*, 22, 713–724.

Teare, R. E., Costa, J., and Eccles, G. (1998). Relating strategy, structure and performance. *International Journal of Contemporary Hospitality Management*, 10(2), 58–77.

Williamson, O. E. (1985). *The Economic Institutions of Capitalism*. New York: The Free Press.

Wren, D. A. (1994). *The Evolution of Management Thought* (4th ed.). New York: Wiley.

Part Four

Functional competencies

Strategic human resource management: high performance people system as core competencies

Kevin S. Murphy[1] and Michael D. Olsen[2]

[1]*University of Central Florida*
[2]*Virginia Tech*

Introduction

In the past two decades scholars have dedicated a tremendous amount of effort to studying the relationship between a firm's performance and its human resource management (HRM) practices. What has emerged from these studies is empirical evidence that demonstrate a linkage between a firm's HRM practices (core competencies) and performance that can give it a competitive advantage. However, what has also become equally clear is that human resource (HR) practices do not operate independently from each other or from the firm's overall strategy. HR practices operate in a complex system of interrelated parts. This system has become known as high performance work practices (HPWP) in the area of strategic human resource management (SHRM). In the hospitality and tourism management field this system is known as a high performance people system (HPPS), which characterizes the unique nature of the hospitality industry.

This chapter outlines the development of a HPPS within the U.S. hospitality industry and demonstrates those practices which should be included in a firm's HRM core competencies. Firms able to implement such systems possessing complementary internal fit have been shown to increase the intangible value of their human capital (employees) and create greater economic value (Delery, 1998). Such organizations can compete more effectively in their industry sector. Studies on HPWP in the service industry have been limited to heavily regulated firms such as banking. These results, however, have limited validity for the hospitality industry which is heavily influenced by customer-driven preferences, trends, and market forces. Therefore, a HPPS for the US hospitality business containing different practices than those develop for the manufacturing-based HPWP system is outlined in the following chapter.

Literature review

There are two streams of literature that are relevant to the discussion of HPPS to be reviewed. The SHRM literature, which has been developing over the past 20 years and uses the resource-based view (RBV) of the firm as its foundation. The hospitality co-alignment model has evolved from the business environmental literature and is fundamentally concerned with bringing a firm's strategy choice and structure into alignment with its environment. Additionally, other important concepts and topical areas will de discussed.

Strategic human resource management (SHRM)

SHRM is a relatively new field in business theory. Deemed to be a macro-oriented approach of (HRM), SHRM is a blue-print of HR allocation set to meet the firm's needs. Wright and McMahan define SHRM as "the pattern of planned human resource deployments and activities intended to enable an organization to achieve its goals" (1992, p. 300). Theoretically, SHRM focuses on the nature of HR and management decision impacting a company's human capital. Strategic and non-strategic frameworks of HRM represent potential beginning points for emergent theoretical models for SHRM.

SHRM researchers have been advocates of the theory that provides support to the relationship between HRM practices, sustainable competitive advantage (SCA), and firm performance. Several SHRM researchers such as, Cappelli and Singh (1992), Wright and McMahan (1992), Pfeffer (1994), Lado and Wilson (1994), Huselid (1995), Jackson and Schuler (1995), Becker (1996), Delaney and Huselid (1996), Boxall (1998), Pfeffer (1998), Schuler and Jackson (2000), Ulrich and Beatty (2001), Lepak and Snell (2002), and others have directly or indirectly made attempts to theorize the effects of single or multiple HRM variables on firm performance. These efforts have led to the incremental development of the SHRM literature that stresses the relationships between the HRM work practices, SCA and firm performance.

There is an emergent body of evidence demonstrating that "the methods used by an organization to manage its human resources can have a substantial impact on many organizationally relevant outcomes" (Delery, 1998, p. 1). The change of focus on organizational resources is noteworthy in that it shifts the traditional emphasis in the field from micro HRM practices to a macro system of practices that the organization uses to manage its human capital. Imbedded in the discussion of HRM systems is the concept of HPWP. The study of HPWP and their importance in SHRM, however, has received less attention in the literature then the traditional HRM issues (Delery, 1998). Confounding the research on HPWP is a general disagreement among researchers on the micro HRM practices which comprise a HPWP system; there is little concurrence among scholars with respect to specifically which HR practices should be incorporated (Guest et al., 2004; Becker, 1996; Rogers and Wright, 1998; Chadwick and Cappelli, 1999). Becker (1996) identify six key unresolved questions in need of future study, with the development of an agreed upon set of HRM practices as the first step. Rogers and Wright (1998) deem the next decade to be critical in the establishment of a clear, sound and consistent construct for firm performance in the field of SHRM. Indeed, construct development and validation of measures is fundamental to the progression of model development (Nunnally, 1978).

The current status of theory on valuating the HR function is "in its infancy and is seriously hampered" (Lev, 2001, p. 75). It may be such a complicated concept and influenced by so many intervening variables that it does not get fully developed for sometime. However, several studies have posited that there is a positive link between HR practices and firm performance (Becker and Huselid, 1998; Becker, 1996; Delaney and Huselid, 1996; Huselid, 1995). In Becker (1996) research, influential HR practices were designated as "best practices". The best practices approach attempts to identify efficient and effective HR practices through benchmarking among firms. For example, a company may compare selection processes, benefit packages, training, compensation, and employee relations practices, and package those exhibiting appropriate internal fit. The difficulty with this type of linkage between an individual HR practice and firm performance is that very few practices operate in isolation.

The universalistic perspective purports that all HR practices and associated outcomes are universal across organizations (Delery and Doty, 1996). In the SHRM field this is the simplest and most straight forward theoretical relationship. What works in one organization is assumed to work in another organization. As in the best practice approach, universalisms look for an HR practice or set of practices that will work in most if not all firms. Pfeffer (1994) proposed 16 most effective practices for managing people and reduced the list to 7 in 1998: employment security; selective hiring of new personnel; self-managed teams and decentralization of decision making as the basic principles of organizational design; comparatively high compensation contingent on organizational performance; extensive training; reduced status distinctions and barriers, including dress, language, office arrangements, and wage differences across levels; extensive sharing of financial and performance information throughout the organization (p. 96).

Delery and Doty (1996) also developed a list of 7 most effective practices for managing people partly based on Pfeffer's original 16: internal career opportunities; formal training systems; appraisal measures; profit sharing; employment security; voice mechanisms; and job definition. Additionally, there are some empirical studies that have investigated the relationship between firm performance and HR systems that are worth describing.

A study by Huselid (1995) evaluated at length the links between of HPWP systems and firm performance. Huselid used HPWP as defined by U.S. Department of Labor (1993) in his study which include: "extensive recruitment, selection, and training procedures, formal information sharing, attitude assessment, job design, grievance procedures, and labor-management participation programs, and performance appraisal, promotion, and incentive compensation systems that recognize and reward employee performance have all been widely linked with valued firm-level outcomes" (p. 641). Based on a national sample of nearly 1000 firms, the results indicate that these "practices have an economically and statistically significant impact on both intermediate worker outcomes (turnover and productivity) and short- and long-term measures of corporate financial performance" (p. 635). Huselid (1995) found considerable support for the hypothesis that investments in such practices are associated with lower worker turnover and greater productivity and business fiscal performance across a wide range of sectors and organization sizes.

In a 1996 study on the impact of HRM practices on perceptions of organizational performance Delaney and Huselid investigated for—profit and non-profit firms to determine if positive associations exist between HRM practices, such as staffing selection, training and incentive compensation, and firm-performance measures. In general the findings supported the view that progressive HRM practices are positively related to perceptual measures of firm performance. A similar study was conducted by Huselid et al. (1997) using publicly available financial data as measures of firm performance. The results support the hypothesis that investments in HR are a potential source of competitive advantage; however, the authors conclude there is still very little understanding of the processes used to achieve this potential or the conditions under which it is realized.

In addition to the empirical studies aforementioned, several authors have proposed conceptual and theoretical frameworks for further exploring this important topic. Wright and Snell (1998) presented a framework that provides a theoretical foundation for understanding the dual roles of both fitting the HR system to the strategic needs of the firm and building the system so as to enable a flexibility in response to a variety strategic requirements over time. The authors contend that firms should promote simultaneously both fit and flexibility in SHRM to create a SCA.

Although, there have now been multiple studies of the effectiveness of internal fit, very little evidence has come to the forefront to suggest that a coherent system of HR practice is needed and of great consequence (Delery, 1998); this is particularly the case in the hospitality industry. HR have the potential, in each organization, to become a competitive advantage; however, a major challenge for SHRM research in the next decade "will be to establish a clear, coherent and consistent construct for organizational performance" (Rogers and Wright, 1998, p. 1).

HPWP systems

There is an emergent body of evidence demonstrating that "the methods used by an organization to manage its human resources can have a substantial impact on many organizationally relevant out comes" (Delery, 1998, p. 1). The change of focus on organizational resources is noteworthy in that it shifts the traditional emphasis in the field from micro HRM practices to a macro system of practices that the organization uses to manage its intangible human capital. Imbedded in the discussion of HR systems is the concept of high performance work practice (HPWP) systems, also referred to as systems of internal fit. The study of HPWP systems and their importance in SHRM, however, has received less attention in the literature (Delery, 1998). Confounding the research on HPWP systems is a general disagreement among researchers on the micro HR practices which comprise the HPWP system (Becker, 1996). Research would seem to imply that not many managers have the expertise needed or know how to 'bundle' or integrate HRM practices into HPWP system that fits the organization's particular context and its developing strategies (Barney and Wright, forthcoming; MacDuffie, 1995). MacDuffie (1995) takes the standpoint that it is a bundle of HR practices rather than any single practice that forms an overall HRM system. Further, MacDuffie posits that it is a single bundle, rather than multiple bundles, that form a comprehensive HPWP system.

According to Guest *et al.* (2004):

One of the distinctive features of contemporary HRM is the claim that some combination of practices has advantages above and beyond the careful application of specific techniques such as sophisticated selection, training or job design. Unfortunately, there is little agreement about which practices should be combined to constitute effective HRM. It seems plausible to expect that theory and empirical research might lead us towards some kind of answer. (p. 79)

Some progress has been made in conceptualizing the content of an HPWP system, demonstrated in the emerging agreement that a HPWP system should be formulated to guarantee that employees obtain high skills, competence, motivation, and the prospect to add discretionary effort. The combined outcome should be value-added performance (Appelbaum *et al.*, 2000; Becker *et al.*, 1997; Delery and Doty, 1996; Huselid, 1995; MacDuffie, 1995).

Finally, the empirical research on HPWP systems has produced results which support the argument that investments in HR are a potential source of competitive advantage; however, there is still very little understanding of the processes used to achieve its' potential or the conditions under which it is realized. Again, there is a general disagreement among researchers on the micro HR practices which comprise the HPWP system and there is little agreement about what practices constitute effective HRM. It seems reasonable to anticipate that research might direct us towards some kind of solution, unfortunately to date; such optimism has yet to be realized.

Sustainable competitive advantage (SCA)

The concept of a SCA emerged in 1984 when Day recommended types of strategies that could help to "sustain the competitive advantage" of an organization (p. 32). The actual term "SCA" was used by Porter (1985) to discuss the generic competitive strategic typologies firms can possess (low-cost or niche) to achieve sustainable competitive advantage. However, it was Barney (1991) who first put forth a formal conceptual definition by suggesting: "A firm is said to have a sustained competitive advantage when it is implementing a value-creating strategy not simultaneously being implemented by any current or potential competitors and when these other firms are unable to duplicate the benefits of this strategy" (p. 102). Hoffman offered the following formal conceptual definition, premised in part on the definitions of each term provided in the dictionary and Barney's work (2000): "An SCA is the prolonged benefit of implementing some unique value-creating strategy not simultaneously being implemented by any current or potential competitors along with the inability to duplicate the benefits of this strategy".

SHRM implies that HPWP systems can contribute to sustained competitive advantage by making possible the development of core competencies that are company explicit, produce multifarious organizational relationships, are rooted in a company's history and customs, and create implicit organizational knowledge (Barney, 1997; Reed and DeFillippi, 1990).

Co-alignment theory

The co-alignment theory conceptualizes the interaction between the four constructs in the model (Figure 12.1). Co-alignment is achieved when the four constructs (environmental events; strategy choice; firm structure; and firm performance) are brought

Figure 12.1
The co-alignment principle.

into alignment with each other under the organizations over-arching strategy. The co-alignment theory states: "if the firm is able to identify the opportunities that exist in the forces driving change, invest in competitive methods that take advantage of these opportunities, and allocate resources to those that create the greatest value, the financial results desired by the owners and investors have a much better chance of being achieved" (Olsen *et al.*, 1998, p. 2).

Environmental scanning (ES) is the first of the four pillars of the co-alignment principle. Pinto and Olsen (1987) defined ES "as the process of probing an organization/s external environment for information which may be directly or indirectly relevant to top management in making decisions of a long term strategic nature" (p. 183). ES is performed at multiple levels such as remote, task, functional, and firm (Olsen *et al.*, 1998).

Strategy choice is the firm's purposeful choice of the *competitive methods* (the second pillar of the co-alignment theory) that will be used to compete in the market place and which should be reflective of the organization's intended strategy. Competitive methods are bundles of goods and services combined in unique ways so as to produce a sustainable competitive advantage. The entire set of a firm's competitive methods is their strategic portfolio of goods and services which should set an organization apart from its competitors. Slattery and Olsen (1984) analysed the environment of hospitality organizations and identified patterns in the relationships between the environment and the organization.

Firm structure is how the business organizes itself so as to efficiently, consistently, and effectively allocate its scarce resources to the implementation of its competitive methods. To do this, the firm must develop or already posses the *core competencies* (the third pillar of the co-alignment theory) needed to carry this out (Olsen *et al.*, 1998). Core competencies are those things which a firm does well and ideally better than anyone else. The combination of competitive methods and core competencies should produce a competitive advantage that cannot be easily copied or substituted and is sustainable. The essence of good strategy is to be able to position the firm to achieve a SCA in one or more areas, which will enable the firm to produce above average returns. To do this the firm must not only be successful in crafting a good strategy, competitive methods, and core competencies, but the firm must be highly successful in the *implementation* (the forth pillar of the co-alignment theory) phase of the plan.

Implementation is a process that occurs within the contextual environment of the firm. The context of each firm is different and this will affect the process in varying ways. This is part of the reason that firms are successful in implementation to varying degrees. Therefore, the implementation of strategy is the outcome of the actions of the firm within its context as those actions impact the activities of the process. The main contextual variables that impact the process according to Schmelzer and Olsen (1994) are perceived environmental uncertainty, firm structure (decision making, formalization, hierarchy), and organizational culture. The process variables that are involved in implementation are information systems, planning and control, project initiation style, resource allocation, method of training, and the outcome variable of rewards. All of these variables can make for a highly convoluted process and a difficult measurement challenge.

The co-alignment theory's last construct is that of firm performance measurement, which leads to the feedback and review loop. West and Olsen (1988) surveyed the foodservice industry to determine whether the relationship between ES, in support of organizational strategy, has an impact on firm performance. The results indicated that higher performing firms engaged in significantly higher levels of ES than lower performing firms when grouped by ROS and ROA. The study demonstrated that companies can improve firm performance through the use of ES in conjunction with organizational strategy in foodservice firms.

High performance people system (HPPS)

The previous sections described in detail the literature, theory, and research on co-alignment and SHRM that are the basis for the development of a construct for the conceptualization of HPPS in the casual theme restaurant sector of the U.S. hospitality industry for management. Firms able to implement such systems possessing universality have been shown to increase the intangible value of their human capital (employees) and create greater economic value (Delery, 1998). In Figure 12.2 a conceptual theoretical model is presented, which expounds on the relationships between the key concepts. Additionally, the model was used as a working theoretical model for the conceptualization of a HPPS for unit-level managers in casual theme restaurants of the US.

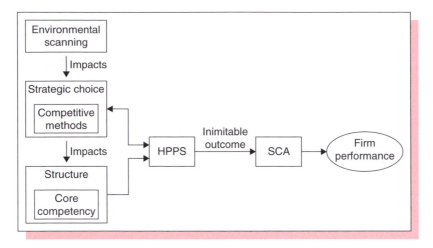

Figure 12.2
Proposed theoretical model.

The framework for the HPPS model, Figure 12.2, is based on previous theoretical literature on co-alignment and SHRM and the findings of exploratory research conducted (Murphy, 2006), which conceptualizes the construct relationships that produce a SCA in the US casual themed restaurant segment for unit-level management. Both the dimensions of HRM work practices and the stakeholder performance outcomes to measure the investments in work practices are included in the framework. The model's design suggests that a decision to invest in work practices is the result of ES and a strategic choice to produce a core competency through the use of intangible human capital, specifically unit management. The selection of specific dimensions in the HPPS construct is based on interviewee's scanning of internal and external environmental forces and reflects the first construct of the Co-Alignment Model Proposition.

The framework theoretical model is underpinned by the Co-Alignment Model and thus it is driven by the central thesis of the Co-Alignment Model. The constructs in the framework are significantly impacted by environmental forces and a need for competitive methods and core competencies to align with these forces to produce a competitive advantage. However, every framework operates within boundaries, which the results of this study suggest are the people management practices or dimensions that comprise a firm's HPPS construct and are important to the firm's value-creation process.

The data from Murphy's 2006 study indicates that the work practice dimensions which comprise a HPPS by mean rank are

Table 12.1 Work Practice Dimensions Which Comprise a HPPS by Mean Rank

Work Practice Dimensions	Mean	Outback
Training and skill development	6.58	X
Information sharing	6.46	X
Employer of choice	6.41	X
Selectivity in recruiting	6.29	X
Measurement of the HR practices	6.21	X
Promotion from within	6.17	X
Quality of work/life	6.09	X
Diversity	6.09	X
Incentive pay based on performance appraisal	5.88	X
Participation and empowerment	5.88	X
Self-managed teams	5.71	X
Employee ownership	5.67	X
High wages	5.63	X

(Table 12.1) Training and Skill Development, Information Sharing, Employer of Choice, Selectivity in Recruiting, Measurement of the HR Practices, Promotion from Within, Quality of Work/Life, Diversity, Incentive Pay Based on Performance Appraisal, Participation and Empowerment, Self-Managed Teams, Employee Ownership and High Wages. These are the relevant dimensions to the casual themed restaurant service industry according to the study's results and are represented in the first construct of the theoretical model (Figure 12.3) labelled SHRM.

According to Huselid (1995), an HPWP system is comprised of an amalgamation of HRM competitive methods and core competencies, which when combined are capable of producing an SCA. However, what this study demonstrates is that a restaurant HPPS is not an amalgamation of competitive methods and core competencies, but a combination of multiple core competencies in support of the competitive methods. The primary competitive method (a bundle of goods and/or services) the HPPS supports is the management team in the casual themed restaurant. They are an intangible component in the guest service experience. The management team is the one that implements and executes the service plan. They hire and conduct the training of service staff to ensure a great guest experience and

277

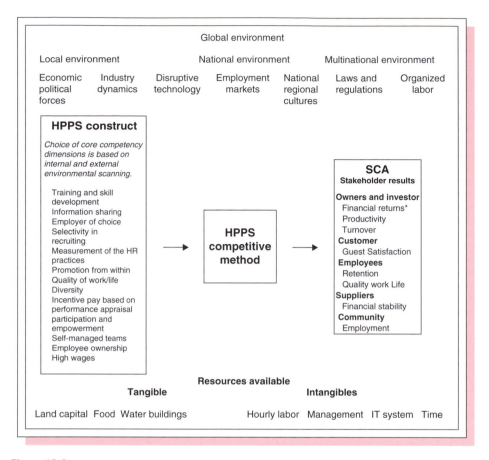

Figure 12.3
Theoretical Model of an HPPS for US Casual Restaurant Unit Management * Note: Financial returns in the model include more than just cash. Financial returns also reflect value creation in market price and accounting profits.

they are the ones to make adjustments to improve the experience when necessary. High performing management is rare, not easily imitable, is value-adding and is difficult to replace. These are the four essential elements of an SCA, rarity, inimitable, value, and substitutability, according to Barney (1991).

Application

"No Rules, Just Right" is the slogan of the dominant player in the steakhouse segment of the U.S. casual restaurant industry. Outback Steakhouse Inc. is a casual dining American restaurant chain based in Tampa, Florida with over 900 locations in 23 countries throughout North and South America, Europe,

Asia, and Australia. It specializes in USDA Choice and other offerings in an Australian-inspired environment. As the name suggests, Outback Steakhouse has an Australian outback theme, exemplified by Boomerangs, stuffed crocodiles, maps of Australia, and paintings by Aboriginal artists. Menu items are largely named after places and animals in Australia and others take their names from pop-cultural references, such as the *Mad Max Burger* and *Grilled Shrimp On The Barbie*. In early 2007 Outback removed some of its Australian flair from the menu. The New York Strip Steak, Rib-eye, Pork Chops, and Mad Max burger are some of the more popular menu items to lose their "Aussie" nicknames. It was founded in February 1988 by Bob Basham, Trudy Cooper, Chris T. Sullivan, and Tim Gannon. It is owned and operated in the United States by OSI Restaurant Partners, and by franchise and venture agreements internationally.

"The most serious issue for employers today, in all industries, is hiring and keeping qualified and capable employees" according to Donald Marshack, senior analyst at the U.S. Bureau of Labor Statistics (BLS) (Pine, 2000, p. 32). The labour shortage is especially critical in the restaurant industry, according to the National Restaurant Association (2002) (NRA) over the last few years operators have consistently identified "finding qualified and motivated labor as their biggest operational challenge" (p. 2). According to Olsen and Sharma (1998) white paper on trends in the casual restaurant industry, there is no reason to believe that the labour situation will get any better "in fact, in the developed world it is likely to become a more formidable task than ever" (1998, p. 62). In a 1999 People Report survey of 50 hospitality companies, the median cost of turnover for a manager is more than $24,000 (Pine, 2000). As Dennis Lombardi, executive vice president of Technomic Inc., told more than 200 HR directors and foodservice operators at the 15th annual Elliot Conference "there is so much competition for employees out there, and we are not the industry of choice" (King, 2000, p. 6). However, some restaurant companies, including Outback Steakhouse, have done a good job with their turnover and compensation packages (Inc. Magazine, 1994). Murphy and Williams (2004) investigate the current management compensation practices for the managing partners of Outback Steakhouse and to identify the relationship between management compensation, intention to turnover, and core competencies for managers at Outback Steakhouse restaurants.

Outback does not use traditional methods to recruit general managers to operate its' restaurants instead it relies on an industry leading compensation package and a chance to own a "piece of the action" with low risk to attract experienced qualified managers. It further tries to boost retention by requiring a $25,000 "buy in" for the GM on their restaurant and having the manager sign a 5-year contract. The work schedule consists of only 55 h a week (5–11 h days) to give the manager a chance to have a life and not incur burnout. Further the manager gets the ability to develop roots in the community by committing to a 5-year deal. With the turnover rate for all management positions at only 9.7% the strategy appears to be working.

The useful life of compensation as a core competency is hard to determine because of many intrinsic factors. First, when dealing with people there are as many variables as there are individuals and predicting how long a restaurant manager will stay with the firm or in the industry before they burnout or decide to leave is difficult. Outback Steakhouse has done a good job of attempting to mitigate this problem so far by performing a careful screening of its' Managing Partners before they take over the management position (Hayes, 1995). All of Outback's managing partners are industry veterans who have worked in the restaurant business for years. Outback does no traditional recruiting of its' managers, in contrast the managers seek them out because of the potential to be a managing partner and to receive a portion of the profits in a successful restaurant and restaurant company. Before a person can become a managing partner they have to go through a 6-month training period as an assistant GM and are evaluated as to their potential to be successful in the Outback system and with the Outback Steakhouse culture (Hayes, 1995).

This core competency would seem to be easily duplicated, but so far no other major casual chain has attempted to duplicate the system of bringing in managing partners rather than general manager "employees" on the scale of Outback. This has enabled Outback Steakhouse to continue to recruit and retain qualified management, which is a key to the success of the concept (Inc. Magazine, 1994). The high compensation and the continued ability to renew the management contracts every 5 years or find a replacement for the departing manager enables Outback to maintain this core competency in the present and far into the future. With the success of this core competency, it seems that some other large casual theme restaurant organizations have realize that in order to grow and create value into the future they need to hire the best general managers and reward them well in order to continue to strive for excellence in staffing and operational performance into the future. Thus, new players to the casual restaurant industry have been adopting some of Outback's practices on a smaller scale.

Outback's operational management system

This for most insiders and outside observers is one of the cornerstones of Outback's success: the ability to hire and retain well-qualified restaurant management by providing managing partners the opportunity to purchase a 10% ownership stake in the restaurants they operate for $25,000 and requiring them to enter into a 5-year contract (Hayes, 1995). By offering this level of commitment and by providing the managing partner with a significant stake in the restaurant (10% of operating cash flows), the company understands it can attract and retain experienced highly motivated restaurant managers. The company also limits most restaurants to dinner only service, which reduces the hours for managers (5 days and 55 h maximum) and employees. This enables the average managing partner to earn $73,600 a year in bonuses from cash flow coupled with a $45,000 base salary for annual cash compensation of $118,600 (Inc. Magazine, 1994). The 13 dimensions of the operational management system at Outback are: ownership equity stake-10%; retirement plan; cash flow bonus-10%; base salary $45,000; stock option 4000 shares vested over 5 years; deferred compensation/end of contract cash out (10% of cash flow for last 2 years times five); medical, dental, and life insurance; vacation/paid time off; quality of work; status as manager/partner; community association/location; job autonomy; job status (http://www.outback.com). These key attributes are as follows.

Monetary

Ownership stake/equity interest: Outback provides managing partners the opportunity to purchase a 10% ownership stake in the restaurants they operate for $25,000 and requires them to enter into a 5-year contract. By offering this level of commitment and by providing the managing partner with a significant stake in the restaurant (10% of operating cash flows), the company believes it can attract and retain experienced highly motivated restaurant managers. After 5 years managing partners can sign up for another contract and purchase an additional equity stake in their unit up to 20%.

Retirement plan: The company offers a 401 K plan to its' managers.

Performance bonus: This is the largest part of many managing partners' annual income. Managing partners earn 10% of the cash flow for the unit in which they are the proprietors. This equates to an average annual income of $118,600, but can go over $160,000 in high performing restaurants.

Base salary: The base salary for managing partners is $45,000, which has remained unchanged for several years since the early 1990s.

Stock options vested over 5 years: Outback managers receive 4000 shares vested over the first 5 years of their contract. If they choose to sign up for an additional 5 years more shares are offered.

End of contract cash-out/deferred compensation: At the end of the managing partners contract they can "cash out" of their restaurant unit for 10% of the last 2 years cash flow times 5, or roll the deferred compensation over. With some cash outs reported to reach as high as $300,000.

Fringe benefits: Medical, dental, life, and disability insurance benefits are provided for the managing partners as part of their employment contract.

Paid time off: Outback managing partners receive vacation and holiday pay as part of their management contract. At the end of their 5-year contract they receive a 1-month paid "sabbatical" at the corporate office in Florida where they get to discuss their future with the principles of the company, relax and decide if they want to negotiate a new contract with Outback.

Non-monetary

Quality of working conditions: The company limits the restaurant to dinner only service, which reduces the hours for managers to an average of 50–55 h/week and a 5-day work week.

Status as a managing partner of the restaurant: Outback believes that restaurant managers have a desire to own a restaurant of their own. So managing partners have their names put above the entrance to their Outback restaurant labelled as the proprietor.

Community association/location: The company believes that a strong community affiliation is important to the success of their Steakhouses and that managers should have say in where they work and live. Also the company's community-based marketing plan calls for their managers to develop strong ties with the community where they live and work.

Job responsibility: Outback managers like most restaurant managers are responsible for a lot, but even more so because their equity stake in the company makes it difficult to walk away if times get tough.

Job autonomy: The outback philosophy is to hire the best managing partners and make them the captains of their own ships while monitoring from afar. This gives the Outback managers a lot of autonomy in running the day-to-day operations of their units.

Ask someone to define compensation, and depending on the life experiences of that person, you will get a range of definitions. The combination of all cash incentives and the fringe benefit mix that an employee receives from a company constitutes an individuals' total compensation according to Lawler (1981). Dibble (1999) expands the definition of compensation to mean the benefits provided by employers that do not have to do with earnings or cash. Even benefits such as employee training and development, though not necessarily viewed by the employee as compensation, are a substitute for money and a major cost for employers. Murphy and Williams (2004) study used a list of compensation items as defined in published literature about Outback Steakhouse (Table 12.2), company published literature and personal interviews with managers with results by mean rank.

The compensation plan for Outback Steakhouse Inc.'s managing partners has significant positive impact on manager

Table 12.2 Outback Compensation Dimensions by Mean Rank

Outback Compensation Dimensions	Mean	Std. Deviation
Ownership stake/equity interest	6.56	0.97
Deferred compensation/end of contract cash out	6.17	1.30
Performance bonus	6.16	1.56
Job responsibility[a]	6.05	1.24
Job autonomy[a]	6.05	1.17
Quality of work conditions[a]	6.03	1.31
Status as a restaurant manager[a]	5.86	1.68
Community association/location[a]	5.80	1.25
Stock options	5.34	1.90
Vacation/time off	5.03	1.65
Base salary	4.91	1.43
Medical, dental, life insurance	4.56	1.66
Retirement plan	4.47	1.92

[a] Non-monetary dimensions.

retention; consequently reducing their intention to turnover to an annual manager turnover rate of 4–5% compared to an industry turnover average for managers of 27% (Inc. Magazine, 1994; Ghiselli *et al.*, 2000). This is in accordance with some of the previous research on manager turnover that the compensation an organization provides clearly influences the decision employees make about the organization and turnover intentions (Lawler, 1987; Mobley, 1982). Additionally, Steers and Porter (1991) support the premise that companies which offer the greatest compensation retain the most employees. Steers and Porter (1991) have found that high reward levels lead to high satisfaction, which in turn leads to lower turnover. The results of Murphy and Williams (2004) study would seem to add credence to the assumption that the compensation plan for Outback Steakhouse managing partners is a value-adding core competency considering the low turnover rate and the industry leading financial performance of their restaurants (Garger, 1999; Inc. Magazine, 1994; Olsen *et al.*, 1998).

Outback believes that the compensation plan they offer is effective in preventing turnover, retaining quality management while helping to attract experienced well-qualified managers and gives the company a value-adding core competency (Inc. Magazine, 1994). The findings of the study shows that Outback Steakhouse's managing partners are highly influenced by the compensation package that the company offers in regards to their intentions to stay with the company. The findings also demonstrate that the managing partners are most influenced by the non-traditional attributes of the plan (deferred compensation, stock option, and ownership stake) as opposed to the more traditional attributes of compensation plans (base pay, insurance, and retirement plans). The managers appear to be overall positively influenced by the compensation plan of Outback. This bodes well for Outback because these well-developed, non-traditional aspects of their compensation plan are a successful core competency for the company.

The study also indicates the factor that would be most influential in the managing partner's decision to leave is a non-monetary element perhaps not addressed by their compensation strategy, quality of life, and quality of family life. While the respondents clearly indicated that it is the monetary aspects of compensation influencing their decision to stay with Outback, they were also equally clear that it is the non-monetary aspects of compensation, quality of work, and life that would most influence their decision to potentially leave. Working 55 h a week, nights, and weekend all the time can start to become burdensome for managers (Bureau of Labor Statistics, 2003). The lack of time spent with family and friends can start to wear on managers as they get older. There is also the risk of burnout as managers decide that they want something more out of life than just being a successful restaurant manager (Mcfillen *et al.*, 1986). For Outback to continue to consider its' compensation plan an industry leader they will need to address these issues in the future.

The continued superior performance of some of the most successful restaurant firms, such as Outback and Cheesecake Factory, has been attributed to unique capabilities for managing HR to gain competitive advantage (Murphy and DiPietro, 2005). On the contrary, to the extent that people management systems hinder the development of new competencies and/or tear down present organizational competencies, they may contribute to firm liability and competitive weakness.

According to Steers and Porter (1991), the research on compensation clearly shows a link between the rewards a company offers and those individuals that are attracted to work and stay with a company. In recent years the benefits available to employees has expanded both in terms of the type of benefits and the amount. Traditionally, restaurant general managers were compensated with a base pay and a business period bonus based on meeting preset goals for revenues and expenses (Muller, 1999). In general, compensation has been divided into monetary and non-monetary incentives, but with the advent of "cafeteria" style plans, where employees get to choose among a variety of options for a set price, the compensation categories have become blurred. Additionally, employees that are in high demand are increasingly acting as their own agents negotiating individual compensation arrangements, much like professional sports players, based on their employment value to the firm.

An analysis of the key points and difficulties to be considered

The HPPS framework implies that the internal and external environmental forces driving change must be identified by scanning environmental events to choose the dimensions of the HPPS construct. The study indicates that there are 13 HRM dimensions applicable to the US casual themed restaurant segment for management (Table 12.1); Training and Skill Development, Information Sharing, Employer of Choice, Selectivity in Recruiting, Measurement of the HR Practices, Promotion from Within, Quality of Work/Life, Diversity, Incentive Pay Based on

Performance Appraisal, Participation and Empowerment, Self-Managed Teams, Employee Ownership, and High Wages are the relevant dimensions to the casual themed restaurant service industry. These dimensions were identified as ones being highly important to the firm and that contain the fundamental elements of a value-adding core competency.

What has come to light from conducting this study is an HPPS construct containing 13 dimensions that are posit to produce an SCA for casual restaurant firms. According to Huselid (1995), an HPWP system is comprised of an amalgamation of HRM competitive methods and core competencies, which when combined are capable of producing an SCA. However, what this study demonstrates is that a restaurant HPPS is not an amalgamation of competitive methods and core competencies, but a combination of multiple core competencies in support of the competitive methods. The primary competitive method (a bundle of goods and/or services) the HPPS supports is the management team in the casual themed restaurant. They are an intangible component in the guest service experience. The management team is the one that implements and executes the service plan. They hire and conduct the training of service staff to ensure a great guest experience and they are the ones to make adjustments to improve the experience when necessary. High performing management is rare, not easily imitable, is value-adding and is difficult to replace. These are the four essential elements of an SCA, rarity, inimitable, value, and substitutability, according to Barney (1991).

A restaurant HPPS is different than a manufacturing HPWP system because its focus is squarely on being a multifaceted core competency that supports the value-adding manager competitive method—management is the intangible competitive advantage which oversees the execution of the production of outstanding food and service to achieve customer satisfaction.

In most high-performance restaurant companies, managers are given the freedom to have control of their work environment within clearly defined frameworks. As John Denopli of OSI stated "they are captains of their own ship" and in charge of their own destiny; "I am here to help them be successful." In these work systems managers are more knowledgeable about their operating environment as they have a clear stake in the restaurants performance. HPPS recognize managers as people who are capable of being key contributors to the success of the organization. Managers are given an opportunity to interact in team meetings, joint problem solving sessions, and information sharing. HPPS and people management systems aid in keeping the morale of the employees at high levels. By involving people, employee involvement systems rest on the interaction between the tangibles and intangibles.

The casual restaurant service sector does not have all of the same work practices that were suggested by previous studies conducted in manufacturing and other regulated industries. Job Design, Employment Security, and Reduced Status Distinctions and Barriers that were included in those previous studies do not seem to apply in the U.S. casual themed restaurant segment for unit managers according to the research results.

This is an important distinction and a significant finding of this study. Over the last several business cycles the U.S. economy has successfully transformed itself from a manufacturing economy to a service and knowledge economy. However, the focus in mainstream accounting practices, academic business research, and government statistics has not significantly evolved with this rapidly changing environmental reality. The future of the U.S. economy clearly rests with the creation of value through the use of intangible knowledge works, whose value is hard to quantify and is highly mobile. Thus knowing what components of an HPPS for intangible, value creating unit-level restaurant managers are required to attract and retain, will ultimately add value to the firm.

Performance measures for HPPS

The difficulty in measuring the effectiveness of an HPPS is its intangibility. Intangibles are qualities in a person or group of people, especially those in an organizational group, which affect performance but are not directly quantifiable. They are often cited as a reason for performance which is surprisingly better or worse than expected. So, how is the immeasurable measured? This is the current dilemma with the valuation of intangibles; although they often far exceed in value "hard or real assets" in today's knowledge economy. As previously stated, this study represents that a restaurant HPPS is a combination of core competencies in support of the competitive methods. The primary competitive method the HPPS supports is the value-adding management team in the casual themed restaurant, which oversees the execution of the production of outstanding food and service to achieve customer satisfaction. The normative definition of a competitive method is:

A competitive method is a portfolio of products and services that is bundled in such a way that it attracts those customers from within the overall demand curve of the industry (Olsen *et al.*, 2006).

This definition would not include a value-adding manager competitive method; however, nearly every casual themed restaurant operator would agree that quality management adds value to the firm and is hard to find in great supply and highly mobile. This realization does not necessarily mean that organizations act on this knowledge by changing their business model to provide for a HPPS. Therefore, what need to be measured are not the core competencies, but the competitive method—management. What an organization really wants to know is whether or not their investment in a competitive method produces acceptable returns. Is their investment in core competencies that support a competitive method worth it? Or should the firm invest its limited resources in other assets, tangible or otherwise?

So what measures should a casual themed restaurant firm use? The results of the study would seem to indicate that a restaurant company use retention, turnover, guest satisfaction, and operational cash flow for financial performance. However, not all stakeholders were fully represented in the performance outcome section of the model (Figure 12.2). The performance metrics need to be reevaluated to determine if employee surveys need to be part of the evaluation process. Additionally, in general, the author feels that the performance dimensions to measure the effectiveness of the work practices and HPPS do not accurately gage the value of these core competencies. This study proposes that a restaurant HPPS is a combination of core competencies in support of the competitive method (management). What needs to be measured is the competitive method not the core competencies. To effectively measure all stakeholders' outcomes in the U.S. casual themed restaurant industry, retention, turnover, guest satisfaction, operational cash flow for financial performance, employee quality of work life, and same store sales should be collectively assessed.

Human capital intangibles

Baruch Lev (2001), a professor at the Stern School of Business at New York University, and a leading authority on intangibles, was commissioned by The Brookings Institution to do a comprehensive study of intangibles in all aspects of business. Dr. Lev wrote barely two pages on HR intangibles and concluded, "the research on human resource expenditures (intangibles) is in its infancy and is seriously hampered by the absence of publicly disclosed corporate data on human resources" (p. 75). The body of literature on HR intangibles is deficient and it is difficult to draw any conclusions from the studies published thus far, especially with public companies not required by the Securities and Exchange Commission (SEC) to disclose significant financial information related to their employees. According to a recent Business Week cover story not much has changed over the last 10 years:

Assessing how much bang for the buck companies get from their spending on intangibles is even harder, especially in the fast-changing knowledge economy. Take employee training. In the old days, that required flying people to a teaching facility, which cost companies a lot of time on top of the cost of the instructors and real estate. Now online learning and other innovations are driving down the cost of training. At IBM the training budget fell by $10 million from 2003 to 2004, a 1.4% decline, while the number of classroom and e-learning hours rose by 29%. Are other companies seeing an equally dramatic decline in the cost of training? No one knows (p. 55).

The idea that individual worker performance has implications for business level results has been widespread among scholars and practitioners for many years (Huselid, 1995). Interest in this area has recently intensified as academics have begun to debate that, as a group, a company's employees can also provide a distinctive source of competitive advantage that is difficult for its competitors to imitate. An employment system that creates a distinct sustainable competitive advantage is an "intangible asset" and it is not carried on the balance sheet, as are traditional assets (plant and equipment). Bill Gates was quoted in an article in the Journal of Business Strategy Review "Our primary assets, which are software and our software development skills, do not show up on the balance sheet at all" (1999). Intangible assets are now worth on average three times more than firm's hard assets, according to the Harvard Management Update Newsletter (Wagner, 2001). Microsoft, for example, reported in 2000 that it had revenue of $23 billion, physical assets of $52 billion, and a market capitalization (number of outstanding common stock shares times their price) of more than $423 billion. That leaves a spread between intangibles and tangible assets of eight fold.

"As innovation accelerates, it is increasingly difficult to measure the source of wealth. The three biggest measurement headaches are human capital, healthcare and computers" (Rohwer, 1999, p. 263). Human capital is basically the ability of employees to generate economic output through the application of their education, knowledge, and skills; it refers to employees' know-how, capabilities, skills, and expertise. "The best known indicator of human intellectual capital value is market to book value" (Dzinkowski, 2000, p. 93). The difficulty with this valuation is that there is no distinction as to what part of the intangible value is representative of human capital and what belongs to other intangibles (trademarks, etc). The other complex issue is that stock market valuations are so volatile and book value of assets does not always represent their true worth. On Friday July 26, 2002, in the midst of a severe stock market slide, Tyco International announced that it had hired Edward Breen, the former president of Motorola, to be its new CEO (Eisner, 2002, p. C1). Tyco's stock shot up 46% that day, worth $7.5 billion in market value, while at the same time Motorola's stock declined $2.5 billion, a $10 billion swing due to the departure and arrival of one man. Is this a demonstration of the power and value of human capital intangibles … or just due to some wild market forces? Most likely the cause is a little of both.

Intangible valuation

According to David Norton, co-developer of the balanced scorecard, the greatest anxiety today for business executives in the new economy is that "human capital is the foundation of value creation" and they do not know how to create, measure, keep it, or ultimately value it (Becker *et al.*, 2001, p. ix). Top-level management realize that they are in a battle for talented employees, but they only seem to know how to manage their human capital like operating costs, something to be cut when the budget gets tight (Becker *et al.*, 2001). The outcome of this paper for intangible value is the advancement of a model to demonstrate the economic value of an HRM intangible dimension and ultimately an HPPS; and additionally to demonstrate why restaurant firms should invest in HRM as a strategy to develop core competencies that produce economic value-added (EVA) for the firm. Intangible EVA is the potential and ability of employees to add additional value above and beyond the cost of the products and services they create while engaged in work activities or work-related activities. "The best known indicator of human intellectual capital value is market to book value" (Dzinkowski, 2000, p. 93).

There are lots of intangibles that have the potential to create value, including skilled employees, specialized training and development, intellectual property, business processes, customer intimacy, corporate culture, brand equity, and many others that do not show up on most balance sheets. Businesses and investors have to understand how to identify the intangibles that contribute to the creation of value; how to measure them to understand the nature of the value they create; and how to improve their value to measurably grow the bottom line. CFOs, COOs, and CEOs are already approaching this challenge from multiple fronts, which is reflected in trends like business intelligence and the balanced scorecard—initiatives that hinge on mapping business processes directly to corporate strategy. Unfortunately, few HR managers are sitting at the strategy table to represent HR's value, because the HR value-creation process is not fully understood or causal.

The fundamental driver shaping current trends in corporate strategy is a shift in how the value of a business is measured. Until the early 1980s, up to 75% of the market value of a business was defined by the tangible assets that appeared on the balance sheet. Today, that number is less than 25%. "Gone are the days when businesses can afford to view people purely as costs. In the 21st century knowledge economy, people must be seen as wealth and capability generators who can profoundly affect market appeal, reputation, and performance. How well businesses measure and then improve know-how greatly influences how successful they are. When it comes to measuring know-how, no one metric or approach can meet all purposes. Several areas commonly explored in existing reporting on intangible value include customer capital, human capital, intellectual capital and relationship capital. Without doubt, the area of measuring business know-how (intangible assets) is undergoing fundamental change" (Allister, 2003, p. 1).

There are numerous concerns with this problem; however, they all can be summarized in two simple statements. How comfortable can the executives be when they cannot identify, and therefore cannot control 90% of the firm's value? Additionally, as value and risk are two sides of the same coin, how comfortable can other stakeholders in the firm, specifically, investors and regulators, be when the leadership cannot identify the major sources of value, and degree of risk?

In the "New Economy," growth is no longer driven predominantly by investments in physical assets, but by investments in intellectual, organizational, and reputational assets. Growing discrepancy between the important role of intangibles on firm's growth and the ability to identify, measure, and account for those assets is a serious potential problem for a restaurant firm.

Concluding comments

The restaurant industry employed an estimated 12 million people in 2005, making it the nation's largest private sector employer providing work for nearly 9% of those employed in the U.S. (http://www.restaurant.org/research/employment/). Many restaurant companies have learn to view their employees from a new perspective, as strategic human capital which possesses intangible assets (knowledge, experience, skill, etc.) that are valuable to the firm. Industry reports and actions suggest that restaurant company's business performance improves and the state of their restaurant workers is raised when these companies implement adopt this strategy. The industry as a whole needs to break-free of the out dated HR paradigm of high turnover and low retention of employees, which is costing the industry billions in replacement costs, lost productivity, service quality, employee know how, and experience (Pine, 2000). Gordon (1991) concluded that "corporate cultures, consisting of widely shared assumptions and values, are, in part moulded by the requirements of the industry in which they operate" (p. 410). The foodservice industry, and more specifically the restaurant segment, is subject to Gordon's exact proposition that the industry norms shape the corporate culture/thinking of individual entities, when it comes to valuing employee retention and experience. Many of the individual firms in the restaurant industry are still stuck in a paradigm of giving to their employees as little as possible, because that's how the business traditionally made money in the past. Those organizations still practicing that mode of HRM operation will need to undergo a fundamental change in philosophy in order to harvest the full potential of their employee's intangible value.

For hospitality executives to effectively use a co-alignment strategy they clearly must begin with an effective ES process that does more than just benchmark competitors for ideas to mimic. Executives must proactively search out ways in which to gain a SCA and compete in the future. Currently, the most prevalent strategy in the industry appears to be that of unit growth. However, at some point in time the restaurant industry will reach a saturation point. Currently there is one restaurant for every 350 Americans. How much further can the industry grow? Those companies that are going to be successful in the future will need to be in co-alignment with the environmental realities of slower unit growth and will have to seek more effective ways to grow profit. They will need to develop new competitive methods and core competencies such as comprehensive HR systems that will yield sustainable competitive advantages.

While past literature in business strategy has consigned the HR function to the implementation stage of strategy, current theoretical approaches argue that HR and the organizational systems that develop them can generate a SCA (Becker, 1996; Barney, 1995). While some classic strategy theory takes a strategic choice view, and suggests that companies select a "generic" strategy to compete in the environment in which they find themselves, recent theorists have viewed organization strategy from a RBV of the firm, arguing that businesses develop SCA only by creating value that is rare and not easily imitated by the competition (Penrose, 1959; Wernerfelt, 1984; Barney, 1991;

Barney and Wright, 1997; de Chabert, 1998). The conventional sources of competitive advantage discussed in the strategic choice literature include factors such as technology, natural resources, productivity improvements, and low-cost leadership. These factors have been shown to create value within an organization. Many have argued that these traditional types of competitive advantages are becoming increasingly scarce, hard to develop, and easy to imitate, particularly in comparison to a well thought out employment systems (Murphy and Williams, 2004). Experienced managers are increasingly leveraging their value to the company and to the restaurant industry by "making a statement about whom they are, where they want to live, how they want to work" (Prewitt, 2000).

"The ability of human beings to learn and thus constantly improve their services, to transfer their knowledge from one domain to another, and to combine other resources in more productive ways makes human beings distinct from other types of resources" (Penrose, 1959, p. 69). Human expertise is viewed as a separate resource class (intangible asset) and as a distinct resource, which adds more of a value-adding element to the organization then through traditional profit generating resources such as the manufacturing of goods. Boxall (1998) uses HR theories to outline the basic elements of a theory of "human resource advantage." Boxall suggests that HR capable of yielding sustained advantage are those which meet the tests of rare value, and relative immobility and superior appropriate ability. Firms which secure ongoing viability in their industry have the potential to build HR advantage through superior human capital and organizational processes. These sources of superiority depend on the quality of interest alignment (firm and employee) and employee development in a firm compared with industry rivals. It is for this reason that HR strategies can become important sources of competitive advantage, now and in the future; "the challenge for management will be creating value through people rather than using them as objects" (Olsen and Zhao, 2002, p. 7).

References

Alexander, S. (1998). No more turnover. *Computer World*, *32*(21).

Allen, R. L. (2000, Jan. 10). Can enhanced employee benefits, marketing end labor shortages, *Nation's Restaurant News*, p. 25.

Barney, J. B. (1991). Firm resources and sustained competitive advantage. *Journal of Management*, *17*(1), 99–121.

Barney, J. B. (1995). Looking inside for a competitive advantage. *Academy of Management Executive*, *9*(4), 49–61.

Barney, J. B. (1997). *Gaining and Sustaining Competitive Advantage*. Reading, MA: Addison, Wesley.

Becker, B. E., and Huselid, M. A. (1998). High performance work systems and firm performance: A synthesis of research and managerial implications. *Research in Personnel and Human Resources Journal*, *16*(1), 53–101.

Becker, C. (1996). Penetrating the surface of empowerment: A guide for teaching the empowerment concept to future hospitality managers. *Hospitality Educator*, *8*(4).

Bohl, D., and Ermel, L. (1997). Responding to tight labor market: Using incentives to attract and retain talented workers. *Compensation and Benefits Review*, *29*(Nov/Dec).

Boxall, P. (1998). Achieving competitive advantage through human resource strategy; towards a theory of industry dynamics. *Human Resources Management Review*, *8*(3).

Bureau of Labor Statistics. (2003). *The 1998–1999 Occupation Outlook Handbook*, Retrieved from http://www.bls.gov/oco/cg/print/cgs023.htm on May 15, 2005.

Conner, K. (1991). Historical comparison of resource-based theory and five schools of thought within industrial organization economics: Do we have a new theory of the firm? *Journal of Management*, *17*(1), 121–154.

Davis, S., and Meyer, C. (1998). *Blur*. Reading, MA: Addison-Wesley.

de Chabert, J. (1998). *A Model for the Development and Implementation of Core Competencies in Restaurant Companies for Superior Financial Performance*. Unpublished dissertation, Virginia Tech.

Delaney, J., and Huselid, M. (1996). The impact of human resource practices on perceptions of organizational performance. *Academy of Management Journal*, *39*, 949–967.

Delery, J. E. (1998). Issues of fit in strategic human resources: Implications for research. *Human Resources Management Review*, *8*(3), 289–309.

Delery, J. E., and Doty, D. H. (1996). Modes of theorizing in strategic human resources management: Tests of universalistic, contingency, and configurational performance predictions. *Academy of Management Journal*, *39*, 802–835.

Dibble, S. (1999). *Keeping Your Valuable Employees*. New York: Wiley.

Ermel, L., and Bohl, D. (1997). Responding to a tight labor market: Using incentives to attract and retain workers, *Compensation and Benefits Review*, American Management Association International, *29*(6).

Frumkin, P. (2000). Lone Star Land-banks 10 lonely sites as it moves to upgrade staff, finances, *Nation's Restaurant News*, *34*(7), p. 110.

Garger, E. M. (1999). Holding on to high performers: A strategic approach to retention. *Compensation and Benefits Review*, *15*(4).

Ghiselli, R., LaLopa, J., and Bai, B. (2000). *Job Satisfaction, Life Satisfaction, and Turnover Intent of Foodservice Managers*. Paper presented at The Council on Hotel Restaurant Institutional Education, New Orleans, LA.

Gray, C. (1998) Holding your own, *Financial Executive*, *14*(5).

Grindy, B. (1998, February). *Customer Loyalty Key to Success. Restaurants USA*, Retrieved from http://www.restaurant.org/rusa/1998/february/fst9802a.html on May 15, 2005.

Hartog, D., and Verburg, R. (2004). High performance work systems, organizational culture and firm effectiveness. *Human Resource Management Journal*, *14*(1), 55.

Hayes, J. (1995). Inside outback: Company profile, *Nation's Restaurant News*, *29*(13), 47–86.

Hickton, M. (2000). *David verses Goliath. National Restaurant Association, Restaurant Report*, Retrieved from http://www.restaurantreport.com/features/ft_davidvsgoliath.html on May 15, 2005.

Horovitz, B. (2002). Quick casual takes place at restaurant table, *USA TODAY*, June 03, 2002.

Huselid, M. A. (1995). The impact of human resource practices on turnover, productivity, and corporate financial performance. *Academy of Management Journal*, *38*, 635–667.

Huselid, M. A., Jackson, S. E., and Schuler, R. S. (1997). Technical and strategic human resource management effectiveness as determinants of firm performance. *Academy of Management Journal*, *38*, 635–667.

Inc. Magazine. (December 1994). Entrepreneur of the year, pp. 40–59.

Jackson, S. E., and Schuler, R. S. (1995). Understanding human resource management in the context of organizations and their environments. *Annual Review of Psychology*, *46*, 237–265.

Joinson, C. (1999). The cost of doing business, *HR Magazine*, *44*(13).

Kapner, S. (1996). Robert Basham: Outback co-founder fuels chain with a get things done attitude, *Nation's Restaurant News*, *30*(40), p. 148.

King, P. (2000). Elliot conference addresses industry's concerns about shrinking labor pool, *Nation's Restaurant News*, *34*(17), p. 6.

Lado, A. A., and Wilson, M. C. (1994). Human resource systems and sustained competitive advantage: A competency-based perspective. Academy of management. *The Academy of Management Review*, *19*(4).

Lawler, E. E. (1981). *Determining Total Compensation: Strategic Issues, Pay and Organization Development*. Reading, MA: Addison-Wesley.

Lawler, E. E. (1987). *The Design of Effective Reward Systems*. Englewood Cliffs, NJ: Prentice Hall.

Lazear, E. (1999). Personnel economics: Past lessons and future directions. *Journal of Labor Economics*, *17*(2).

Linstone, H., and Turoff, M. (1975). *The Delphi Method: Techniques and Applications*. Massachusetts: Addison-Wesley Publishing Company.

Linstone, H. A., and Turoff, M. (1979). *The Delphi Method*. Boston, MA: Addison-Wesley.

Marvin, B. (1994). *From Turnover to Teamwork*. New York: Wiley.

Mcfillen, J., Riegel, C., and Enz, C. (1986). Why restaurant managers quit (and how to keep them). *The Cornell Hotel and Restaurant Administration Quarterly*, *27*(3).

Miles, M. B., and Huberman, A. M. (1994). *Qualitative Data Analysis: An Expanded Sourcebook*. Thousand Oaks, IL: Sage.

Mobley, W. H. (1982). *Employee Turnover: Causes, Consequences, and Control*. Reading, MA: Addison-Wesley.

Muller, C.C. (1999). The business of restaurants: 2001 and beyond, *Hospitality Management*, *18*(4).

Murphy, K.S. and DiPietro, R.B. (2005). Management compensation as a value-adding competitive method for casual theme restaurants, *FIU Hospitality Review*, *22*(2).

Murrmann, S. K. *et al.* (1987). The level of compensation and employee benefits for entry level managers in the hospitality industry survey. The Virginia Tech Center for Hospitality Research and Service.

National Restaurant Association, (2002). *Industry Studies: The Restaurant Industry 2010*, http://www.restaurant.org/research/

National Restaurant Association, (2003). *Forecast, 2003 Executive Summary*, Retrieved from http://www.restaurant.org/research/forecast.cfm on May 10, 2005.

Nunnally, J. (1978). *Psychometric Theory* (2nd ed.). New York: McGraw-Hill. p. 245

Ohlin, J. B., and West, J. J. (1994). An analysis of fringe benefit offerings on the turnover of hourly housekeeping workers in the hotel industry. *International Journal of Hospitality Management*, *12*(4).

Olsen, M. D. (1995). *Environmental Forces, Competitive Methods and Industry Performance—A Study of Multinational Chains in the Hotel Industry, into the New Millennium: The White Paper on the Global Hospitality Industry*, International Hotel and Restaurant Association, Paris, France.

Olsen, M. D., and Sharma, A. (1998). *Forces Driving Change in the Casual Theme Restaurant Industry.* Paper presented at the International Hotel and Restaurant Association Conference, Paris, France.

Olsen, M. D., West, J. J., and Tse, E. C. (1998). *Strategic Management in the Hospitality Industry* (2nd ed.). Boston, MA: Wiley.

Olsen, M. D., and Zhao, J. (2002). *Forces Driving Change in the Foodservice Industry and Competitive Methods of Multinational Foodservice Firms.* IH & RA White Paper, Paris, France.

Outback Inc., (1998). *Annual report,* Retrieved from http://www.corporate-ir.net/ireye/ir_site.zhtml?ticker=osi&script=700&layout=11 on June 10, 2005.

Outback Inc., (2005). *News Releases,* Retrieved from http://www.outback.com/companyinfo/pdf/madduxreport_sept2004.pdf on June 13, 2005.

Papeiernik, R. (2002). Technomic: 100 largest chains' sales growth matched '00's pace. *Nation's Restaurant News,* June 3, 2002, p. 12.

Papiernik, R. (1999). National Restaurant Association: Restaurant industry 2010, the road ahead, *Nations Restaurant News, 33*(44), pp. 1, 6.

Papiernik, R. (2000). Boston chicken: All over but the carving. *Nation's Restaurant News,* May 22, 2000, p. 3.

Patil, P., and Chung, B. G. (1998). Changes in multiunit restaurant compensation packages. *The Cornell Hotel and Restaurant Administration Quarterly, 39*(3).

Penrose, E. T. (1959). *The Theory of the Growth of the Firm.* New York: Wiley.

Pfeffer, J. (1998). Seven practices of successful organizations. *California Management Review, 40*(2), 96–124.

Pfeffer, J., Hatano, T., and Santalainen, T. (1995). Producing sustainable competitive advantage through the effective management of people. *The Academy of Management Executive, 9*(1), 55.

Pine, B. (2000). Lending a hand. *Restaurants USA, 20*(3), 31–35.

Porter, E. (1985). *Competitive Advantage: Creating and Sustaining Superior Performance.* New York: The Free Press.

Prahalad, C. K., and Hamel, G. (1990). The core competence of the corporation. *Harvard Business Review, 68*(May–June), 79–91.

Prewitt, M. (September, 2000). Studies find operators create employee turnover problem, *Nation's Restaurant News, 34*(36), p. 8.

Prewitt, M. (October, 2000). MUFSO 2000: Conference probes labor recruitment woes, solutions, *Nation's Restaurant News, 34*(41), pp. 1, 6.

Pugh, D. S., Hickson, C. R., Hinings, C. R., and Turner, C. (1969). The context of organizational structures. *Administrative Science Quarterly, 16*(March), 91–114.

Raleigh, P.R. (1998). Employee theft and turnover not inevitable, *Nation's Restaurant News, 32*(18), pp. 46, 114.

Reed, R., and DeFillippi, R. J. (1990). Casual ambiguity, barriers to imitation, and sustainable competitive advantage. *Academy of Management Review, 15*(1), 88–102.

Roseman, E. (1981). *Managing Employee Turnover: A Positive Approach.* New York: AMACOM.

Schmelzer, C. D. (1992). *Case Study Investigation of Strategy Implementation in Three Multi-unit Restaurant Firms.* Unpublished doctoral dissertation. Virginia Polytechnic Institute and State University, Blacksburg.

Schmelzer, C. D., and Olsen, M. D. (1994). A data based strategy implementing framework for companies in the restaurant industry. *International Journal of Hospitality Management, 13*(4), 347–359.

Schmidgall, R. S., and Bechtel, C. (1990). ESOP's: Putting ownership in employees hands. *The Cornell Hotel and Restaurant Administration Quarterly, 30*(4).

Slattery, P., and Olsen, M. D. (1984). Hospitality organizations and their environments. *International Journal of Hospitality Management, 3*(2), 55–61.

Steers, R. M., and Porter, L. (1991). *Motivation and Work Behavior.* New York: McGraw Hill.

Sullivan, J. (21 December 1999). Human resources propel the future of foodservice. *Nation's Restaurant News*, pp. 72, 74.

Tabacchi, M. H., Krone, C., and Farber, B. (1990). A support system to mitigate manager burnout. *The Cornell Hotel and Restaurant Administration Quarterly, 31*(3).

The Wild New Workforce. (1999). December 6. *Business Week.*

U.S. Department of Labor, (1993), *High Performance Work Practices and Firm Performance,* Washington, DC: U.S. Government Printing Office.

Van Houten, B. (1997). A piece of the pie, *Restaurant Business, 96*(13).

Venkatraman, N., and Prescott, J. E. (1990). Environment–strategy coalignment: An empirical test of its performance implications. *Strategic Management Journal, 11*, 1–23.

Wasmuth, W. J., and Davis, S. W. (1983). Managing employee turnover: Why employees leave. *The Cornell Hotel and Restaurant Administration Quarterly, 24*(1).

West, J. J., and Anthony, W. (1990). Strategic group membership and environmental scanning: Their relationship to firm performance in the foodservice industry. *International Journal of Hospitality Management, 9*(3), 247–268.

West, J. J., and Olsen, M. D. (1988). Environmental scanning and its effect on firm performance: An exploratory study of the foodservice industry. *Hospitality Education and Research Journal, 12*(2), 127–136.

Woods, R. H. (1999). Predicting is difficult, especially about the future: Human resources in the new millennium. *Hospitality Management, 18*.

Wright, P. M., Dunford, B. B., and Snell, S. A. (2001). Human resources and the resource based view of the firm. *Journal of Management, 27*(6).

Wright, P. M., and Snell, S. A. (1998). Toward a unifying framework for exploring fit and flexibility in strategic human resource management. *Academy of Management Journal, 23*(4).

CHAPTER 13

Investing in information technology to grow firm value

Daniel J. Connolly

University of Denver

The perennial question of any business is "How does an organization add value?" Value can be defined from many different perspectives and may result from tangible and intangible factors. Principal stakeholders include shareholders (investors), customers, and employees. Shareholders typically measure value in terms of economic return on their investment based on some level of perceived risk. For customers, value is assessed in terms of a price–value relationship; that is, how much they received in terms of product and services for the price they paid. For employees, value is measured by salary and by the intrinsic rewards of the job. Yet, one of the most elusive questions with respect to information technology (IT) is "How can value be measured?" This question is especially important given the growing costs, capital intensity, and competitive requirements to invest heavily in IT and is the subject of this chapter. Hospitality business professionals must be able to successfully answer this question to create compelling business cases, to evaluate and make appropriate strategic and resource allocation decisions, measure and monitor the success of IT projects, and hold IT staff accountable.

IT typically ranks among the top five investments of most organizations, yet one of the least understood areas of the business (Lutchen, 2003). The prevailing attitude shared by many business executives is that IT overpromises and under-delivers (Betz, 2006). In the words of Maizlish and Handler (2005, p. 9):

IT investments represent a profound hole in companies. There are no other investments within a company that occupy such a large and growing expenditure yet lack disciplined management, processes, and performance measurements.

As a result of assertions such as these and other factors (e.g., the Sarbanes–Oxley Act), corporations recognized the need for increased scrutiny and accountability of their IT function and now experience tremendous pressure to achieve tangible and sustainable results (Weill and Ross, 2004). Adding fuel to the fire is the polemic debate Nicholas Carr created in 2003 regarding the strategic importance of IT in business (Carr, 2003). His controversial article calls into question the value IT plays in firms and its ability to create competitive advantage. While there are merits to some of his arguments, it is difficult to imagine any hospitality business operating in today's complex and competitive environment without the use of IT. IT is an essential ingredient to any hospitality business and an important part of any organization's competitive methods (Piccoli, 2004). Moreover, the IT requirements of today's marketplace are raising the level of investment and managerial skills required to compete successfully. What is important to note from Carr's article is that IT alone is insufficient in providing strategic value. What matters is how IT is used within organizations and what it enables. The value of IT can only be realized when it is well aligned with business strategy, when business processes are transformed to take advantage of IT, and when people are able to use IT and the information it provides to act in ways that competitors cannot (e.g., to do things faster, better, different and/or cheaper than competitors).

In order for a firm to achieve advantages and value from IT requires complementary relationships among the firm's resources and capabilities. Mata *et al.* (1995) refer to this as the resource-based view of the firm. According to their work, a company achieves competitive advantage through the culmination and convergence of a series of events, resources, experiences, and underlying management processes. In other words, competitive advantage is the result of not only how a firm competes (i.e., the strategies and competitive methods selected) but also the assets it has in which to compete. There is no one contributing factor but rather a series of ingredients or idiosyncratic resources that, when combined, provide a competitive edge in the marketplace. Plimpton (1990) terms this hidden competitive edge as the "X Factor." For many organizations, the integration of software applications and IT with the organizational structure provides the source of competitive advantage (Adcock *et al.*, 1993). Because of its tacit nature, the competitive advantage and its contributing factors are difficult to identify and, therefore, hard to duplicate. The resulting competitive advantage can then be sustained for as long as it remains inimitable and not obsolete, a period that is becoming shorter all the time in today's hypercompetitive marketplace. Because sustainability is difficult, firms should look to creating a sequence of advantages over time (Wiggins and Ruefli, 2005).

The literature is rich in examples of successful IT applications and their contributory role in a firm's success. For example, the work by Hiebeler *et al.* (1998) highlight best practices in 40 well-known and leading firms, including several from the hospitality industry such as Walt Disney, Ritz-Carlton, and Hyatt Hotels. In almost all cases, these authors recognize IT, either explicitly or implicitly, as a critical success factor and contributor to what makes companies stand out among others in their industries. IT is often deployed to help organizations grow revenues, cut costs, improve management decision making and controls, enhance guest services, and facilitate information reporting and communications. What the literature is less clear about, however, are the direct contributions provided by IT and a formula for success in how executives decide to invest in IT, the methods they employ, and the criteria they use to evaluate and select the appropriate investments, particularly in the hospitality industry. Strategic IT planning and investments have a long history of beleaguering industry professionals (Caldwell, 1998; Post *et al.*, 1995; Applegate *et al.*, 1996; Dreyfuss, 1995; Liao, 1994; Laberis, 1994; Diebold, 1987; Sprague and McNurlin, 1986; Parsons, 1983). It is believed that these problems result largely from the lack of suitable measurement tools, techniques, and criteria, not from any theoretical shortcomings (Saunders and Jones, 1992).

On the surface, IT investment decisions seem straightforward. All projects should be accepted that add value to the firm. In reality, however, the process is much more complex due to the difficulties in defining and measuring value and the expected and actual contributions provided by IT. It does not help that in many firms, spending on IT is viewed as discretionary and, therefore, among the first to be reduced during times of capital rationing (Antonucci and Tucker, 1998). The decision-making process is further complicated by subsequent issues such as build versus buy (or hybrid) decisions for software and lease versus buy decisions—which add to the dimensions of the analysis.

Investment in IT is important to nearly every aspect of an organization since it impacts customer service, transaction processing capabilities, employee performance, and so on. Surprisingly, however, many executives are ill-prepared to make sound decisions regarding IT investment and strategy (Weill and Broadbent, 1998; Weill, 1991). Executives' inability to effectively estimate cash flows, timing, and an IT project's useful life increases the uncertainty—and, hence, the risk— surrounding each investment. Consequently, they tend to shy away from important IT investment decisions, but when they do chose to select an IT project, the results are often mixed despite their best efforts. Commonly published statistics for IT across industries suggest that upwards of three-fourths of all IT projects are late, over budget, or unable to deliver the proposed functionality (O'Brien, 1997) or offer no appreciable business returns (Neelakantan, 1996). The hospitality industry's track record as a whole with respect to IT is, at best, mixed and adds to management's scepticism towards IT.

Practices rooted in traditional capital budgeting methods

The most common approach to IT investment is the capital budgeting process, which relies on traditional financial measures and the evaluation of cash flows based on the time value of money using discounted cash flow techniques (Bacon, 1992). General limitations to capital budgeting theory as it applies to investments in IT include: (1) a false assumption that all cash flows are known (i.e., that they can be predicted and quantified), (2) an invalid pretence that all contributions from IT (both good and bad) can be quantified, expressed in monetary terms, and measured by financial criteria, and (3) failure to account for organizational and behavioural factors (Bacon, 1992; Hubbard, 1999). The shortcomings of discounted cash flow techniques in particular are as follows: (1) benefits not easily quantifiable tend to be ignored; (2) financial analysis focuses mostly on cost displacement (i.e., labour and material savings) and tends to omit strategic implications such as new products and services or enhancements to existing ones; (3) in situations involving high perceived risk, unjustly high hurdle rates (rates of return) are set to compensate; (4) opportunity costs for forgoing an investment or IT project tend not to be considered, (5) analysis tends to be biased towards short-term returns, and (6) IT investments tend to pervade an organization and rely on interactions among different IT investments and different departments within the organization (Clemons and Weber, 1990; Weill, 1991).

Unfortunately, popular financial models such as net present value (NPV) and discounted cash flow analysis are inadequate for estimating the financial benefits for most of the technology projects under consideration today. While the hospitality industry has disciplined models and sufficient history to determine the financial gains or success of opening a new property in a given city, it lacks the same rigorous models and historical data for technology, especially since each technology project is unique. Although this problem is not specific to the hospitality industry, it is particularly problematic since the industry tends to be technologically conservative and unwilling to adopt new technology applications based on the promises of its long-term merits if it cannot quantify the results and calculate a defined payback period. When uncertainty surrounds the investment, when the timing of the cash flows is unpredictable, and when the investment is perceived as risky, owners and investors will most likely channel their investment capital to projects with more certain returns and minimal risk. Thus, under this thinking, technology will always take a back seat to other organizational priorities and initiatives. Efforts must be made to change this thinking and develop financial models that can accurately predict and capture the financial benefits derived from technology.

Until recently, most technology investment decisions have been considered using a support or utility mentality that stems from a manufacturing paradigm. Under such thinking, business cases could be built around an application or technology's ability to reduce costs or create labour savings. However, management's attitudes towards technology have been shifting in recent years. The more technologically savvy hospitality companies are looking to IT to build strategic and competitive advantages. These types of investments yield results over time, and seldom in the short run. This is problematic among owners and investors who demand more immediate results. Moreover, it is difficult to quantify and calculate the tangible benefits of technology when it is used for strategic purposes.

Sabherwal and King (1995) identify five decision-making processes: planned, provincial, incremental, fluid, and political. In the hospitality industry, it seems that there are six prevailing philosophies regarding IT investment. All projects tend to fall in one of the following six categories: (1) essentialness to survival, (2) an act of faith (or gut feeling) that an investment will prove beneficial to the firm over the long term, (3) projects with an intuitive appeal and seemingly obvious outcomes, (4) projects that are required or mandated (either by law, by regulation, or by top management), (5) a response to moves by competitors to achieve parity or protect market share, and (6) paralysis by analysis in situations involving high degrees of risk and uncertainty, perceived or actual.

More often than not, decisions related to IT tend to be made on an ad hoc basis because of the difficulties in evaluating IT investment decisions and judging their strategic benefits in advance of implementation (Antonucci and Tucker, 1998; Farbey et al., 1992; Clemons and Weber, 1990; Diebold, 1987). In many firms, formal justification procedures simply do not exist, and where they do exist, they are not always followed or enforced; instead, a project champion is left to determine the approach(es) deemed appropriate and sufficient to gain project approval and funding (Farbey et al., 1992). With respect to overall IT budgeting, firms tend to use simple approaches to establishing IT budgets such as developing guidelines based on existing budgets (some percentage of the current year's budget, which is often determined through a series of negotiations by senior executives and IT management) or benchmarking IT expenditures with those of competitors so as to maintain competitive parity. Needless to say, these approaches demonstrate little rigour and may lead to inappropriate or ineffective investment decisions, especially when resources must be allocated to multiple, contending projects and involve large sums of capital. Betz (2006) calls for a more sophisticated approach to IT management and oversight with specific focus on the development of effective and efficient IT management processes, discipline measures, and rational decision making. He emphasizes the need for better overall governance and accountability, particularly when it comes to people, priorities, and performance.

Unfortunately, IT is a complex entity to manage, and IT projects are often difficult to substantiate. The benefits of IT are not always obvious or certain, take years to realize, and are sometimes elusive. Because technology pervades a firm's value chain (Porter, 1985), it is difficult—if not impossible—to measure benefits derived from the technology, attribute benefits directly to the technology, or establish causal relationships. Moreover, the study of IT on firm performance is a difficult and complicated task due to the many confounding variables involved (e.g., organizational structure and organizational processes) and the many sources of extraneous variance (Hildebrand, 1997; Loveman, 1991; Bakos, 1987; Chakravarthy, 1986; King, 1983). Since there is a great deal of ambiguity surrounding performance (Anderson, 1984), it is difficult to establish a causal link between IT and firm performance.

In the hospitality industry, absence of this link and concrete evidence makes it more challenging to sell hospitality executives on the merits, capabilities, and benefits of IT—especially when greater emphasis is placed on IT as a support role or utility function rather than as a strategic weapon (Cho, 1996). This lack of clarity begs the question: What factors should executives consider when making IT-related investment decisions? There is often scepticism surrounding IT investment decisions due to the intangible returns and benefits derived from the technology itself, and when competing for resources and capital, IT often loses out to more tangible and visible projects that seemingly offer greater certainty and less risk. For example, one hotel IT executive of a leading, international hotel chain once reported at an industry workshop how he competed for and lost funding for an IT project to a physical facility upgrade. Instead of funding an IT initiative, senior executives favoured marble in guest bathrooms because it was viewed to have an immediate and direct impact on the hotel chain's guests. While one cannot defy this logic, it is representative of the emphasis placed on tangibility and the short-term mentality of industry leaders. It is this short-term thinking that fails to capture the long-term strategic potential of IT applications and plagues the development and advancement of IT throughout the industry.

The traditional approaches to assessing value are derived from accounting and finance practices that focus on physical assets supported by financial capital, but in an information-driven economy, these factors are clearly no longer sufficient; one must also include employees and customer relationships in the equation (Cline and Blatt, 1998) as well as the intangible factors. This holistic view will provide a more complete picture of value derived from IT investments.

Loveman (1991) suggests that because business executives are unable to effectively measure IT costs and benefits, they cannot make informed decisions regarding IT resources and investments—which, in turn, lead to misallocated resources and ineffective or unrealized benefits. Companies must have a clear view of how IT can fit in an organization, allocate resources, and invest according to this view.

Using a multivariate approach

To mitigate the limitations of financial methods when evaluating IT investment decisions, a more comprehensive or holistic approach is needed. The literature suggests that a cluster of metrics reflecting multiple dimensions and disciplines is better than a single measure when evaluating IT to provide a more robust assessment. These metrics can (and probably should) be quantitative as well as qualitative. Parker *et al.* (1988) identify six classes of value derived from IT: return on investment (ROI), strategic match, competitive advantage, management information support, competitive response, and strategic IS architecture. Bacon (1992) uses this framework of value to identify a set of 15 criteria classified in three categories (Table 13.1) and then develops a survey to ascertain what criteria are considered when making IT investment decisions.

Bacon (1992) approaches IT investment decisions from the standpoint of the criteria used, not the processes followed. In a similar vein, Semich (1994), Shein (1998), and Madden (1998) suggests a multiple-criteria approach, building upon the balanced scorecard technique first popularized by Kaplan and Norton (1992, 1996). Using this approach, most of the analysis can be done using a simple spreadsheet to group and rank organizational priorities among each of four categories: financial, internal business processes, customer service, and organizational learning and innovation.

Farbey *et al.* (1992) propose a benefits-oriented perspective to evaluating IT projects and investments. Under this

Table 13.1   IT Project Selection (Investment Decision) Criteria

Category	Measure
Financial criteria	
Discounted cash flow	Net present value
	Internal rate of return
	Profitability index
Other financial	Average/accounting rate of return
	Payback method
	Budgetary constraint
Management criteria	Support explicit business objectives
	Support implicit business objectives
	Response to competitive systems
	Support management decision-making
	Probability of achieving benefits
	Legal/government requirements
Development criteria	Technical/system requirements
	Introduce/learn new technology
	Probability of project completion

Source: Bacon (1992, p. 338).

approach, benefits derived from an IT application are expected to fall within one or more of the following categories (listed by the authors in order of increasing impact):

1. *Efficiency*: Creates savings (or avoidance) of time, manpower, money, or other resources of the firm.
2. *Functionality*: Provides the ability to process or complete new tasks or activities or improves upon the quality in which the existing ones are done.
3. *Communications*: Connects different systems and enables the exchange of information.
4. *Management*: Improves the quality and capabilities of management and enhances decision making.
5. *Strategy*: Supports corporate objectives and creates opportunities for competitive advantage.

In yet another approach, Benjamin *et al.* (1984) provide a simple framework for considering IT investments based on the strategic opportunities they pose. The criteria of this framework are based on the competitive marketplace and a firm's internal operations. They are:

1. IT's ability to significantly alter the way a firm does business to create competitive advantage.
2. IT's role in providing internal improvements and efficiencies.

Rockart (1979), on the other hand, addresses the process rather than the specific criteria. He introduces the term critical success factors, the defining elements of a firm's competitiveness and organizational performance. He suggests that critical success factors should determine a firm's priorities and needs because these, when done "right," are what make firms flourish. In his work, Rockart presents the process of interviewing top-level executives to identify a firm's critical success factors. Boynton and Zmud (1984), Geller (1984), and Shank *et al.* (1985) later employed this technique.

The critical success factors technique is a strategic approach involving high-level executives of the firm. Davenport *et al.* (1989) propose a somewhat similar methodology called the principles approach, or what Weill and Broadbent (1998) refer to as management by maxim. With this technique, senior executives articulate the firm's basic philosophies regarding the firm's business and its usage of IT through a set of management principles (maxims) that capture how IT should be used to achieve organizational goals and objectives. These principles then guide IT-related decisions and investments. The objective of the methodology is to force strategy to drive technology initiatives and to bridge the communications gap between senior management and technical experts.

Interestingly, despite the rapid change of technology and the newer capabilities afforded by technology, the principal reasons for implementing IT have remained relatively stable over time (Grover *et al.*, 1997). These include such goals as growing revenues, cutting costs, improving management decision making and controls, enhancing guest services, and facilitating information reporting and communications. Despite this stability in objectives, there is no one best solution, process, or set of criteria for evaluating IT investment options because the range of circumstances is so broad (Farbey *et al.*, 1992).

The use of IT throughout a firm should reflect that firm's strategic plan. The methods employed must balance short- and long-term needs with appropriate levels of risk and return using a portfolio approach (Maizlish and Handler, 2005; Applegate *et al.*, 1996; McFarlan, 1981; Thorp and DMR's Center for Strategic Leadership, 1998; Weill and Broadbent,

1998; Weill, 1991; Weill and Olson, 1989). The administration of these portfolios requires the use of fundamental management practices and business concepts, with the overall objective focused on creating value for a firm through supporting current strategies and by enabling new ones (Weill and Broadbent, 1998; Thorp and DMR's Center for Strategic Leadership, 1998). Like any financial investment portfolio, an IT portfolio must be actively managed with continuous monitoring and suitable investment levels to meet a firm's goals and objectives and to create a balanced set of risk-return profiles. Moreover, firms cannot afford to ignore the opportunity costs and strategic implications of failing to accept a given investment opportunity. Complacency is seldom an option since competitors will quickly alter the competitive landscape with their own moves and initiatives and consequently force action by sleeping firms and those attempting to avoid it.

Implicitly, all IT investment decisions are designed to improve strategic value, business performance, and ROI—unless of course, they are made to comply with regulatory, legal, or other government requirements. Realization of the benefits derived from IT applications comes with time, other changes throughout an organization, and complementary resources. IT alone does not generate benefits. However, the tools and methods for evaluation and IT appraisals to capture IT's contribution to these benefits are ill-defined and lacking, making it difficult to apply the necessary rigour and analysis for objective, fact-based decisions and allocations of firm resources.

As the above discussion illustrates, no single metric can adequately measure or capture the contributions of IT. Assessing the impact of IT should not rely on univariate metrics but instead must look at a composite of measures using multiple techniques to provide a more holistic assessment. Multiple measures are almost always preferred to a single measure because of the richness that can be captured. Since a single measure cannot sufficiently assess the impact of IT (e.g., costs, benefits, organizational impact, etc.), King and McAulay (1997) suggest the use of multivariate and multi-method measures to capture the diverse needs of multiple stakeholders, to provide criteria that can be rank ordered, and to offer a source of triangulation. To that end, a composite of quantitative and qualitative measures should be used to create a balanced scorecard approach (Semich, 1994; Kaplan and Norton, 1992, 1996; Shein, 1998; Madden, 1998). In the words of Weill and Broadbent (1998, p. 24):

Mangers make decisions about information technology investments based on a *cluster of factors* [italics added], including capabilities required now and in the future, the role of technology in the industry, the level of investment, the clarity with which technology investments are viewed, and the role and history of information technology in the firm.

In the words of Farbey *et al.* (1992, p. 116):

The organization wishing to sharpen its IT investment decision-making must first recognize that there are evaluation techniques other than ROI. It must then try to find which technique is most suitable for its IT investment.

Why measures matter

IT, when applied appropriately, can have a significant impact on a company's service levels and overall firm performance, but when a project is poorly conceived, the impact to the organization can be catastrophic (Bowen *et al.*, 2007; Maizlish and Handler, 2005). Moreover, selecting too many IT projects at one time or the wrong mix of projects can also lead to disastrous results (Ross and Weill, 2002). Therefore, when contemplating any significant IT investment, it is important to apply rigour and follow a formal and disciplined process to ensure the *right* mix of projects, commitment from the organization, and alignment with the business strategy. These, in turn, will lead to success-ful outcomes and the creation of business value (Holland and Skarke, 2008; Chan and Reich, 2007; Peak *et al.*, 2005). According to Diebold (1987, p. 590), one should analyze and quantify all IT projects/investments to the fullest extent possible to decrease the level of uncertainty and risk while lessening the leap of faith required by company executives. Bacon (1992) and Farbey *et al.* (1992) postulate that the criteria used in evaluating and mak-ing IT investment decisions are important because they deter-mine which projects are accepted and the level of funding and resources they receive. Ultimately, they become instrumental in determining and measuring the overall success and effective-ness of the decisions. The assumption is that the criteria used will ensure that only the *right* projects are accepted, while all others are rejected. These authors suggest the following signifi-cant implications regarding the criteria used:

1. The criteria used (or omitted) and the manner in which they are used (or not used) impact which decisions or projects are funded or rejected (thus, defining the mix of projects adopted and the pace at which they are adopted).
2. The criteria provide justification and set expectations within the firm for the application, system, or technology.

3. The criteria provide a basis for comparison of multiple projects competing for a finite set of resources.
4. The criteria impact how a firm attempts to maximize ROI and any ensuing cost-benefit analysis.
5. The criteria used affect how a firm balances multiple stakeholder requirements and needs.
6. The criteria provide a set of measures so a firm can monitor and control project and judge its degree of success.
7. Evaluation and subsequent measurement and comparison with actual achievements or impact provide a basis for learning which can be factored into future evaluation processes.

Common questions related to the IT function in a firm are (1) is the company spending too much money on IT, and (2) is the organization gaining appropriate returns from its investment in IT (Kaplan, 2005; Ross and Weill, 2002). Weill and Ross (2004) argue that the ability to derive value from IT is directly correlated to the effectiveness of a firm's IT governance process. Governance, as defined by Weill and Ross (2004), deals with what decisions should be made, by whom they should be made, the criteria upon which they should be based, and the accountability metrics used to monitor and measure outcomes. Since resources for IT are finite and subject to supply, demand, and costs, firms must have an effective governance process in place (Lutchen, 2003; Weill and Ross, 2004). The extant literature on IT governance reveals two common patterns of decision making: attribute-based (with the focus on characteristics surrounding the IT project and decision-making processes) and stage-based (which emphasizes the various steps through which a decision must move, the actors involved at each stage, and the timing) (Sabherwal and King, 1995).

Given the capital intensity, business impact, and risks associated with IT projects, the decision-making and approval process tends to be complex, multi-faceted, and conducted over a period of time with a number of hoops and hurdles to jump (Xue *et al.*, 2008). Decision making for IT investments typically requires a series of steps that begin with ideation and concludes with a go/no-go decision (Boonstra, 2003). Figure 13.1 provides a typical example of the various process stages IT projects must go through for prioritization and approval. Each stage gate represents a series of hurdles which must be cleared prior to advancing to the next level.

How decisions are analyzed and carried out can vary by firm depending upon IT governance (processes and actors), IT investment characteristics (such as costs, risks, technical complexity, and strategic importance), external forces (e.g., environmental

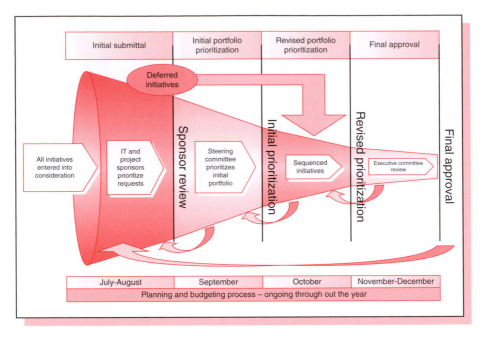

Figure 13.1
An illustrative example of the various stage gates IT projects must pass. (*Source*: Adapted from Tobin, 2007)

threats, regulatory requirements, and competitor moves), organizational structure (including the degree of formalization, centralization, and hierarchical management), and IT function power (which is affected by organizational culture and the clout, reputation, and credibility of the IT organization, among other things) (Xue *et al.*, 2008).

Setting priorities and investment strategies in IT are difficult processes. Since few formal methodologies exist, these processes are as much an art as a science, causing many firms to struggle and fail (Williamson, 1997). The lack of methodologies for determining the value of IT further complicates the process. Financial theory suggests measuring financial returns on a risk and time-adjusted basis (Hamel and Prahalad, 1991), and in most cases, firms rely on financial measures such as ROI, NPV, and internal rate of return (IRR). However, more often than not, the financial rationalization fails to capture the complete picture in terms of customer satisfaction, service, quality, employee satisfaction, productivity, or strategic positioning (Williamson, 1997; Bharadwaj and Konsynski, 1997).

The most popular thinking and prolific theories regarding the use and value of IT come from the Harvard Business

School, which is dominated by the works of Michael Porter (Porter, 1980, 1985; Porter and Millar, 1985). Porter's works are frequently cited in the IT literature as the theoretical underpinnings for studying IT. Applying this school of thought, the frameworks used to measure the strategic significance of IT are value chain analysis, Porter's industry and competitive analysis (ICA) framework or *Five Forces* model (e.g., create economies of scale, barriers to entry, switching costs, links to customers and suppliers, etc.), and Porter's generic strategies (i.e., low-cost producer, product differentiation, or market niche focus).

McFarlan (1984) proposed a strategic grid to evaluate a company's use of IT. Based on the strategic impact of existing systems and those under development, firms could be ranked in one of four categories: support, factory, turnaround, or strategic. Investment decisions can then be made based on consideration of a firm's current standing in the grid with respect to where it wants to be positioned. McFarlan (1984) also suggested five criteria useful when deciding resource allocations with respect to IT applications:

1. System rehabilitation and maintenance
2. Experiments with new technology
3. Competitive advantage
4. Maintenance or regaining of competitive parity
5. ROI

A firm's IT should be treated as any financial investment portfolio; that is, as a collection of assets that, when managed well, will generate suitable returns on investment (Kaplan, 2005; Jeffery and Leliveld, 2004; Weill and Broadbent, 1998; Weill, 1991; Weill and Olson, 1989). Just like with any financial portfolio, one must balance both short- and long-term needs of all stakeholders as well as risk and return while maintaining appropriate levels of investment to achieve a firm's objectives. McFarlan (1981), Applegate *et al.* (1996), and Thorp and DMR's Center for Strategic Leadership (1998) also use a portfolio metaphor, proposing that, as in finance, firms create a technology portfolio to help diffuse risk, particularly with respect to new projects. When embarking on new IT initiatives, firms should consider other projects currently underway and factor in the risks of the new project in terms of three dimensions: project size (in terms of budget, staff, scope, complexity, and development time), experience with technology, and project structure. Clemons and Weber (1990) elaborate on the topic of risk and suggest that there are six types that should be considered with respect to IT: technical risk, project risk, functionality risk, internal political risk, external environmental risk, and systemic risk. Hence, a sixth category, risk, should be appended to McFarlan's list.

There is growing recognition that intangible benefits and aspects of IT increasingly contribute to the IT's overall value and importance in today's knowledge-based economy. This is why Bharadwaj and Konsynski (1997) suggest that intangible factors such as strategic flexibility, risk avoidance, and growth potential receive greater consideration when evaluating IT investment decisions. Williamson (1997) offers the following as suggested criteria for IT investment decisions:

- Alignment with the business strategy: Consideration for how well the proposed IT project fits with the company's overall business strategy.
- ROI: The anticipated return on the IT investment.
- Risk: The ability to deliver the proposed project, fulfilling the requirements within a timely fashion. Assessments should be made to determine both technical and organizational risks.
- Business readiness: The overall preparedness of the firm to adopt the new technology and make the necessary changes required to implement it.
- Regulatory or mandated changes: Changes that are required due to necessary changes in the business environment.
- Business values: The anticipated changes brought on by the new IT application are consistent with the firm's corporate value system.
- Cost assessment: The best estimate for the project's total cost.
- Sponsorship: The project has support from the user community and an overall product champion.
- Common sense: Intuitively, the project makes sense.

The quest for determining the economic life and payoff from an IT project may very well be an exercise in futility in the minds of some (Hibbard, 1998). Could this be the equivalent of the search for the Holy Grail? Hildebrand (1997) writes of the difficulties in measuring the value of IT because of the many intangible variables. She suggests that IT value is best measured not by hard numbers but by anecdotal evidence based on the following criteria: alignment with business strategy, affordability, flexibility, scalability, cost-effective solutions (i.e., price/performance), dependability, reliability, the ability to accommodate new technologies, service levels, responsiveness to changes in the environment, the ability to deliver projects on time and within budget, support, organizational credibility, innovation and organizational learning, and financial performance (increased revenue, decreased costs, and ROI).

Apostolopoulos and Pramataris (1997), Bharadwaj and Konsynski (1997), Grover *et al.* (1997), Brynjolfsson and Hitt (1996), Semich (1994), Saunders and Jones (1992), Brady *et al.* (1992), and Diebold (1987) among others, also support greater emphasis on the "soft" benefits of IT, including factors such as strategic advantage, service, quality, timeliness, improved decision making, added flexibility, employee satisfaction, and so on in the overall benefits analysis. Indeed, evidence that this shift in focus is surfacing. For example, research by Thyfault *et al.* (1998) suggest that in many companies today, customer loyalty is driving IT investment decisions, not ROI.

Building a business case for IT

Given the high costs and risks typically associated with IT projects, it is necessary for organizations to have a formal, rigorous process for evaluating, approving, and justifying IT projects. This is especially true with the increased scrutiny and level of accountability brought on by the Sarbanes–Oxley Act, which requires strict financial reporting and fiscal responsibility. However, since each IT project tends to be unique in terms of purpose, scope, and objectives, approval processes may vary and decisions may need to be made on a case-by-case basis using some ad hoc criteria or methods.

Based on a series of studies across multiple industries, Weill and Olson (1989), Weill (1991), and Weill and Broadbent (1998) suggest that not all IT investment decisions are alike but rather can be defined by five basic categories: strategic, informational, transactional, infrastructural, and threshold. These authors then suggest that firms apply a contingency theory approach to decision making, where the type of investment and the context of the investment determine the criteria to be used in evaluating that investment (Table 13.2). They posit that there is generally one prevailing measure for each category. However, other authors show that reliance on a single measure can be misleading since it cannot possibly capture all of the complexities of IT.

As Farbey *et al.* (1992) so eloquently state, there are multiple approaches to evaluating IT, and each technique is suitable to a set of circumstances. The challenge for any organization is to select the appropriate methodology and criteria given the situation and desired objectives. A firm must balance rigour with efficacy. To assist firms in achieving this balance, Farbey *et al.* (1992, 1994) present an effectual process that can be followed to determine the contextual setting, capture the relevant characteristics, and match a project with the most appropriate evaluation method. It is important to note that timing can change

Table 13.2 A Simplified Approach to IT Investment Analysis

Investment Category	Description	Examples	Prevailing Measure(s)
Strategic IT	IT decisions designed to alter a firm's products and services or change the way a firm competes in its industry to create competitive advantage and build market share; the overall objective is to drive sales.	Customer relationship management (CRM) Loyalty programme system Central reservation system (CRS) and revenue management system (RMS) integration Web site Mobile (m-) commerce In-room amenities	Revenue and market share growth rates to capture long-term goals related to competitive advantage.
Informational IT	IT geared towards the development of a firm's information and communications infrastructure to provide better information in the hands of a firm's decision makers for managing and controlling the business.	Accounting Business intelligence (BI) Balanced Scorecard Data mining and decision support tools Digital signage	Return on assets to measure medium-term goals for improved decision making and firm performance.
Transactional IT	IT that supports the firm's operations and typically involves repetitive transactions; the primary foci are cost reduction, productivity, efficiencies, and labour savings.	Point-of-sale (POS) Property management system (PMS) Sales and catering Self-service kiosks Energy management Procurement Time and attendance	Indirect labour to capture reductions in labour resulting from the use of IT; productivity and efficiency metrics.

Infrastructural IT	IT that provides the foundation and support infrastructure necessary for shared information technology services and capabilities. The evaluation criteria are typically based on the investment's utilitarian attributes.	Operating system upgrades Hardware upgrades Wired and wireless networks Security	Focus tends to emphasize the IT infrastructure's utility, cost savings, and/or (strategic) enabling capabilities. Traditional accounting measures (e.g., NPV, IRR, and payback) are used and often combined with subjective evaluations.
Threshold IT	IT investment required to compete in a given industry, without which a firm cannot survive; the investment is mandatory or a competitive necessity.	Sarbanes-Oxley compliance Payment Card Industry Data Security Standards (PCI DSS) compliance In-room Internet access	No measure is suggested since the investment is required for a firm to enter, compete, or remain in a marketplace; the investment should be treated as a sunk cost.

Sources: Adapted from Weill and Olson (1989, pp. 13–15), Weill (1991, pp. 4–5), and Weill and Broadbent (1998, pp. 212–220).

perspective and how one views a certain type of technology (in terms of investment category) and the level of risks (perceived or actual) associated with that technology vis-à-vis the maturity lifecycles of both the technology and the organization itself.

Regardless of the type of project, the deliberation should be rigorous, deliberate, and as objective as possible to ensure the firm is appropriately using its resources, aligning its IT initiatives to its business strategy, and mitigating risk. The launch of a new IT initiative often begins with some informal discussions between people within an organization regarding an idea or recognition of an organizational problem or need. After the idea builds interest and momentum, it is channelled into the company's budgeting process. When time comes to appropriate funding for a specific capital project, a formal business case must be developed, presented to the executive committee, and approved for funding. The process can become political at times, with individual executives becoming passionate over certain issues. One hospitality executive once described the process in his company as "interesting with lots of lobbying and horse trading taking place." In the end, however, sound reasoning and judgment must prevail to allow only the *best* projects to emerge and win funding.

Because many hospitality companies have historically had poor track records when it comes to IT project success and benefits realization, executives tend to carefully scrutinize requests for new IT initiatives and place difficult hurdles in the way to ensure only the most viable projects get approved—and understandably so. The justification process is typically a multi-step process that involves multiple people, levels, and departments in the organization. The decisions are confounded by the number of different stakeholders (e.g., guests, employees, franchisees, and shareholders) that must be satisfied and their often conflicting needs. Decisions are most commonly committee-based, and the process itself can be difficult due to the many unknowns involved, the inability to quantify benefits, prior blunders and credibility issues, and limited history/benchmarks that can be used for reference.

Following a traditional approach to capital budgeting, the business case begins with an executive overview or summary of the situation and includes a needs/benefits analysis. The business case goes on to state the objectives, scope, and timing of the project; provide rationale or justification for the project; assess the marketplace in terms of opportunities, threats, risks, and competitor activity; discuss the financial benefits and ROI; and suggest a recommended course of action. The components of a typical business are depicted in Table 13.3 below.

Table 13.3   Proposed Business Case Content/Structure

---

1. Executive summary
2. Problem/opportunity statement
3. Project definition and scope
4. Needs analysis and alignment to company strategies
5. Competitor activity assessment and industry trends analysis
6. Project budget and funding request
7. Key assumptions
8. Cost–benefit analysis, including financial analysis, cash flows, and net present value (NPV)
9. Risk assessment
10. Alternatives considered
11. Recommendations
12. Project work plan and timeline
13. Signatures of approval
14. Appendices (as needed)

The business case guides executives through the analysis process and is the basis for informing executive judgment used in making the ultimate decision. It ensures that the IT project is properly aligned with the firm's business strategy, a requisite for achieving a successful outcome. The degree of rigour in the process and reliance on tangible measures tends to vary according to organizational attributes such as size, structure, culture, firm strategy, and industry positioning. These variables can be labelled under the construct context variables, which are moderating variables that frame the situation in which an IT decision is to be made and the circumstances surrounding that situation and decision. Context variables, derived from the environment in which a firm operates, set the stage for how the process is carried out, moderating both the evaluation process and the final decision.

Context variables give rise to another category or construct of variables called process variables. Process variables define the actual evaluation and decision-making processes, which are governed by a number of factors. These include the methodology and techniques used to evaluate the alternatives and the ensuing decisions, the participants involved, the actual evaluation and decision criteria, the level of formality of the process, degree of rigour, etc. Process variables can vary according to IT project type or classification. Process variables, in turn, influence project variables contained in the project variables construct. Project variables also influence process variables and can be directly tied to the IT project or investment decision under consideration. These are the specific attributes or characteristics of a project that define its strengths and weaknesses, opportunities, costs, benefits, and risk. Project variables are defined by the criteria established for the process and lead to a go/no-go decision for the project in question. These consist of quantitative and qualitative, tangible and intangible measures. For example, all of the companies studied indicate the importance of NPV, payback, and strategic alignment as three important decision criteria for any IT project.

The relationships between context, process, and project constructs are depicted in Figure 13.2. The external environment drives the strategy and the context. This is consistent with the strategic management literature which describes firms as living organisms that must be responsive to their environment. It also echoes the teachings of the co-alignment principle. Simply stated, the co-alignment principle suggests that if a firm understands the environmental events affecting its business and shaping the future of its industry, plans and develops its strategies so as to exploit these environmental opportunities and minimize any threats, and appropriately allocates and aligns its resources (e.g., people, capital, technology, etc.) through consistent investment to create product and service offerings (i.e., competitive methods), it will outperform industry players and receive competitive advantage (Chandler, 1962; Thompson, 1967; Bourgeois, 1980; Venkatraman and Prescott, 1990; Olsen *et al.*, 1998). Intuitively, given the concepts expressed in the co-alignment process, the context should drive strategy and the process, which, in turn, guides the project (Kearns and Sabherwal, 2006/2007). In reality, the relationship between process and project is likely to be dyadic, or two-way. Oftentimes, the project may drive the process (Farbey *et al.*, 1992). For example, when a project's benefits

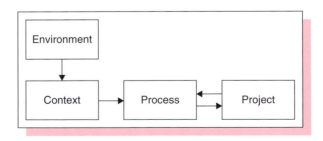

Figure 13.2
The relationship between the context, process, and project constructs.

are obvious, the evaluation process may be streamlined and relaxed. Alternatively, when a project is vague or exhibits a high degree of risk, the process used will likely be more deliberate and calculated.

Identification of the important and appropriate variables is a prerequisite step in closing the measurement gaps commonly found in IT projects, reported by leading scholars (e.g., Mahmood and Mann, 1993; Saunders and Jones, 1992) and often cited by industry practitioners. By clarifying what needs to be measured, one can begin to explore how best to measure these variables; develop suitable tools, techniques, and instruments; and extend this new knowledge—from theory to application—to include all IT projects, regardless of type (i.e., strategic, informational, transactional, infrastructural, or threshold).

Table 13.4 provides a listing of the key context, process, and project constructs and variables associated with IT investment decision making. Since the specific measures used may vary by company and, according to contingency theory, are contextual depending upon the nature of the project and the organization in which the project is under consideration, the variables listed represent a starting point for organizations wishing to develop a balanced scorecard approach (Kaplan and Norton, 1992, 1996) to project evaluation.

Concluding remarks

IT is an important resource vital to a firm's success. No longer can it be viewed simply for its support and utility roles dominant in tactical applications, which focus on the use of IT to gain efficiencies, reduce costs, decrease labour, and improve productivity. Instead, IT is increasingly playing a strategic role in organizations, where it either creates competitive advantage or enables new business opportunities. Attention is now being given to IT's ability to differentiate products and services, to create new product and service offerings, and to build and sustain core competencies. As such, one must treat IT expenditures as capital investments that will add value over the long term, not as period expenses (Applegate et al., 1996; Weill and Broadbent, 1998). Their applications and impact must be considered in a wider context, that of the entire organization.

The convergence of powerful computers, intelligent software, and high-speed, global telecommunications networks is creating a new climate for conducting business throughout the world. To survive and thrive in the long run, the firm of the future will need to be a learning organization, one that must always reinvent itself to create value. How a hospitality company rises to

Table 13.4 Context, Process, and Project Constructs and Variables

Context Variables	Process Variables	Project Variables
Firm strategy	Evaluation	Business considerations
Organizational	and approval	Competitive advantage
structure	processes:	Financial performance
Organizational	methodology,	Growth rate
infrastructure	techniques, and	Leverage/economies of scale
Degree of	measures	Strategic alignment
fragmented	Critical success	Enabling capabilities
ownership	factors	Customer service
Organizational	Process formality	Customer satisfaction and loyalty
culture	Participants and	Opportunity costs and cost avoidance
Internal politics	decision makers	impacts
Company size	Level of analysis	Improved quality of information
and geographic	Degree of rigour	Enhanced decision making
dispersion	Levels of approval	Financial
Organizational	Evaluation and	Net present value (NPV)
maturity (life cycle	decision criteria	NPV as a percentage of present value
stage)	Role of	invested
Industry positioning	quantitative vs.	Payback
Resources,	qualitative data	Cost–benefit analysis
capabilities, and	Length of	Cash-on-cash invested
core competencies	evaluation period	Cash flows
Portfolio of products	Business case	Impact on earnings per share (EPS)
and services	format and	and stock multiples
IT portfolio and	content	Value creation/economic value added
infrastructure	Ranking process	(EVA)
Perceived level of		IT
environmental		Resource availability
uncertainty		Architectural fit
Perceived level		Technology life cycle
of competitive		Functional and technical requirements
intensity		Reliability
Attitudes towards		Response time
risk		Ease of use
Timing		Flexibility, growth, and migration paths
Compensation and		Project
rewards structure		Perceived need
		Classification of project
		Measurement and evaluation criteria
		Project sponsor/champion
		Organizational readiness
		Staffing
		Costs
		Benefits
		Useful life
		Risk
		Project risk
		Technical risk
		Business risk
		Hurdle rate
		External
		Alternatives
		Competitive positioning and market
		share
		Competitors' moves and industry
		response

the challenges and opportunities presented by IT will be a key determinant of success.

With escalating costs and investment capital required to support today's complex technologies and infrastructures, hospitality executives must employ sound logic when allocating corporate resources to ensure their decisions will bring value to their firm. No longer can they simply rely on "gut feel" or responses to competitor activity. Instead, they must take a more discriminating approach and identify which technology decisions will truly add value to the firm. Only those clearly able to demonstrate value-adding potential should be adopted. In today's context, adding value implies that each decision made will result in a return for the firm and its stakeholders that is in excess of the cost of capital used to invest in that decision, the opportunity costs, and inflation and is commensurate with the level of risk that must be assumed for the given investment.

Not all technology investments have easily calculable paybacks or some other economic measures because it is nearly impossible to assess a value to information and knowledge. Because the tools are limited and fail to value the intangible aspects, such as the lifetime value of the consumer and the strategic positioning of the firm, decisions cannot be made on quantitative data analysis alone, but that does not mean that rigour and accountability should be relaxed. It just means that executives should employ a variety of criteria or metrics when evaluating and making IT investment decisions.

Seldom is the IT decision-making process entirely rational. Perhaps the term rational is better described by degrees of rationality rather than in absolute terms. It is extremely difficult if not impossible to achieve perfection and exactness when calculating the financial returns and benefits of IT projects. Therefore, some element of subjectivity will always come into play. Accuracy, like rationality, comes in degrees or orders of magnitude. It is important to come as close as possible—or at least get in the ballpark—and improve the process with each new project. What seems to matter most are the processes, measures, and level rigour required. The most significant benefits are (1) a culture that fosters rational decision making; (2) an emphasis on value creation, linking actions and resources to strategic objectives; and (3) attention to costs and benefits. Additionally, the structure, process, and rigour create accountability. Finally, as a result of following the process, an organization develops targets and a baseline for subsequent measurement, thus leading to greater focus, better project management, cost containment, and ultimately, a higher probability of success.

The decision-making and resource allocation processes are not entirely scientific. It is as much an art as it is a science. Financial calculations and analysis are important, but they are not the end-all. While traditional, rational, textbook methodologies are used, they are often insufficient in addressing the problem at hand because these are not always textbook cost-benefit analysis problems. For many of the projects under consideration, the process is too complex and time-consuming with little patience or forgiveness from the marketplace. Therefore, instinct rather than hard numbers drives most of the decisions. Executives must do their best to evaluate every project/funding decision within certain parameters, namely the available information, resources and time, to determine which one(s) will have the highest probability of succeeding. However, the resulting decisions are nothing more than collective, calculated best guesses, akin to hedging bets. In the end, the business case and good business judgment must prevail. In other words, management judgment is informed by measurements, forecasts, and the business case in hopes that both rationality and integrity of the process can be upheld, which, in turn, leads to greater confidence in the decision.

References

Adcock, K., Helms, M. M., and Jih, W.-J. K. (1993). Information technology: Can it provide a sustainable competitive advantage? *Information Strategy: The Executive's Journal*, Spring, 10–15.

Anderson, E. (1984). *The Sales Person as Outside Agent or Employee: A Transaction Cost Analysis (Report no. 84-107)*. Cambridge, MA: Marketing Sciences Institute.

Antonucci, Y. L., and Tucker, III. J. J., (1998). Responding to earnings-related pressure to reduce IT operating and capital expenditures. *Information Strategy: The Executive's Journal*, Spring, 6–14.

Apostolopoulos, T. K., and Pramataris, K. C. (1997). Information technology investment evaluation: Investments in telecommunication infrastructure. *International Journal of Information Management*, 17(4), 287–296.

Applegate, L. M., McFarlan, F. W., and McKenney, J. L. (1996). *Corporate Information Systems Management: The Issues Facing Senior Executives* (4th ed.). Chicago, IL: Irwin.

Bacon, C. J. (1992). The use of decision criteria in selecting information system. *MIS Quarterly*, 16(3), 335–354.

Bakos, J. Y. (1987). *Dependent Variables for the Study of Firm and Industry-level Impacts of Information Technology*. Proceedings of the Eighth International Conference on Information Systems, Pittsburgh, PA, pp. 10–23.

Benjamin, R. I., Rockart, J. F., Scott Morton, M. S., and Wyman, J. (1984). Information technology: A strategic opportunity. *Sloan Management Review*, *Spring*, 3–10.

Betz, C. T. (2006). *Architecture and Patterns for it Service Management, Resource Planning, and Governance: Making Shoes for the Cobbler's Children*. San Francisco, CA: Morgan Kaufmann.

Bharadwaj, A., and Konsynski, B. R. (1997). Capturing the intangibles. *Information Week*, September 22, pp. 71–73, 75.

Boonstra, A. (2003). Structure and analysis of IS decision-making process. *European Journal of Information Systems*, *12*, 195–209.

Bourgeois, III. L. J., (1980). Strategy and environment: A conceptual integration. *Academy of Management Review*, *5*(1), 25–39.

Bowen, P. L., Cheung, M.-Y. D., and Rohde, F. H. (2007). Enhancing IT governance practices: A model and case study of an organization's efforts. *International Journal of Accounting Information Systems*, *8*(3), 191–221.

Boynton, A. C., and Zmud, R. W. (1984). An assessment of critical success factors. *Sloan Management Review*, *Summer*, 17–27.

Brady, T., Cameron, R., Targett, D., and Beaumont, C. (1992). Strategic IT issues: The views of some major IT investors. *Journal of Strategic Information Systems*, *1*(4), 183–189.

Brynjolfsson, E., and Hitt, L. (1996). The customer counts. *Information Week*, September 9, pp. 48, 50, 52, 54.

Caldwell, B. (1998). Executive briefing: Senior managers get IT-enlightened. *Information Week*, March 23, pp. 2ER–3ER.

Carr, N. G. (2003). IT doesn't matter. *Harvard Business Review*, *81*(5), 41–49.

Chakravarthy, B. S. (1986). Measuring strategic performance. *Strategic Management Journal*, *7*, 437–458.

Chan, Y. E., and Reich, B. H. (2007). IT alignment: What have we learned? *Journal of Information Technology*, *22*(4), 297–315.

Chandler, A. D. (1962). *Strategy and Structure: Chapters in the History of Industrial Enterprise*. Cambridge, MA: MIT Press.

Cho, W. (1996). *A Case Study: Creating and Sustaining Competitive Advantage Through an Information Technology Application in the Lodging Industry*. Unpublished doctoral dissertation, Virginia Polytechnic Institute and State University, VA.

Clemons, E. K., and Weber, B. W. (1990). Strategic information technology investments: Guidelines for decision making. *Journal of Management Information Systems*, *7*(2), 9–28.

Cline, R. S., and Blatt, L. A. (1998). Creating enterprise value around the customer…Leveraging the customer asset in today's hospitality industry. *Arthur Andersen Hospitality and Leisure Executive Report*, 5(1), 2–11.

Davenport, T. H., Hammer, M., and Metsisto, T. J. (1989). How executives can shape their company's information systems. *Harvard Business Review, March–April*, 130–134.

Diebold, J. (1987). Criteria for information technology investment. *International Journal of Technology Management*, 2(5/6), 583–595.

Dreyfuss, J. (1995). Rethinking the customer. *Information Week*, January 30, p. 28.

Farbey, B., Land, F., and Targett, D. (1992). Evaluating investments in IT. *Journal of Information Technology*, 7, 109–122.

Farbey, B., Land, F., and Targett, D. (1994). Matching an IT project with an appropriate method of evaluation: A research note on 'Evaluating investments in IT'. *Journal of Information Technology*, 9, 239–243.

Geller, A. N. (1984). *Executive Information Needs in Hotel Companies*. Houston, TX: Peat, Marwick, Mitchell & Co.

Grover, V., Fiedler, K. D., and Teng, J. T. C. (1997). Corporate strategy and IT investments. *Business and Economic Review*, 43(3), 17–22.

Hamel, G., and Prahalad, C. K. (1991). Corporate imagination and expeditionary marketing. *Harvard Business Review, July–August*, 81–92.

Hibbard, J. (with Violino, Bob, Caldwell, Bruce, and Johnston, Stuart J.). (1998). Software gains capital treatment. *Information Week*, January 12, pp. 18–20.

Hiebeler, R., Kelly, T. B., and Ketteman, C. (1998). *Best Practices: Building you Business with Customer-focused Solutions*. New York: Simon & Schuster.

Hildebrand, C. (1997, August 1). The nature of excellence. CIO [On-line]. Available: http://www.cio.com/archive/080197_overview_content.html

Holland, D., and Skarke, G. (2008). Business & IT alignment: Then & now, a striking improvement. *Strategic Finance*, 89(10), 43–49.

Hubbard, D. (1999). The IT measurement inversion. *CIO Enterprise, April 15*(Section 2), 26–31.

Jeffery, M., and Leliveld, I. (2004). Best practices in IT portfolio management. *MIT Sloan Management Review*, 45(3), 41–49.

Kaplan, J. D. (2005). *Strategic IT portfolio management*. Washington, DC: Pittiglio Rabin Todd & McGrath (PRTM), Inc.

Kaplan, R. S., and Norton, D. P. (1992). The balanced scorecard—Measures that drive performance. *Harvard Business Review, January–February*, 71–79.

Kaplan, R. S., and Norton, D. P. (1996). Using the balanced scorecard as a strategic management system. *Harvard Business Review, January–February*, 75–85.

Kearns, G. S., and Sabherwal, R. (2006/2007). Strategic alignment between business and information technology: A knowledge-based view of behaviors, outcome, and consequences. *Journal of Management Information Systems, 23*(3), 129–162.

King, M., and McAulay, L. (1997). Information technology investment evaluation: Evidence and interpretations. *Journal of Information Technology, 12*, 131–143.

King, W. R. (1983). Evaluating strategic planning systems. *Strategic Management Journal, 4*, 263–277.

Laberis, B. (1994). Impossible dream: Linking information systems with corporate goals and the evolution of the chief information officer position. *Computerworld*, October 17, p. 24.

Liao, J. (1994). *A Theoretical Model of IS Planning and Business Strategy*. Proceedings of the Decision Sciences Institute, USA, 2, pp. 858–860.

Loveman, G. (1991). Cash drain, no gain. *Computerworld*, November 25, pp. 69–70, 72.

Lutchen, M. (2003). *Managing IT as a Business: A Survival Guide for CEOs*. Hoboken, NJ: Wiley.

Madden, J. (1998). Vendors help IT measure up with variations on the Balanced Scorecard. *PC Week*, September 28, p. 76.

Mahmood, M. A., and Mann, G. J. (1993). Measuring the organizational impact of information technology investment: An exploratory study. *Journal of Management Information Systems, 10*(1), 97–122.

Maizlish, B., and Handler, R. (2005). *IT Portfolio Management: Step-by-step Unlocking the Business Value of Technology*. Hoboken, NJ: Wiley.

Mata, F. J., Fuerst, W. L., and Barney, J. B. (1995). Information technology and sustained competitive advantage: A resource-based analysis. *MIS Quarterly, 19*(4), 487–505.

McFarlan, F. W. (1981). Portfolio approach to information systems. *Harvard Business Review, September–October*, 142–150.

McFarlan, F. W. (1984). Information technology changes the way you compete. *Harvard Business Review, May–June*, 98–103.

Neelakantan, S. (1996). Tech goofs. *Forbes*, December 30, pp. 18–20.

O'Brien, T. (1997). Redefining IT value: Novel approaches help determine the right spending levels. *Information Week*, April 7, pp. 71–72, 76.

Olsen, M. D., West, J. J., and Tse, E. C. (1998). *Strategic Management in the Hospitality Industry* (2nd ed.). New York: Wiley.

Parker, M. M., Benson, R. J., and Trainor, H. E. (1988). *Information Economics: Linking Business Performance to Information Technology*. Englewood Cliffs, NJ: Prentice Hall.

Parsons, G. L. (1983). Information technology: A new competitive weapon. *Sloan Management Review, Fall*, 3–14.

Peak, D., Guynes, C. S., and Kroon, V. (2005). Information technology alignment planning: A case study. *Information & Management*, 42(5), 635–649.

Piccoli, G. (2004). Making IT matter: A manager's guide to creating and sustaining competitive advantage with information systems. *CHR Reports*, 4(9), 5–21.

Plimpton, G. (1990). *The X Factor*. Knoxville, TN: Whittle Direct Books.

Porter, M. E. (1980). *Competitive Strategy: Techniques for Analyzing Industries and Competitors*. New York: The Free Press.

Porter, M. E. (1985). *Competitive Advantage: Creating and Sustaining Superior Performance*. New York: The Free Press.

Porter, M. E., and Millar, V. E. (1985). How information gives you competitive advantage. *Harvard Business Review, July–August*, 149–160.

Post, G. V., Kagan, A., and Lau, K.-N. (1995). A modeling approach to evaluating strategic uses of information technology. *Journal of Management Information Systems*, 12(2), 161–187.

Rockart, J. F. (1979). Chief executives define their own data needs. *Harvard Business Review, March–April*, 81–93.

Ross, J. W., and Weill, P. (2002). Six IT decisions your IT people should not make. *Harvard Business Review*, 80(11), 85–91.

Sabherwal, R., and King, W. R. (1995). An empirical taxonomy of the decision-making processes concerning strategic applications of information systems. *Journal of Management Information Systems*, 11(4), 177–214.

Saunders, C. S., and Jones, J. W. (1992). Measuring performance of the information systems function. *Journal of Management Information Systems*, 8(4), 63–82.

Semich, J. W. (1994). Here's how to quantify IT investment benefits. *Datamation*, January 7, pp. 45–46, 48.

Shank, M. E., Boynton, A. C., and Zmud, R. W. (1985). Critical success factor analysis as a methodology for MIS planning. *MIS Quarterly*, 9(2), 121–129.

Shein, E. (1998). Formula for ROI: IT is gauging project performance to produce tangible results for business. *PC Week*, September 28, pp. 73, 76, 79.

Sprague, R. H., Jr., and McNurlin, B. C. (Eds.). (1986). *Information Systems Management in Practice*. Englewood Cliffs, NJ: Prentice Hall.

Thompson, J. D. (1967). *Organizations in Action*. New York: McGraw-Hill.

Thorp, J. DMR's Center for Strategic Leadership (1998). *The Information Paradox: Realizing the Business Benefits of Information Technology*. Toronto: McGraw-Hill.

Thyfault, M. E., Johnston, S. J., and Sweat, J. (1998). Customer service: The service imperative. *Information Week*, October 5, pp. 44–46, 50, 52, 54–55.

Tobin, J. (2007, October 23). Presentation made at the University of Denver, Denver, CO.

Venkatraman, N., and Prescott, J. E. (1990). Environment-strategy coalignment: An empirical test of its performance implications. *Strategic Management Journal*, 11(1), 1–23.

Weill, P. (1991). The information technology payoff: Implications for investment appraisal. *Australian Accounting Review*, 4, 2–11.

Weill, P., and Broadbent, M. (1998). *Leveraging the New Infrastructure: How Market Leaders Capitalize on Information Technology*. Boston, MA: Harvard Business School Press.

Weill, P., and Olson, M. H. (1989). Managing investment in information technology: Mini case examples and implications. *MIS Quarterly*, 13(1), 3–18.

Weill, P., and Ross, J. (2004). *IT Governance: How Top Performers Manage IT Decision Rights for Superior Results*. Boston, MA: Harvard Business School Press.

Wiggins, R. R., and Ruefli, T. W. (2005). Schumpeter's ghost: Is hypercompetition making the best of times shorter? *Strategic Management Journal*, 26(10), 887–911.

Williamson, M. (1997). Weighing the nos and cons. CIO [Online]. Available: http://www.cio.com/archive/041597_need_content.html

Xue, Y., Liang, H., and Boulton, W. R. (2008). Information technology governance in information technology investment decision processes: The impact of investment characteristics, external environment, and internal context. *MIS Quarterly*, 32(1), 67–96.

Strategy execution and implementation— achieving strategic goals through operations

Peter Jones[1] and Alan Parker[2]*

[1]*Associate Dean (International) and ITCA Chair of Production and Operations Management, Faculty of Management & Law, University of Surrey, Guildford, Surrey, UK*
[2]*CEO Whitbread PLC*

*Alan Parker is a Visiting Professor at the University of Surrey.

Introduction

In the strategic management literature there is broad agreement on the difference between corporate strategy, business strategy, and operations strategy. In essence, these can be considered as a hierarchy. Corporate strategy is devised by large firms in order to provide an overall plan for the firm. Within the firm, there may be a number of different businesses, for each of which a strategy is devised. For instance, Accor has hotels, travel agency, and restaurant coupons among its portfolio of businesses. Once a business strategy has been set, each of the functional areas within the business—marketing, human resources, finance, and operations—devises its own strategies, as illustrated in Figure 14.1.

In manufacturing businesses, these functional strategies have clear demarcation between them, even though they need to be integrated with each other. This is largely because the production of goods is separate, in terms of both time and place, from the purchase and consumption of these goods. However, in services, and especially the hotel business, production and consumption are simultaneous—the hotel "produces" a room which is "consumed" by the guest during their stay. Moreover, the customer comes into direct contact with employees delivering the service. It is therefore more difficult in services to differentiate between functional strategies, as illustrated in Figure 14.2. These two concepts—the hierarchy of strategies and overlap between functional strategies in service firms—are clearly demonstrated in the case study of Whitbread PLC, later in this chapter.

Operations management in small, medium, and large firms

Having established the notion of a hierarchy of planning and control, as illustrated in Figure 14.1, we need to consider whether all businesses engage in all three levels of planning. Research (Jones et al., 2004) in small and medium sized enterprises (SMEs) suggests that they do not. SMEs have no need for complex planning processes because they manage relatively small businesses operating in local markets, over which the owner can often have direct, personal control. As firms grow larger they tend to separate out the levels identified in Figure 14.1. One particular feature of such growth in hospitality is that firms expand geographically, beginning to operate a number of units in a number of locations. Clearly, a key feature of operations management (OM) and its alignment with strategy is the management of such chain operations. This leads to the concept of multi-unit management (Jones, 1999).

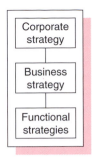

Figure 14.1
Hierarchy of planning and control in firms.

Figure 14.2
Relationship between functional planning in service firms.

One model of growth in service industries is that of the service firm life cycle (SFLC) (Sasser *et al.*, 1978). This assumes that service firms follow an S-shaped curve similar to that of the product life cycle. Sasser *et al.* (1978) suggest four stages in this cycle:

1. Entrepreneurship
2. Multi-site rationalization
5. Growth
4. Maturity

Implicitly this model assumes that such firms remain focused around a single concept or brand. McDonalds growth in the North America is the archetype of such a firm.

At each stage of the cycle, the issues that face the operations function (as well as marketing, human resources, finance, and administration) change. This has best been explained in the hospitality industry by Olsen *et al.* (1992). A synopsis of such changes is provided in Table 14.1. It is clear from this table that as the firm moves from the first through to the maturity stage,

335

Table 14.1 Issues and Policies of OM During the Service Firm Life Cycle

	Entrepreneurial	MSR	Growth	Maturity
Strategic focus	Concept development	Product/service development	Geographic growth	Reducing unit costs
Work organization	Owner plays central role	Flat hierarchy develops	Addition of functional specialist	
Cost control systems	Little or none	Trial and error	Systems begin to be developed	Systems designed and implemented
Production systems	Limited technology	Production technology selected	Process design emerges	Productivity and efficiency of major concern
Production management	Top-down communication	Informal—task uncertainty remains	Communications systems developing	Task uncertainty removed
Quality	Few specifications—output variable	Standards emerge—implementation variable within units	Variation between units	SOPs in place—standards across chain actively managed

Source: Based on Olsen et al. (1992).

there is a shift from straightforward OM to *strategic* operations management (SOM).

There are strong reasons why single concept firms might go through the SFLC, based largely on the concepts of economies of scale and organizational learning. However, many firms do not follow the SFLC. First of all, some do not go beyond the first stage and remain SMEs, while some do grow but fail or are taken over along the way. However, some pursue a different *strategy*—they become multi-concept chains. One example of this is Lettuce Entertain You Enterprises (LEYE), a Chicago-based chain which in 2004 operated 25 different restaurant concepts in 39 locations. These concepts ranged from quick service through mid-priced up to fine dining, and represented cuisine from all four corners of the globe. Clearly this firm's business strategy, and hence its operations strategy, is quite different to that of single concept chains.

Strategic operations management in practice

Firms make strategic choices to compete on cost or to differentiate or a combination of these. In order to differentiate, the firm needs to offer something different to or better than its competitors in a range of performance criteria. Slack *et al.* (2007) identify five performance criteria: quality, speed, dependability, flexibility, and cost. To these might also be added originality of design and/or function. However, these are not mutually exclusive. In many cases, quick service restaurant chains have to ensure that they provide fast, reliable products and services at low cost; while customers of boutique hotels expect not just originality of design, but also reliability and high standards.

Hence, few firms compete on a single criterion—they bundle these together to create an operations strategy that they believe will lead them to have competitive advantage over their competitors. Different combinations of policies and practices reflect the markets, processes, and technologies of different industries. Such operations strategies vary widely from one industry sector to another. However, in some cases, they are given generic names to reflect that the strategy can be applied across different sectors. Some examples of such operations strategies are provided in Table 14.2. An example of such a strategy, evident in many industries, is *mass customization*. In manufacturing, this refers to the idea of customizing products to individual consumer needs even though they are manufactured on mass production lines. BMW and Swatch have based their strategy on such an approach. This approach requires consumers to give up a little, in terms of speed of delivery, in order to have

Table 14.2   Operations Strategies in a Range of Industries

Industry	Operations Strategy	Example of Firms
Textiles	Planned product response	Claudel Lingerie Inc.
Grocery	Efficient consumer response	Tesco Stores
Watches/bicycles	Mass customisation	Swatch, China Bicycle Co.
Electronic goods	Time-based competition	Sony, Matsushita
Automobiles/food manufacturing	Just-in-time production	Toyota
Clothing/electronics	Strategic postponement	Benneton, Dell computers

Source: Based on Lowson (2002).

greater flexibility. This strategy also exists in hospitality, and has done so for many years, since this is essentially the strategy adopted by Dave Thomas at Wendys in 1969 and Burger King with their "have it your way" strategy from 1974. It could be argued that this strategy is also evident in coffee shops, such as Starbucks, given the wide variety of hot drinks that can be made from basic and small combination of ingredients.

Operations strategies in hospitality

It is clear from Table 14.2 that there are no hospitality examples, although mass customization is apparent in this industry. This is partly because there has been little research into the nature of SOM in this industry, and partly because industry itself is not always aware of what its operations strategy is. Nonetheless, some operations strategies are clearly evident in some sectors.

Location, location, location

Conrad Hilton's famous words—identifying the three most important factors in the success of a hotel—are as valid today as they were when he said them. The issue is not so much as to the importance of location, but whether or not it is considered part of the operations strategy of a firm. Due to overlap between business, marketing, and operations strategy in the hospitality industry, each could claim location as significant to it. Its importance to operations is based on the need to ensure that the physical infrastructure is utilized to its full capacity in order to get the best return on investment and minimize variability of demand. Hence, hoteliers and restaurateurs are quite concerned to ensure their operations are located to maximize the potential level of business. This can be specified in terms of foot fall (number of pedestrians walking past), number of passing cars, population within a certain travel time, or some other similar criteria.

Just-in-time manufacturing

In flight catering, since the late 1990s, the larger flight-catering firms have been adopting a "just-in-time strategy" (Jones, 2004). Based on practices developed in Japan in car assembly plants, flight kitchens now routinely use *kaizan*, *kanbans*, and *poka-yoke* in their operations. Kaizan refers to the concept of continuous improvement, especially in relation to operational processes. A kanban is a bin for holding exactly the right amount of any stock item to facilitate swift and even flow. And poka-yokes are "mistake proofing" systems or failsafe devices designed to ensure that all processes lead to the desired output. Together, these ideas and other related polices have enabled flight caterers to reduce cycle time (the time it takes to undertake a process), reduce waste, reduce inventory levels, cut costs, and be more reliable. Such an operations strategy is vital at a time when the world's major airlines have reduced their demand for in-flight meals in the face of stiff competition from low-cost or budget airlines and passenger demand has been erratic due to environmental issues, such as 9/11, SARS, and the Gulf War.

Production-lining service

Fast food is another industry in which the operations strategy is clear. Although operators in the industry no longer like this term and prefer to be known as quick service, the term "fast food" is used here deliberately to describe the strategy that has led to phenomenal success. For what Ray Kroc recognized was that the McDonald brothers had devised a way of working (an operations strategy) that gave competitive advantage. They had devised a system for selling hot meals to customers as if they were a retail product to be sold off the shelf (which is why originally the restaurants were called stores). This required a hot food product that could be quickly prepared and wrapped in advance of customer orders, and could stay in good condition so that it was ready for sale. The product also had to be hand held so that it could be eaten outside the restaurant as well as inside it. The hamburger was the perfect product. Fast food is fast because of these characteristics. Linked to speed of delivery is also the idea that there must be high sales volume. If perishable product is waiting on the shelf ready for sale then customers must flow through the door at a high rate. To attract customers in large numbers the product must be inexpensive. The product must also be quick and easy to produce; hence, menu and dish variety are reduced to ensure food production can be simplified. Today, many of these simple tasks have actually been automated. In discussing trends in services, Levitt (1972) used fast food as the prime example of "production-lining"—a service business.

Ubiquitization

Fast food as an operations strategy was so successful that it actually created an entirely new industry sector. The firms that adopted the strategy *and* successfully implemented it gained competitive advantage and grew to become market leaders, in some cases achieving a global market position. But because the strategy was developed in the 1950s, these firms needed to continue seeking new strategies. In the 1990s, another strategy emerged called the "ubiquitization" strategy—fast food was to be served everywhere. This was achieved by thinking of alternative ways of marketing and delivering the product. While the store or restaurant continues to operate it also serves as a central production and/or distribution centre for other sales channels, such as home delivery, kiosks, carts, and even vending machines. Rather than the customer coming to the food, the food goes out to the customer. This strategy was made possible by the development of new technologies. Better catering equipment allowed hot food to be held in better condition more safely for a longer time, and information technology allowed managers to track sales and monitor performance at a distance. A feature of this strategy was the way in which chains modified their approach to multi-unit management. Restaurant managers became market managers, responsible for a range of different types of outlet. They were "empowered" and the spans of control by area management were greatly increased, from 12 up to 30 units in some cases. This example neatly illustrates the concept that a strategy requires a fit between all elements of operations. In this case, changes in the process and technology also required changes in marketing and human resources.

Self-service

Production-lining tends to be applied to the service worker, whereas "self-service" applies similar concepts to the customer, that is, tasks are simplified, processes may be automated, and control is built into activities. There are many examples of this in the hospitality industry—self-service check-in and check-out in hotels, drink dispensing in cafeterias, hotel mini bars, online reservations, and so on.

Innovation

Another operations strategy is innovation. This is essentially the strategy adopted by multi-concept restaurant chains. Their strengths and competitive advantage lie in their ability to develop new concepts and make them work. LEYE is not just an operator, it also offers consulting services on "corporate services, operational systems, service and hospitality, training and development, culinary development, concept creation, product development, and operator research" (LEYE Consulting, 2004). For instance, the company employs an "Artistic and Creative Director." Her primary responsibilities include "concept ideation, attribute development, and food product stylization … (based on) concept board development, historical and social research, material selection and menu writing."

Total quality management (TQM)

No discussion of SOM could be complete without reference to TQM. Many firms in the hospitality industry like to think that they have successfully adopted this strategy, but only one has undoubtedly done so—the Ritz Carlton hotel company. During the 1990s Ritz Carlton won the prestigious Malcolm Baldridge award not once, but twice. Much has been written about TQM, and in hospitality it is one of the most researched topics, along with yield management (Jones and Lockwood, 1998). Despite this, TQM remains difficult to achieve in a service environment, largely because it is so complex. TQM includes concepts such as quality control and quality assurance but must be adopted across the organization, both back-of-house and front-of-house, and from the boardroom to the shop floor. The challenge of this strategy may be exemplified by Ritz Carlton who identified that their housekeeping operation alone experienced 70,000 errors per one million transactions. Their TQM goal became to reduce this level to "six sigma," that is 4.3 errors per million, and in so doing provide 100% customer satisfaction and save the company substantial cost.

Capacity control

Finally, we have to consider whether or not hotel revenue management is a strategy or not. Since one of the major challenges facing a service firm is the unpredictability of demand, devising a system that manages this certainly has strategic importance. Hence, revenue management is not a strategy unless it is part of a capacity control strategy. One firm that has successfully implemented this strategy is Center Parcs (Jones, 2002). This European firm operates resort villages aimed at the short break market. It is only possible to book a villa at one of their villages for a 3-day weekend (Friday through Monday) or a 4-day midweek break (Monday through Friday), or combination thereof. By restricting bookings to these days, Center Parcs is able to achieve annual occupancy rates of 92–95% in villages that can accommodate in excess of 3000 guests. Supporting this strategy is a sophisticated forecasting, advanced reservations, and operating systems designed to manage housekeeping on the changeover days (Mondays and Fridays) when more than 600 villas may have to be made ready for new guests.

It should be noted that just as strategic goals are not mutually exclusive, so are the strategies, although implementing more than one operations strategy at a time is very challenging. Nonetheless, firms who have adopted capacity control might also be implementing TQM; chains with high rates of market penetration (ubiquitization) may also be seeking to innovate, and so on. This is illustrated in the Whitbread PLC case study that follows.

Operations strategy in practice: Whitbread PLC

In 2005, Whitbread was the United Kingdom's largest hospitality firm, employing 60,000 people with a turnover of £1500 million. A feature of Whitbread was its management of very strong brands in different segments of the hospitality industry. These brands were[1]

- Marriott Hotels—Whitbread was corporate franchisee of Marriott for the United Kingdom
- Premier Travel Inn—the United Kingdom's largest chain of budget hotels
- TGIFridays—another United States-based brand operating in the casual dining segment

---

[1]Since the end of 2005, Whitbread's corporate policy has been to dispose of some of these brands in order to focus on and grow two key brands—Premier Travel Inn and Costa Coffee.

- Pizza Hut—an international brand operating in the quick service segment
- Costa Coffee—the United Kingdom's second largest chain of coffee shops
- David Lloyd Leisure Centres—originally founded by the British tennis player of that name

Whitbread's overall mission and strategy is to be "best in class" in each segment in which it operates. This requires a focus on quality and the delivery of brand standards. Underpinning this is also a commitment to being the "best in class" hospitality employee, supported by a strong organizational culture. The culture is expressed through *"the Whitbread Way-four Principles that guide us in everything we do."*

- We believe in people and teamwork
- We believe in caring for guests
- We believe in passion for winning
- We believe in continuous improvement

Whitbread's operations also face the challenge of fixed capacity. Hence, another key feature of their operations strategy is maximizing occupancy or visits to each of their operations. A major influence on this is the sites they have selected for the location of their operations. Another approach to this is to develop customer loyalty by making people become "members." This strategy is adapted across each brand, so "membership" can be either required (as in the case of David Lloyd Leisure Clubs), or partially through loyalty/reward cards (Marriott, Pizza Hut, and TGIFridays), or top-up cards (Costa Coffee). These schemes, as well as internet-based reservation systems, provide each brand with an increasingly large database of customer contact details, especially email addresses, which enables the brand to engage in so-called one-to-one marketing. The same databases are also being used to measure guest satisfaction, and hence monitor service quality and brand standards.

To implement this operations strategy, there are some corporate-wide policies and procedures, as well as brand-specific ones. These are based on a standard "template," as illustrated in Figure 14.3. User and attitude research is carried out in order to establish the specific strategy for each brand. From this, tactics are devised, based on product and service standards. The tactics then need to be implemented, which in the Whitbread case is called "orchestration." This element of the template might include product remodelling and maintenance, the guest recommendation system, customer guarantee,

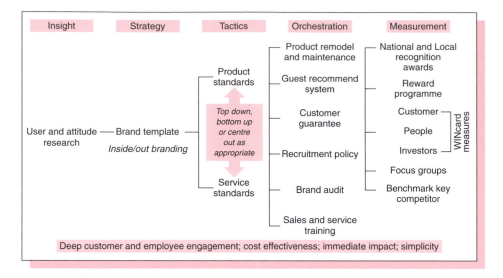

Insight	Strategy	Tactics	Orchestration	Measurement
			Product remodel and maintenance	National and Local recognition awards
		Product standards	Guest recommend system	Reward programme
		Top down, bottom up or centre out as appropriate	Customer guarantee	Customer
User and attitude research	Brand template *Inside/out branding*		Recruitment policy	People / Investors (WINcard measures)
		Service standards	Brand audit	Focus groups / Benchmark key competitor
			Sales and service training	

Deep customer and employee engagement; cost effectiveness; immediate impact; simplicity

Figure 14.3
Whitbread's brand template.

employee recruitment policy, brand audit, and employee training. Linked to this orchestration is the idea of measurement and the specific tools that might be used to monitor delivery on these items.

Measurement is based on the *balanced scorecard*, originally developed by Kaplan and Norton (1996). In Whitbread's case, the three main elements are based on key stakeholder groups—investors, customers, and employees. Routinely, seven items are measured. Six of these are across all brands, namely revenue, profit, customer satisfaction, health and safety, and employee satisfaction, while one is specific to the brand. The brand-specific item is usually related to some measure of usage (room occupancy, seat turnover, customers per day, and so on). Linked to this is *benchmarking*—comparing the performance of operating units against each other.

Marriott UK

In 2005, there were more than 70 Marriott Hotels operated by Whitbread on a corporate franchise agreement with Marriott Corporation. These are generally large four-star hotel properties aimed largely at the corporate and business market. Eleven of them were the Courtyard brand, aimed at a slightly lower market segment. Marriotts's quality and service strategy is based heavily on the approach developed by Marriott in the United States. Employees are called "associates," and there is a strong service-oriented organizational culture. Capacity is managed through a revenue management system, similar to that used by other international hotel chains.

Premier Travel Inn

It is now the United Kingdom's largest hotel chain, with 470 properties located mainly on major highways and on the outskirts of cities and towns. In this market segment, guests have little or no contact with employees, except at check-in and check-out. Food and beverage provision is not in the hotel itself, but in an adjacent stand-alone, branded restaurant. The operations focus is on product quality, that is to say the standard of cleanliness and facilities in the bedroom. This is demonstrated by Premier Travel Inn's "Good Night Guarantee," which states—"*we guarantee you a clean, comfortable room and friendly and efficient service-in fact everything you need for a good night. And if we don't live up to our promise, we'll give you your money back—guaranteed.*" In this segment, the chain has a basic price for all rooms. In 2005, this was £45 for out-of-town properties and slightly more for city centre or high-demand properties. Nonetheless, the chain achieved high average occupancies and hence revenues, although not engaged in revenue management.

TGIFridays

This brand is a global player in the casual dining segment and the U.K. chain has 46 restaurants. This U.S. brand was one of the first themed restaurant chains to develop the dining experience based on a wide range of dishes ("*flexibility*") and a fun environment. Key to this experience is the TGIF staff who contribute greatly to the ambience. The chain, as a result, has always had a highly distinctive and strong organizational culture that reinforces the service ethos and greatly facilitates the delivery of brand standards globally.

Pizza Hut

Pizza Hut is a well-known global brand in the pizza quick service segment, with over 500 units in the United Kingdom. There are four distinct categories of restaurants:

- Full service: dine-in and takeaway: these offer our full menu for both casual dining and a takeaway experience.

- Restaurant-based delivery: dine-in, takeaway, and delivery: these offer the full-service experience as well as delivery to their customers who live within the designated trade zones.
- Express: eat-in and takeaway: this is a new concept that is being developed by the company within food halls and leisure parks across the United Kingdom. These offer an informal, quick service experience with a reduced menu.
- Home service: delivery and takeaway: these restaurants offer both a delivery and a takeaway experience. The menu is specific to this concept, and delivery is offered to customers living within the designated trade zones.

Costa Coffee

This brand competes in the United Kingdom against global brand leader Starbucks and U.K. brands such as AMT, Ritazza, and Café Nero. Like Pizza Hut, Costa competes on the basis of *"speed"* and *"reliability."* It is rapidly expanding in the United Kingdom and by the end of 2007 will have 750 outlets.

David Lloyd Leisure Centres

This chain of sports and leisure centres is the United Kingdom's largest player in this market, with 69 centres around the United Kingdom and over 300,000 members. Across the chain, DLL has around 10,000 exercise machines and over 100 swimming pools (of which half are indoor). The racquets facilities are unrivalled in the United Kingdom with 500 tennis courts (over half of which are indoor), as well as 100 badminton and 85 squash courts. Additional facilities include health and beauty spas, club lounges with free internet access, crèches, nurseries, and specialist sports shops. Members may use these facilities, but also have one-to-one coaching sessions or participate in a wide variety of classes— each centre offers over 40 exercise classes per week. David Lloyd Leisure employs some 5000 team members including an expert health and fitness team of over 500 and more than 200 tennis professionals.

Whitbread's operations strategies

A number of strategies were identified in this chapter— location, JIT manufacturing, production-lining, ubiquitization, self-service, innovation, TQM, and capacity control—some of which can be seen to put into practice by Whitbread.

The two key strategies it has adopted have been *location* and *ubiquitization*, along with some *innovation*. For all of its brands, Whitbread have very clear criteria for locating their operations and selecting appropriate sites. Linked to this is ubiquitization, the other key feature of the chains—especially in the mass market. Premier Travel Inn and Costa Coffee are being grown rapidly to ensure that there are units in every part of the United Kingdom to enable country-wide access to an outlet. Likewise the Pizza Hut chain had four different types of outlets designed to enable pizza to be served and eaten not only in a sit-down restaurant setting but also in takeaway and home delivery system. The takeaway market is also important for the Costa Coffee brand. Finally, innovation is also important in order to keep brands fresh and appealing to the market. New products are often linked to marketing campaigns and special promotions. This can be seen in Pizza Hut and Costa Coffee by the introduction of new menu items and special offers.

JIT, production-lining, and *self-service* have been adopted in a number of brands—Costa Coffee and Travel Inn—usually to simplify and speed up service. But this has been as a result of operational improvements rather than as key strategic moves. *Capacity control* is important for all the brands, but Whitbread has not developed unique ways of managing this strategically in an effort to gain competitive advantage. And while the company is concerned with maintaining brand standards and delivering reliable products and services, it has not adopted a *TQM* strategy towards this.

Finally, it should be remembered that the operations is only one area that is managed to achieve competitive advantage. Firms can also compete on the basis of marketing and human resources. This is certainly the case with Whitbread. With popular brands, the firm is clearly competing through marketing, and its use of the balanced scorecard underlines the high value it places on its human resources and human resource strategy. Interestingly it is largely through the operations function—specifically the area manager—that all these strategies are integrated and managed. Area managers are particularly concerned with ensuring that each unit meets brand standards. For instance, they conduct quality audits, follow up on mystery shopper reports, and investigate customer complaints. They are also heavily involved in the recruitment, selection, and training of staff within the units. Hence operations is clearly not separate from marketing and human resources throughout the firm.

Key elements of strategic operations implementation

As the examination of Whitbread's operations strategy and its operations demonstrate, it is important to differentiate between *SOM* and OM. Many firms in the industry have introduced new policies, procedures, and ways of operating that include forecasting, electronic point of sale, inventory controls, process reengineering, quality circles, empowerment, continuous improvement programmes, and so on. Each of these may have had benefits for the firms concerned, but they are not a strategy unless integrated with each other *and* the firm's business strategy.

However, since implementation of strategy is just as important as planning, it is useful to look in more detail at the specific policies and procedures that are the ingredients of a strategic recipe. This recipe may be made up of key tactical activities; core competences, processes, and capabilities; resources; and technologies (Lowson, 2002). It is suggested here that the key generic elements of one or more operations strategy in hospitality are as follows.

Benchmarking

In order for organizations to be able to assess their level of performance, they are increasingly recognizing the importance of benchmarking themselves against others, either in the same industry or learning from other industries, as we saw in the Whitbread case. Benchmarking can take place in two ways: either in terms of performance benchmarking or in process, sometimes known as best practice, benchmarking. Hotels have used comparative data on average room rates and occupancy for many years to assess their rooms' performance. A recent innovation has been the introduction of an internet-based system that facilitates this comparison in real time. Other systems such as the U.K. Institute of Hospitality's *Hospitality Assured* scheme allow comparison against a national standard and the identification of those operations with the best practice in their field.

Continuous improvement

Rapidly changing consumer tastes and expectations, competitor action, and advancements in technology all require the operator to continuously improve the delivery of service to their customers. Continuous improvement (CI) includes both improving the product/service and improving the process. The former requires continuous research into customer requirements and their level of satisfaction; while process improvement adapts and refines existing designs to be more effective and efficient. Some of the tools used to achieve CI include menu engineering, customer satisfaction surveys, time and motion study, variance analysis, and mystery shopping.

Cycle time reduction

This is typically achieved by removing waste from the system. Japan achieved global dominance in a wide number of industry sectors such as motorcycles and electronic goods through the work of the Japanese guru Taiichi Ohno, one-time Chief Engineer for Toyota. He identified seven types of waste:

1. doing too much
2. waiting
3. transporting
4. too much inflexible capacity or lack of process flexibility
5. unnecessary stocks
6. unnecessary motions
7. defects

One way to identify improvements that can be made is to create a "blueprint" or flow process chart for the operation. This means identifying each stage in the process and looking for opportunities to reduce waste: to eliminate stages, simplify or automate stages, or do two or more things at once. The focus of CI tends to be on employees and customers, whereas that of cycle time reduction tends to be on technology and systems.

Demand forecasting

Most hospitality operations are subject to variable demand from customers. Efficient and effective operations seek to both forecast what this demand will be and operate systems designed to manipulate it. Hotels and restaurants typically have reservations systems, and most hotel chains have revenue management systems in place (except in the budget sector where the room tariff is less dynamic).

Design of cross-functional processes

The efficient operation of any system is at its weakest at the interface between subsystems. The experience of the typical hotel guest involves interaction with a number of staff from different departments—porterage, front desk, housekeeping, room service, and so on. As long ago as 1948, Whyte (1948) showed how dysfunctional the relationship could be between restaurant serving staff and chefs. More recently Anthony Bourdain (2000) in his book provided several examples of alienation between these two groups of employees. One way to tackle this is to change the design of the process to remove such interfaces (the other way is to employ staff to work across these boundaries—see multi-skilling below). For instance, some flight catering operations now have managers responsible for market segments controlling the total process, that is, inventory, hot and cold production, and tray/trolley assembly.

Integrated information and communications technologies (ICT)

Many of the core competences discussed here, such as demand forecasting, continuous improvement, logistics, and temporal employee flexibility, are enabled by ICT, which provides the immediate and accurate exchange or sharing of data. Such information systems are increasingly provided on a common platform, which is often linked to the internet, as we saw in the Whitbread case. In other industries, the impact on operations has been highly significant. For instance, retailing has been transformed by internet shopping, the archetype of which is Amazon.com. Similar effects have been seen in financial services and travel distribution. The hospitality industry has not been as affected, except with regards its sales and marketing activity, due to the nature of hospitality which depends on the personal interaction of the consumer with the provision, that is, hotel customers sleep in beds!

Logistics

This refers to the efficient and effective transportation, handling and storage of materials, sometimes inside the organization but also across the supply chain. Through the use of ICT it is now possible for electronic point of sale (EPOS) devices to link directly to suppliers, so that inventory is renewed in precise response to consumer demand, thereby minimizing stock-outs and overstocking.

Multi-skilling

Multi-skilling is the selection and training of staff so that they are able to work in more than one job position within the operation. Multi-skilling is not the same as multitasking, where employees are deployed across a range of activities in which they are not necessarily trained. Multi-skilling is adopted for several reasons:

- More efficiently scheduled staff, especially during relatively quiet periods of operation.
- Increased staff retention, especially among part-time employees.
- Improved team working.

Most fast food employees are multi-skilled, but this is increasingly being adopted across all sectors. This is sometimes known as functional flexibility.

Temporal employee flexibility

Functional flexibility firms may also adopt temporal flexibility. This approach plans and controls employees' work hours in order to match labour cost as closely to revenue generation as possible. Different forms of temporal flexibility include the employment of full-time, part-time, and casual staff; flexible work hours for employees; and overtime and annual hours contracts.

Training

Employees are typically trained to perform tasks directly related to their function—either technical or interpersonal. As part of a strategy however, training may go beyond this to include training staff in skills such as problem solving, decision making, and creativity. For instance, manufacturers such as Harley Davidson train their employees in techniques such as statistical process control.

The future of strategic operations management

It is relatively easy to identify potentially new OM policies, practices, and technologies that might lead to new ways of doing things, but predicting new *strategic* operations policies is much more difficult. In many industries, the internet has had a major impact on strategy, for instance Amazon.com has revolutionized book retailing. A key role of the internet is to provide a common platform to enable the integration of data from a variety of sources. Hospitality firms are beginning to use this in order to better manage *labour scheduling*. Even in

351

highly successful hotel chains it is often department heads or supervisors that devise staff rotas using simple pen and paper systems. By the time labour cost is calculated it is too late to do anything about it. But the internet can provide an interface that enables all managers with scheduling responsibility to do so in a standard way. Moreover, it can provide immediate feedback to these managers as to the likely outturn of their decision by forecasting labour cost against forecast revenue. Moreover, more senior managers can examine aggregate data or the schedules themselves to see that the plan does not lead to excessive cost. One trial in an international chain found that internet-based labour scheduling leads to a 25% reduction in labour cost in housekeeping alone.

In the future, other new strategies may emerge. This may be due to firms' thinking of new ways to combine the ingredients of operations into a new "recipe," that is, strategy, or through the invention or adoption of new technology which enables firms to manage their operations in ways that were previously not possible.

Conclusion

It might seem slightly surprising that SOM is relatively little discussed in the hospitality industry and not much researched. This is partly because of the "blur" between operations, marketing, and human resources, and partly because it is difficult to separate managing operations from managing operations *strategically*. Nonetheless, when this is attempted, as in this chapter, it becomes apparent that firms have developed and adopted a strategic approach to how they manage their operations, which has contributed greatly to their success. The Whitbread case illustrates how a company can compete at a number of levels—at the corporate level, for instance though merger, acquisition, and disposal of other firms; at the business unit level, by having an integrated strategy based on operations, human resources, and marketing; and specifically through operations, by adopting the right location strategy, ubiqitization, or other operations strategies.

References

Bourdain, A. (2000). *Kitchen Confidential*. London: Bloomsbury.

Jones, P. (1999). Multi-unit management in the hospitality industry: A late twentieth century phenomenon. *International Journal of Contemporary Hospitality Management*, 12(3), 155–164.

Jones, P. (2002). Center Parcs UK. *Tourism and Hospitality Research: Surrey Quarterly Review*, 4(2), 174–182.

Jones, P. (2004). Flight Catering operations and organization. In P. Jones (Ed.), *Flight Catering* (pp. 148–165). Oxford: Elsevier.

Jones, P., and Lockwood, A. (1998). Hospitality operations management. *International Journal of Hospitality Management*, 17(2), 183–202.

Jones, P., and Lockwood, A. (2000). Operating systems and products. In R. Brotherton (Ed.), *The UK Hospitality Industry: A Comparative Approach* (pp. 46–69). Oxford: Butterworth Heinemann.

Jones, P., Lockwood, A., and Bowen, A. (2004). UK hospitality and tourism SMEs: Differentiation by size, location, and owner style. *Tourism and Hospitality Planning & Development*, 1(1), 7–11.

Kaplan, R. S., and Norton, D. P. (1996). *The Balanced Scorecard*. Boston, MA: Harvard Business School.

Levitt, T. (1972). Production line approach to service. *Harvard Business Review*, 50(5), 20–31.

LEYE Consulting (2004). In: Jones, P. (2006) *Strategic Operations Management*, unpublished. Guildford: University of Surrey.

Lowson, R. H. (2002). *Strategic Operations Management: The New Competitive Advantage*. London: Routledge.

Olsen, M. D., Tse, E., and West, J. J. (1992). *Strategic Management in the Hospitality Industry*. New York: Van Nostrand Reinhold.

Sasser, W. E., Wyckoff, D. D., and Olsen, M. (1978). *The Management of Service Operations*. Boston: Allyn and Bacon.

Slack, N., Chambers, S., and Johnston, R. (2007). *Operations management* (5th ed.). Harlow: Prentice Hall.

Whyte, W. F. (1948). *Human Relations in the Restaurant Industry*. New York: McGraw-Hill.

Part Five

Decision-making

Leadership in the hospitality industry

Joseph J. West[1] and Sabina Tonarelli-Frey[2]

*[1]Dean, School of Hospitality and Tourism Management,
Florida International University
[2]President STF Consulting, Inc.*

In this chapter, we introduce the topic of leadership and its importance to the hospitality and tourism industries. One need only scan the current headlines to understand the importance of leadership and its impact upon the hospitality organization. There are as many examples of failed leaders as there are of successful leaders. For every J. W. Marriott, the visionary force behind Marriott Corporation there is a Steven J. Heyer, disgraced former Chief Executive Officer of Starwood. Mr. Marriott built the world's largest lodging company from an A&W Root Beer Stand in Washington, DC. Mr. Heyer was terminated from leading one of the world's largest lodging companies for inappropriate conduct with underlings. For every Ray Kroc, the legendary driving force of McDonald's, there is a Joe Micatrotto, former Chief Executive Officer of Buca Incorporated. Ray Kroc envisioned the future and led a small hamburger company in its metamorphosis into the world's largest hospitality company. Joe Micatrotto took a small Italian restaurant company, built it up, took it public, and then along with several other corporate officers used it as his piggy bank. He and two other executives were indicted for fraud. He pled guilty to a lesser charge and was sentenced to federal prison as well as fined heavily. What is the difference between these diametrically opposite high profile hospitality leaders? We are sure that they all felt that it was "their company"—but that is where the similarity ceased. Messer's Marriott and Kroc understood their responsibility to the stakeholders of "their company," while Heyer and Micatrotto did not. Therein lies the rub. As the global environment continues its dynamic change, leaders face untold challenges. If they are unable to completely understand their role, they set themselves up for failure and perhaps disgrace.

In examining the current state of the hospitality industry one discerns that the hospitality leader of today must be different. There is no more autocratic "my way or the highway" approach to obtaining productivity gains from today's workforce. As Harold Leavitt (2005) notes "… authority… has never been enough to guarantee effective management, and it is certainly not enough to handle middle manager's jobs today." He goes on to state that due to the fast-changing, speeding world, managers must become equipped with many more skills and competencies than were required in the past. Managers now need imaginative, persuasive, visionary, and inspirational skills—the skills many label leadership. Leavitt states now is the time for managers to become leaders and develop their leadership skills.

In today's business environment, human capital has become the most important asset of hospitality firms. As the hospitality business environment becomes more and more complex, organizations need employees capable of adapting to change and able to grasp the complexity of their jobs. Bill Darden, founder of Red Lobster Restaurants and the namesake of Darden Restaurants once remarked: "I am convinced that the only edge we have on our competition is the quality of our employees as reflected each day by the job they do." His words have even greater perspicacity for the future. Employees (human capital) follow leaders because leaders inspire them, motivate them, encourage them to be the best that they can be. Managers must develop their leadership skills including the ability to effectively implement new programmes, the ability to solve new and unique problems, and the ability to communicate to their followers the future they—the leader—desires to create. Today's and tomorrow's leaders must possess the ability to motivate their followers to build the future of their organizations. Leadership is not riding the organization into the future determined by others. Leadership is about building the future that one envisions, creating the organization necessary to excel in that future, and then making the vision reality.

How does one go about developing ones leadership skills? What skills constitute the construct that we call leadership? Are there really leadership skills which can be learned and honed? Are leaders born with the requisite traits and not made? These are a few of the questions we will address in this chapter.

What is leadership?

Leadership is a social phenomenon which has occurred throughout the world, regardless of culture. From the earliest times through today people have identified leaders—individuals who inspire followers. There is evidence to suggest that leadership is a social process which can impact the success of business organizations. Day and Lord (1988) demonstrated that executive leadership can account for 45% of the variance in an organization's performance. Effective leaders create shared values, beliefs, and vision in an organization. They are also capable of focusing their follower's attention on the important issues facing the organization as well as changing their follower's understanding of the situation.

It is important to understand that leadership must exist at all levels of the organization. Leadership is not simply a function of the CEO. It must be found throughout. There is no longer a gulf between managers and leaders. All managers must be leaders. It was once said that "Managers do things right and leaders do the right thing." That is no longer the case. Within today's hospitality organization, much is accomplished by the front line service employees who must make decisions on the spot. They can not wait for a manager to solve the problem. This environment requires that service employees possess the knowledge necessary to make the correct decisions. They are knowledge workers. Drucker defined knowledge workers as "... Knowledge workers are neither bosses nor workers, but rather something in between—resources who have responsibility for developing their most important resource, brainpower, and who also need to take more control of their own careers" (Edersheim, 2007). As we look towards the continuing shift to a world based upon knowledge workers, we posit that hospitality leaders must recognize that this changes the type of individual who is employed in the hospitality industry. This shift to the knowledge revolution is similar to the shift from agriculture to the industrial revolution. As the industrial revolution changed the face of the globe, so too will the knowledge revolution. This means that hospitality workers entering during this revolution will have their value to the hospitality organization based upon not only what they can do but also upon what they know. For the most part, these types of individuals cannot be led by autocratic styles from the top. They must be inspired by the leadership they encounter at all levels within the hospitality firm. In this scenario, many employees emerge as leaders of groups or teams throughout the organization, especially as hospitality firms become more decentralized and decision is pushed to the lowest levels of the organization.

Peter Drucker states that leadership can be learned. He goes on to note that effective leaders understand four basic points:

1. leaders have followers—without followers who share the same values and vision there can be no leader;
2. leaders are highly visible—they set the example for their followers behaviour. It is up to the leader to develop the culture of the organization through their actions, whether symbolic or dynamic;
3. their followers do the right thing—leadership is not a popularity contest. Successful leadership is results oriented, it accomplishes the mission of the organization;
4. leaders have responsibility not rank. As we noted in the introduction, the difference between successful leaders such as Marriott and Kroc and the fallen leaders such as Heyer and Micatrotto is the understanding of the personal responsibility of leadership. The trappings of leadership can quickly ensnare the unwary and lead to their ultimate failure (Drucker, 1996).

At the end of his life, Peter Drucker realized that today's business leaders had to provide three types of leadership—strategic leadership, moral leadership, human leadership—and strike the appropriate balance between them (Edersheim, 2007). This ability to balance takes courage. As Edersheim notes, it takes courage to do what is right. There are so many temptations faced by hospitality leaders. How does one turn against short-term profits which ensure large bonuses in order to invest in the long-term success of the organization? Courage. What does it take to break the rules in an industry full of "me too" firms and innovate? Courage (Edersheim, 2007).

What traits are required of successful CEO's in today's dynamic environment? In her conversations with Peter Drucker shortly before his passing, Edersheim reported that he thought that there were three leadership behaviours unique to a successful CEO:

1. A wide field of vision which enables them to see the whole—the inside and outside of the organization—combined with the perspicuity to challenge organizational assumptions about the present and the future. Drucker held that most businesses fail not due to things being done poorly but due to the fact that the assumptions upon which the organization has been built no longer fit the present and the future. It is up to the CEO to ask and answer what needs to be done;

2. Willingness to assume accountability for their imprint on the organization's character, values, and personality. The CEO must realize that they set the tone of the organization. Drucker was always dismayed when the CEO's embroiled in scandals such as the Enron debacle proclaimed that they were unaware of what was happening within their organization. He thought that this was anathema—why have a CEO if they were not responsible for the actions of the organization? They were willing to accept the plaudits, they must be responsible for the shortcomings;

3. Understand the influence the CEO has upon individuals and the organization as a whole. Drucker posited that the CEO must understand that the key role they play in the organization is a personal one. It is up to them to develop the relationships with people both inside and outside the organization in order to establish a mutual confidence and the creation of a community. This is something that of necessity falls to the CEO (Edersheim, 2007).

Leadership then can be defined as the process used by an individual to influence group members towards the achievement of a goal or goals. It is important to note that most authors think that these individuals must view the influence as legitimate, by this we mean that the influence is reasonable and justifiable given the situation. According to Howell and Costley this definition requires five core characteristics of an effective leader:

1. Leadership is a process or a pattern of behaviours directed towards achievement of group goals. It is not a single act or even a series of acts performed only in certain situations. It is continuous until the group goals have been achieved;
2. The actions of the leader are designed to influence people to modify their behaviour. As their behaviour is influenced towards the group goal they become followers and the leader's position is recognized by the group. It is important to remember that without followers there is no leader, only a voice crying in the wilderness. It is also critical to remember that successful leaders must be successful followers at some time in their lives;
3. While leadership activities may be shared among individuals during the course of the day, a single individual must be recognized among the group as the overall leader responsible ultimately for the achievement of the group's goals;
4. Followers must view the leader's influence as legitimate. The legitimacy may be formal such as their position in the organization or informal because of their interaction with the other members of the group;
5. The leader's influence is directed towards the achievement of group goals. There are two separate scenarios of group goals—in one, the leader plays an important role in setting the group's goal and in the other, the leader inherits established group goals. In either case, the most important concept is that there is a goal which the group is seeking to achieve with the assistance of the leader (Howell and Costley, 2006).

When all is said and done, how do we know that a leader is successful? Most management scholars measure a leader's effectiveness against two metrics:

1. individual follower's behaviours such as job performance. This metric usually examines such measures as employee productivity, performance appraisals either by supervisors or external examiners. Other behaviours may also be measured such as employee satisfaction, commitment to the organization, and motivation. These behaviours most typically measure the most immediate impacts of a leader's behaviour upon the group;

2. group or organizational outcomes indicate the effectiveness of the leader's behaviour on the group or organization as a whole. Measures of success may be profitability, increased market share, or low employee turnover.

In the end it is the accomplishment of group goals within the norms and mores of society which defines the effectiveness of the leader. Follower satisfaction means little if the group's goals are not achieved. Many failed organizations have had satisfied employees. It must be remembered that ultimately the leader is responsible for the achievement of the group's goals. It is the leader to whom the followers look to provide the necessary support and resources to achieve the shared goal.

Leadership traits

Until recently, most people believed that leaders were born and not made. Successful leaders were thought to have inherited the necessary personal characteristics which enabled them to achieve beyond their peers. Early researchers focused upon the characteristics which they identified as traits. These traits were defined as permanent characteristics which did not change no matter the situation faced by the leader. During the first three quarters of the twentieth century, much research was published concerning these traits. Researchers developed a list of personal characteristics which they posited provided the leader the ability to be successful. Some of these traits included height, social status, energy, aggressiveness, assertiveness, and popularity. However, it was discovered that this theory had several flaws:

1. most researchers could not agree upon which of the leadership traits were the most important;
2. most of the published research compared leaders to followers. There was little attempt to distinguish between effective and non-effective leaders;
3. there was no universal agreement on either the definition of the individual traits or their measurement;
4. there was no measurement of how much or how little of each trait was necessary to predict leadership success (Howell and Costley, 2006).

While the theory of the leader being born not made has been largely discredited, there is some validity to the idea that effective leaders do possess certain common traits. Most researchers agree that effective leaders do possess high levels of intelligence and cognitive ability. Intellect is a driver of outstanding performance while cognitive ability—big picture thinking, creativity, and long-term vision—enables the leader to achieve group goals. Creativity is an illusive concept. It is difficult to describe but usually we know it when we see it. Many argue that only a few are creative, that it is something with which they are born. Others suggest it can be learned. We argue the latter. If one is able to truly expand their perceptual window, see patterns of change in the big picture, and are motivated and excited by the thought of developing something new, it is easy to be creative. It is important that hospitality leaders work at expanding their cognitive and perceptual skills. The leader of tomorrow will be required to personally grow through the acquisition of knowledge and experience. As we move towards a knowledge or information society, this need is no longer a desirable objective, it is mandatory. Leaders must be able to the use their intellectual power to lead creative change if they expect to remain the spiritual and rational leaders of their organizations.

We agree that there are other personal traits which can assist the leader in their quest towards the goal. However, these traits depend on the situation for their effectiveness—they are not universally applicable to all situations in which leaders may find themselves. It appears that traits such as fluency of speech, self-confidence, adaptability, and assertiveness assist effective leaders in a fairly broad range of situations. Most of the traits we have identified can be developed by the leader. Fluency of speech, assertiveness, social ability are all skills which can be honed with practice. The one trait which is difficult to enhance is native intellect. It is virtually impossible for individuals who lack basic intelligence to become effective leaders.

It seems that while some of these traits can assist a leader in certain situations, their effectiveness varies with the situation. They are contingent—which supports our position that leadership can be learned. It falls to the leader to recognize the situation and employ the traits appropriately.

Leadership behaviours

Since we have argued that leadership can be learned and that there are few universal leadership traits, how do we differentiate effective leaders from ineffective ones? Largely through their leadership behaviour. There are numerous behaviours among which leaders can choose. Which are effective are based upon the situation and follower characteristics. Once again, effective leadership behaviours similar to effective leadership traits are contingent or situational. If this is the case, then effective leaders must vary their behaviours as the situation or followers change. This mandates that the leader possesses the intellect necessary to accurately assess the situation and choose from among a repertoire of leadership behaviours. Once again demonstrating that effective leadership can be learned. This contingency theory of leadership posits that the most effective leadership behaviour depends on the situation. It follows then that leadership training is important and is a key to successful leadership.

In today's dynamic hospitality environment there seems to a number of leadership behaviours which enable individuals to successfully lead their organizations. We will examine five such patterns of behaviour which can be applied to most of the situations faced by today's hospitality leader. We caution you that these behaviours are not usually used independently of one another nor are they mutually exclusive. An effective leader will probably use a number of the behaviours at the same time as required by the situation. The five behaviour patterns are:

1. Supportive—this pattern demonstrates the leader's concern for follower needs, open communication and follower development. One of the primary goals of organizational leaders is to develop their followers to the point that the organization functions at peak performance. In addition, the effective leader must work to develop their successor. A sign of ineffective leadership is the decline in organizational performance upon leadership succession;
2. Directive—this pattern refers to the assignment of tasks to followers. To assure the successful completion of those assignments, the leader must ensure that the methods to be utilized are understood by followers, that lines of communication are open and clear, that there are specific goals and expectations of performance understood by all. This behaviour is related to organizational structure and is necessary until all members of the organization possess a clear understanding of what is expected of them and are capable of meeting those expectations;
3. Participative—this behaviour is demonstrated by the level of follower participation in decision making and goal setting utilized by the leader. This behaviour ranges from one-on-one interactions to group interaction in an effort to elicit input for decision making. This behaviour is appropriate when there is knowledge possessed by the group which the

leader can effectively utilize in decision making. This behaviour has an implicit understanding that when participation is requested it will be valued by the leader. Symbolic use of participation by the leader can result in group dissatisfaction and poor morale and performance;

4. Reward and punishment—this behaviour is necessary because the leader must signal to the followers whether they are positively or negatively impacting the organization. When followers positively impact the organization, the effective leader must provide them with some form of reward. The rewards can range from a simple word of praise to more tangible actions such as bonuses and promotions. It follows that followers who negatively impact the organization must also be acknowledged in a manner which will encourage them either to modify their behaviour to a more acceptable level or leave the organization. This type of behaviour must be based upon performance if it is to be effective. To base it upon the whim of the leader, is to turn it from a positive impact to a negative impact upon the organization;

5. Charismatic—this behaviour is best demonstrated by the leader as they communicate their vision of the future and serve as a role model to their followers. Max Weber defined charisma as the influence based upon the exceptional characteristic of the individual person. In his nineteenth century industrial revolution setting, he juxtapositioned behaviours of managers of large political and manufacturing organizations which he named bureaucratic against the behaviour of heroic or revolutionary leaders who had successfully advocated actions to resolve crises which he named charismatic (Weber, 1947). This characterization continues today as charismatic leadership behaviours are defined as behaviours which elicit extreme devotion, commitment, or trust from followers. The leaders who through the power of their personal characteristics are able to motivate their followers to follow their vision of the organization utilize charismatic leadership behaviour. Reverend Martin Luther King, Jr. was such a leader. He possessed little power except for his spirit and his vision. Yet he was able to bring about great change to society.

Emotional intelligence

In the middle 1990s, Daniel Coleman introduced the concept of "emotional intelligence" to the leadership literature. His research of 200 large, global companies led him to posit that while the traditional qualities associated with successful leadership—intelligence, toughness, and vision—were necessary but not sufficient for effective leadership (Coleman, 1998).

He believed as we do that different situations call for different types of leadership behaviours and that the personal styles of effective leaders varied greatly throughout the world. The overwhelming number of researchers agree that effective leaders must possess intelligence but they disagree on the other necessary qualities. Coleman reports that all of the effective leaders he studied possessed one trait in common—emotional intelligence. He studied the competency models used to predict leadership potential of employees of 188 global companies. These models had been designed by asking senior managers at the companies to identify the common characteristics that were typical of their organization's outstanding leaders; in addition objective measures were used to identify those leaders who positively influenced the performance of their units. Star leaders were interviewed and tested. As a result, the researchers developed a list of 15 characteristics which were linked to highly effective leaders in the companies. Coleman divided these characteristics into three constructs: intelligence, technical skill, and emotional intelligence. He found that while the first two—intelligence and technical skill—were important, emotional intelligence seemed to be twice as important as the others in effective leadership. He also discovered that as the leader rose higher in the organization, emotional intelligence increased in importance at the expense of technical skill. Coleman (1998) maintains that individuals can develop their emotional intelligence.

Since emotional intelligence is important to the success of a leader and it can be developed in most intelligent people, we thought that it should be discussed in this chapter. Coleman holds that there are five components of emotional intelligence:

1. Self awareness—effective leaders understand themselves. They understand their emotions, strengths, and weaknesses, their needs, and their drives. They are honest with themselves and their followers. They are neither overly critical nor overly hopeful. They understand what they value and their goals. This understanding enables them to make decisions which are in alignment with their values and goals. Self awareness enables leaders to be candid with themselves and others. This is important since effective leaders must make decisions that require them to candidly assess their capabilities as well as the capabilities of their followers and their organization;

2. Self regulation—effective leaders control themselves in a manner which frees them from their emotions and feelings. While they still feel their emotions they are able to separate them from the actions necessary for success. This is important because leaders who are in control of their emotions create an environment conducive to productive behaviour from their followers. In addition, in this environment of constant and unpredictable change, they are able to adapt to the environmental dynamism. Much of the negative behaviour exhibited in organizations can be traced to impulsive behaviour on the part of the leaders. The executives in Buca, Incorporated did not plan on defrauding the company, it occurred due to their impulsive behaviour. Once they began down the slippery slope their behaviours became even more impulsive. As a result of their lack of self regulation, they were imprisoned and the company was nearly destroyed;

3. Motivation—this is a trait common to all effective leaders. They are driven to achieve for the sake of achievement. They have an innate desire to excel. They desire to stretch in order to develop themselves. They embrace the challenge and exhibit a passion for whatever it is they are attempting. It is a characteristic of motivated people that they maintain an aura of optimism which is infectious to their followers. Not only are they optimistic they are also committed to the organization. These two attributes—achievement and commitment—are fundamental to effective leadership;

4. Empathy—this is demonstrated by the leader's thoughtful consideration of follower's feelings as part of their decision-making process. This does not mean that the needs of the followers are placed before the needs of the organization to achieve its goals. It simply means that when important decisions are made, the needs of the employees are taken into consideration. Empathy is important in today's business environment due to the increasing importance of knowledge workers and the need to retain them, the increasing use of teams, and the global expansion of large companies;

5. Social skill—this quality is demonstrated by the leader's ability to develop relationships both inside and outside the organization. Socially skilled people are adept at a number of important leadership behaviours—leading teams to attain their objectives, developing partnerships with entities necessary for the survival of the organizations, and establishing effective networks to support their initiatives. No leader is alone. They all need to accomplish their goals through others and it is their competency with social skills which enables them to be effective (Coleman, 1998).

It is apparent that emotional intelligence as defined by Coleman is important to successful leadership. While these attributes seem to be innate, they can be learned. It requires hard work and commitment. It is not easy for the inwardly focused individual to develop social skills but it can be accomplished. It is important that potential leaders honestly examine themselves and evaluate their level of effective emotional intelligence.

Ethics and leadership

Ethics has been defined as "the discipline of dealing with what is good and bad and with moral duty and obligation" (Dictionary, 1996). While philosophers have studied ethics for centuries, it has now become a critical business issue. It is no wonder when we examine the recent headlines of executive misbehaviour. The Human Resource Institute's 2003–2004 Major Issues Survey found that among North American companies ranking 120 issues facing managers today, ethics was among the top three most important in terms of impact on the company (American Management Association, 2006). The American Management Association reported that business leaders reported that they believe that ethics has a great impact upon their brands and reputation as well as customer trust and investor confidence (American Management Association, 2006). This is of particular interest to leaders in the hospitality industry where customer trust and investor confidence is of the utmost importance. In the hospitality industry, brands are everything. Any actions that adversely impact the image of a hospitality brand are to be avoided at all costs. Thus hospitality leaders should be very interested in business ethics. The number one reason for ethical behaviour in the hospitality enterprise is protection of the company's reputation. It is the leader who models and supports ethical behaviour in their organization that has the most impact on the company's ethics.

In a survey of 1665 executives around the world, researchers discovered that 95% of the respondents indicated that the ethics of the CEO play a meaningful role in the way that business is conducted throughout the company (Verschoor, 2006). Their findings indicated that while personal ethics are important, corporate culture is critical. Their respondents were in concert with the Human Resource Institute's findings that most of today's business leaders thought that strong ethical practices in business help build brands, win over customers, and save money in the long run. When we speak of unethical behaviour in organizations we mean not only the headline catching activities such as Cendant and Enron, we also mean employee activities such as:

1. inflating sales forecast numbers to senior management and investors;
2. taking office supplies home;
3. inflating company sales to win a client;
4. charging personal expenses to the company account.

Reasons employees have given for such actions include:

1. I do so much for the company that they do not pay me for, they owe it to me;
2. I did it because of the pressure from senior management to increase my performance;
3. I did it to buy time and keep my job.

Obviously, these are not the actions of individuals whose behaviours reflect the corporate culture of an ethical company. In a 2005 report on their ongoing research in business ethics of employees in for-profit, non-profit, and governmental sectors in the United States, the Ethics Resource Center (2005) found that little had changed during the 11 years they had been conducting their research. The Center surveyed more than 3000 employees for their research. They found that in spite of increasing implementation of formal ethics programmes, positive outcomes remained unchanged or declined. The Center reported that 52% of employees responding to the survey witnessed misconduct in the workplace, with 36% of them reporting multiple instances of misconduct. Of those who witnessed the misconduct only 55% reported it to management, a decline of 10% from the 2003 survey (Ethics Resource Center, 2005). In 2005, 10% of the employees reported pressure to compromise their or company standards. These findings should ring alarms in the minds of hospitality leaders. Unethical behaviour does have an impact on organization morale and performance.

The insightful hospitality leader understands that managers and employees in the industry are constantly placed in situations which test their ethical behaviours. Employees handle large amounts of cash and credit cards, control large inventories of food and liquor, have access to guest rooms, and also engage in complex service exchanges with guests and suppliers. Given this scenario, it is important for hospitality leaders to establish ethical codes of conduct for their organizations. However, Stevens (2001) reported that approximately 50% of hotel companies published ethical standards compared to 80% for mid-to-large American companies.

While all can agree that stealing money is unethical, there is great disagreement on other actions such as sexual harassment, racism, competitor information, etc. It falls to the leader to develop the code of conduct by which the actions of the followers as well as the leader will be judged. It is up to the leader to build the ethical culture which will minimize the need for a compliance based infrastructure. Research has found that when employees think that something will be done to correct unethical behaviour they are more likely to report it to the proper authority (Stevens, 2001). The leader must focus upon what situations exist within their organizations which either prevent employees from doing the right thing or keep employees from taking appropriate action when they observe other employees not doing the right thing. The role of corporate culture is increasingly recognized as an important influence on ethical behaviour. Steven Cutler, recently retired Director of the Securities & Exchange Commission's (SEC) Division of Enforcement, stated the manner of how the SEC viewed the CEO's responsibility for ethical behaviour in their organizations had changed. He stated "We're trying to induce companies to address matters of tone and culture. ... What we are asking of that CEO, CFO, or General Counsel goes beyond what a pep walk or an enforcement action against another company executive might impel her to do. We're hoping that if she sees that a failure of corporate culture can result in a fine that significantly exceeds the proverbial 'cost of doing business,' and reflects a failure on her watch—and a failure on terms that everyone can understand: the company's bottom line—she may have a little more incentive to pay attention to the environment in which her company's employees do their jobs" (Gebler, 2006).

The SEC clearly expects more of CEO's and their impact on corporate culture than they did in the recent past. Corporate culture goes beyond ethics training programmes and compliance infrastructure. Culture can not be developed in the corporate offices and then implemented by the human resource department. Corporate culture is the sum total of the shared values and behaviours of all of the company's employees, managers, and leaders. The leader can move an organization towards ethical behaviour only when they understand the full range of values and behaviours needed to meet their ethical goal. The leader must understand how their managers deal with ethical issues and how the values they (the leader) demonstrate impact upon their manager's behaviours. The leader must understand the pressures that all the members of their organization are under and how they react to those pressures. The leader must understand how the lines of communication work throughout the organization and if they are effective in developing a sense of accountability and purpose among the managers and employees. These are great challenges for today's hospitality leaders. It is no wonder that we see the failures in leadership that we are seeing today.

Gebler (2006) states that leaders must understand how the myriad of human behaviours and interactions fit together in the organization in order to see the whole picture of corporate culture. He presents a Culture Risk Assessment Model to assist CEO's in assessing the ethical corporate culture in their organizations. He states that over 1000 organizations in 24 countries have utilized the model and McKinsey & Co. has adopted it as its method of choice for mapping corporate cultures and measuring progress towards culture change. The model is based upon the principle that all values can be categorized in one of seven constructs. The constructs are grouped by level and the levels grouped by commonality. Levels 1, 2, and 3 relate to the organization's basic needs, level 4 relates to accountability while levels 5, 6, and 7 focus upon the common good. The levels are defined as:

1. Financial stability—if the organization is not financially stable unethical or illegal behaviours can be rationalized. Organizations which are struggling for survival frequently do not focus a lot of attention on how they conduct themselves. CEO's in struggling organizations must be confident that their managers understand and stay within the desired ethical boundaries;
2. Communication—the key is to clearly communicate the correct messages which enhance good relationships between employees, customers, and suppliers. The CEO must effectively communicate a vision which creates a sense of loyalty among employees as well as creating a sense of connection between the organization and its customers in order for the organization to successfully attain this level;
3. Systems and processes—the CEO must ensure that they have implemented strong internal controls and established clear standards of conduct in order for the organization to successfully operate at this level. It is important that the internal controls are viewed as the opportunity to create more efficient, timely processes. However, the leader must be cautious of being too focused upon processes which can lead to bureaucracy and eventual degradation;
4. Accountability—the CEO must focus on creating an environment where managers and employees take responsibility for

their actions. For the creation of an ethical corporate culture, the environment must be such as all employees think that they have a personal responsibility for the integrity of the organization. In order for the organization to successfully reach this level the leader must invite employee participation in the building of the processes and develop a feeling of trust throughout the organization;

5. Alignment—in order for the organization to operate at this level the CEO must create a shared vision of the future as well as a shared set of corporate values. The shared vision provides employees with an accepted organizational purpose, while the shared values provide them with guidance for decision making;

6. Social responsibility—at this level it becomes apparent to stakeholders that the organization is making a difference in society through its products and services and its involvement in the community. Organizations operating at this level are dedicated to becoming good responsible corporate citizens;

7. Sustainability—to be successful at the highest level, CEO's must ensure that their organization's employees accept the highest levels of ethical behaviour in all of their relationships with other employees, customers, suppliers, and all other stakeholders (Gebler, 2006).

Organizations may be successfully operating at some levels and not at others. For example an organization may have fully developed values around 5, 6, and 7 but be lacking in levels 1, 2, and 3. These organizations probably possess visionary leaders and externally focused social programmes but lack the core systems which ensure that higher level commitments are imbedded in the day-to-day operations. It is up to the leader to bring about the necessary changes in levels 1, 2, and 3 to ensure that the ethical standards are upheld in the daily operations of the organizations.

In this section, we have attempted to communicate the importance of ethics in the hospitality firm of today and the future. Ethical behaviour is a moving target, which requires commitment and focus on the part of the leader. It is clear that society no longer condones nor rewards unethical corporate behaviour and holds the CEO responsible for the actions of their organization.

Summary

In this chapter we have introduced the reader to the concept of leadership and our point of view that effective leadership can be learned. Effective leaders are highly visible, take responsibility for their actions, and have followers who do the right thing. Leaders are goal oriented, judged by the actions of their followers, they glory in the strength of their followers, and they are intolerant of poor performance. Effective leaders understand that leadership is situational and they must either modify their behaviour or the situation to successfully attain their goals. They realize that in addition to intelligence and technical skills, they must possess emotional intelligence if they are to be effective in today's complex environment. They understand that emotional intelligence is essential if they are to lead the knowledge workers of today and tomorrow. Above all, effective leaders understand that they are responsible for the ethical behaviour of their organizations.

References

American Management Association. (2006). *The Ethical Enterprise*. New York: American Management Association.

Coleman, D. (1998). What makes a leader? Reprinted in: Inside the mind of the leader. *Harvard Business Review* (November and December).

Day, D. V., and Lord, R. G. (1988). Executive leadership and organizational performance: Suggestions for a new theory and methodology. *Journal of Management*, *14*(3), 453–464.

Dictionary, Merriam-Webster. (1996). Springfield, MA: Merriam-Webster.

Drucker, P. (1996). *The Leader of the Future* (p. xii). San Francisco, CA: Jossey-Bass.

Edersheim, E. H. (2007). Peter Drucker's 'Unfinished Chapter': The role of the CEO. *Leader to Leader*, *2007*(45), 40.

Ethics Resource Center. (2005). *How Employees View Ethics in their Organizations*. Washington, DC: Ethics Resource Center.

Gebler, D. (2006). Creating an ethical culture. *Strategic Finance*, *87*(11), 29.

Howell, J. P., and Costley, D. L. (2006). *Understanding Behaviors for Effective Leadership*. Upper Saddle River, NJ: Pearson/Prentice Hall.

Leavitt, H. J. (2005). Hierarchies, authority, and leadership. *Leader to Leader*, *2005*(37), 55.

Stevens, B. (2001). Hospitality ethics: Responses from human resource directors and students to seven ethical scenarios. *Journal of Business Ethics*, *30*(3), 233.

Verschoor, C. C. (2006). Strong ethics is a critical quality of leadership. *Strategic Finance*, *87*(7), 19.

Weber, M. (1947). *The Theory of Social and Economic Organization*. New York: Free Press.

CHAPTER 16

The organizational culture and its role in executing strategy

Chris Roberts

*Hospitality and Tourism Management,
Isenberg School of Management,
University of Massachusetts Amherst,
90 Campus Center Way, Flint 206,
Amherst, MA 01003*

Introduction

Leading an organization to success in the competitive environment requires a strategy that is thoughtful, intentional, and with specific goals in mind. As equally importantly as that, though, is having an organization that internally understands and supports the strategy, and has the resources necessary to implement it (Doz and Prahalad, 1988). These three elements (understanding, support, and resources) are the lynchpins to successfully enacting the strategy and generating the desired outcomes (Kotter and Cohen, 2002).

Leadership typically focuses attention on the organization internally to decide how to organize the business, who should perform which functions, and where such activities are to take place. Such organizational design decisions are necessary to create a functioning system of operations (Nadler and Tushman, 1997). In addition, however, intentionally examining the organization's culture and making decisions about how to sculpt or influence it is a key step in creating the internal understanding and support needed for leadership's strategic plans and activities. Thus, the organization's internal culture and design form the bedrock of the organization's ability to perform. That is, who works with whom, who talks with each other (both formally and over the water cooler), who controls resources, and who makes internal decisions can expedite or stifle any well-intended strategic plans (Alexander, 1985; Beckhard and Pritchard, 1992).

Strategic impacts upon the organization

Organizational culture

A simple definition of organizational culture is the shared beliefs and values that result in expected behaviours and norms among the members. The organizational culture has three levels: artefacts, stated values, and assumptions.

Artefacts are symbols, buildings, legends, ceremonies, rituals, and an internal language. These artefacts develop over time and information about them is passed along from worker to worker. The symbols can be company logos, or uniforms or other manner of dress that people wear, or badges and awards for certain kinds of performance. Some symbols might become revered while others might be more fun in nature. Regardless, the symbols take on meaning that endears themselves to those within the organization.

The buildings typically become part of the culture, as it is the "home" for workers while at work. Status is often conveyed based upon location within the building. Neighbours know the visual look of the building within the community so that eventually workers become identified with the physical facility. Usually a building changes little over time, so its image to the workers becomes a core part of their identity.

Legends, ceremonies, and rituals, both formal and informal, become a key method by which the organizational culture is communicated among members. The histories of those who went before the current members (the legends) act as either role models or warnings of what not to do. Ceremonies are useful processes to recognize members for their accomplishments and to hold their performances up for all to see and emulate. Rituals are patterns of behaviour that members recognize as acceptable behaviour and could include how people address or greet one another, or how parking spaces are allocated. Regardless of the scope of the ritual, its role becomes known within the organization and members are expected to honour it.

Language is a key aspect of any organizational culture as it forms the basis for communicating values, ideals, and concepts. Each industry seems to develop language unique to its products and processes, such as discussing products by code numbers rather than actual names or referring to locations by abbreviations (LAX for Los Angeles International Airport is an example). Firms within those industries seem to advance some of the common industry jargon to fit local conditions. For instance, within the Bell Telephone Company the common, simple home telephone service became known internally as POTS, or plain old telephone service.

Organizational culture is a powerful force within firms. It provides members with a sense of identify, helps to create commitment towards goals and strategies, gives members a framework for understanding what happens within the organization, and acts as a control mechanism to guide behaviours and attitudes.

Organizational design

As noted, how the business is organized forms the basis for effective operations (Adler, 1999; Leavitt, 2003; Nadler and Tushman, 1997). The lines of authority for decision-making and for communicating must be clearly delineated so that all employees, from the front line workers and support staff, to the office of the GM, can efficiently and effectively learn what it is each person is to do, and how to adapt and change to fit with organizational needs. Functions are often organized into departments such as production, shipping and receiving, sales and marketing, etc. This certainly helps the various functions, or departments, understand better how to interact with one another. Such formalization of the organization is often necessary to create the needed efficiency for competitive effectiveness.

However, this can often be an overlooked aspect as a new strategy is employed, especially of a firm that has been in business for some time. The established lines of authority and communication might have become so deeply entrenched that sheer inertia keeps the system operating in the same manner in spite of efforts to change it. How can that happen? Essentially, processes become embedded into the daily operations of the company. Forms, routines, and procedures abound in many organizations, and such practices often drive the flow of operations. While senior management might have a vision about how the organization is to operate under a new strategy, learning all of the various "nuts and bolts" to tweak is usually beyond the working knowledge of leadership. Thus, having members of the strategy development team that are experts on the organization's design can be an essential aspect of developing a strategy implementation plan. Further, having that internal expert on the strategy formation team can be valuable, too, as the expert can help inform the decision makers what the firm might be capable of in terms of change, and what time frames are possible.

The role of leadership

While there are many different definitions of leadership, the majority indicated that it is the ability to set directions for a group, gain member's commitment, and influence them to achieve group goals. It is having the courage to identify needed action and initiate change. In return, followers expect their leaders to be competent, honest, knowledgeable, and inspiring.

Leaders, then, are strong influences upon the organizational culture (Bridges, 1991). The policies and procedures they design, the strategies they conceive, and the attitudes and values they adopt set the tone for how other members are expected to act. The goals of the organization also influence the culture, for if the goals are respected and valued the members often exhibit pride in being a part of that organization. The strategies formulated by management should respect the firm's value sets that are embedded within its culture. The strategies should either be incrementally adjusted to conform with and support existing culture, or plans should be developed to gently mould the culture so that it becomes aligned with the new strategies. It is a responsibility of management to understand the organizational culture well enough to anticipate its influences upon the organization and to anticipate how to harness that power to support corporate strategies.

Managing change

Preparing members of an organization for change is a large task unto itself (Deal and Kennedy, 1982; Jick, 1993; Kilmann *et al.*, 1985). A direct edict from authority rarely is sufficient to enact any change throughout an organization. Simply put: in general people prefer the safety and security of the known, or the tasks and internal routines of operations that they have mastered and execute with confidence. Thus, such people are typically resistant to any change that would put that safety, security, and competence at risk.

Change can be considered incremental or radical. Incremental change is often considered linear; that is, it is focused upon small improvements or adjustments to existing procedures and processes. Radical change, in contrast, is often transformative. It can be multidimensional and can modify or greatly change the basic systems, structure, thinking, and attitudes of members of the firm. Major strategic initiatives are often of this type.

For a change to be successful, there is a critical mass of individuals that must be identified as those whose support is both vital and necessary. This critical mass should be the smallest group of people possible, for it is they who can best enact the change, and who must influence others to also become committed to the change. These individuals are the change agents who accept the responsibility to enacting the change. They not only should not just be from the senior management team but rather should be from many levels throughout the organization. For it is their collective influence that can educate and convince others within the firm to adapt and accept change.

Such successful changes often do not come from broad concepts that originate from the top of the organization. Rather, such ideas for change often originate at the fringes of the firm and have champions who focus recourses on improvements. Such change processes often call for existing members to first let go of their previous understandings, listen to the new concepts, and learn to build the improvements into systems. Lewin (1947) provided the classic description of this as an "unfreeze, move forward and re-freeze" process.

It is key, then, that managers desiring to make changes understand that change is a process, not an event or directive. The process typically involves (1) identifying the need for change, (2) forming a guiding coalition, (3) developing a shared vision, (4) creating an implementation plan, (5) identifying potential resistance and how to secure participation, (6) communicating the change throughout the firm, (7) enacting the change, and then (8) evaluating the change.

Of these steps, keeping in mind throughout the process the impact upon organizational culture is paramount to the success of the change process. Step five (above) centres upon this concept. How people within the organization relate to one another, how they feel about their work and their organization, are key internal motivators. Managers must think ahead of the likely impact that any change may have upon those perceptions that workers hold dear. For if the intended change does not nurture or enhance those ideals, and does not offer acceptable replacements for what might be lost, then the resistance may be so great that the change will not be successful (Olson and Eoyang, 2001).

An example of this can be seen in the firm that clamped down upon a morning coffee break. In this particular firm, employees were in the habit of arriving to work at 8 am as expected, but then taking a coffee break about 8:45 for about 30–45 min. It was not a scheduled break for any of the employees. Not every employee took that coffee break every day. It would often depend upon the work demand of the morning. However, large numbers of employees could be found in the employee cafeteria at that early hour. A new senior manager joined the organization, and upon witnessing this phenomena, issues a directive that all supervisors were to limit employees to scheduled break times only. The manager's intended result was to improve productivity by having workers spend more time performing their function. The result was not an improvement in productivity but rather a slow but steady breakdown in morale that was in direct proportion to quality defects in production.

What the senior manager did not realize was the extent of informal networking and relationship building that happened during the morning coffee breaks. Many employees from different departments spent the time interacting, chatting about some work situations and/or problems while building friendships in a pleasant, non-threatening environment.

These relationships enabled the workers to more easily work through challenges later in the day as they were more comfortable with one another, knew who to contact to get answers, and because they knew they would have that opportunity to see one another again at another morning break. The change in culture from one that was relaxed and supportive of employee networking shifted to one focused upon efficiency. The value of the internal networking eroded over time. Employees felt a loss as a "perk" of the job had been taken away and nothing given to replace it. The internal culture became more stifled and insular. Formal channels of communication and decision-making were now used to resolve issues, which took more time, as employees were less familiar with one another and each other's issues. Thus, while employees might be spending more time at their workstations, the overall performance of the firm suffered rather than improved. Even a "minor" change such as this can have a tremendous impact upon the organization's culture and therefore its ability to perform.

Psychological contract and commitment

Entry into any organization or group begins with an agreement about membership, responsibilities, and rights. Many of the terms of belonging are stated, such as when to show up, how long to stay, what to do when there, who to ask questions, and who to follow for commands and directions. Benefits for belonging and performing acceptably are also usually articulated such as rate of the pay and related compensation factors, work location and tools, supplies, etc. However, often there are "unwritten rules" that either are unspoken or are assumed. It is usually expected that the new member will learn these unwritten rules over time and through experience.

Together, these agreements form what is called the psychological contract. That is, it is a set of expectations created through initial interactions when joining a group. It is a key opportunity to include information about the organization's strategy and to explain how the new member's group function fits within that strategy as well as what the new member can do to contribute in a constructive manner.

Many lower level employees are often unaware of the organizational strategy or, if known, how his or her individual actions make a difference in achieving the strategy. This time of entry into the organization when the psychological contract is being developed is a prime opportunity to build an awareness of the strategy and set an expectation of activities to positively contribute to it.

Many new employees are focused upon immediate concerns such as where do I work, how much will I get paid, who will I work with, how will I be trained to do my job, etc. During this period of time the worker is often somewhat anxious about fitting into the existing set of other workers, and of becoming successful at the task at hand. Information about the corporate strategy is often lost or forgotten during this initial period of welcome. Later, after having become established within their position within the firm, patterns of thinking and behaviour likely become set into routines and an awareness of the larger industry environment and competitive positioning of the organization might seem beyond the realm of that employee's sphere.

Thus, organizations might consider regular internal information campaigns that inform and renew interest and commitment in strategic initiatives. The psychological contract creates an expectation of actions and behaviours. Building an awareness of the role of strategies into that initial contract could well build a regular sense of participation and commitment for individual workers.

Methods to shape internal culture to fit new strategies

There are many tools available to leaders of an organization to enact a change in the internal culture. Most of the tools can emerge from a keen understanding of what members value. An awareness of the components of organizational culture can give managers an opportunity to make either incremental or radical changes so that a new strategy can be blended into the organizational climate. A clear understanding of the written and unspoken rules, the assumptions, the rituals and legends, and the accepted practices of behaviour all can be used to identify features of the culture to influence.

The structure of the organization can be used to begin a change in culture (Galbraith *et al.*, 2002). If the organization is traditional in design with many layers of management, the slow introduction of cross-divisional teams can begin to break down the rigid barriers of a functional structure. The occasional application of a matrix organization where some employees have both direct and dotted-line reporting relationships with other departments can also begin to blur the formal organizational lines of authority and communication (Bartlett and Ghoshal, 1990). The intentional but slow injection of these different structural aspects can begin to soften a climate of command and control into one of more cooperation and collaboration (Bryan and Joyce, 2005; Sy and D'Annunzio, 2005).

The opposite might be needed as well. An organizational climate may be too fluid and easy-going for the forecasted future and the strong demands of a new strategy. A disciplined approach to sales and production might be needed to handle a dramatic increase in volume. Concerns about managing quality control could also be reasons for a focus upon the care employees use to perform their functions. Employees may be asked to more carefully adhere to work schedules and/or to reduce some of their casual interactions. The introduction of an annual employee review process with elements related to schedules, error rates, goal attainment, etc., would likely convey a message that more attention to detail is needed. Any change, of course, will be meet with some resistance, but as noted above, focusing upon the identification of a critical mass of key influencers within the organization, gaining their understanding and commitment for the change, can be a tremendous help in its implementation.

In addition to changes in organizational structure, other efforts can be made to help shape the informal culture. The general ambience of employee break areas, workstations, offices, and public areas within the facility can be decorated differently to reflect desired attitudes built into new strategies. Simple posters can be printed that express a quick "sound bite" about a new attitude or behaviour and posted in high traffic areas. Leaders can include some of these sound bites in their routine communications with both internal and external stakeholder groups. Values can be openly expressed, and emphasis placed upon the specific values that are most desired and useful for the new strategies. Even legends of past successes can be brought forward again, only this time with an emphasis upon the aspects of the situation that are appropriate for the new competitive attitude needed to implement the intended strategy.

The assumptions underlying deeply held beliefs could also be used to influence a cultural change. For instance, a large, public state university has a culture that seems to assume a value of choice. That is, employees seem to believe they have choices to make in just about all aspects of their jobs—especially the faculty. While this concept of choice is not written in documents or spoken about in official communications, it seems to be commonly understood that employees have a choice and a related role in decision-making. Therefore, management does not just arbitrarily make decisions and announce them. Instead, issues are brought forward into public arenas (such as the faculty senate or the daily campus newspaper) and options for action discussed in open forums. Employee input is sought. Given this background of a deeply held belief in choice, few employees expect to have managers dictate orders to them. Employees expect to be consulted and be part of the decision process, even if they are not formally empowered to actually make a final decision.

In this climate, introducing a new strategic direction for the organization requires preparing the culture for a change. It might include informing the employees about the need for change; about the financial or competitive forces that are impacting the way business has been conducted in the past versus what is happening now, and why the past behaviours would not be sufficient for the future. The timing of decision-making might become more compressed as competitive pressures require the institution to react quicker than it has in the past, and employees would need to have this explained to them. The time to have open forum discussions and elicit input from the entire community may no longer be possible. These types of explanations deal with the unspoken assumptions that drive the present culture of choice and help members understand why those assumptions can no longer be used, why they may not have the opportunity to choose as they have in the past, and why new processes and actions are needed.

Summary and conclusion

Organizational culture is recognized as one of the most powerful forces in determining an organization's success. Resistance to goals and strategic plans from those within the organization can doom such efforts before they have any opportunity to succeed. Therefore, understanding what constitutes an organizational culture and how to influence it is a key aspect of effectively formulating and implementing strategic plans.

As discussed, leaders have many tools available to them to help guide and shape their organization's culture. A key starting point is developing a deep awareness of the components of the culture that are highly valued, and carefully using those aspects to reshape attitudes and behaviours. Formal tools such as organizational design in structure, lines of authority and communication are possibilities. Informal tools such as legends, traditions, ceremonies, and rituals can also be used to enact change.

Notice, however, that some of the cultural aspects may be considered so important to the members that they take on a sense of having become sacred. For example, a past leader may be held in such high regard that any attempt to show what that person accomplished (and how he or she might have been done it) is not appropriate for today's condition could backfire. Members may resent any implication that the icon of the past would not be sufficient for today. Thus, any effort to influence a change in culture should be carefully examined to anticipate resistance and should be introduced slowly.

New strategies often call for major changes within an organization. Members typically do not desire radical change as it generally creates a threatening environment filled with uncertainty. Members generally like the comfort of the known and the established patterns of acceptable behaviours within the firm. The angst created by rapid change can overshadow the efforts needed to implement any new strategic plans. Thus, great care should be exercised in making changes to an organization's culture driven by strategies, and it should be done slowly so that members have time to absorb the change and adapt.

Case study

Steven Davis was quietly stunned at the behaviour of the employees—both managers and staff—throughout the entire company. He had been hired as the new General Manager and today marked the start of his fourth month in the position. Davis was stunned because he learned that none of the employees were used to making decisions and were clearly not comfortable doing so. He found himself GM of a resort with mangers who were order-takers but not thinkers or risk takers.

Reston Hotel and Resort is a premier property located in Hilton Head, SC. As an upscale resort, the majority of their customers are economically and socially in the upper stratus of American society. The hotel had been open and operating for slightly more than 30 years. Robert "Bert" Tanner, whose family originally helped build the town of Hilton Head, founded the company fresh out of high school using some family oceanfront land as collateral for a loan to build the hotel. With a careful mix of salesmanship, support from his family, and an eye for product quality and consistency, Bert had developed his 250-room resort into one with sales exceeding $400 million annually and employed more than 420 people.

Bert Tanner had been diagnosed with Parkinson's disease about 8 years ago. The first 5 years after he learned the news had been rather uneventful in terms of his health and he had been able to run the resort with his usual vim and vigour. Bert ran a tight ship and made all of the decisions. He was deeply involved in everything: no detail, or project, or advertisement was too unimportant for him. Some employees used the phrase "ruled with an iron fist" to describe his leadership style. However, all loved him dearly and believed passionately in his vision and ability to lead the company. For these workers, Bert *is* the company.

But the past 3 years had become very difficult for Bert. The disease had taken its toll on him physically and he simply could not do as much work as he had been used to doing. However, Bert was not a person to willingly let go of his "baby." He had built the resort from scratch by himself and he was not interested in finding a successor. For Bert, hiring a successor was tantamount to resigning. The hotel was his life and he had no desire to leave. In fact, he had named the resort in honour of his mother (Reston is her maiden name), demonstrating how emotionally invested he is in the company.

Eighteen months ago Bert stopped coming into the office every day. At first he tried to work daily for 4+ hours, but that proved to be too taxing. After a few weeks of that, he changed to coming in two or three times a week, staying for no more than 1 to 2 hours at a time. Bert had not shared authority with any of his managers so he still needed to review and approve projects, spending decisions, sign cheques, etc. The paperwork kept building up but Bert was not able to handle it all in a timely manner. As a result, the business generally slowed down. Workers sometimes waited weeks for a decision to proceed. Although deeply concerned about the health of the business, the employees were so deeply attached to Bert, so enamoured by his charisma, that none were willing to confront Bert with the situation and ask for a new leader.

Finally the day arrived that Bert simply could not get to the office. The board of directors held a meeting with him at his home and Bert finally acknowledged that he was not able to run the resort anymore and they should seek a new GM. While there was relief among the board members that this difficult step had been taken, they now faced an even more daunting challenge: how to find a new leader.

Given that Bert was such a forceful leader, his board of directors was basically a sounding board and rubber stamp agent. The members knew they had been invited to the board to provide gentle advice—and strong disagreements with Bert were not desired. Thus, the board members were not used to "taking charge" and had no process for working among themselves without Bert.

The search took the board about 8 months to complete. The first 3 months were wasted while the board members cautiously jockeyed for position. None were willing to be seen quickly stepping into the leadership for fear of being accused of pushing Bert out of the company. Finally, a search committee was formed and given the charge to find a new GM. The search committee interviewed a number of executive headhunting firms and finally selected one to undertake the task.

Out of that cumbersome search process emerged Steven Davis. Steven had learned about the resort's history during the interview process and certainly had everything he had heard about Bert confirmed by the employees he spoke with while visiting the property. With 25 years of experience in lodging management and having led two other mid-sized resort hotel complexes in another part of the country, Steven's experience appeared to make him a good fit with Reston Hotel and Resort.

The first 3 months on the job were hectic, as Steven needed to complete two key tasks at once. First, he had to learn about the resort's operations in detail so that he could make informed decisions. That took quite a bit of time and a number of detailed conversations with various people throughout the property. Second, he had to handle the backlog of decisions that were desperately needed in a number of departments. The second task was very difficult, as he had not yet completed the first task of learning the operations thoroughly. It was a delicate balancing act made especially difficult since none of the managers were comfortable with making recommendations or with handling lower level issues. Everyone waited for Steven to give them directions and to make decisions.

Steven's dilemma, then, was how to transform the organizational culture from one that idolized the founder who had centralized all decision-making into a hotel that encouraged a sharing of the responsibility and authority needed to operate the well-established business. From what Steven could assess, the resort continued to be profitable merely because of a long-standing reputation in the resort community and not because of any particular new business or general increase in demand. It made him realize that the resort could be much more efficiently lead if all decisions did not have to flow through his office. With that improved efficiency resources could then be used to increase sales and grow the business. The question for Steven then was what to do to change the culture so that these deeply entrenched, long-standing employees became willing to "take charge" without damaging the reputation, admiration, and success of Bert Tanner so that the resort would continue to be a success under his leadership.

Questions for discussion

1. Who should Steven Davis include in his efforts to transform the resort's internal culture? Why? Who should he exclude initially? Why?
2. What are some of the terms or phrases Steven should use when discussing this with the employees? Should he prepare different approaches for managers than that of the non-management staff?
3. Steven decided he needed a plan of action to make this change. Develop a conceptual action plan for him. Remember to include a timeline and benchmarks for measuring progress.

References

Adler, P. S. (1999). Building better bureaucracies. *Academy of Management Executive*, *13*(4), 36.

Alexander, L. (1985). Successfully implementing strategic decisions. *Long Range Planning*, *18*(3), 91–97.

Bartlett, C. A., and Ghoshal, S. (1990). Matrix management: Not a structure, a frame of mind. *Harvard Business Review*, *68*(4), 45.

Beckhard, R., and Pritchard, W. (1992). *Changing the Essence*. San Francisco, CA: Jossey-Bass.

Bridges, W. (1991). *Managing Transitions: Making the Most of Change*. Reading, MA: Addison-Wesley Publishing Company.

Bryan, L., and Joyce, C. (2005). The 21st century organization. *McKinsey Quarterly*, *3*, 24–33.

Deal, T., and Kennedy, A. (1982). *Corporate Cultures: The Rites and Rituals of Corporate Life*. Reading, MA: Addison-Wesley Publishing Company, Inc.

Doz, Y., and Prahalad, C. K. (1988). A process model of strategic redirection in large complex firms: The case of multinational corporations. In A. M. Pettigrew (Ed.), *In the Management of Strategic Change*. Oxford: Basil Blackwell.

Galbraith, J. R., Downey, D., and Kates, A. (2002). *Designing Dynamic Organizations*. New York: AMACOM.

Jick, T. D. (1993). *Implementing Change. Managing Change: Cases and Concepts*. Boston, MA: Irwin. p. 200

Kilmann, R., Saxton, M., Serpa, R. *et al.* (1985). *Gaining Control of the Corporate Culture*. San Francisco, CA: Jossey-Bass Publishers, Inc.

Kotter, J. P., and Cohen, D. S. (2002). *The Heart of Change: Real Life Stories About How People Change their Organizations*. Cambridge, MA: Harvard Business School Press.

Leavitt, H. (2003). Why hierarchies thrive. *Harvard Business Review, 81*(3), 96–102.

Lewin, K. (1947). Frontiers in group dynamics. *Human Relations, 1*(1), 5–41.

Nadler, D., and Tushman, M. (1997). *Competing by Design*. New York: Oxford University Press.

Olson, E. E., and Eoyang, G. H. (2001). *Facilitating Organization Change: Lessons from Complexity Science*. San Francisco, CA: Jossey-Bass/Pfeifer.

Sy, T., and D'Annunzio, L. (2005). Challenges and strategies of matrix organizations: Top-level and mid-level managers. *Human Resource Planning, 28*(1), 39–48.

CHAPTER 17

Measuring co-alignment

Marcia H. Taylor[1] and
Michael D. Olsen[2]

[1] East Carolina University
[2] Virginia Polytechnic Institute
and State University

Introduction

Traditionally, understanding how firms can outperform their competitors was the focus of researchers in the field of strategic management (Barney, 1991; Porter, 1980, 1985). Conversely, in today's dynamic and uncertain environment, strategy is about achieving sustainable competitive advantage (Olsen *et al.*, 1998). Moreover, what the literature does not offer is a comprehensive business model, developed empirically, that offers managers a blueprint to accomplishing sustainable competitive advantage. Instead, the literature offers a number of schools of thought about strategy, but little in the way of a comprehensive model (Mintzberg *et al.*, 1998). This paper attempts to address this situation using the co-alignment theory of strategy as the underpinning to this effort.

The concept of fit or alignment has been offered by scholars as a way of achieving sustainability. Researchers such as Fuchs *et al.* (2000), Powell (1992), and Olsen *et al.* (1998) view the alignment between the environment of the firm, strategy choice, firm structure, and firm performance as the primary approach to sustainability. Their conclusions resulted from a variety of research approaches across different contexts, often testing the financial consequences of organizational alignment in concert with the effects of industry market share, generic strategy, and strategic membership group.

The co-alignment theory suggests that, to gain competitive advantage, firms must identify the opportunities in the forces driving change in their environment. Firms should invest in competitive methods that take advantage of these opportunities, and allocate resources and capabilities to the competitive methods that have the ability to create the greatest value and the financial returns desired by owners and investors (Olsen *et al.*, 1998). According to Olsen *et al.* (1998), because of the complexity and the dynamism of the hotel industry's environment, the competitive methods utilized must reflect the environmental forces present. These competitive methods are value-adding dimensions of the firm's overall strategy (Olsen *et al.*, 1998).

In trying to conduct research relative to the entire co-alignment theory, the researcher is faced with many challenges. First, strategy is a dynamic process that involves decision making by executives who are subject to both objective and emotional dimensions in guiding firms forward. In addition, firms are subject to contextual forces, both internal and external, which can change the strategic direction of the business on short notice. Thus, research into the relationships among all four constructs must reflect these conditions often ruling out the use of coarse-grained, cross-sectional, and quantitative methodologies. The researcher really must enter into the domain of the firm and study it in depth in order to understand the complexities and nuances of the situation and do so ideally over a longitudinal basis. This necessitates qualitative, interpretive research methods.

In addressing these theoretical and methodological needs, this paper reports the result of a multiple case study of five hotels testing the application of the co-alignment theory in the context of the Jamaican hotel industry. The purpose of this study was to understand the types of competitive methods used by independently owned (non-chain affiliated) hotels in Jamaica, in their bid to obtain and sustain competitive advantage, and to test whether there was co-alignment with the environment, strategy choice, and firm structure, leading to improved firm performance. Measures were also developed to actually estimate the degree of co-alignment among the firms in the research study.

Literature review

The co-alignment approach is not new to strategic management research. In fact, it predated the positioning approach, which dominated the 1980s (Powell, 1992). Since then, the main foci of strategy research over the past two decades are the positioning concept, which is market oriented (Porter, 1980, 1985) and centres on the external positioning of the firm against its competitors, and the resource-based view (RBV), which is operational (Barney, 1991) and focuses on the execution of the strategy (Fuchs et al., 2000). Although the desired end result for firms adopting one or both concepts is to gain competitive advantage, according to Fuchs et al. (2000), both views developed independently of each other.

Fuchs et al. (2000), Olsen et al. (1998), and Powell (1992) have attempted to address the gap between the external (marketing and positioning) and internal RBV theories on sustained competitive advantage in the literature by showing how alignments within certain elements in the organization can be a source of sustainable competitive advantage. The alignment to be achieved comes from matching the forces driving change in the environment; the strategy choices made by the enterprise, firm structure (how it allocates resources), and firm performance (Figure 17.1).

Olsen et al. (1998) applied the co-alignment theory to the context of the hospitality industry. They developed a co-alignment

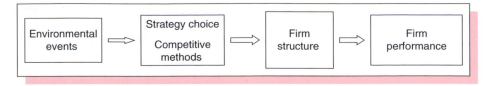

Figure 17.1
The co-alignment principle.

model that demonstrated the importance of the alignment with all elements of the strategic management concept. In addressing the importance of the co-alignment theory, Olsen *et al.* (1998) suggested that for organizations to be successful, they must marry their competitive methods or company's strategy with the opportunities and threats created by the forces driving change and allocate resources accordingly.

As the model suggests, the first construct is the environment of the firm. This environment is generally grouped into two categories—the remote and the task environments. The manager is expected to develop an environment scanning system to gather information about what the firm should be investing in to take advantage of the opportunities presented by these forces and avoid threats that may be posed.

The strategy choice construct refers to the competitive methods firms invest in to achieve their objective, and the choices made are based on environmental scanning activities. Also, the competitive methods chosen are the ones that generate the highest levels of cash flow for the firm (Olsen *et al.*, 1998). According to Olsen *et al.* (1998), in the hospitality industry, competitive methods are made up of portfolios of products and services designed to bring the unique resources and capabilities (core competencies) of the firm together in order to achieve competitive advantage.

The term "firm structure" in the co-alignment model refers to the ability of the firm to effectively implement its strategy. Olsen *et al.* (1998) define strategy implementation as the "the process of allocating resources on a consistent basis to the products and services that produce the highest levels of cash flow to equity and will continue to do so well into the future" (p. 206). They also suggest that before resources can be allocated, an internal analysis must be done to identify the core competencies of the firm (this is consistent with the RBV of the firm).

Firm performance is measured by both financial and behavioural measures. The assumption is that an evaluation of the firm's performance will reflect the most valuable competitive methods. Snow and Hambrick (1980) suggest that the performance of a firm may vary according to whose viewpoint is taken, the time period observed, and the criteria used. However, it is generally agreed that cash measures are better predictors of success in hotels (Murthy, 1994). Using cash measures can depict the added value provided by each competitive method to the firm's total cash flow.

The most comprehensive studies on the co-alignment theory in the hospitality industry were published by the International Hotel and Restaurant Association in 1995 and 2000 (Olsen, 1997; Olsen and Zhao, 2000). The White Papers reported the competitive methods utilized by multinational hotel companies over two periods of time during the 1990s. They were based on secondary research and were industry-wide studies addressing generic forces driving change and firm responses to these forces. The key events in the environment were examined, the competitive methods employed identified, and their performance analysed (Olsen, 1997). Using secondary data, Olsen (1997) was able to identify the forces driving change and analysed how firms reacted to the changes and their subsequent financial performance. While inferences were made with respect to co-alignment, no actual measures of this construct were utilized.

Given the supportive evidence to date in favour of co-alignment, in both the hospitality literature and the general literature on strategy, this study set out to address the following guiding proposition:

Firms that achieve greater alignment between competitive methods and firm structure, contingent on the objective of the owners, perform better than those that did not.

Three constructs of co-alignment were used to test this proposition—strategy choice, firm structure, and firm performance. The first construct of the co-alignment theory—the environment—was taken into consideration. The assumption was made that because Jamaica is an island nation, hotels are subject to similar environmental forces emanating from the remote and task environments of the firm, and should therefore be held constant. Holding the environment constant suggested that the same forces in the remote and task environment affected all the hotels equally.

Methodology

Five independently owned and operated resorts in five different tourist resort locations in Jamaica were used as a part of a case study to investigate a way to measure alignment. The idea was to test whether the co-alignment model applied to different types of operations. Because of the lack of information that would allow for the isolation of the cash flow streams associated with each competitive method, matrices were used to measure the degree of co-alignment between the resort's competitive methods and the core competencies.

Data collection

At each resort, the general manager/managing director was interviewed along with other key managers (food and beverage director, rooms division manager, human resources manager, marketing and sales director, and the financial controller). The same questions were asked at each interview. Each interview was supplemented by direct observations of managers and employees at work and their actions and reactions in regards to the implementation of the competitive methods.

Surveys were administered to current guests to capture how the guests viewed the resort and their perception of the competitive methods employed (Table 17.1). Specific questions on the resort's competitive methods were developed based on the answers received from management during the interviews. Information collected from secondary data was also used to verify information collected from the interviews.

Matrices

To test the degree of co-alignment between the resorts' competitive methods and core competencies, information collected at interviews, direct observations, secondary data, and comments listed on the guests' surveys were entered into matrices to show the relationships and assess the alignment. Each entry into each cell reflected whether or not the evidence gathered in the research process demonstrated alignment. If the evidence was present, it was assigned a point value of 1, and each cell had the potential of four points (one point for supportive evidence found in each of the following: for appearing in the interviews, secondary data, guest survey comments, and direct observations). Points received were divided by the total possibilities (Table 17.2 for an example of the matrix used) in each matrix as determined by the list of competitive methods and core competencies identified for each hotel. If a hotel was in perfect alignment it would have four points in each cell, one from each source of information. The total points possible in each cell were then divided into

Table 17.1 Constructs, Propositions, and Research Questions on Co-Alignment

Proposition	Constructs	Sub-Proposition	Questions
Firms that achieve greater alignment between competitive methods and firm structure, contingent on the objective of the owners, performed better than those that did not.	Strategy choice	The forces driving change in a firm's industry determine the strategy choice/ competitive methods.	1. How are competitive methods chosen? 2. What competitive methods are used to gain competitive advantage? 3. What is the relationship between the strategy choice, firm structure, and firm performance?
	Firm structure	Firms that are in alignment should allocate resources to the implementation and development of core competencies that support the competitive methods chosen.	4. What investments are made to best utilize the competitive methods? 5. What resources, human or material, are allocated to the competitive methods? 6. How are the resources aligned so that there is no compromise in achieving the mission of the hotel? 7. What core competencies are identified? 8. How do the contextual and process variables affect implementation and expectation of the competitive methods?
	Firm performance	Firms that are in alignment with the environment, strategy choice, and firm structure should find a higher level of performance.	9. How does management evaluate investment decisions that support the competitive methods? 10. How is the success of the competitive methods measured? 11. What cash flow is generated from each competitive method? 12. What return on invested capital is utilized by the hotel? 13. How do guests, relative to the competitive methods employed, perceive the hotel?

Table 17.2 Example of Competitive Methods and Core Competencies Matrix

Core Competencies	Competitive Methods		
	"Green Hotel"	Physical Product	Quality Service
Guest comment cards	*Used to improve or correct greening policy. (1)[b]*	*Comments or recommendations are used to improve the physical structure and landscape. (1)[b]*	Ratings for each department are circulated each month. Positive and negative comments are discussed in department meetings and used as tools for training. (1)
Information technology	*Incorporated in the system. (1)[a]*	*Facilities are wired for easy access in all areas. (1)[a]*	Used effectively for repeat guest history, preferences, and other features that help to recognize the repeat guest. (1)
Training and development	Training is continuous for all employees in recycling, reusing, and reducing. *There is a monthly EMS training in each department. (2)[b]*	*Maintenance and grounds training are similar to the staff members who have direct contact with the guests. (1)[b]*	There are three levels of training: new employees, line staff, and supervisory and management staff. The objective is to manage the customer service process, both internally and externally. *Monthly training for all employees in the delivery of customer service.[b]* *Highly motivated and competent staff. (3)[c]*

[a] Observation.
[b] Secondary data.
[c] Guests' comments.

the points earned in each cell to obtain a percentage of total possible. A score of 100% would indicate perfect alignment.

Prior to this attempt to assess alignment between strategy choice and structure, little was revealed in the literature as to what percentage of alignment would be necessary to support the proposition that firms would perform better if they were properly aligned. The process of using four separate sources of evidence with respect to the alignment between competitive methods and core competencies provided content validity and placed a rigorous standard on the measurement of alignment.

Measuring co-alignment in hotels

Measuring co-alignment in hotels involves collecting information from internal sources, external sources, and guests. The following method can be used to determine alignment between the firm's core competencies and the competitive methods that have been implemented.

To measure co-alignment, the following steps are suggested:

Internally, collect the following information that the company uses to market to its employees, its customers, and other stakeholders.

1. Mission of the company—does the mission reflect your goals?
2. Strategic plan
3. Employee manual
4. Training material
5. Brochures
6. News letter
7. Advertisement
   a. TV
   b. Newspapers
   c. Magazines
   d. Internet
8. Outcomes of internal self-studies, that is, balanced scorecard, six sigma, and process reengineering
9. Websites
10. Supervisory observations
11. Quality control systems
12. Intranets
13. Job descriptions
14. Performance evaluation systems
15. Decision-making processes
16. Compensation systems
17. Budgets and the budgeting process

18. Annual reports
19. Minutes of management meetings
20. Production systems

The purpose of this exercise is to verify that the messages you are sending to all stakeholders are in line with your competitive methods and that you are allocating resources to the competitive method that has the greatest value to the company.

Externally, collect the following information that is available in the media (secondary information) about the company:

1. Travel writers' articles
2. News articles
3. Internet blogs
4. Assessments by third parties such as TripAdvisor.com and J. D. Powers and Associates
5. Entries on Utube or MySpace
6. Customer guides like Michelin, Mobil, and AAA

Identify what others are saying about your company and how the company is perceived by the media. Is it in line with the competitive methods?

The guests will always give feedback on their stay. Collect information from the following sources:

1. Comment cards
2. Guest complaint logs
3. Guest surveys (if available)

What do the guests identify as value to them? Are they the same as your competitive methods? The guests should identify the same values that you are selling to them. The comment cards will reflect what they liked best and where their expectations were not met. Guest complaint logs will identify where you have the greatest challenges and where you should allocate your resources.

After collecting the above information, use a matrix to show the relationships and assess the alignment (Table 17.2). In the first column, list the core competencies of the firm and on the first row list the firm's competitive methods. The next step is to match each item of information with the (horizontally) core competency identified and with the (vertically) competitive methods, by entering the information in the matrix cell. Assign a value of 1 to each entry. Each cell has a potential of one point for each item of information used in the analysis, from the internal information, the external information, and the guests. The final step is to add the points in each cell and divide by the total possibilities. The total will identify the percentage of alignment. A score of 100% will indicate perfect alignment.

Table 17.1 shows an example of the co-alignment between the core competencies at one resort. In this matrix, the total possible score equalled 36 points (nine cells by four reflecting all the sources used in this example) and the total score earned was 12. The percentage of alignment was 33.3%, signifying a small degree of alignment between the core competencies and the competitive methods.

The steps outlined above are designed to assist managers in testing for co-alignment between the firm's competitive methods (strategies) and the core competencies. The matrix will identify where there is alignment within the company and whether the resources allocated are adding value. It will also identify the areas where resources need to be allocated.

This method to test for alignment requires managers to be cognizant of what they are telling their employees, what message are they sending about the company, and how others perceive them. It will also tell managers whether what they perceive as value is in fact perceived as value to their guests through the impact of guest comments.

Conclusion

Using five resorts to test alignment revealed several important issues to be addressed by the management in a competitive environment:

1. Scanning is a concept that has limited scope in the managers' conceptual skills portfolio. The only evidence of scanning was the focus on the competition, although no consistency was found, and the customers, through the use of comment cards.
2. Even in the best-performing firms, the degree of alignment is low—37%. This confirmed the complexity of hospitality enterprises that provide hundreds of products and services that can be and are often combined in unique ways. It also demonstrates that reaching perfect alignment is a rather significant accomplishment, and maintaining it is perhaps nearly impossible. Thus the low performance by Resorts A, B, and C suggests that managers can be modest in their objectives regarding alignment, while keeping in mind the longitudinal aspect of keeping things in alignment.

3. In resorts A, B, and C where some alignment was found, only basic accounting systems are used which do not allow for the tracking of investments made in competitive methods. Managers, therefore, can only use "gut instincts" on what create value and is not capable of explaining why the alignment was reached.

4. Managers have little understanding of the evaluation process with respect to investments in competitive methods. Therefore, they rely on accounting data which do not give immediate feedback.

Recommendations

Because of the lack of recorded information that would validate alignment, based on the investment of resources, matrices were developed as a method to measure alignment. Using the information gathered from management, observations, guests, and secondary sources, it was possible to test alignment between the competitive methods, as stated by management, and competitive methods, as recognized through the different sources investigated. The matrices were used to measure the alignment and confirmed the relationship between co-alignment and performance. However, the case studies suggest that much still needs to be done to improve upon the achievement of co-alignment within hospitality establishments.

The following recommendations for managers within hospitality establishments are drawn from the study of the five resorts:

1. Managers who wish to gain sustainable competitive advantage cannot rely on conventional wisdom when making decisions on strategic choice and the allocation of resources, but should instead strive to examine environmental trends that have the potential of positively affecting their establishment.

2. Given that reaching perfect alignment is a significant accomplishment, although difficult to achieve, managers must constantly monitor their performance by ensuring that their competitive methods are visible to guests and observers, and must be at the forefront of their decision to invest their resources.

3. To ensure the creation of business value by the competitive methods, the use of discounted cash flow methods should be used as the dominant metric for assessing value. This would allow for a more accurate measurement using operating statistics.

Using the matrix approach will assist managers in identifying alignment between core competencies and competitive methods.

References

Barney, J. B. (1991). Firm resources and sustained competitive advantage. *Journal of Management, 17*(1), 99–120.

Fuchs, P. H., Mifflin, K. E., Miller, D., and Whitney, J. O. (2000). Strategic integration: Competing in the age of capabilities. *California Management Review, 42*(30), 118–147.

Mintzberg, H., Ahlstrand, B., and Lampel, J. (1998). *Strategy Safari*. New York, NY: The Free Press.

Murthy, B. (1994). *Measurement of the Strategy Construct in the Lodging Industry, and the Strategy Performance Relationship*. Unpublished Dissertation, Virginia Polytechnic Institute and State University, Blacksburg, VA.

Olsen, M. D. (1997). *Hotel Industry Performance and Competitive Methods: A Decade in Review, 1985–1994*. Paris, France: International Hotel and Restaurant Association. pp. 27–49

Olsen, M. D., Tse, E. C., and West, J. J. (1998). *Strategic Management in the Hospitality Industry* (2nd ed.). New York, NY: Wiley.

Olsen, M. D., and Zhao, J. L. (2000). *Competitive Methods of Multinational Hotel Companies—a Five Year Review, 1995–99*. Paris, France: International Hotel and Restaurant Association. pp. 31–45

Powell, T. C. (1992). Organizational alignment as competitive advantage. *Strategic Management Journal, 13*, 119–134.

Porter, M. (1985). *Competitive Advantage: Creating and Sustaining Superior Performance*. New York, NY: The Free Press.

Porter, M. E. (1980). *Competitive Strategy: Techniques for Analyzing Industries and Competitors*. New York, NY: The Free Press.

Snow, C. C., and Hambrick, L. G. (1980). Measuring organizational strategies: Some theoretical and methodological problems. *Academy of Management Review, 5*(4), 527–528.

Part Six

Implementation

Innovation and strategy implementation: the key challenge in today's competitive atmosphere

Sander Allegro[1] and Rob de Graaf[2]

[1]*Hotelschool The Hague, The Netherlands*
[2]*University of Groningen, The Netherlands*

Introduction

Innovation has taken the modern business world by storm. Any self respecting firm will stress its importance in their mission statement, vision, and other strategy document. In today's volatile business world, innovation is often seen as inevitable; if we do not change our products or services, the way we produce them and deliver them, we will not be able to survive! The hospitality industry does not have a great reputation in the field of innovation. Its conservative nature combined with its capital-intensive structure that requires payback horizons of over 25 years has not been driving innovation.

Most innovation in the hospitality industry has been introduced by outsiders. Individuals who looked at the industry with an outsider's perspective and were not hindered by reigning paradigms.

In this chapter we will look into three innovation concepts that help make the right decisions around innovation: scenario thinking, the innovator's dilemma, and the development of new services. These concepts have been used in industry for many years and have increased product and service sales and profits. They are applicable to the hospitality industry as well.

We will also present a case study of Qbic hotels, a truly innovative concept that was introduced in the European hotel market.

Relevant innovation and strategy concepts

Introducing strategic innovations into practice has long been the subject of study in literature. Many concepts have been published to improve the so called "hairy back end" of innovation, the part after the project is executed and needs to be introduced to the market and the organization, as reviewed by Hultink *et al.* (1997).

However, in the hospitality industry the problem may not only be in the area of the hairy back end but in the entire innovation process or the lack of it. Especially more comprehensive or radical innovations are scarce in the hospitality industry, according to Dialogic (2005).

Many organizations in the hospitality industry are very busy with daily operations, and only very few have distinguishable processes or departments for innovation of the services they offer. When innovations are introduced into the market it is either by large organizations such as hotel chains or by new entrants which have a completely new business model, such as *easyHotel*.

easyHotel

easyHotel is part of the easyGroup of companies based in London which also includes the leading European low cost airline, easyJet. easyHotel opened its first hotel in London in August 2005 and a second one in Switzerland in September 2005. It offers short-stay travellers a safe and quality option at around £40 a night in central London, about half the price of other branded budget hotels. Designed for city centres, it offers consumers a recognized brand that delivers a standardized high quality product and banks on customers accepting small (60 square feet!), no-frills, and simply furnished rooms. All easyHotel bookings are taken by credit card through the easyHotel.com website.

The rest of the market will only embark on innovation when there is no other choice to maintain in business (e.g., internet reservations) or buy innovative solutions from suppliers, which usually focus on improving efficiency and effectiveness (Dialogic, 2005). Most lack the vision on how the future looks and how they can best position themselves in it.

In case this vision is present, the timing of the introduction of the innovation is hard to determine and therefore innovations miss their window or effect. And in case vision and timing are well defined, the innovation does not get to market quickly enough or at all because no processes are used to execute the innovation project and introduction.

To address this issue three mayor innovation theories are used in to review their application to the hospitality industry:

- Scenario thinking by Van der Heijden (2005)
- The innovator's dilemma by Christensen (2006)
- New service development by Johnson *et al.* (2000)

These three theories are chosen because they address the problems stated from different angles: scenario thinking from the point of the future environment, the innovator's dilemma from the point of technological innovation, and new service development from the point of the process. Combining these three perspectives provides a broad and powerful set of tools which enable managers in hospitality to see opportunities for innovation, know when they should embark on an innovation journey, and finally provides insight in how the innovation process should be addressed and executed.

Furthermore, these theories are all built from analysing the daily practice of innovation. Many cases have been studied as input for these theories and they are continuously being deployed and validated in practice. Every sector has its own preference, e.g., scenario thinking is used widely in the energy business; the innovators dilemma is popular in electronics, and structured innovation processes are common in software and financial industries. Applying the theories to hospitality industry is relatively new; it is interesting to see how they can be applied to implement innovation and strategy.

First each of the theories is described briefly in this section, and then the next section applies the theories to an innovative new offering in the hospitality world: *Qbic hotels*. In this section each of the theories will be reviewed along the following items:

- Definition
- Process
- Focus
- Insight
- Result
- Value for hospitality industry

Scenario thinking

Definition • • •

Scenarios are possible futures. In scenario thinking, the scenarios differ quite strongly to show that the future may have various faces. The scenarios are built along identified uncertainties in the market and society that impact the business substantially. Scenarios are not the result of extrapolated trends or actions, but truly independent. Scenarios focus on creating insight in future circumstances in which the ambition of an organization should be realized.

Process • • •

The process by Van der Heijden is very structured. First focus is placed on the present and past situation of the organization. In this step an analysis of its current issues and determined whether they are intrinsic or extrinsic to the organization. Then the focus is put on the external issues, taking in opportunities and threats of the environment and market of the organization.

Next the ambition or goals of the organization are defined. Amazingly, many organizations struggle with this step. A time period is set at which these goals need to be complied with (anywhere from a few years up to half a century).

Based on the goals and their timeframe, issues, opportunities, and threats are reviewed once more. Those that have a high uncertainty with regards to where they may end up at the set time are selected. Then these are analysed to determine the impact on the core question. Usually the two uncertainties with highest impact on the goals set are chosen to draw up a scenario space. Examples frequently used in practice are economic prosperity and fierceness of competition.

Then scenarios are developed, first in general terms as in the example of Figure 18.1, then in more detail providing a story about the scenarios, sketching the key developments, positioning of actors, and the impact on the goals that are set.

Now the scenarios are developed, ideas on how to reach the goals set can be developed. This can either be done looking back from each of the scenarios to the present situation of the organization, or by plain brainstorming about how the goals defined can be reached. These ideas are developed into various options the organization can choose from.

Options that are robust, help in realizing the goals in at least 50% of the scenarios and in the remaining 50% they should not have a negative impact, so be at least neutral. To make options more robust, combinations of options are often needed. Eventually the robust options can be translated into innovation plans for the organization. Of course the feasibility of these options or innovation plans needs to be carefully assessed. Those that are most feasible are chosen as a strategy for the company.

Finally, a monitoring system is defined to assess where the defined uncertainties may be going over time. Themes are

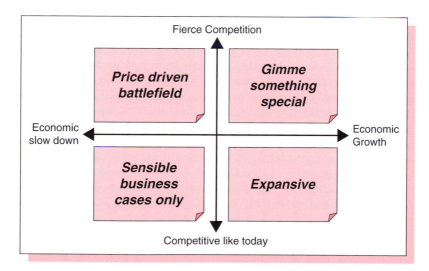

Figure 18.1
Example uncertainties and scenarios.

identified which are being reviewed frequently to see how the future is getting shape. Strategies based on robust options should be able to adapt to the developments in the market and the larger environment or context of the organization.

Focus • • •

Scenarios focus an organization on the future. They do not foretell what is going to happen, but provide different types of futures that an organization should be prepared for. This provides the context in which innovative ideas (options) can be evaluated and ensures that only robust options are developed. This way the scarce resources for innovation, which are even scarcer in the hospitality world, can be put to work on innovations that will be successful in future.

Insight • • •

Scenario thinking provides insight in the future circumstances and into which options for new services to pursue. Scenario thinking is essentially a management tool to assess innovation need and opportunities. Also the option of just doing what we always did can be evaluated. This may result in being a non-robust option, which means a more innovative strategy to providing hospitality is needed.

Result • • •

The result of a scenario thinking exercise is better a vision of the future. Strategies on how to be successful in the future are developed, tested and improved to become robust. Essentially an organization is better prepared to deal with future circumstances and knows which developments to monitor closely.

Value for hospitality industry • • •

The hospitality industry is quite vulnerable to changes in environmental and the market factors, such as the economy, new competitors in its market, and availability of good staff. If a hotel for instance is able to attract guests, employees, etc. even in low times, the chances for success are much higher. Better insight in the kind of opportunities in the future helps in defining what kind of innovations are needed and if they really contribute to the long-term goals of the hotel.

Innovator's dilemma

Definition • • •

The innovator's dilemma is essentially the choice of doing small stepwise innovations (typical for successful incumbents) or deciding that a jump to a radically new idea, technology, concept, etc. is needed (typical for successful new entrants). The innovator's dilemma is especially of interest when new technologies emerge which enable product or service delivery in a different way, but can also be used for new concepts like the one presented in the case study in this chapter.

Process • • •

Performances of various technologies and concepts change over time. When faced with the question if a certain technology or concept should be developed further or that resources should rather be put towards new technologies concepts is the essence of Christensen's theory.

To find out if a certain technology or concept is still viable for further development, its maturity should be reviewed. Mature technologies or concepts develop relatively slowly, where new ones have the potential to outperform the existing ones over time. If the performance of a product or service can radically improve in terms of value for money, the technology or concept below it may be a disruptive one. Figure 18.2 illustrates the disruption (Christensen, 2006).

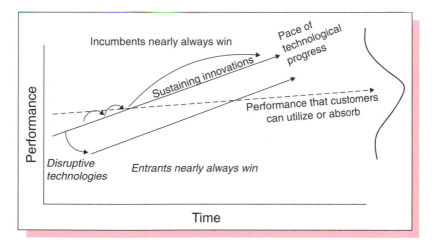

Figure 18.2
Absorption of disruptive technologies.

A good example is how EasyJet and other low cost carriers found their way to the traveller through a new medium: internet. Business processes could radically be redesigned and automated, thus delivering the same value (flight from A to B in economy class) for much less money. Here the internet can be seen as a successful disruptive technology where new entrants are more successful than their incumbent competitors. Market share was lost by the incumbents, but more importantly a new market was addressed, providing flights at such low prices that they were attainable for almost everyone.

Analysis of current and rival technologies to determine their maturity and growth potential is the key process of dealing with the innovator's dilemma. Henderson (Journal of Product Innovation Management, 2006; 23: 5–11) argues that the competencies for being able to identify possibly disruptive technologies (or concepts) and to define appropriate responses to it are scarce and hard to develop when at an incumbent.

Keeping an open mind towards the market and underlying factors, such as technology, is a good start. Quarterly scans of market developments are now being carried out at some incumbents to be able to see changes coming. Educational programmes are adapted to suit these new needs, and consultants are often hired to help out. Most important factor to analyse is the fact how customers can see their needs fulfilled by a certain proposition, which Christensen calls absorption.

Focus • • •

The innovator's dilemma is all about timing. For incumbents this means when to move to a new concept and not to further develop the existing one. Business processes need to be redesigned and take more time than a new design from scratch. However, missing the disruption may cause strong falls in revenues and profits. For new entrants it is a great opportunity as incumbents usually need more time to adopt a new technology. They should however be aware that introducing a new technology or concept too early, will not deliver the required value for money. So timing is key for both.

Insight • • •

The innovator's dilemma provides insight in how new technologies or concepts can change the way we (need to) do business. Being aware what kind of role you have (incumbent or entrant) and how your business processes may be affected, provides a competitive advantage to competitors.

Result ● ● ●

If the innovator's dilemma is managed well, timing certain radical(ly needed) innovations will be improved. Business processes can be adapted in a timely and controlled manner when incumbent and success for new entrants in the market will be higher. Even the boundaries to enter the market can be lowered or fade away completely if disruptive technologies take hold of the market.

Value for hospitality industry ● ● ●

The hospitality industry is known for its lower levels of innovation. Exaggerating, refurbishment is the most radical innovation done. Usually the concept is not really changed. Therefore the industry is vulnerable to new entrants which have a good timing in moving to new technologies or concepts to deliver value to their guest. Young entrepreneurs can this way really enter when their timing is right and take part of the market by surprise. Developing skills to identify possibly disruptive technologies and concepts may support incumbents to embark on more radical innovation.

New service development

Definition ● ● ●

The process of developing new to the organization services, with four phases:

1. Design (of the concept behind the service)
2. Analysis (of the business viability)
3. Development (of the service derived from the concept)
4. Full launch (of the appropriately tested service)

This process is based on the model by Johnson *et al.* (2000), which was refined by Brackel (2006) as illustrated in Figure 18.3.

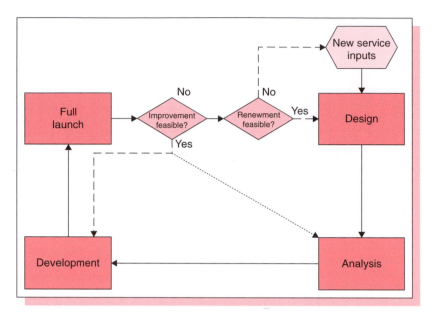

Figure 18.3
New service development flow.

Process • • •

This full process of new service development is adaptable for incremental and radical innovations.

- Incremental innovations are usually executed in the left side of the model above. Launched services are evaluated if they have improvement potential and changes are then implemented through a light weight development process. Sometimes there is a formal analysis of the improvement in case it cannot be done along with the current operational tasks and assigning of resources is necessary.
- For more radical innovations (new services) the design and analysis phases must be executed. If the same approach for incremental innovations is used, the new service can only be successful by chance or luck. The issue here is that concepts for the new service need to be developed first, then compared and possibly combined, and then tested to enable a sensible analysis process. In many service organizations, the left side of the model can be identified, the right side is usually absent, which means that the organization is somehow stuck with the incremental innovations.

All phases are worked out in detail in the work by Brackel (2006). As the focus of this chapter is on the more innovative side of this model, the design phase is illustrated below.

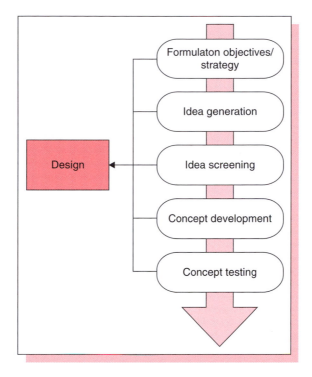

First the outset of a good strategy is needed. This is a major issue in many service organizations, due to their strong operational focus. Scenario thinking as illustrated before may be very helpful in defining a robust strategy. When generating ideas, disruptive technologies and concepts need to be considered. In screening the scenarios can be used again, this time to assess the robustness of the generated ideas. Here combining ideas brings a lot of value. Then, one or more concepts need to be developed. This means the first detailing of the new service starts, and that also the operational processes to provide the service are being designed. Finally, in concept testing, the customers (in case of hospitality many times the guests) are provided the conceptual service to find out how it fits with their needs. This customer involvement is essential for the evaluation of the developed concept, as a service is always created on the spot with the customer. This is one of the essential differences with new product development, where for instance simulations can be used to see how the product performs in practice.

Focus • • •

The focus of new service development is to have a structured process that enables both incremental and more radical innovations of the service portfolio of an organization. A formalized development process provides support in areas where most operations-oriented organizations do not perform well: tasks that are not directly related to their daily practice. However, using the knowledge and experiences that staff, guests, external experts, etc. can apply in this process, provides a strong advantage over other service companies that are stuck on the left side of the model, not knowing which process to use in a particular situation.

Insight • • •

New service development provides a complete and comprehensive model for innovation in the service sector. The main difference with product development is the required participation of the customer or guest in the process. This is the only way to verify if new innovative concepts will work, and how they will need to be designed both from the customer's and from the organization's perspective.

Result • • •

When a new service development process is deployed, a more mature innovation process is created and successfully introducing new services is a process that can be managed much better. Formalized processes lead to better performing innovations, in terms of time to market, customer satisfaction, and operational effort.

Value for hospitality industry • • •

The new service development model and process provide the hospitality industry with a way to mature their processes regarding innovation. This way they will be able to address more radical innovations if needed to fulfil their strategy. New service development institutionalizes innovation, makes clear what kind of activities need to be executed, and what tools can be used. It provides a framework for the hospitality industry to increase its success through innovation.

Case study

Innovation case study: Qbic hotels

A designer boutique hotel room that assembles in 4h in any empty space and which only requires running water and a hole in the floor for drainage. No long construction projects; an instant design room at an amazingly low cost. And the best part is: should the owner wish to use the space for a different purpose? The hotel room disassembles even faster. This is the story of Qbic hotels (http://www.qbichotels.com), an initiative of innovative Dutch hotel entrepreneur Paul Rinkens. Rinkens has left his mark on the hotel industry with the development of several successful concepts that have one thing in common: innovation is key.

Box 1: the Cubi

The key element of the Qbic design concept consists of the cube-shaped living spaces, appropriately called Cubi (Photo). Each Cubi measures $7\,m^2$ and features an astonishingly practical configuration, individually designed, and built with attractive materials; "living room," extra long Hästens bed, Philip Starck design bathroom elements, TV, radio, safe and wireless internet, and an ingenious work-and-dine set provide a state-of-the-art living environment.

Innovation and hospitality appear to be natural enemies. Innovation involves taking risks, breaking the "rules" and daring to challenge the status quo. Hospitality operations are about risk avoidance, sticking with the rules, and protecting the status quo. Many hotel chains are experiencing the "innovator's dilemma" as documented by Clayton Christensen. Christensen tries to explain how it can be that outstanding companies that stay in close touch with their markets, listen to their clients, and invest pro-actively in technology still stand the chance of failing. Christensen shows us that real breakthrough innovation is often initially rejected by customers. And this scares the well-established corporations in the industry. That may explain why most innovation in the hospitality industry is initiated by outsiders. Entrepreneurs that are not stuck in the reigning industry paradigms, but that bend the rules and create new entrepreneurial space. Although Qbic founder Rinkens is a hotelier by profession, he still managed to keep the outsider's perspective.

Box 2: paradigms

Paradigm is a term from ancient Greek referring to standard models used in certain settings. The Oxford English Dictionary defines paradigm as "a pattern or model, an exemplar. Joel Barker was the first person to popularize the concept of paradigm shifts for the corporate world. Barker defined the term paradigm as any set of rules or regulations that defines boundaries and tells you how to behave within those boundaries." The fact that people tend to resist change and often appear to be unable to see and accept change is caused by the conclusion that we view the world around us through paradigms. And applying Barker's definition, we behave accordingly. The hospitality industry is full of paradigms. "The customer is always right" maybe the most powerful one. According to Barker, paradigms are changes. Barker begins by introducing paradigm shifters—the people that bring in the idea for the new paradigm and paradigm pioneers—the people who will have to develop the paradigm. In order to create the much sought after new competitive space, entrepreneurs must shift paradigms.

The Qbic hotel concept is ground breaking in many ways. It bends the rules with regard to all three major stakeholders in hospitality; the guest, the employee, and the owner. The guest is used to the paradigm that top design and good location come at a high cost. Qbic challenged these principles. Although the concept uses top designer brands like beds from Swedish-based Haestens and bathroom fittings by French designer Philip Starck, the concept is still relatively low cost as the manufacturing of the hotel room can be done in an assembly plant setting, away from the hotel.

In most cities of the world, locations for new hotels are scarce. Empty office buildings on the other hand are a lot easier to find. The solution that allows for hotel rooms to be installed in empty office spaces brings about a whole new world of potential hotel locations without requiring costly refurbishments in the building, and all while maintaining a great amount of flexibility for the owner of the real estate. Should the office market turn out to be more favourable than the hotel market, the spaces can be turned back into office spaces overnight.

This feature is highly beneficial to the owner, who also likes the limited investment cost involved in transforming an office building into a hotel. And last but not the least the employees. For these stakeholders Qbic provides mainly bad news. Apart from a few housekeepers and a host, the hotel hardly requires any human input. Reservations are made online by guests, directly into the reservation system. Check in is possible via unmanned self service kiosks in the hotel lobby. Food and beverage is available via vending machines or by independent entrepreneurs who offer restaurant and bar facilities on the premises.

Many hoteliers condone the concept. Checking in via self service kiosks is unacceptable in the reigning paradigms of the industry. But Qbic has proven to be successful. Its first branch in Amsterdam was fully booked from day one. The internet savvy traveller that so many hotel chains seek to enthuse, appears to embrace the concept, and they are not the only enthusiasts. The concept has drawn the attention of people from all parts of the world including organizing committees of major sports events such as the Olympics. The Qbic concept provides the possibilities to set up state-of-the-art hotel facilities on a temporary basis.

The Qbic hotels case shows us that innovation in hospitality requires breaking through the existing paradigms and overcoming the innovator's dilemma. Companies and individuals that aim for success better create a new competitive space for themselves in which they can become the instant market leader.

Information technology, service reliability, effectiveness, and flexibility are critical factors behind business initiatives. Qbic's mission is to continually improve the development of systems and global infrastructure.

Analysis

In this section, the three concepts—scenario thinking, The innovator's dilemma by Christensen, and new service development will be applied to the Qbic case. With regard to scenario thinking, the Qbic case clearly shows how a thorough scan of the environment can help create business innovation. The founders of Qbic took 16- and 17-year-old consumers as their focal point, arguing that this group will produce tomorrow's traveller. Furthermore they analysed the real estate market, concluding that most European cities experience a great demand for new hotel locations that turn out to be mighty scarce. Faced with this challenge the developers mirrored this challenge and asked themselves what type of real estate was widely available. The answer was found in the office market, a market that experiences a situation of oversupply. In terms of the concept of scenario planning, the developers of Qbic turned the otherwise certainty—the location—into an uncertainty. This helped them in developing a robust solution. Last but not the least the scenario of flexibility—the option to change the purpose of a building in a relatively short time at relatively low cost—proved to be a vital factor in risk reduction which in turn helped tremendously in acquiring the required capital.

When analysing the Qbic hotel case by using the concept of disruptive technology, a number of applied technologies can be identified. Construction of hotel rooms has been replaced with assembly techniques that are commonly found in the manufacturing industry. Factory produced components can be easily assembled in the hotel's location, saving a considerable amount of time and money. The production method allows for overseas production of components.

In its market approach the Qbic concept uses revenue management systems that allow for optimization of revenue. The system rewards early bookings, while last minute bookings come at a premium which is contrary to the most commonly applied system that awards last minutes.

The application of self service internet and kiosk check in services in a design hotel environment is another innovation that helps in realizing a considerable cost cutting as no staff are required for this otherwise labour-intensive process.

When looking at the Qbic case from the new service development perspective, the concept clearly shows the long-term perspective that was taken by taking 16–17 year olds as a main focus group. This leads to choices like leaving out workspace and telephone lines, as these travellers are likely to be bringing along their own handheld telecommunication devices that allow for maximum freedom.

The adoption of manufacturing processes as in use in production technology, allowed for a considerably lower initial investment required for establishing the hotel. At the same time this choice of method forced the developers to follow a more structured development process than normally in use in product development in the hotel industry. Last but not the least the concept was tested shortly by a group of randomly chosen travellers who helped in establishing the final design. The industrial design of the Cubi itself allows for opportunities for continuous improvement.

Conclusion

Innovation comes from outside the organization: opportunities, technology, new business concepts, etc. Scenario thinking helps in providing you with views of the future in which you want to realize your strategic goals. Analysing the blocking factors and seeing robust opportunities of overcoming them (i.e., that will work in multiple scenarios and not just one). This is just as applicable to hospitality industry as in other industries. The case of Qbic shows that many opportunities lie there to be taken up and that the way of implementing can be quite straightforward and successful.

Disruptive concepts or technologies are also applicable to the hospitality sector. Providing a combined set of existing technologies and stepping away from the traditional hotel design provides excellent value for money in the Qbic case. Who can reject a €39 deal for a Hästens bed and a Philip Starck bathroom at 3 min walking distance from your business meetings the next morning? Taking adolescents as a starting point, numerous services can be left away, like a phone in the room. Wireless internet and using your own mobile phone are sufficient for the modern day communication needs.

Finally, a structured new service development process provides a valuable framework for knowing what to do when, especially as innovation processes are not as main stream as in other industries. A structured development process will certainly offer support for personnel involved but not working with innovation routinely. It also provides the timing of when to involve potential customers, in this case guests in the process. Testing the concept, as was done by Qbic by using family and friends is certainly an option, as this enables you to address their findings before the service is completely developed.

Summarizing, the hospitality industry seems to be locked in a position where incumbents do small adaptations to their service portfolio. However, the case shows that radical innovation is a possible and, at times, needed way forward in hospitality. As incumbents still have the major part of the market they may have a lot to loose, when they are not able to apply the concepts illustrated in this chapter in their business processes. Faculty and students in hospitality management universities should therefore review and apply the concepts above whenever applicable. Of course, this is not the only way to success, but it may help them along.

References

Brackel, W. A. (2006). Towards improvements for new service development to gain competitive advantage, Master Thesis, University of Groningen.

Christensen, C. M. (2006). The ongoing process of building a theory of disruption. *Journal of Product Innovation Management, 23*, 39–55.

Dialogic (2005). *Innovatie in de horeca, onderzoek naar de innovativiteit van de Bedrijfstak.* Zoetermeer: Bedrijfschap Horeca en Catering (in Dutch).

Henderson (2006). The innovator's dilemma as a problem of organizational competence development performance. *Journal of Product Innovation Management, 23*, 5–11.

Hultink, E. J., Griffin, A., Hart, S., and Robben, H. S. J. (1997). Industrial new product launch strategies and product development performance. *Journal of Product Innovation Management, 14*, 243–257.

Johnson, S. P., Menor, L. J., Roth, A. V., and Chase, R. B. (2000). A critical evaluation of the new service development process: Integrating service innovation and service process design. In J. A. Fitzsimmons and M. J. Fitzsimmons (Eds.), *New Service Development: Creating Memorable Experiences.*

Van der Heijden, C. J. (2005). *Scenarios: The Art of Strategic Conversation.* Chichester: Wiley.

CHAPTER 19

Strategy models and their application to small- and medium-sized enterprises

Amit Sharma

*School of Hospitality,
The Pennsylvania State University,
223 Mateer Building,
University Park, PA 16802*

Introduction

Small businesses have been part of social and economic fabric of nations since the beginning of economic activity. Still, most business strategy literature that currently exists is from the perspective of larger businesses. One of the reasons for this bias was the emergence of large businesses in the 19th century as a source of economic progress. The complexity of bringing together factors of production on a large scale intrigued economists and later business strategists. However, as there appears to be resurgence of interest in entrepreneurship, especially through small businesses, it is vital to revisit small business strategy process to understand how current theories can be applied to the investigation of small businesses. The purpose of this chapter is to understand why strategy theories and models are not commonly applied to small businesses. Given this understanding can hospitality small business literature be strengthened? The paper uses evidence from two recent hospitality small business case studies and tests the application of two leading strategy models—Michael Porter's generic strategies model (1985) and Olsen *et al.*'s (1998) co-alignment principle—to assess their applicability on small businesses. This paper argues that as most hospitality strategy literature is based on strategy models with a lesser emphasis on small businesses, by default the emphasis has been on studying large businesses even though hospitality and tourism industries as such include a larger number of small businesses. Therefore, to strengthen hospitality strategy literature and in favour of studying small businesses, researchers will need to expand the existing models and theories. This will also have implications on methodological approaches. Resulting argument is that earlier strategy models and theories may have (unintentionally) excluded small businesses resulting in the dire need for a parallel stream of literature focused solely on small businesses. However, given that both small and large businesses exist for similar purposes, to maximize wealth for their owners, then attempts should be made to reduce this polarized approach.

Recent studies also have shown that small businesses, especially hospitality businesses such as hotels and restaurants have the potential to not only contribute to a nation's economic development but to its entrepreneurial activity (Sharma and Upneja, 2005; Sharma, 2006a). Therefore, strengthening the stream of literature that evaluates strategic processes of such businesses is not only essential but also a much overlooked aspect of hospitality research.

Literature review

There are a total of over 150 theories and models of business strategy. How many of these were developed in view of special characteristics and circumstances facing small businesses? It is not possible to review all of these theories and models in this chapter, instead two leading models, one from mainstream strategy literature and the other from hospitality strategy literature, were evaluated to assess their applicability to small business research. Strategy literature applicable to small businesses is, at best, scattered and limited. For instance, of the strategy articles available for reference in leading management research databases (over 115,000), only 1% (1034) were devoted to small businesses (ProQuest, 2007). Of these almost 50% were published in the last decade. The following review of key studies related to small business strategy will further highlight the difficulty of categorizing this research under themes.

Earlier studies of small business strategy were highly applied. For instance, Van Auken and Ireland (1980) proposed an input–output approach to small business planning. The paper was significant in proposing a practical forward-thinking strategic approach for small businesses. Similarly, Brasch (1981) proposed a mode for practitioners to decide on an organizational structure for marketing export entry. Proposed choices were very practical and involved different ways for the firm owners to invest in marketing resources. The growing popularity of information technology prompted Allaway *et al.* (1988) to present a framework for small retailers make effective promotion mix decisions using "off the shelf PC-driven software." An interesting aspect of this study was that it used an actual store data analysed through a case study approach, and emphasized the use of computer technology to improve effectiveness of small business decision-making. Other studies related to information technology that followed on these earlier works were that of Drozdow and Carroll (1997). They proposed practical tools such as PC-based simulations for family firms to help them develop their strategies. Hall and Mestler (1997) evaluated software available for small business strategic planning. An example of operational analysis was Bassin (1990) who presented the use of economic order quantity (EOQ) technique to manage inventories in small retail businesses, stressing that inventories is a financial investment and how they can be managed using this technique with limited operational assumptions and simple methodology. Such studies set the tone of small business investigations to be not only very practical in their application but also problem-oriented.

Slowly, however, the focus evolved from more analytic aspects of operations and technology to behavioural, human aspects of the entrepreneur and the management, and the more traditional strategy concerns of the environment, organizational configuration, and their alignment. Variyam and Kraybill (1993) investigated a broad choice of small business strategies, and the influence of managerial human capital on business strategy. The study found that firm size impacts certain strategy choices and that managerial human capital had a significant influence on the choice of strategies by small businesses. Hatton and Raymond (1994) evaluated the organizational effectiveness framework in context of small businesses to assess the congruence and mates of key variables such as environment, strategy, technology, task, structure, and individual. Around the same time Morrison (1994) investigates the strategic alliance behaviour of small hotels and found that cooperative alliances was a necessary aspect of strategic choices that hotels would need to consider due to rapid environmental changes, particularly due to emerging "electronic markets." Nwachukwu (1995) found that CEO's locus of control in small businesses was related to the business's structured differentiation, and that this was related to its economic performance. The study results emphasized that more focus needs to be on CEO judgment and small business performance rather than evaluating strategy processes.

Some studies have also looked at small businesses in relation to larger ones. For instance, Audretsch et al. (1999) investigated the theories that explain the existence of small firms in context of larger firms. A key conclusion of this study was that small firms do not compete directly with larger firms, particularly due to their larger price-cost differences versus that of the larger firms. Instead, the smaller firms tend to develop product niche strategies unlike that of larger firms. However, Benrud (2002) explored how small firms competed with larger ones on the basis of low price and low quality of products. Similar issues were investigated by Darrow et al. (2001) using the generic strategy framework to identify strategy options available for small hardware stores due to rapid environmental changes from big hardware stores taking control of the marketplace. The study identified critical success factors to help small hardware stores remain competitive even as they face these environmental changes. This also happens to be among the only studies to have used the generic strategy framework proposed by Porter (1985). More recently, Hollenstein (2005) investigated the factors that determined the choice of internationalization strategies of small businesses. Small businesses were found to be different than the larger ones in that they primarily rely on capabilities related to incremental innovations whereas the larger firms relied on their assets.

The impacts of strategy on various aspects of small businesses began with investigations into profitability and productivity. Roper (1999) evaluated small business growth and profitability and found that turnover growth and profitability were only weakly related. Other significant findings were that profitability was related to strategy choice, and both growth rates and profitability did not show any long-term persistence. Gunasekaran *et al.* (2000) evaluated causes of low productivity through a small business case study and proposed ways to enhance productivity in such businesses. This paper was significant in evaluating the strategies that would enhance productivity of small businesses. These earlier works laid the foundations to more thorough evaluation of small business strategy.

More recently, small business strategy literature has continued to evolve, attracting attention of research from various perspectives. Beal (2000) investigated the alignment between environmental scanning and strategy choice of small firms. The study found that broad-based environmental scanning had an influence on strategy choice; however, found no relationship to the frequency of environmental scanning. Gelderen *et al.* (2000) found that personal strategies of owners/founders of small business start-ups were related to performance and environmental uncertainty. Certain strategies were found to be more effective and high/low environmental uncertainty was also found to be related to certain types of strategies. From the financial perspective Lopez-Gracia and Aybar-Arias (2000) used credit rationing and pecking order theory approaches to show that financial behaviour of SMEs was influenced by size and business sector. The study found that size influenced self-financing strategies and business sector influenced short-term financial policy. Similarly, Reid and Smith (2000) investigated factors that made a new business start-up successful and found that above all the one factor that was successful for small businesses was the entrepreneur's pursuit of the highest return on investments. Other factors important for success were entrepreneur's realistic assessment of its abilities and long-term planning. Limited work has been done to evaluate information strategies. One such example is Levy *et al.* (2002) who investigated the process of information systems (IS) investment strategies of small firms. Investment in IS was found to be dependent upon various factors including stages of growth, entrepreneur/owner's values and experiences, and even the industry sector of the business. Davies (2001) investigated competitiveness constraints in manufacturing firms and proposed a model for these firms to minimize resource constraints through clustering inter-firm linkages in South Africa. Arasli (2002) evaluated the perceptions of hotel middle management executives towards total quality management (TQM) philosophy and how resolving these internal management conflicts could enhance overall readiness of these businesses to adopt TQM strategies. A recent study by Rasheed (2005a) investigated the moderating effect of environment construct on foreign entry mode and performance of SMEs. Results of the study suggested that firms experience higher international revenue growth rates using no-equity based foreign market entry modes "in growing domestic environments." Alternatively, international revenue growths are higher for equity-based entry modes when firms take on higher foreign market risks. Gibbons and O'Connor (2005) studied the influence of small business characteristics on their strategic planning processes. The study concluded that entrepreneurial firms adopted more formal strategic planning processes while the conservative firms adopted more incremental processes. Davis and Wood (2005) demonstrated the importance of financial forecasting by developing a model that would evaluate financial aspects of strategic decisions. The model is shown to be applicable to a number of industries including travel agencies, food brokers, and the study emphasizes the value it creates for various organizational stakeholders. And more recently, Cressy (2006) investigated why most firms tend to die within the first few years of trading. Among the key theoretical propositions of this study were that most firms die early because the market value fall below the opportunity cost of staying in business, and those entrepreneurs that are high on management human capital (MHC) tend to have higher absolute profits than those low on MHC.

Small business strategy literature, influenced by studies from entrepreneurship, also investigated issues specific to owners, managers, and their decision-making aspects. Sonfield *et al.* (2001) investigated gender comparisons in strategic decision-making in context of the Entrepreneurial Strategy Matrix. Like previous studies, this investigation also reported significant differences between female and male entrepreneurs' satisfaction with venture performance, where male were found to be more satisfied. Jocumsen (2004) studied small businesses' marketing strategy decision-making processes. The study concluded that small businesses make strategic decisions on the basis of performing three tasks: "information gathering/ research," "financial analysis and assessment," and "internal matters." An interesting observation was that these tasks were conducted non-sequentially and preceded by "decision initiation" and followed by final commitment." Likewise, Kickul and Gundry (2002) studied the relationship between small firm owner's personality, strategic orientation, and innovation. The study found that small business owners' proactive personality was linked to strategic orientation that allowed the firm to change in respond to its surrounding environment. Entrialgo (2002) investigated and found links between strategy choice and managerial characteristics such as functional experience and formal education, while no links between age and tenure to strategy choice. The study emphasizes that the co-alignment between managerial characteristics and strategy choice has performance implications for the small businesses. Linking business characteristics to strategy, Chetty and Campbell-Hunt (2003) conceptualized a theoretical model to explain different paths to internationalization by integrating internationalization theories and SME characteristics. An implication of this study was emphasis on firm characteristics such as demographic aspects, management style, and competencies. Rasheed (2005b) investigated small business entrepreneurs' strategic choices when faced with either growth or retrenchment. Combining previous theories of strategy choice with the perceptions of entrepreneurs regarding their access to resources and past profitability, the study proposed that entrepreneurs essentially remain aggressive and choose growth strategies, whether their perceptions of resource accessibility and past profitability was high or low. Payne *et al.* (2005) empirically analysed cognitive maps of small business leaders to understand the influence of these maps on organization's attributes and actions. Results of this investigation suggested small business leaders could develop two distinct polar orientations through their self-identity with the organization, overall assessment of external stakeholders, and their perception of the environment. An important conclusion of the study was that small business leaders should be mindful of their orientations and biases as these could influence the behaviour and performance of their organizations.

Increasingly the idea of resources and competency development has attracted attention of researchers. For instance, Clarke and Turner (2004) extended the resource-based view (RBV) and proposed a knowledge management (KM) strategy for small- and medium-sized businesses to develop competitive advantage. The study concluded that in addition to KM SME biotechnology firms also used intellectual property also as complementary source of a competitive advantage. Gurau (2004) used the value-added chain methodology to assess competitive advantage of SMEs in the biopharmaceutical sector. This study resulted in a theoretical model that described stages and factors influencing strategic positioning of SMEs in the value-added chain of this sector. Wilson and Stokes (2005) studied the distinction between and the importance of entrepreneurs managing creativity and innovation. The study highlighted that managing these two aspects were different and would require entrepreneurs to develop internal skills such as effective communication, and also effective promotional strategies and external focus. Similarly, Adewole (2005) used Porter's (1985) five forces model to understand the challenges in the supply chain of small manufacturing businesses. Bretherton and Chaston (2005) investigated the resource dependency behaviour of small firms using strategic alliances. Results of the study found that firms were clearly using strategic alliances at various stages of the value chain to access resources and capabilities. In an applied study, Reynolds and Lancaster (2006) presented practical and low-cost marketing methods for small entrepreneurial firms to maximize profitability through increased sales and increased consumer satisfaction. This study was valuable in presenting a theory-based practical approach that small firms could apply without allocating large resources in a research and development budget. Cooper *et al.* (2005) investigated customer relationship management (CRM) aspects of family businesses and compared them with non-family businesses. The results of their study suggested that family businesses were less likely to place a high importance on CRM compared to non-family businesses and were likely to use less sophisticated strategies too, more traditional and less risky ones. However, they were unable to conclude whether these different approaches yielded significantly different effectiveness of CRM strategies between family and non-family businesses.

Small business research in hospitality literature remains limited and fragmented, especially in context of operational dynamics (Buick, 2003). Models used to analyse manufacturing industries revealed that hotel entrepreneurs employed business-oriented strategies to optimize performance and that these strategies were in close association to their individual backgrounds (Glancey and Pettigrew, 1997). Among other studies of small hotels and restaurants profitability and revenue analysis, pricing policies, and the level of investments in fixed assets include Kaufman *et al.* (1996) and Poorani and Smith (1995). Operators' previous experience, marketing resources, and capital structure mix were some of the factors found to influence performance of these businesses, including the skills and educational levels of operators and employees (Romer, 1986, 1990). Even though on-the-job training was largely prevalent in hotels and restaurants, there remains inconclusive evidence to suggest that such efforts yielded successful results (Worsfold and Griffith, 2003; Zhang *et al.*, 2002). Among other factors (like entrepreneurship activity, innovation, etc.) recent evidence shows that economic growth from small businesses can be derived from their linkages with the rest of the economy (Sharma, 2006a).

This rather brief, yet significantly representative review of small business strategy literature from both mainstream strategic management research as well as hospitality strategy literature shows that small business strategy studies have been limited, fragmented, and lacked focus in their direction. On one hand the lack of focus is evident in the difficulty of categorizing them in similar themes, and on the other hand, it at least shows evidence of a general evolution of perspectives in the study of small businesses.

Small business strategy studies of hospitality businesses are especially limited and fragmented. This literature stream remains in its nascent stages. There could be a number of reasons why small business strategy literature has lagged behind in its size, content, and complexity compared to studies conducted for larger businesses. One possible explanation is that leading strategy models and theories fall short of presenting evolved perspectives to study small businesses. Given that mainstream strategic management literature has developed within these leading theoretical conceptualizations, it may have led to ignoring application of these theories to small businesses. If this is indeed one possible reason, then it would be worthwhile understanding how some of the leading models have fallen short in their application to small businesses. With this knowledge at least researchers could be conscious of theoretical limitations as they approach to study strategic management behaviour of organizations. Furthermore, those researchers particularly interested in small business research can attempt to apply mainstream strategic management theories to small businesses so that small business studies can become increasingly mainstream research and not frowned upon by "mainstream researchers."

Purpose statement

As stated earlier, the purpose of this chapter was to investigate whether the partial scope of leading strategy models and theories contributed to weak literature on small business strategy. Therefore, this chapter evaluated two leading strategy models to see whether they were appropriate for studying small businesses. Given the context of this chapter, the focus was on hospitality businesses such as hotels and restaurants. Case study evidence from two recent projects was taken to evaluate the applicability of the selected strategy models.

Methodological approach

The three components of the descriptive methodological approach in this paper were: two leading strategy models; case study evidence from two small businesses; and the framework for evaluating the application of strategy models against the case study evidence. The two leading strategy models selected for this assessment was Michael Porter's generic strategies (1985) (Figure 19.2) and the co-alignment principle Olsen *et al.* (1998) (Figure 19.1). The reason for selecting Porter's (1985) model was that it has, so far, been one of the most influential models in strategy and management literature. It therefore presented itself as a significant and an interesting candidate to assess its applicability to the study of small businesses, especially since it has been scarcely applied to study small businesses.

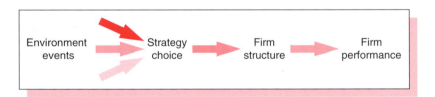

Figure 19.1
The co-alignment principle.

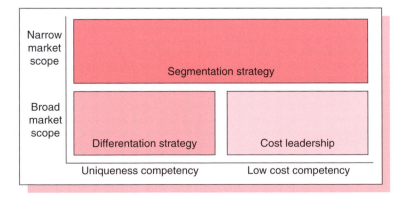

Figure 19.2
Generic strategies.

The co-alignment principle (Olsen *et al.*, 1998) remains the only strategy conceptualization in the field of hospitality and tourism and its application is increasingly gaining acceptance. Therefore it was thought appropriate to evaluate its applicability to small businesses as it lead future developments in the area of hospitality strategy.

The two case study evidence used in this paper was of a restaurant and a hotel, both small and independently owned businesses. To increase the coverage of evidence the small restaurant case study was based in North America (Sharma, 2006b) and the small hotel case study was based in a sub-Sahara African nation (Sharma and Sneed, 2007). Both these case studies were based on actual evidence from previously conducted projects. Each of these case study discussions was contextual to the strategies adopted by the businesses to develop competitive advantage.

The restaurant was located in a small mid-western town in North America. Its product and service mix could be categorized as exclusive, with an average food check at $30–50 for dinner. The chef was highly qualified and trained from one of the best culinary institutions in the world. He also owned and managed the restaurant along with a partner managing the service side of the restaurant. The eventual competitive strategy adopted by this restaurant was the use of fresh and locally grown foods that appealed to its customer base and also distinguished it from other less exclusive eating out options. The strategy proved to be successful. The hotel was located in a large city in a sub-Sahara African nation. Its owner had retired after a run of mismanagement and loss making of the property. At that time the owner transferred the property to his daughter who had taken control of its day-to-day management. The current owner was not highly trained in hotel management but was energetic and committed to making the property a business and financial success. However, given the already intense competition in the market she thought it was best to focus on certain untapped segments of the market. Her eventually adapted strategy was to focus on non-profit and non-governmental agency clients that were visiting the city and the country on development projects. As there were no hotels solely focusing on such markets and their needs, the strategy had begun to show success.

Given these two case studies and their contextual strategy choices, the two strategy models (Porter, 1985; Olsen *et al.*, 1998) were used to describe the hypothetical process that would eventually lead to the selection of respective strategies. This descriptive process was then evaluated using a framework to assess whether issues appropriate to small businesses were identified by the models as each of the businesses adopted their respective strategies.

The framework for evaluating the applicability of the two strategy models was adopted from D'Amboise and Muldowney (1988). The framework proposed evaluated small business management theories with the criteria that appropriate models should include certain constructs. According to this framework, theories to study small businesses must include constructs of environment, organizational configuration, managerial characteristics, success–failure criteria, evolution, behaviour of persons operating within that specific environment, and problem-orientation. Therefore, this framework was applied to the descriptive strategy process of each of the case study to assess whether each of the models possessed the required constructs to study small businesses. Results of the evaluation were coded as "yes" if the model had the appropriate constructs, "none" if the constructs were missing and "implicit" if the constructs were not explicitly defined but were inherent in the model. This evaluation helped identify constructs that were missing in each of the models to study small businesses. Results were discussed to assess implications for small business strategy result and development of appropriate theories and models for such studies.

Application of Porter's generic strategies (1985)

Porter (1985) proposed three generic strategies commonly used by businesses: market segmentation, differentiation strategy, and cost leadership. The selection of either of these strategies by the businesses, Porter suggested, will be based on *strategic scope* and *strategic strength* within the market. Strategic scope defined the size and composition of the intended target market and strategic strength comprised of the core competencies that the business possessed (Figure 19.1). This schema of the model was applied to each of the small business case studies under focus.

First the small restaurant's strategy was described using Porter's generic strategy model. The strategic scope of the restaurant would refer to its customer base, its size, and its composition. The target customer base in the restaurant's geographic area comprised of a near-by university town and increasingly aging population of baby-boomers. The composition of this target market would be described as high in education and disposable income level. The size of this target market would also be described as high for this restaurant especially due to the lack of other high-price eating out options. Therefore this model would describe the target market as broad on the strategic scope dimension. The chef and owner's core competencies were also relatively high and unique. Similarly, the level of core competencies required to prepare the exclusive meals were also relatively high. Therefore on the strategic strength dimension the core competencies would also be described as unique. Based on the matrix location of this business on both these dimensions (Figure 19.1) Porter's (1985) model could conclude that a differentiation strategy would be most suitable for the restaurant. The focus on using locally grown and fresh foods was a differentiation strategy that was eventually used by the restaurant.

Second, the small hotel's strategy was described using Porter's generic strategy model. Given the intense competition in the market place, the hotel was facing already narrow market segments. The high-priced hotels had already captured the top-end of the market leaving the rest of the hotels, including the smaller ones, with the more price-sensitive customers. Therefore, for the small hotel under focus, composition of the market would have been described as highly price-sensitive customers. The size of this market was also narrowing due to the increased competition in the market place. Therefore, this hotel's target market would have been labelled narrow on the strategic scope dimension. As the hotel had recently changed ownership, the current owner was attempting to make a financial success of the property. The current owner did not possess any specific skill set necessary to operate and manage a hotel, even though managing a multi-activity business like a hotel required certain level of competencies. Therefore, even though her strategic competency would have been labelled low cost, certain unique competencies were required to successfully manage the hotel property. On the basis of these two labels on the strategic scope and strategic competency dimensions, Porter's strategic model could also have concluded that the small hotel pursues a market segmentation strategy.

Application of Olsen *et al.*'s (1998) co-alignment principle

The co-alignment model (1998) was presented earlier. Its key components include: environmental scanning, strategy choice, resource allocation, and performance evaluation (Figure 19.2).

The restaurant case study could be described using each of these components of the co-alignment model. *Environmental scanning* stage of the process would require the restaurant to effectively scan its environment to assess opportunities, challenges, and other characteristics of its business, task, and remote environments that would eventually help shape *strategic choices*. These components of the environment would help the restaurant describe its target market, competitive environment, supplier environment, and other remote aspects of the environment that may influence strategic choices. Given the previously described geographic location of the restaurant, the owner's exclusive skill set, the target market's description and its composition as high in education and disposable income levels would be included. The lack of restaurants catering to such a clientele would also be noted. Therefore, the transition from environmental scanning to strategy choice stage would guide the owner to consider an exclusive product/service mix that would cater to such a consumer. At the strategy choice stage the owner could have the choice to consider an exclusive product/service mix as a competitive method to create that competitive advantage. If this strategy is pursued, the next stage, *resource allocation*, would aid the owner to evaluate the resources required to implement such a competitive method. Among the resources required would be production and service skills needed for developing an exclusive product/service mix. Given that these skills existed, and if others were found to be present too, the owner could proceed to evaluate the *financial performance* of the competitive method in the last recommended stage of the co-alignment principle.

A similar hypothetical description could be developed for the hotel case study using these components of the co-alignment principle. In the *environment scanning* stage, the owner would scan its business, task, and remote environments to identify opportunities and challenges for developing effective competitive methods. Among most obvious characteristics of the environments would be the increased presence of international hotels, low level of tourist traveller market in the city, high volume of development-aid related market, and lack of good quality low-priced accommodations. Within the growing development-aid traveller market, another observation would be that while most aid-agencies provided lucrative contracts to hotels and paid close to rack-rates, the smaller non-profit and non-governmental agencies (NGOs) supported largely by volunteers were unable to pay these high room rates of international standard hotels. This then could be recognized as a logical opportunity to pursue in the demand side of the market. Given a lack of quality accommodation in the small hotel sector, the owner could consider this as a viable competitive method to pursue in the short to medium term, especially when government's need for support from such NGOs was not expected to diminish. Such could be the hypothetical description of an environmental scan leading to a *strategy choice* for creating a quality product/service mix for price-sensitive NGO travellers to the city. If this choice of a competitive method was eventually selected the *resource allocation* stage would help the owner evaluate the resources required for implementing such a competitive method. Two obvious resource requirements would be the development of appropriate quality product/service mix that would appeal to the price-sensitive NGO traveller and developing relationships with appropriate NGOs so that they may consider this hotel as their preferred accommodation in the city. Given the low level of professional skill required to develop relationships with appropriate NGOs, and the possibility of hiring a skilled manager to develop the product/service mix the owner could proceed to the next stage of *evaluating* this competitive method's *financial performance*.

These then would be the hypothetical applications of both the leading strategy models in context of two selected actual case studies and the actual strategies that were eventually pursued by these businesses. The next task was to evaluate these descriptions to assess how well models performed in their description of strategy process of a small business.

Evaluation of strategy models to assess small business fit

The evaluation framework used in this paper suggested that small businesses strategy models include constructs of environment, organizational configuration, managerial characteristics, success–failure criteria, evolution, behaviour of persons operating within that specific environment, and problem-orientation. This framework was used to assess whether the applied description of the two selected strategy models these various constructs or not. If the constructs appeared in each models' application to the case studies then the observation was coded "yes." If the constructs did not appear in the description of models' application then the observation was coded "none." Where the construct was not explicitly defined but inherent the observation was coded "implicit."

Porter's generic strategies

The generic strategies model proposed by Porter was applied to the two small businesses case studies. The hypothetical description of this application suggested how this strategy model would be implemented in an actual scenario. This

439

description could be evaluated to assess whether the model included constructs of environment, organizational configuration, managerial characteristics, success–failure criteria, evolution, behaviour of persons operating within that specific environment, and problem-orientation.

The construct of environment was included in the description of this model's application as the two dimensions of *strategic scope*. Similarly organizational configuration was summed up in a single dimension labelled *strategic strength*. There appeared to be no description of managerial characteristics other than those required in strategic strength dimension. There was also no success–failure criteria included in the implementation description. Similarly, there was no reference to evolution of the business in the implementation of the model. Behavioural aspects of the owner/manager were also not included in implementation of this model. Finally, the model was oriented towards solving an inherent problem of developing competitive advantage.

The co-alignment principle

The co-alignment principle proposed by Olsen *et al.* (1998) was applied to the two small businesses. The hypothetical description of this application suggested how this strategy model would be implemented in an actual scenario. This description could be evaluated to assess whether the model included constructs of environment, organizational configuration, managerial characteristics, success–failure criteria, evolution, behaviour of persons operating within that specific environment, and problem-orientation.

A well defined and developed construct of environment was included in the model. Organizational configuration was also included and highlighted at the *resource allocation* stage. Managerial characteristics did not appear in the hypothetical description. The model clearly referred to success–failure criteria during its final stage *performance evaluation*. There was no description of evolutionary aspects of the business. Behaviour of persons operating with that specific environment was not explicitly observable. However, *environmental scanning* and *strategy choice* stages did provide observable managerial characteristics of perception and choice. If such perceptions towards the environment and strategic choices could be observed longitudinally they have the potential of sketching strong behavioural patterns of individual managers and owners. Finally, there was an inherent problem orientation, that of developing a competitive advantage.

Table 19.1 Strategic Evaluation of Small Businesses

Criteria	Generic Strategies (Porter, 1985)	The Co-Alignment Principle (Olsen et al., 1998)
Constructs of environment	Yes	Yes
Organizational configuration	Yes	Yes
Managerial characteristics	None	None
Success–failure criteria	None	Yes
Evolution	None	None
Behaviour of persons' operating within that specific environment	None	Implicit
Problem-orientation	Implicit	Implicit

Gaps in strategy models

On the basis of the above evaluation of the two strategy models under focus, some interesting gaps were identified. Porter's (1985) generic strategies model, while clear in describing many aspects of the strategy process, was unable to identify managerial characteristics, clearly defined success–failure criteria, evolution of the business, and behaviour of persons operating within that specific environment. There also existed an inherent problem-orientation in the model of developing a competitive advantage. The Olsen et al.'s (1998) co-alignment principle did better than the Porter's model in that it defined clear success–failure criteria and had certain implicitly described behavioural aspects of persons operating within that specific environment. However, it too was unable to identify managerial characteristics and evolution of the business.

To summarize, both models while included certain key constructs to study small businesses, they also fell short of studying managerial characteristics, individual behaviours, and business evolution that would be useful in strategic evaluation of small businesses (Table 19.1).

Gaps and missing case study information

Given these gaps identified in the strategy models, how critical or essential is the information that would be considered lost? Let us take the example of managerial characteristics and individual behaviours in the case of both the small business case studies: the North American restaurant and the sub-Saharan Hotel. Both owners of these establishments had strikingly different managerial characteristics but could be said to demonstrate similar individual behaviour towards such decisions as taking risks. The restaurant owner appeared to be more "hands-off" in his management technique towards his subordinate staff members in the kitchen, whereas the hotel owner tried to overlook every aspect of day-to-day management of the hotel. However, both were willing to take the risk to commit resources to a strategy that was relatively different than that being pursued by competitors. The restaurant owner committed time and resources to develop relationships with local farmers to develop reliable supply chains of various food products. As the success rate of developing these relationship was less than 100% this process was a continuous one. Furthermore, the initial stages of local farm relationship development included a lag time—before farmers could respond to specific product/quality needs of the owner. Similarly, the hotel owner had to commit competitive prices for developing the new market segment of price-sensitive NGO travellers. This was in spite of her stressed financial resources partly due to the recent renovations to the existing establishment and in part due to committing resources to re-establishing the image and presence of the property since it is "close to financial and market ruin" with the previous owner.

The evolutionary aspect of both businesses was also not highlighted in the strategy implementation description through the two models. For instance, the growth objectives of both owners were strikingly different. The restaurant owner was not interested to expand beyond the current premises or even increase its capacity, while the hotel owner had already increased capacity of its accommodation and was working on increasing the capacity of its conference and banqueting services. She was also open to consider future possibilities of additional properties but was realistic to continue focusing on making a success of the current property.

Finally, while both models had an implicit problem orientation it is not clear whether either of the models would have successfully identified the reasons why respective strategies were chosen. That is, the real issues that motivated these individuals to select their respective strategies would probably not be explicitly identified. Both the restaurant and hotel owners were new entrepreneurs trying to establish themselves in their relatively new working environment. While the restaurant owner had required technical skill levels, he lacked experience of owning and managing a business. The hotel owner, on the other hand, did not posses any technical knowledge of managing the hotel but had the general sense of business ownership by association to her father, the previous owner of the hotel. Therefore, while both owners were new entrepreneurs they were both facing strikingly different challenges.

The question is whether ignoring this information would have been critical in understanding the strategic process of both these small businesses. Referring back to literature on small businesses, the most critical aspect of small businesses are the owners that create, lead, manage, and grow the businesses. All the information that was missing in the strategy description through the two models pertains to the owners and their behaviours. Therefore trying to understand the strategic process of small businesses without an in-depth understanding of owners could have provided only a limited view of how they selected strategies and why these strategies were successful (or not).

Then how do we study small business strategy?

Clearly neither of the two strategy models evaluated in this research yielded a perfect fit for small business strategy. Yet the two together show promising signs of studying small business, and above all, depict an evolutionary process in strategic management thinking. Porter's (1985) generic strategies included the building blocks of an organization, that is, organizational configuration and environment. Recent studies of small businesses have tried to explore various aspects of organizational configuration. Still more work is required to open in this black box to understand how businesses configure themselves in bringing together resources critical to developing a competitive advantage. Such applications of the model will clearly enhance our understanding of the underlying principles of small businesses. Olsen *et al.*'s (1998) co-alignment principle added important elements of success–failure criteria, behaviour of persons' operating environment, and problem orientation, all critical constructs to study small businesses. Some of these constructs appeared implicitly in the model further allowing flexibility in their application to study small businesses. The behavioural environment of persons as a construct has the potential of incorporating managerial characteristics and the relationship of these characteristics to other aspects of the strategy process. Similarly, if this process of co-alignment can be studied over time it could add an evolutionary dimension to study small business behaviour. The two models together show an evolutionary process of strategic management thinking as successive models enhance our understanding of phenomenon less emphasized in previous ones. Future strategic management models for small businesses would not only benefit from incorporating existing constructs but could also extend their conceptualization and operationalization to incorporate additional dimensions.

Implications

So where does this all lead us in trying to understand why hospitality strategic management literature has continued to lack focus on small businesses? The purpose of this paper was to understand why strategy theories and models are not commonly applied to small businesses? To answer this question, two leading strategy models were applied to two small business case studies.

The descriptive strategy implementation process was evaluated using a framework to assess whether strategy models would be appropriate for small businesses. It was found that while these two models would be appropriate to study certain aspects of small businesses, issues pertaining to characterizing the business owners or the entrepreneurs would be less effectively understood using either of the two models. More specifically, the aspects of small businesses that require further explicit elaboration as constructs were managerial characteristics, behavioural aspects, business evolution, and problem-oriented strategy processes. The potentially missing information from the descriptive implementation of the two models was also evaluated for its importance. It was suggested that this information would have been critical in understanding the strategy process of these small businesses.

This short fall of current strategy models to effectively study small businesses could be one of the reasons why small business strategy literature, especially in hospitality industries, has lagged behind other mainstream studies. This has obviously led to the development of a parallel literature on small businesses. While that in itself is not of concern, the parallel literature continues to be anecdotally labelled as "non-mainstream." This could have and may continue to discourage researchers to pursue investigation of small businesses. While none of the two models studied in this paper appeared to be a perfect fit to study small business, together the two provided insights into how these models can be further extended in their conceptualizations to study small businesses or to develop extended models.

Another dimension that must be considered is can the current state-of-the-art of research support small business studies. In view of the conceptual gaps identified in the two models, constructs characterizing individuals, particularly owners or the entrepreneurs would need to be studied. Such characterizations would include managerial and behavioural aspects of the individuals, evolution of the businesses, and studying-specific problems. In essence this would require longitudinal, sample specific, possibly even context- and time-specific research. The analytical techniques required for some of these investigations may not necessarily be driven by probabilistic models but non-probabilistic, computational mathematical and statistical models, and may be even largely descriptive case study type approaches. This then highlights another challenge that exists in state-of-the-art of current research: the limited application of wide variety of methodological designs available to study the nature of problems and challenges facing small businesses. Several issues will need to be addressed in this context. Primarily, small business studies may not be large data driven analytical investigations but small sample specific analyses. Longitudinal study designs may imply larger resource commitment in terms of time and financial resources. This may discourage the use of large mail survey driven research and longer and in-depth commitments from the research teams. Such resources will need not only in-house commitments but also possibly external research funds. If external research funds are to be acquired for such studies it would automatically imply that studies are designed to provide solutions to problems that are not only context specific but applicable to business and society in general. Therefore, while at one-level investigations will need clear problem-orientation at another level research may still strive to be generic in nature. Implications of such research strategies will be on the choice of statistical methods, research designs, and most importantly reporting and application of solutions and results.

To summarize, the investigation through this discussion suggested that one possible reason strategy literature for small businesses is limited and fragmented is that leading models and theories may require additional constructs and conceptualizations to study small businesses. If the models focused in this investigation were found to be short of certain constructs to study small business, then it is also likely that other strategy models and theories may have limited conceptualization of the small business phenomenon. A related implication discussed was that methodological variety has and remains limited to study small businesses. Descriptive, case study-based research, and small sample datasets continue to be frowned at. Unfortunately these remain the leading modes to conduct small business research. This limitation

445

may also have contributed as an obstacle in furthering small business strategy research. Finally, hospitality small business strategy literature continues to be nascent particularly because the limited application of mainstream models have been used for these studies. Yet, this investigation found that the co-alignment principle, based in hospitality context, could be an appropriate model to study small business strategy with minor extensions of its conceptual boundaries. However, as stated earlier, this must also be coupled with a broadened scope of methodological variety in the study of small businesses. At the least, this investigation should provide researchers with the conscious knowledge and tools to assess mainstream strategy models and theories for their appropriateness to study small businesses. If gaps in other models can be identified researchers could fill these gaps and still try to investigate small businesses. This would hopefully not only increase the incidence of small business strategy research, but may also bring it closer to "mainstream strategy literature."

Conclusions

Small businesses are critical for economic growth, innovation, and entrepreneurship, yet literature to study strategic processes of these businesses remains limited. The fragmented state of small hospitality business strategy literature is of concern. One of the possible reasons why strategy studies in context of small hospitality businesses are few could be because leading strategy models and theories may require conceptual extension of their current constructs required to study small businesses. Another possibility suggested was that methodological variety has also been limited. Therefore, if hospitality strategy literature is to be strengthened to include small business studies, then a conscious effort needs to be made to increase conceptualizations of small businesses when using current models and theories, in addition to exploring new models. Methodological variety must also be explored as small businesses studies are not without special challenges. Given that a large share of worldwide hospitality industries is comprised of small businesses, efforts to strengthen this line of research will yield fruitful results to understand hospitality business phenomenon.

References

Adewole, A. (2005). Developing a strategic framework for efficient and effective optimisation of information in the supply chains of the UK clothing manufacture industry. *Supply Chain Management*, 10(5), 357–366.

Allaway, A., Mason, J. B., and Moore, T. D. (1988). A PC-based approach to promotion mix analysis and planning for small retailers. *Journal of Small Business Management, 26*(3), 14.

Arasli, H. (2002). "Diagnosing whether northern Cyprus hotels are ready for TQM: an empirical analysis". *Total Quality Management, 13*(3), pp. 347–364.

Audretsch, D. B., Prince, Y. M., and Thurik, AR. (1999). Do small firms compete with large firms? *Atlantic Economic Journal, 27*(2), 201–209.

Bassin, W. M. (1990). A technique for applying EOQ models to retail cycle stock inventories. *Journal of Small Business Management, 28*(1), 48.

Beal, R. M. (2000). Competing effectively: Environmental scanning, competitive strategy, and organizational performance in small manufacturing firms. *Journal of Small Business Management, 38*(1), 27–47.

Benrud, E. (2002). Challenges of existing in a market as a small, low-quality producer. *Small Business Economics, 18*(4), 269–280.

Brasch, J. J. (1981). Deciding on an organizational structure for entry into export marketing. *Journal of Small Business Management (pre-1986), 19*(000002), 7.

Bretherton, P., and Chaston, I. (2005). Resource dependency and SME strategy: An empirical study. *Journal of Small Business and Enterprise Development, 12*(2), 274–289.

Buick, I. (2003). Information technology in small Scottish hotels: Is it working? *International Journal of Contemporary Hospitality Management, 15*(4), 243–247.

Chetty, S., and Campbell-hunt, C. (2003). Paths to internationalisation among small- to medium-sized firms: A global versus regional approach. *European Journal of Marketing, 37*(5/6), 796–820.

Clarke, J., and Turner, P. (2004). Global competition and the Australian biotechnology industry: Developing a model of SMEs knowledge management strategies. *Knowledge and Process Management, 11*(1), 38–46.

Cooper, M. J., Upton, N., and Seaman, S. (2005). Customer relationship management: A comparative analysis of family and nonfamily business practices. *Journal of Small Business Management, 43*(3), 242–256.

Cressy, R. (2006). Why do most firms die young? *Small Business Economics, 26*(2), 103.

D'Amboise, G., and Muldowney, M. (1988). Management theory for small business: Attempts and requirements. *The Academy of Management Review, 13*(2), 226–240.

Darrow, W. P., King, A. B., and Helleloid, D. (2001). David vs. Goliath in the hardware industry: Generic strategies and critical success factors as revealed by business practice. *The Mid-Atlantic Journal of Business*, *37*(2/3), 97–109.

Davies, T. A. (2001). Enhancing competitiveness in the manufacturing sector: Key opportunities provided by inter firm clustering. *Competitiveness Review*, *11*(2), 4–15.

Davis, H. M., and Wood, D. D. (2005). A commission-based management spreadsheet model: Strategies to increase stockholder returns for an insurance agency. *Journal of Education for Business*, *80*(3), 139–144.

Drozdow, N., and Carroll, V. P. (1997). Tools for strategy development in family firms. *Sloan Management Review*, *39*(1), 75–88.

Entrialgo, M. (2002). The impact of the alignment of strategy and managerial characteristics on Spanish SMEs. *Journal of Small Business Management*, *40*(3), 260–270.

Gelderen, M. V., Frese, M., and Thurik, R. (2000). Strategies, uncertainty and performance of small business startups. *Small Business Economics*, *15*(3), 165–181.

Gibbons, P. T., and O'Connor, T. (2005). Influences on strategic planning processes among Irish SMEs. *Journal of Small Business Management*, *43*(2), 170–186.

Glancey, K., and Pettigrew, M. (1997). Entrepreneurship in the small hotel sector. *International Journal of Contemporary Hospitality Management*, *9*(1), 21–24.

Gunasekaran, A., Forker, L., and Kobu, B. (2000). Improving operations performance in a small company: A case study. *International Journal of Operations & Production Management*, *20*(3), 316–335.

Gurau, C. (2004). Positioning strategies in the value-added chain of the biopharmaceutical sector: The case of UK SMEs. *The Journal of Consumer Marketing*, *21*(7), 476–485.

Hall, O. P., Jr., and Mestler, C. (1997). Putting business planning software to the test. *The Journal of Business Strategy*, *18*(1), 42–45.

Hatton, L., and Raymond, B. (1994). Developing small business effectiveness in the context of congruence. *Journal of Small Business Management*, *32*(3), 76.

Hollenstein, H. (2005). Determinants of international activities: Are SMEs different? *Small Business Economics*, *24*(5), 431–450.

Huseyin, A. (2002). Gearing total quality into small- and medium-sized hotels in North Cyprus. *Journal of Small Business Management*, *40*(4), 350–359.

Jocumsen, G. (2004). How do small business managers make strategic marketing decisions? A model of process. *European Journal of Marketing*, *38*(5/6), 659–674.

Kaufman, T. J., Weaver, P. W., and Poynter, J. (1996). Success attributes of B&B operators. *Cornell Hotel and Restaurant Administration Quarterly*, 21–33.

Kickul, J., and Gundry, L. K. (2002). Prospecting for strategic advantage: The proactive entrepreneurial personality and small firm innovation. *Journal of Small Business Management*, *40*(2), 85–97.

Levy, M., Powell, P., and Yetton, P. (2002). The dynamics of SME information stations. *Small Business Economics*, *19*(4), 341.

Lopez-Gracia, J., and Aybar-Arias, C. (2000). An empirical approach to the financial behaviour of small and medium sized companies. *Small Business Economics*, *14*(1), 55–63.

Morrison, A. J. (1994). Marketing strategic alliances: The small hotel firm. *International Journal of Contemporary Hospitality Management*, *6*(3), 25.

Nwachukwu, O. C. (1995). CEO locus of control, strategic planning, differentiation, and small business performance: A test of a path analytic model. *Journal of Applied Business Research*, *11*(4), 9.

Olsen, M. D., Tse, E. C. Y., and West, J. (1998). *Strategic Management in the Hospitality Industry*. New York: Wiley.

Payne, G. T., Kennedy, K. H., Blair, J. D., and Fottler, M. D. (2005). Strategic cognitive maps of small business leaders. *Journal of Small Business Strategy*, *16*(1), 27–40.

Poorani, A. A., and Smith, D. R. (1995). Financial characteristics of bed-and-breakfast inns. *Cornell Hotel and Restaurant Administration Quarterly*, October, 57–63.

Porter, M. E. (1985). *Competitive Advantage*. New York: The Free Press.

ProQuest (2007). *Search of "Strategy" and "Strategy AND Small Business,"* retrieved in July 15, 2007.

Rasheed, H. S. (2005a). Foreign entry mode and performance: The moderating effects of environment. *Journal of Small Business Management*, *43*(1), 41–54.

Rasheed, H. S. (2005b). Turnaround strategies for declining small business: The effects of performance and resources. *Journal of Developmental Entrepreneurship*, *10*(3), 239–252.

Reid, G. C., and Smith, J. A. (2000). What makes a new business start-up successful? *Small Business Economics*, *14*(3), 165–182.

Reynolds, P. L., and Lancaster, G. (2006). A scheme to increase profitability in entrepreneurial SMEs. *Journal of Small Business and Enterprise Development*, *13*(3), 395–410.

Romer, P. M. (1986). Increasing returns and long-run growth. *Journal of Political Economy*, *5*(94), 1002–1037.

449

Other-Ref: Romer, P. M. (1990). Endogenous technological change. In E. Mansfield and E. Mansfield (Eds.), *The Economics of Technical Change. Elgar Reference Collection. International Library of Critical Writings in Economics*, Vol. 31. Aldershot, UK: Elgar. (Distributed in the U.S. by Ashgate, Brookfield, VT, 1993; pp. 12–43. Previously published in 1990.)

Roper, S. (1999). Modeling small business growth and profitability. *Small Business Economics, 13*(3), 235–252.

Sharma, A. (2006a). Economic impact and institutional dynamics of small hotels and restaurants in Tanzania. *Journal of Hospitality and Tourism Research, 30*(1), 76–94.

Sharma, A. (2006b). Economic costs and benefits of marketing local foods for independent restaurants and growers/producers in Iowa. Submitted to *the Leopold Center for Sustainable Agriculture at Iowa State University*.

Sharma, A., and Sneed, J. (2007). Production efficiency analysis of small hotels in Tanzania. *Journal of Services Research* (accepted for publication).

Sharma, A., and Upneja, A. (2005). Factors influencing financial performance of small hotels in Tanzania. *International Journal of Contemporary Hospitality Management, 17*(6), 504–515.

Sonfield, M., Lussier, R., Corman, J., and McKinney, M. (2001). Gender comparisons in strategic decision-making: An empirical analysis of the entrepreneurial strategy matrix. *Journal of Small Business Management, 39*(2), 165–173.

Van Auken, P. M., and Ireland, R. D. (1980). An input–output approach to practical small business planning. *Journal of Small Business Management (pre-1986), 18*(000001), 44.

Variyam, J. N., and Kraybill, D. S. (1993). Small firms' choice of business strategies. *Southern Economic Journal, 60*(1), 136.

Wilson, N. C., and Stokes, D. (2005). Managing creativity and innovation: The challenge for cultural entrepreneurs. *Journal of Small Business and Enterprise Development, 12*(3), 366–378.

Worsfold, D., and Griffith, C. J. (2003). A survey of food hygiene and safety training in the retail and catering industry. *Nutrition and Food Science, 33*(2), 68–79.

Zhang, L., Cai, L. A., Liu, W. H., Zhang, L., and Liu, W. H. (2002). On-job training-a critical human resources challenge in China's hotel industry. *Journal of Human Resources in Hospitality and Tourism, 1*(3), 91–100.

Part Seven

Strategy and multiunit issues

Factors influencing entrepreneurial orientation of ethnic minority small- and medium-sized hospitality enterprises

Levent Altinay[1] and Fevzi Okumus[2]

[1]*Oxford Brookes University Business School, Gipsy Lane Campus, OX3, OBP Headington, Oxford, UK*
[2]*Rosen College of Hospitality Management, The University of Central Florida, Universal Blvd., Orlando, FL 32819*

Introduction

Small and medium-sized enterprises (SMEs) account for over 95% of businesses in Organisation for Economic Co-operation and Development (OECD) countries and 60–70% of employment and generate a large percentage of new jobs in most countries (OECD, 2000). For example, there were an estimated 4.3 million small business enterprises in the United Kingdom at the start of 2005 employing approximately 22 million people (more than half of the employment—58.7%). They had an estimated annual turnover of £2400 billion (National Statistics, 2006). However, SMEs continue to face major problems including lack of financing, difficulties in exploiting technology, rapid changes in the business environment, lack of management skills, and poor HR management skills (OECD, 2000). Perhaps because of such challenges, it is claimed that a small percentage of new SMEs survive for more than 5 years (OECD, 2000).

In many developed countries, ethnic minority-owned SMEs are responsible for a considerable percentage of new business start-ups. This ratio is around 9% in the United Kingdom. These SMEs represent almost 7% of the total business stock (Bank of England, 1999). According to Osborne (2005), in 2004 ethnic minority entrepreneurs set up 50,000 new businesses—up a third from the figure in 2000 of 32,000—and they now account for 11% of all new firms. In a speech made in November 2002, Nigel Griffiths, the former Minister of Small Firms in Britain, claimed "Ethnic minority businesses are amongst the most entrepreneurial in society. There are 250,000 ethnic minority enterprises in the UK, contributing £13 billion a year to the British economy" (Griffiths, 2002). It is estimated that there are 100,000 ethnic minority-owned businesses in London, employing around 800,000 people (Ethnic Minorities and the Labor Market, 2003). Similar statements can be made about ethnic minority businesses in many cities in European countries as well as in the United States and Canada.

Ethnic minority SMEs face fierce competition not only from the other ethnic minority businesses but also from the mainstream businesses and brands. In the United States, many of the major retailers, groceries, banks, and other service providers have already adopted their business strategies to target ethnic minority consumers, leading to an increase in competition for ethnic entrepreneurs (Gore, 1998; Mummert, 1995). In the United Kingdom, with the increasing number of ethnic consumers, mainstream marketers tend to adapt their marketing strategies to target increasingly diverse consumers (Jamal,

2005). In the past, ethnic minority businesses competed only against their ethnic counterparts for survival. In today's world, competition is also with mainstream businesses that sell ethnic products such as Chinese Food, Turkish Delight, Chicken Biryani, and Japanese Sushi and also continuously seek ways to attract the "second generation immigrants" whose needs and wants are more aligned with those of the host country. It is also known that many ethnic minority SMEs in the United States and Europe target tourists visiting the host country.

Self-employed immigrants are highly concentrated in the tourism and hospitality industry (OECD, 2000). Particularly the independent restaurant sector, which includes restaurants, takeaways, and cafes, has been a popular activity for ethnic minority businesses in many developed countries. This can perhaps be explained by the relatively low entry barriers, such as the low financial start-up capital required compared to the other sectors (Basu and Altinay, 2002), low skill requirements (Basu and Goswami, 1999), and the cultural business tradition of ethnic groups (Basu, 2004; Basu and Altinay, 2002). Ethnic minority businesses in the tourism and hospitality industry have been traditionally reluctant to allocate time and financial resources for a strategic approach to managing their businesses (Altinay and Altinay, 2006). However, due to rapid changes in the business environment and fierce competition, they now need to adjust their entrepreneurial orientation by continuously monitoring the internal and external environments and finding creative ways to survive and prosper. This involves not only analysing the customer needs in the market but also adjusting the firm's strategies according to the competitors' moves; including the ones from the mainstream market.

To date, there has been limited research on entrepreneurial orientation of ethnic minority-owned SMEs in the tourism and hospitality industry. Given this, this chapter aims to discuss factors influencing entrepreneurial orientation of ethnic minority SMEs in this industry. This chapter begins by explaining the concept of entrepreneurial orientation. The following section evaluates the relationship between the cultural attributes of a business owner and the entrepreneurial orientation of the firm. This section also discusses whether the differences in the cultural backgrounds of the entrepreneurs lead to any differences in their reliance on their ethnic resources, in other words, on the use of ethnic capital, labour, advice, and customers in the hospitality industry. Finally, it draws on a number of conclusions and discusses several implications for small ethnic minority business owners and policy makers.

Entrepreneurship and entrepreneurial orientation

Entrepreneurship usually involves opening a new business and/or buying an existing one. It normally requires investing financial resources and time, which means a risk is associated with this move. Different reasons can be given to why some people are more successful in opening and running business and why people choose to become entrepreneurs. According to Basu (2004) and Basu and Altinay (2002), these reasons include making profit, the desire to take risk, having a spirit of adventure, having access to information or knowledge, the desire to create new products, and having no other choices but to choose self-employment. It appears that people become entrepreneurs due to one or more of the above reasons.

Entrepreneurial orientation refers to "the methods, practices, and decision-making styles managers use to act entrepreneurially" (Lumpkin and Dess, 1996, p. 136). As a strategic choice, entrepreneurial orientation is an embedded organizational philosophy that drives decision making and behaviour towards creating new goods, new methods of production, new markets, or diversification of the business into a new industry (Stevenson and Jarillo, 1990). These definitions suggest that while responding to developments in the market, organizations need to reflect propensity to engage in entrepreneurial behaviours, namely innovation, proactiveness, risk taking, and autonomy. Innovativeness refers to seeking new and creative solutions to problems and needs that can lead to new products and markets (Covin and Slevin, 1991). An example for prosperity to innovate in restaurants would be encouraging the employees, the chefs in particular, to come up with new dishes in order to meet and exceed the expectations of current and potential customers. Proactiveness involves shaping the environment by introducing new products, technologies, processes, and administrative techniques (Lumpkin and Dess, 1996). In the tourism and hospitality industry, we can see many examples of proactiveness ranging from Southwest Airlines' no frill and low cost concept in the United States, to a small pizza owner being the first one in a region doing home delivery to those customers who seek for convenience.

Risk taking involves the willingness to devote significant resources to new initiatives which have a reasonable chance of costly failure (Rugman and Hodgetts, 2000). Risk in broad sense occurs whenever anyone makes a choice and the potential outcomes involve uncertainty (Thompson, 1999). For organizations, uncertainty derives from political, economic, regulatory, and legal actions of government as well as global changes that can threaten the ability of the firm to map out and pursue strategic choices (Covin and Slevin, 1991). There is also uncertainty associated with competition. SMEs in the catering sector in particular should change their menus on a regular basis, take the risk of dropping off some of the offers from the menu, and introduce the new ones. For example, introducing Mexican food to your fast food restaurant menu in Europe may have a reasonable chance of costly failure because unlike in the United States, there are not many Mexican-origin people living in Europe or Americans may like to try more Mexican food than Europeans. However, changing consumer taste in Europe might indicate that there are opportunities for business growth if one was to introduce Mexican food or one Mexican dish in the menu. Here, you are taking a relevant risk that has a good business potential.

Autonomy refers to the organization's willingness to delegate responsibility to individuals or a team to take an independent action in bringing forth an idea or a vision and carrying it through to completion (Lumpkin and Dess, 1996). In the tourism and hospitality industry, autonomy is typically understood as a technique where front-line employees resolve problems immediately without management approval or intervention (Lashley, 2001). This is important since in a hotel, café, or restaurant, customers' demands cannot be kept "on hold" for long. Employees should have the authority to decide how to respond to customers' requests. For example, if owners of ethnic minority SMEs want their employees to deliver customized services to the customers, employees should have the authority to touch the feelings of the customers by solving problems and offering discounts or giving complementary foods and drinks.

In the ethnic minority SMEs context, innovativeness may entail using employees, suppliers, and information within and outside of the firm's ethnic enclave, and offering new products and services to customers. Again, even offering products or services from the home to the host country targeting home country residents may be considered as partly an innovation. Proactiveness may encompass increasing market share by serving co-ethnic customers, home country citizens as well as tourists. Ethnic minorities would heavily rely on capital from their relatives and co-ethnics at business start-up in order to avoid paying interest (Basu and Goswami, 1999). Risk taking in ethnic minority businesses is often related to different levels of resource commitments, and modes of financing such as banks and other financial institutions (Altinay and Wang, 2007). The other question is whether ethnic minority-owned SMEs delegate power to family or non-family members as a form of empowerment. Autonomy involves the ability to delegate responsibility to non-family members or to non-ethnics in terms of decision making, spending money, and resource allocations.

Creating an entrepreneurial orientation that leads to survival and business growth is a more multifaceted task. It requires an effective management of the interdependence between a firm and its environment. A number of factors influence the entrepreneurial orientation of a firm. According to Covin and Slevin (1991) a firm behaviour of entrepreneurship consists of three levels of variables—environmental, organizational, and individual. Various external environmental conditions including political, economic, and sociocultural factors stimulate or impede entrepreneurial activity. For example, the growing demand for healthy options stimulated entrepreneurial activities in the catering sector and triggered off the need for innovations in this area. Business strategy, organizational structure, organizational culture, and organization's resources and capabilities can affect the ability of the firm to engage in entrepreneurial activity. For example, standardized business strategies limit innovative solutions and the flexibility to adapt to the changing environment leads to missed business opportunities (Hall, 1991).

Reacting to changes in the environment requires moving the decision-making authority away from centralized structure towards a decentralized authority. In order to be capable of adequately responding to changes in dynamic environments, organizations often decentralize decision-making authority, have minimal hierarchical levels or structural layers, and adopt free-flow communication channels (Caruana *et al.*, 2002). These attributes permit flexibility and rapid decision making, and thus make a positive impact on an organization's opportunity seeking performance. In addition, organizational structure and culture should support and facilitate generation of new ideas. Internal resources and capabilities are also portrayed as essential foundations for business owners to develop their ventures. These resources include management skills, strategic planning, and capable human capital. The strategic combination of these valuable and unique resources creates competitive advantage and permit successful competition (Barney, 1991).

In SMEs, entrepreneurial orientation is grounded in the values, intentions, and actions of the individual who is in charge. In fact, a small firm is simply an extension of the individual entrepreneur, and therefore influenced by the inherent characteristics of the entrepreneur (Lumpkin and Dess, 1996). Bamberger (1982) suggests that owner's values and backgrounds are important determinants of a small firm's culture and its business practices. He states that "The manager's value systems determine whether a firm pursues the objective of growth or independence, diversifies, enters foreign markets, adopts an active or passive behavior on the market" (p. 46). An ethnic minority-owned small firm is simply an extension of the owner, and therefore influenced by the inherent characteristics of the entrepreneur. In other words, owners are the key stakeholder group and one needs to pay particular attention to their backgrounds in order to be able to understand the entrepreneurial orientation of ethnic minority SMEs.

There may be numerous factors influencing ethnic minority entrepreneurship; however, the relevant literature suggests that cultural attributes of the entrepreneur including ethnicity, religion, language, education, and experience play important roles in developing entrepreneurial abilities and contributing to the survival of the entrepreneur's business (Altinay and Altinay, 2006; Basu and Altinay, 2002; Basu and Goswami, 1999; Ucbasaran *et al.*, 2003; Westhead and Cowling, 1995). These factors influence the four constructs of entrepreneurial orientation, namely, innovation, proactiveness, risk taking, and autonomy, and thus the growth of the ethnic minority firm. The following section discusses the main factors influencing entrepreneurial orientation in ethnic minority SMEs.

Factors influence entrepreneurial orientation in ethnic SMEs

As noted above, there may be numerous other factors influencing entrepreneurial orientation in ethnic SMEs. However, ethnicity, religion, language proficiency, education, and previous experience particularly emerged as the main factors from an extensive literature review. Therefore, it was decided to focus particularly on these factors in this section. In short, this section aims to answer how cultural background (ethnicity, religion, proficiency in the host country language, education, and previous experience) can influence entrepreneurial orientation, in particular the use of ethnic capital (extent of risk taking), reliance on co-ethnic labour (extent of innovativeness and autonomy) and advice (extent of innovativeness), and targeting co-ethnic customers (extent of proactiveness) (Figure 20.1).

Cultural background of the owner and the access to capital—risk taking

Ethnic minority entrepreneurship literature suggests that cultural background (ethnicity in particular) and religion of owners can influence the entrepreneurial orientation of their firms. For example, Bonacich (1973) claimed that immigrants are more

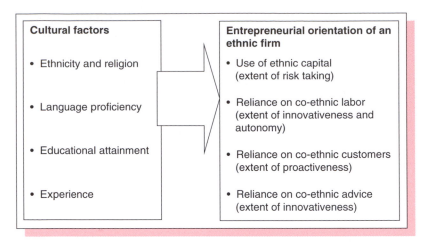

Cultural factors	Entrepreneurial orientation of an ethnic firm
• Ethnicity and religion	• Use of ethnic capital (extent of risk taking)
• Language proficiency	• Reliance on co-ethnic labor (extent of innovativeness and autonomy)
• Educational attainment	• Reliance on co-ethnic customers (extent of proactiveness)
• Experience	• Reliance on co-ethnic advice (extent of innovativeness)

Figure 20.1
Cultural background of an owner and entrepreneurial orientation of an ethnic firm.

entrepreneurs than local residents since they work hard and support each other. Bonacich also recognized that some immigrant communities have more entrepreneurial characteristics compared to other communities such as the Jews, Armenians, Chinese, and East African Asians who would likely to become entrepreneurs and open businesses when they immigrate to other countries.

Korean immigrants differ from other immigrant groups such as European and Asian immigrants in the United States in terms of their high education level, job occupations, religion, urban and middle class origin, strong informal networks (high reliance on family labour, co-ethnic employees), and high degree of sectoral concentration, which enabled them to strengthen their ethnic solidarity and allowed access to significant amounts of capital when they immigrated to the United States (Park *et al.*, 1990; Yoon, 1997). In contrast to the Korean entrepreneurs in the United States, Chinese entrepreneurs lack human capital skills, labour market information, and money to invest on arrival in the United States. Therefore, Chinese immigrants were found to be relatively more disadvantaged compared with other immigrant groups in the United States (Kwong, 1997; Zhou, 1992). Therefore, the business success rate of Chinese businesses is lower than that of Korean businesses (Zhou, 1992). However, there is still limited empirical evidence about the success rate of various ethnic minority businesses in the tourism and hospitality industry.

In the United Kingdom, Pakistanis seem to be less successful than Indians in self-employment because of cultural factors, for example the influence of religion which prohibits the payment of interest on (bank) loans. Pakistanis who wish to live according to Islamic values are less willing to integrate with Western culture and consequently have not performed as well as non-Muslim businesses (Rafiq, 1992; Smallbone *et al.*, 1999). It appears that the religion of the owner may constitute a barrier to capital access from banks and the Muslim managers rely on the capital from co-ethnics for their business start-ups and entrepreneurial activities. Contrary to these practices, there are other Muslim entrepreneurs such as Turkish and Turkish Cypriots who seem to be pragmatic. They borrow money from financial institutions especially if alternative modes of finance are unavailable (Basu and Altinay, 2002). Therefore, it is difficult to generalize for all immigrant communities that religion alone plays an important role in accessing the capital for investment. Other factors such as cultural background, education, and the immediate need for capital may influence decisions to find capital and take risks.

For the ethnic minority business owners the ability to communicate with others in the host country language is an important factor in finding capital. This is because it has a significant impact on social and economic integration (Levent *et al.*, 2003). Ethnic minority business owners who can communicate in the host country language can have a higher level of personal confidence to seek capital from banks and other financial institutions and rely less on co-ethnic capital. In the tourism and hospitality industry, entrepreneurs need capital to start up their businesses. These entrepreneurs' business ideas may range from a small takeaway shop or coffee shop to a restaurant. Similarly, small business owners who develop new ideas and concepts need capital to sustain growth. In most cases, they need capital to expand the capacity or to open another branch. There may also be cases that new ideas are either postponed or totally cancelled because of the entrepreneurs' level of education leading to a confidence or ability problem to develop proposals for loan application from banks or other financial institutions. Educational attainment also helps business owners improve their knowledge about business and equips them with the skills to apply for funds from banks and evaluate the risk associated with any investment decision (Basu and Goswami, 1999).

The entrepreneur's previous work experience in the field prior to opening a new venture is also an important factor that influences how the entrepreneur handles the start-up and the growth of the business (Hatch and Dyer, 2004). For example, in the catering industry, there are many owners who worked either as waiters/waitresses or as chefs before they started up their businesses. Previous experience significantly diminishes the risk and influence positively the individual's intentions of founding a business (Goedhuys and Sleuwaegen, 2000). Previous experience facilitates the creation of networks which affect fund raising to start up their businesses. Informal networks such as friends and relatives can give them the opportunity to raise capital with minimum interest and also without going through the bureaucratic obstacles of financial institutions. In case they ask banks for loans, previous experience can also give them credibility in the eyes of lenders.

Finding capital at the lowest cost is an important factor both at the start-up and growth stages of an ethnic minority-owned business. There is no consensus about the influence of co-ethnic capital on ethnic minority firms' growth. Some researchers argue that reliance on co-ethnics for financial loans can be a barrier to business growth. This is because such a practice allows some flexibility to the business owners and thus leads to a "lax" management style (Altinay and Altinay, 2006). Contrary to these views, some argue that the business survival of ethnic minority entrepreneurs depends on the access to cheap family labour and close community networks, which may offer low-cost capital (Barrett *et al.*, 2002; Basu and Goswami, 1999; Basu, 1998). In ethnic SMEs business in the tourism and hospitality industry, the "widespread" approach appears to rely on the informal networks for financial loans at the start-up to minimize the risk and the cost of borrowings. Once the business starts to grow, then the business owners apply for financial loans from banks to sustain growth. These practices aim to reduce the risk of borrowings.

Cultural background of the owner and the use of ethnic labour force

Cultural background and the religion of the owner in particular may affect the use of human resources management practices of the ethnic minority businesses in some cultures (Gudmundson and Hartenian, 2000). Owners of ethnic SMEs might have a strong preference for hiring candidates from their own religion and cultural background, even though the candidates may be less qualified to perform certain duties. The reliance on employees from their own religion and national culture may reflect the owner's attempt to strengthen what they call "brotherhood" within their own community. A high reliance on co-ethnic labour may imply that entrepreneurs belonging to that ethnic group have a strong cultural identity that they wish to preserve (Altinay and Wang, 2007). Language difficulties can also influence the recruitment practices of the ethnic minority business owners. Those entrepreneurs who do not have good command of host country language may have to rely mainly on co-ethnic labour force and delegate responsibility to only their co-ethnics in order to be able to manage the firm (Levent *et al.*, 2003). This, however, may raise further challenges and problems.

Having or not having education and training in the field can have implications on recruitment. The owners with good education can break out of the ethnic enclave and recruit qualified people outside of their ethnic community. This in return can assist ethnic minority entrepreneurs both to integrate with the wider community and also to exploit the skills and mindsets of the outsiders. Those entrepreneurs who have attained higher level of education have the mindset and the skills to recruit people outside of the ethnic community and empower them to expand the breadth of perspectives and ideas. Looking at the nature of the hospitality industry, one can easily see that hospitality firms accommodate customers from diverse groups with different nationalities and cultures. The entrepreneurs with higher educational attainment usually develop the analytical and managerial abilities to screen the applicants and recruit better candidates in order to accommodate the diversity in consumers' culture-bound service and product preferences. Therefore, it should not come to us as a surprise to see a highly educated Greek-owned restaurant offering contemporary Chinese food experience to a diverse group of customers with its Chinese chefs and a group of waiters and waitresses from different nationalities and backgrounds.

The competitiveness of small and medium-sized businesses in the catering industry very much depends on their ability to differentiate themselves on the quality of the service they offer (Altinay and Altinay, 2006). They are, therefore, in need of employees who possess enough knowledge about the operations of the industry and the skills to deliver quality service which would meet and exceed customers' needs and expectations. Previous experience of the owners can also help them to find unique ways to differentiate their businesses from competitors. In particular, previous experience of owners can help assess the quality and suitability of potential employees for specific positions.

Cost of labour is the largest component of overhead costs in tourism and hospitality operations (Burgess, 2001; Harris, 2003). Therefore, ethnic minority SMEs in this industry tend to employ family members and co-ethnic employees especially at the start-up. This gives them a competitive advantage over their counterparts because family members and co-ethnic labour enable them to reduce their labour costs and maintain a wage lower than the average payroll. In addition, immigrant entrepreneurs can have access to co-ethnic labour who are ready to work under less favourable economic conditions due to lack of qualifications, making it difficult for them to obtain employment in the mainstream job market or even due to their illegal status (Waldinger *et al.*, 1990). More importantly, in the case of ethnic minority-owned tourism and hospitality firms, recruitment of co-ethnic employees who know the ethnic products can help them inform the customers about the ethnic products. This can help ethnic minority business owners differentiate themselves at the service level. Increasing the proportion of the "co-ethnic labour force" can add "ethnic flavour" to what they offer to customers. This may be seen as an innovation and competitive advantage for ethnic minority SMEs.

In the foodservice sector, it is important that employees know enough about the products in order to be able to inform the customers about what they experience (Seo *et al.*, 2001; Stephenson, 1995). In the case of an ethnic catering outlet, offering an "authentic food and drink" or an "authentic experience" can inevitably require employing a "co-ethnic labour force" who knows about the cultural dimension of the food and food-serving experience. Having said that, there are many ethnic minority-owned hospitality firms which suffer from the consequences of recruiting relatives and co-ethnics because such a practice encourages nepotism in management and promotion issues. In addition, they cannot break out into the mainstream or tourist market because of the heavy reliance on co-ethnic labour. Recruiting a nationally diverse workforce can help them expand the breadth of perspectives and ideas available to the organization in making decisions and richer wider customer segments (Cox, 1991).

Empowerment of employees and managers is an important issue in tourism and hospitality organizations since it can lead to higher customer satisfaction and increased profits and sales (Baum, 2006; Lashley, 2001; Nickson, 2007). Empowerment provides employees with a sense of autonomy and control in the service process and this produces a positive emotional state from which stems additional commitment and effort. In turn, this produces better service quality and more satisfied customers, together with increased sales and more profits. Immigrant entrepreneurs make maximum use of family labour as not only the members of the family provide cheap labour support but also they can be empowered believing that it is their family business and they have to succeed (Waldinger *et al.*, 1990).

Family members, therefore, will try to reduce cost and offer better service and, when necessary, can take the ownership of problems and opportunities when the owner of the business (or head of the family) is not present.

However, in most of the small ethnic minority tourism and hospitality firms owners/managers prefer to have a "hands on management approach" and tend to centralize the decision making. Such a management approach neither gives a sense of authority and control to the employees (particularly non-family members) nor stimulates employee commitment to the workplace and the job. In turn, this brings about de-motivation in employees, lower service quality, and a decrease in sales and growth. Empowering non-family members in particular can help the ethnic minority businesses both to integrate with the wider community, including customers, suppliers, businesses, and banks, and also to exploit the skills and mindsets of those outsiders (Altinay and Altinay, 2006).

Cultural background of the owner and choosing ethnic customers as target market

There is an ethnic as well as religious loyalty between ethnic businesses and their clients (Levent *et al.*, 2003). Religion, in particular, can be a source of trust and confidence between customers and the owner, which can create more-than-average loyalty and relationships between the ethnic firm and its customers. This intra-cluster ethnic loyalty offers potential competitive advantage for ethnic firms because the emotional attachment will bring the mutual trust that all long-term relationships need to have (Altinay and Wang, 2007). However, this comparative advantage may also create some barriers for break-out strategies in terms of new opportunities to expand the business and opening to new and non-traditional markets (Levent *et al.*, 2003). In the catering sector in particular, there are some Muslim business owners who are not willing to break out of their religious territories and, for example, sell alcohol or serve pork dishes if demanded by customers. Such a practice may limit their ability to sell products to this customer group and thus weaken their position against the firms that are prepared to diversify their products and services to accommodate customers' needs. However, it is very common to see ethnic restaurants in many big cities worldwide selling halal food that aim to target Muslim customers.

Fluency in host country language and familiarity with the culture undoubtedly provide the ethnic minority entrepreneurs with opportunities in the wider mainstream customer market. For example, a study investigating business strategies of Turkish businesses in the United Kingdom showed that the survival and growth of Turkish businesses operating in the catering sector was highly dependent on meeting the expectations of existing and future customers (Altinay and Altinay, 2006). However, the business owners who had language difficulties could not communicate with customers other than the co-ethnics. Therefore, they received support from their children, who are mainly the second generation of immigrants, to facilitate the communication. In this study, it became apparent that communication with different stakeholder groups, particularly with customers, is a key to the successful operations of the catering businesses. Ethnic minority entrepreneurs need to possess good host country language communication skills in order to be able to break into the mainstream market successfully (Altinay and Altinay, 2006).

Owners and managers of ethnic minority businesses in the tourism and hospitality industry need to gather market intelligence in order to respond the changing customer trends. A higher level of education develops both the analytical ability and the computational skills of the entrepreneur to gather market intelligence and break out into the mainstream market, as well as communication skills to target a wide range of customer groups. In terms of the level of education, there seem to be differences among immigrant groups. For example, in the United Kingdom it was found that 25% of working-age Indians had higher educational qualifications, compared with 12% Pakistanis and Bangladeshis, and 29% Chinese. Similarly, the unemployment rate among Indians is 7.6%, compared with 17.1% for Bangladeshis and Pakistanis (Office for National Statistics, 2001). One may also claim that the level of education among ethnic minority groups may be very different between the first and second generation of each immigration group.

In terms of expanding a business, recent research found a positive effect of one's educational level on the likelihood to perceive entrepreneurial opportunities (Clercq and Arenius, 2006). For example, the Greek Kailis brothers attribute their success as exporters of lobster and other seafood to their secondary/tertiary qualifications which, they maintain, better equipped them to remain flexible and open to market forces and opportunities (Peters, 2002). Previous experience can also assist owners to identifying new market opportunities (Perez and Pablos, 2003) and diversify their products and services. In circumstances where the context of the new business is similar to the one where the entrepreneur gained earlier, s/he might be able to capitalize on the previous relationships with customers and suppliers in their operations (Haber and Reichel, 2007).

Ethnic minority businesses rely heavily on selling ethnic products to co-ethnic markets particularly at the initial stages of the business where it gives an additional advantage (Ram and Hillin, 1994; Waldinger *et al.*, 1990). This is particularly the case in the catering sector where dealing with co-ethnic customers influences business growth because the business owner is always around to assert control over the operations, especially in addressing customer problems. However, heavy reliance on co-ethnic customers and failure to attract customers from the mainstream market can be the main constraint to business growth (Basu, 1998; Jamal, 2005; Smallbone *et al.*, 1999). For example, if an ethnic minority business owned by an Indian stays within the community and sells only chicken biryani to Indian customers, then their business growth will be limited. In other words, inability to attract customers from outside of the Indian market by diversifying their product range will be the key constraints on the growth. Therefore, to enable the growth of a business, a strategic "breakout" into the mainstream market of local residents is needed. In addition, ethnic minority SMEs in many cities and urban tourism destinations such as London, Berlin, Paris, New York, Orlando, and Toronto do target not only their ethnic markets and local residents but also tourists visiting these cities. This implies that the owners of these SMEs not only need to have a good understanding of the needs and expectations of tourists from main tourism markets but also should be able to learn some key words and expressions from different languages and prepare menus in several languages.

Cultural background of the owner and the use of ethnic advice

Ties between people with the same religion and ethnic background are most likely to be realized through financial loans and giving trusted advice (Feld, 1984; McPherson *et al.*, 2001). People socialize with friends, relatives, and associates and ask advice from these parties who belong to the same religions and ethnic background. For example, there are many Indian-, Chinese-, Korean-, and Turkish-owned catering businesses in the United States and United Kingdom whose information gathering requirements may be satisfied by contacts from social/informal "networks." There is little, if any contact with "formal" support bodies such as trade associations, Chambers of Commerce, and other business links. Even if there are such associations, advice is usually gained through organizations or individuals with an affinity to the operations of firms who have an owner/manager from the Indian, Chinese, Korean, or Turkish community with similar religious and ethnic background.

Proficiency in the host country language affects the extent they use mainstream business support agencies. Ethnic minority-owned SMEs often rely on self-help and co-ethnic sources of advice because they do not have a good command of host country language, which results in lack of effective communication with the support agencies. Due to language barrier, they may not even be aware of trade associations and support agencies. In the United Kingdom, a series of workshops and short courses are being held by local councils and business support agencies for the ethnic minority restaurant and café owners about food hygiene, environmental sustainability, and management training (Wealden Food and Safety Bulletin, 2005). However, most of the time council and mainstream business support agencies do not communicate in the language of the ethnic minority group and such a practice acts as a barrier for the dissemination of the information on business support issues for those entrepreneurs who do not feel comfortable with the language of the host country.

In the context of business planning and development, business owners have regular meetings with banks and venture capitalists and receive feedback on their applications for financial loans (Richbell *et al.*, 2005). Education can contribute to the development of good relationship with a credit officer (banker), as can good interpersonal skills (Basu and Goswami, 1999; Storey *et al.*, 1989). It is also possible that owners with good education have a higher level of personal confidence to seek advice from banks, financial institutions, and mainstream business advisers (Coleman, 2005; Rogers *et al.*, 2001; Young, 2002). Previous experience further creates a "cognitive framework" that facilitates pattern recognition and therefore favours the identification of sources for advice and information. Ethnic minority business owners who have had experience of gaining advice from financial institutions, banks, and other consultancy firms might find it easier to collect information or get advice from these sources. Contrary to these, the ones who have had only the experience of getting advice from their informal networks such as family members and friends tend to rely solely on these sources (Altinay and Altinay, 2006).

Information support is important for business growth in every industry (Storey *et al.*, 1987). Ethnic minority entrepreneurs rely very little on mainstream institutional information from banks, accountants, business advisors, and support service providers (Fadahunsi *et al.*, 2000; Marlow, 1992; Ram and Sparrow, 1993). Instead, informal social networks such as family members and friends are more common (Basu, 1998; Fadahunsi *et al.*, 2000). From the business growth point of view, the research suggests that information about markets is very important for growth and the businesses that maintain strong ties and informal networks have advantages compared to their counterparts (Basu and Altinay, 2002; Werbner, 1990; Waldinger *et al.*, 1990). For example, there are small ethnic minority tourism and hospitality firm owners who seek advice from business consultants especially for their start-ups. This however raises their cost of operations and impact upon the growth negatively. The ones who rely on the advice and information from the informal networks have comparative advantage over the others because they shave costs off the advice/information element of the value chain at the start-up. However, it is important to note that these firms might need advice from mainstream institutional information from banks, accountants, business advisors, and support service providers in order to improve their marketing, human resource, financial, and operations practices in the growth stage of their operations.

Conclusions and recommendations

This chapter aimed to discuss and evaluate factors influencing entrepreneurial orientation of ethnic minority SMEs in the tourism and hospitality industry. From the above discussions, we can draw a number of conclusions for the academics and propose implications for the practitioners and policy makers. First, owners of ethnic minority SMEs play a crucial role in setting a direction and influencing the culture and management of these firms. Therefore, one needs to understand and evaluate the cultural background and skills of their owners even before providing specific recommendations for these ethnic firms. The background and competencies of the owners very much determine the extent an ethnic minority-owned SME can operate proactively, communicate, innovate, take risks, and delegate autonomy to the employees and managers.

Second, the growth of SMEs is a process that has two main stages, namely, start-up and growth. It is clear that cultural background, religion, language skills, education, and work experience of the business owner influence these two important stages. Therefore, owners of ethnic minority-owned SMEs need to consider and appraise their cultural attributes and skills even before they start up the business. These factors are the antecedents of the set-up and growth of a business that they should possess prior to the start-up of a business. For example, an adaptation of cultural and religious background to the changing global economic conditions could help them further exploit their multifarious cultural heritages and contribute to the economic and social development of a broad-based community.

Third, accumulated experience of working as an employee, manager, or an entrepreneur in the related field can help them prevent or solve customer and employee–management issues by drawing on a "cognitive framework" that facilitates pattern recognition and favours identification of solutions and opportunities. Fourth, those owners who have a higher level of language proficiency of the host country and business education are better equipped to communicate and understand bankers, employees, suppliers, and customers, gather market intelligence, and develop appropriate strategies. In return such skills then lead to better performance and a higher growth in their businesses. The owners with a higher level of education (i.e., business degree) possess the mindset and the skills to adopt a more professional approach to human resources, marketing, finance, and strategic development. More specifically, they can invest more into employee training, offer incentives to their employees to retain them, use various marketing channels (not only ethnic newspapers or radio) to target the diverse consumer groups, and make more use of recent technological innovations in operations and marketing. The ability to communicate with customers, employees, bankers, and other stakeholders in host country's language is an important factor which in turn has a significant impact on their ability to attract customers and access necessary resources such as business advice and start-up bank loans.

Finally, for ethnic minority SMEs in the tourism and hospitality industry, competition is no longer about gaining and increasing market share, but also about finding employees who are well trained, dedicated, and keen to be a part of operations and the strategic direction of the company. On the one hand, customer expectations are rising across the range and the competition is intensifying to gain market share and, on the other hand, the tourism and hospitality industry is struggling with the general shortage of skilled staff (Baum, 2006; Hospitality and Catering Industry Report, 2003). In a labour-intensive industry, competitive advantage requires having employees who are equipped with the necessary skills and competences and empowering them to deliver optimum service quality. However, it is a great challenge for the SMEs to recruit skilled labour force as the industry is faced with skills shortages.

In addition, skilled employees prefer to work for larger companies that offer better payment and benefits, employee reward schemes, and career opportunities (Small Business Research Trust, 2001).

In terms of recommendations for owners and policy makers, we believe that the owners of ethnic minority SMEs should continuously reconsider the strategic position of their firms in the competitive market. This certainly requires the adoption of the entrepreneurial orientation of their firm that would allow change and align the firm's activities with the dynamic environment. Such a strategic move necessitates the notion of openness to new ideas. Operating within the community and targeting only their co-ethnic customers by working closely with co-ethnic suppliers, relying solely on co-ethnic capital, co-ethnic employees, and co-ethnic advice might offer them a "secure" environment for business opportunities, particularly in the early stages of their business development. It is more likely that they will survive with their socioculturally embedded attributes, including education, language, religion, and experience. However, in order to be able to compete, they need to align their entrepreneurial orientation with the changes in the broader environment. This can only be done by integrating their cultural attributes to the social, economic, and cultural realities of the host country and the global markets. Ethnic minority business owners who have been reluctant to allocate time and financial resources for personal development in the past should now start investing in the development of their business and communication skills. They should further invest in recruiting, training, and empowering their entrepreneurial employees while encouraging accountability. Another alternative would be developing succession plans for their children who are culturally more integrated with the host country and investing in their education.

Policy makers and members of local councils should establish and use the right mechanisms to help these ethnic minority business owners so that they can improve their skills in communication, negotiation, finance, marketing, and strategic planning. For ethnic minority business owners, especially for the first-generation immigrants, doing business in another country might mean a radical cultural shift in their business mentality. Specific workshops on marketing, leading people, communication, finance and accounting, and strategic planning can be helpful for the current and potential ethnic entrepreneurs. Certainly depending on their ethnic background and language proficiency, these workshops can be delivered in multiple languages. These training workshops can be broadcast on local TVs. However, it is also possible that owners of some ethnic minority SMEs may still be in the early stages of cultural shock and therefore need to have a better understanding of the host county culture and business environment before attending workshops and training programs on marketing, communication, finance, accounting, and strategic planning. There is no doubt that their survival and success can contribute to the economy and social well-being of the country.

Community-based organizations and ethnic accountants should be supported by the government to help integrate these business owners into the host county business environment. Among various channels "ethnic accountants" are perhaps one of the most appropriate ones as ethnic minority business owners are reluctant to attend the workshops organized by the local council and business development units because of the "time constraint." However, they seem to spend a considerable amount of time (both social and formal occasions) with their accountants. It is also important that both community-based organizations and government policy makers target ethnic minority SMEs with growth potential and help them develop succession plans as well as the appropriate human resource, marketing, operations, finance, and strategic management practices to change the value systems in their firms and secure long-term growth.

As noted earlier, there have been limited conceptual and empirical studies looking at ethnic minority SMEs. Given this, this area offers many research opportunities. For example, researchers can empirically investigate how far the cultural background of owners influences the entrepreneurial orientation of ethnic minority SMEs in tourism and hospitality organizations. Comparative studies can be undertaken looking at problems and success factors of SMEs from various cultural backgrounds in one country or in several countries. Research studies can also look at marketing, human resource management, finance, and strategic planning practices of ethnic SMEs in different sectors of the tourism and hospitality industry. Providing empirical evidence about why entrepreneurs from some cultures in certain sectors are more successful and what the success and failure factors in this journey are would be helpful to academics, practitioners, government officials, and policy makers.

References

Altinay, L., and Altinay, E. (2006). Determinants of ethnic minority entrepreneurial growth in the catering sector. *The Service Industries Journal, 26,* 203–221.

Altinay, L., and Wang, C. (2007). *Socio-cultural Background, Entrepreneurial Behavior of the Firm and its Growth*. Paper presented at the First International Colloquium on Ethnic Entrepreneurship: Changing Faces of Ethnic Entrepreneurship, Bradford University School of Management. 22nd–23rd March, pp. 230–250.

Bamberger, I. (1982). Value systems, strategies and the performance of small and medium-sized firms. *European Small Business Journal, 1*, 25–37.

Bank of England. (1999). *The Financing of Ethnic Minority Firms in the United Kingdom. A Special Report*, London: Bank of England.

Barney, J. (1991). Social theory forum: The resource based model of the firm: origins, implications and prospects. *Journal of Management, 17*, 97–114.

Barrett, G., Jones, T., McEvoy, D., and McGoldrick, C. (2002). The economic embeddedness of immigrant enterprise in Britain. *International Journal of Entrepreneurial Behavior and Research, 8*, 11–31.

Basu, A. (1998). The role of institutional support in Asian entrepreneurial expansion in Britain. *Journal of Small Business and Enterprise Development, 5*, 317–326.

Basu, A. (2004). Entrepreneurial aspirations amongst family business owners: An analysis of ethnic business owners in the UK. *International Journal of Entrepreneurial Behavior and Research, 10*, 12–33.

Basu, A., and Altinay, E. (2002). The interaction between culture and entrepreneurship in London's immigrant business. *International Small Business Journal, 20*, 371–394.

Basu, A., and Goswami, A. (1999). Determinants of South Asian entrepreneurial growth in Britain: A multivariate analysis. *Small Business Economics, 13*, 57–70.

Baum, T. (2006). *Human Resource Management for Tourism, Hospitality and Leisure: An International Perspective*. London: Thomson Learning.

Bonacich, E. (1973). A theory of middleman minorities. *American Sociological Review, 38*, 583–594.

Burgess, C. (2001). *Guide to Money Matters for Hospitality Managers*. Oxford, UK: Butterworth Heinemann.

Caruana, A., Ewing, T., and Ramaseshan, B. (2002). Effects of some environmental challenges and centralisation on the entrepreneurial orientation and performance of public sector entities. *The Service Industries Journal, 22*, 43–58.

Clercq, D., and Arenius, P. (2006). The role of knowledge in business start-up activity. *International Small Business Journal, 24*, 339–358.

Coleman, S. (2005). Is there a liquidity crisis for small, black-owned firms? *Journal of Developmental Entrepreneurship, 10,* 29–47.

Covin, J., and Slevin, D. (1991). A conceptual model of entrepreneurship as firm behavior. *Entrepreneurship: Theory and Practice, 16,* 51–67.

Cox, T. (1991). The multicultural organization. *Executive, 5,* 34–47.

Ethnic minorities and the labor market. (2003). *Cabinet Office Strategy Unit Report.* March. Strategy Unit, Admiralty Arch, The Mall London.

Fadahunsi, A., Smallbone, D., and Supri, S. (2000). Networking and ethnic minority enterprise development: Insights from a north London study. *Journal of Small Business and Enterprise Development, 7*(3), 228–240.

Feld, L. (1984). The structured use of personal associates. *Social Forces, 62,* 640–652.

Goedhuys, M., and Sleuwaegen, L. (2000). Entrepreneurship and growth of entrepreneurial firms in Cote D'Avoire. *Journal of Development Studies, 36,* 123–146.

Gore, J. P. (1998). Ethnic marketing may become the norm. *Bank Marketing, 30,* 12–15.

Griffiths, N. (2002). Engaging ethnic enterprise conference February 13, *Department of Trade and Industry,* from http://www.dti.gov.uk/ministers/speeches/griffiths

Gudmundson, D., and Hartenian, S. (2000). Workforce diversity in small business: An empirical investigation. *Journal of Small Business Management, July,* 27–36.

Haber, S., and Reichel, A. (2007). The cumulative nature of the entrepreneurial process: The contribution of human capital, planning and environment resources to small venture performance. *Journal of Business Venturing, 22,* 119–145.

Hall, H. R. (1991). *Organisations: Structures, Processes and Outcomes.* London: Prentice Hall International Editions.

Harris, P. (2003). *Profit Planning.* Oxford, UK: Butterworth Heinemann.

Hatch, N., and Dyer, J. (2004). Human capital and learning as a source of sustainable competitive advantage. *Strategic Management Journal, 25,* 1155–1178.

Hospitality and Catering Industry Report. (2003). *Qualifications and Curriculum Authority.* Retrieved April 15, 2004, from http://www.qca.ork.uk

Jamal, A. (2005). Playing to win: An explorative study of marketing strategies of small ethnic retail entrepreneurs in the UK. *Journal of Retailing and Consumer Services, 12,* 1–13.

Kwong, P. (1997). *Forbidden Workers: Illegal Chinese Immigrants and American Labor*. New York: The New Press.

Lashley, C. (2001). *Empowerment: HR Strategies for Service Excellence*. Oxford, UK: Butterworth Heinemann.

Levent, B., Masurel, E., and Nijkamp, P. (2003). Diversity in entrepreneurship: Ethnic and female roles in urban economic life. *International Journal of Social Economics*, *30*, 1131–1161.

Lumpkin, G., and Dess, G. (1996). Clarifying the entrepreneurial orientation construct and linking it to performance. *Academy of Management Review*, *21*, 135–172.

Marlow, S. (1992). Take-up of business growth training schemes by ethnic minority-owned small firms. *International Small Business Journal*, *10*, 34–46.

McPherson, M., Smith-Lovin, L., and Cook, M. (2001). Birds of a feather: Homophily in social networks. *Annual Review of Sociology*, *27*, 415–444.

Mummert, H. (1995). Reaching ethnic markets. *Target Marketing*, *18*, 14–17.

National Statistics (2006). *National Statistics Press Release*, DTI. Small Business Service Analytical Unit, UK.

Nickson, D. (2007). *Human Resource Management for the Hospitality and Tourism Industries*. Oxford, UK: Butterworth Heinemann.

OECD. (2000). Small and medium-sized enterprises: Local strength, global reach, Policy Brief, OECD. Retrieved July 15, 2007, from http://www.oecd.org/dataoecd/3/30/1918307.pdf

Office for National Statistics (2001). *Labor Market Trends*. London: Office for National Statistics. 109(1)

Osborne, H. (2005). Ethnic minority businesses surge ahead. Retrieved January 24, 2006, from http://money.guardian.co.uk/work/story/0,1456,1491828,00.html

Park, I., Fawcett, J., Arnold, F., and Gardner, R. (1990). *Korean Immigrants and U.S. Immigration Policy: A Predeparture Perspective*. Hawaii, East-West Center Occasional Papers, Population Series, No. 114.

Perez, J., and Pablos, P. (2003). Knowledge management and organizational competitiveness: A framework for human capital analysis. *Journal of Knowledge Management*, *7*, 82–91.

Peters, N. (2002). Mixed embeddedness: Does it really explain immigrant enterprise in Western Australia? *International Journal of Entrepreneurial Behavior and Research*, *8*, 32–53.

Rafiq, M. (1992). Ethnicity and enterprise: A comparison of Muslim and non-Muslim owned Asian businesses in Britain. *New Community*, *19*, 43–60.

Ram, M., and Hillin, G. (1994). Achieving 'break-out': Developing mainstream ethnic minority businesses. *Small Business and Enterprise Development*, *1*, 15–21.

Ram, M., and Sparrow, J. (1993). Minority firms. *Racism and Economic Development*, *8*, 117–129.

Richbell, M., Watts, D., and Wardle, P. (2005). Owner-manager and business planning in the small firm. *International Small Business Journal*, *24*, 496–514.

Rogers, C., Gent, M., Palumbo, G., and Wall, R. (2001). Understanding the growth and viability of inner city businesses. *Journal of Developmental Entrepreneurship*, *6*, 237–254.

Rugman, M., and Hodgetts, M. (2000). *International Business: A Strategic Management Approach*. London: Prentice Hall.

Seo, W., Wildes, J., and DeMicco, J. (2001). Understanding mature customers in the restaurant business: Inferences from a nationwide survey. *Journal of Restaurant and Foodservice Marketing*, *4*, 81.

Smallbone, D., Fadahunsi, A., Supri, S., and Paddison, A. (1999). *The Diversity of Ethnic Minority Enterprises*. Paper presented at the RENT XIII, London, November 25–26.

Small Business Research Trust. (2001). *Natwest SBRT Quarterly Survey of Small Business in Britain*. Retrieved February 10, 2005, from http://www.natwest.com/global_options.asp?id=GLOBAL/MEDIA

Stephenson, S. (1995). Training your staff to sell the menu. *Restaurants and Institutions*, *105*(6), 140–142.

Stevenson, H. H., and Jarillo, J. C. (1990). A paradigm of entrepreneurship: Entrepreneurial management. *Strategic Management Journal*, *11*(5), 17–27.

Storey, D., Watson, R., and Wynarczyk, P. (1989). *Fast Growth Small Businesses: Case Studies of 40 Small Firms in Northern England*. Research Paper 67, Department of Employment, London.

Thompson, J. (1999). The world of entrepreneur—A new perspective. *Journal of Workplace Learning*, *11*, 209–224.

Ucbasaran, D., Wright, M., and Westhead, P. (2003). A longitudinal study of habitual entrepreneurs: Starters and acquirers. *Entrepreneurship and Regional Development*, *15*, 207–228.

Waldinger, R., Aldrich, H., Ward, R. et al. (1990). *Ethnic Entrepreneurs*. London: Sage.

Wealden Food and Safety Bulletin (2005). *All Change…. For the Better*. A Newsletter from the Food and Safety Team of Wealden District Council 17.

Werbner, P. (1990). Renewing an industrial past: British Pakistani entrepreneurship in Manchester. *Migration*, *8*, 7–41.

Westhead, P., and Cowling, M. (1995). Employment change in independent owner-managed high-technology firms in Great Britain. *Small Business Economics*, 7, 111–140.

Yoon, J. (1997). *On my Own: Korean Businesses and Race Relations in America*. Chicago, IL: University of Chicago Press.

Young, M. (2002). An examination of information sources and assistance programs available to minority-owned small businesses. *Journal of Developmental Entrepreneurship*, 7, 429–444.

Zhou, M. (1992). *Chinatown: The Socioeconomic Potential of an Urban Enclave*. Philadelphia, PA: Temple University Press.

Conclusion

The authors of this handbook clearly provide a critical view of hospitality strategic management. They present a vision of the hospitality and tourism industry in the year 2015 and discuss the forces driving the hospitality and tourism industry. They explain the systems of environmental scanning that a hospitality company should be equipped with so that the leaders of the company can steer the organization through vibrant, dynamic, and complex environments in order to identify opportunities, invest in competitive methods, allocate resources to these competitive methods to achieve proper execution of strategy, and create the greatest long-term value for all the stakeholders of that organization. They argue that the resource-allocation process constitutes how the firm actually implements and executes its strategy. In order to accurately allocate resources to its strategic priorities or chosen competitive methods, a company needs to clearly analyse its functional competences in terms of its human resources system, information technology system, operations management system, marketing management system, and its organizational culture. It must also understand the vital role of its intangible assets, such as branding, human capital, management know-how, innovation, and entrepreneurship in strategic management. The authors believe that as the hospitality and tourism industry becomes globalized, both strategic alliances and partnerships, and outsourcing may help to lessen the resource shortage and provide opportunities for a company to expand to other parts of the world.

Today's business environment is very complex and ever-changing. Leaders of the hospitality and tourism industry face many challenges. The economy is becoming global. The emerging markets, such as China and India, are attracting the majority of foreign direct investments. The flood of business and leisure travellers from these emerging markets to the

Western world and within the markets creates huge opportunities for the multinational hospitality and tourism companies and small-medium firms. On the other hand, these companies are encountering issues, such as how to better serve these very knowledgeable customers, whose culture, language, and behaviour are different. Meanwhile the industry is experiencing a labour shortage, especially of smart employees equipped with knowledge of high technology. Managers must know how to deal with the fast-changing technological advancement, how to shoulder the responsibility of corporate citizenship and environmental protection, and how to prepare for possible future terrorist attacks. The acceleration of uncertainty requires the leaders of companies to anticipate future events and make more accurate strategic decisions. Tomorrow's managers need to understand the forces driving change, create a vision of the future, translate the vision into proper strategies, properly allocate resources to the strategies, and lead their companies to success.

Index